Women in Management

Women in Management
Current Research Issues Volume II

Marilyn J. Davidson and Ronald J. Burke

SAGE Publications
London • Thousand Oaks • New Delhi

First published 2000

SAGE Publications Ltd
6 Bonhill Street
London EC2A 4PU

SAGE Publications Inc.
2455 Teller Road
Thousand Oaks, California 91320

SAGE Publications India Pvt Ltd
32, M-Block Market
Greater Kailash - I
New Delhi 110 048

British Library Cataloguing in Publication data

A catalogue record for this book is available
from the British Library

ISBN 0 7619 6602 1
ISBN 0 7619 6603 X (pbk)

Library of Congress catalog card number available

Typeset by SIVA Math Setters, Chennai, India.
Printed in Great Britain by Athenaeum Press, Gateshead

Contents

PART III: OCCUPATIONAL STRESS AND BLACK AND ETHNIC
        MINORITY ISSUES

PART IV: THE FUTURE – ORGANIZATIONAL AND GOVERNMENT
        INITIATIVES

Notes on Contributors

Ella J. Edmondson Bell, Associate Professor, Department of Management, Belk College of Business Administration, University of North Carolina at Charlotte, Charlotte, NC 28223, USA.

Reena Bhavnani, Lecturer, Department of Sociology, City University, Northampton Square, London EC1V 0HB, UK.

Diana Bilimoria, Associate Professor, Department of Organizational Behavior, Weatherhead School of Management, Case Western Reserve University, Cleveland, OH 44106–7235, USA.

Ronald J. Burke, Editor, Professor in Organizational Behaviour/Industrial Relations, Faculty of Administrative Studies, York University, 4700 Keele Street, North York, Ontario M3J 1P3, Canada.

Catherine Cassell, Lecturer in Organization Behaviour/Human Resource Management, Sheffield University Management School, 9 Mappin Street, Sheffield S1 4DT, UK.

David L. Collinson, Reader in Organizational Analysis, Industrial Relations and Organizational Behaviour Group, Warwick Business School, University of Warwick, Coventry CV4 7AL, UK.

Cary L. Cooper, BUPA Professor of Organizational Psychology and Health and Pro-Vice Chancellor External Relations, Manchester School of Management, University of Manchester, Institute of Science and Technology, PO Box 88, Manchester M60 1QD, UK.

Angela Coyle, Professor, Department of Sociology, City University, Northampton Square, London EC1V 0HB, UK.

Marilyn J. Davidson, Editor, Professor of Managerial Psychology, Manchester School of Management, University of Manchester Institute of Science and Technology, PO Box 88, Manchester M60 1QD, UK.

Sandra L. Fielden, Director of the Centre for Business Psychology, Manchester School of Management, University of Manchester, Institute of Science and Technology, PO Box 88, Manchester M60 1QD, UK.

Jeff Hearn, Professorial Research Fellow, Faculty of Economic Studies, University of Manchester, Oxford Road, Manchester, UK. Visiting Professor in the Universities of Abo Akadeni, Finland, and Oslo, Norway.

Andrew Hede, Professor of Management and Dean of Business, University of the Sunshine Coast, Maroochydore DC, Queensland 4558, Australia.

Paul G.W. Jansen, Professor of Industrial Psychology, Faculty of Economics, Department of Business Administration, Vrije Universiteit Amsterdam, De Boelelaan 1105, NL 1081 HV, Amsterdam, The Netherlands.

Paul L. Koopman, Professor of Organizational Psychology, Faculty of Psychology, Department of Work and Organizational Psychology, Vrije Universiteit Amsterdam, Van der Boechorststraat 1, NL 1081 BT Amsterdam, The Netherlands.

Jacqueline Laufer, Professor, Département Management et Ressources Humaines, HEC School of Management 1 rue de la Libération, 78351 Jouy-en-Josas, Cedex, France.

Mary C. Mattis, Vice-President of Research and Advisory Services, Catalyst, 120 Wall Street 5th floor, New York 10005, USA.

Judy McGregor, Professor, Department of Human Resource Management, College of Business, Massey University, Palmerston North, New Zealand.

Debra L. Nelson, Professor of Management, College of Business Administration, Oklahoma State University, Stillwater, OK 74078, USA.

Stella M. Nkomo, Professor, Department of Management, Belk College of Business Administration, University of North Carolina at Charlotte, Charlotte, NC 28223, USA.

Carole Pemberton, Career Matters, 78 Waldegrave Road, Brighton BNI 699, UK.

Gary N. Powell, Ackerman Scholar and Professor of Management, University of Connecticut, Box U–41, 368 Fairfield Road, Storrs, Connecticut 06269–2041, USA.

Astrid M. Richardsen, Associate Professor and Department Head, Department of Psychology, University of Tromsø, N–9037, Tromsø, Norway.

Linda K. Stroh, Professor, Institute of Human Resources and Industrial Relations, Loyola University Chicago, 820 N. Michigan Avenue, Chicago, IL 60611, USA.

Cheryl Travers, Lecturer in Organizational Behaviour/Human Resource Management, The Business School, Loughborough University, Ashby Road, Loughborough, Leics LE11 3TU, UK.

David Tweed, Lecturer, Department of Management Systems, College of Business, Massey University, Palmerston North, New Zealand.

Stacey J. Valy-Durbin, Training and Development, The Fort James Corporation, Deerfield, IL 60015, USA.

Arup Varma, Associate Professor, Institute of Human Resources and Industrial Relations, Loyola University Chicago, 820 N. Michigan Avenue, Chicago, IL 60611, USA.

Claartje J. Vinkenburg, Management Consultant, Berenschot – The Change Factory, Bernadottelaan 13, NL 3527 GA Utrecht, The Netherlands.

Susan Vinnicombe, Director of Graduate Research and Director of the Centre for Developing Women Business Leaders, Cranfield School of Management, Cranfield University, Cranfield, Beds. MK43 0AL, UK.

Jane V. Wheeler, Assistant Professor, Department of Management, College of Business Administration, Bowling Green State University, Bowling Green, OH 43403, USA.

Barbara White, Honorary Lecturer in Psychology, Department of Psychology, Eleanor Rathbone Building, University of Liverpool, Bedford Street South, Liverpool L69 7ZA, UK.

Acknowledgements

I would like to acknowledge and thank two important mentors in my life – Art Veno and Cary Cooper. I hope I can now do for others, what they did for me.

Marilyn J. Davidson

I would like to acknowledge the general support provided by the School of Business, York University and the specific assistance of Mary Amati in co-ordinating manuscripts and correspondence. I am also grateful to our international contributors. Finally, I owe a debt of gratitude to Donald DeRosa and William Weitzel, friends and colleagues, who have been there for the past 30 years.

Ronald J. Burke

1

Women in Management: Current Research Issues Volume II

Marilyn J. Davidson and Ronald J. Burke

The overall aim of this book is to present a second edition of our successful publication, *Women in Management: Current Research Issues* (Davidson and Burke, 1994). This book includes a comprehensive overview of the current international research findings pertaining to women in management which were not included in the first volume, as well as new and relevant research initiatives as we reach the millennium. Like its predecessor, this volume brings together an international group of eminent contributors who highlight the major issues facing women in management, in addition to the individual, organizational and government consequences.

The book is divided into four sections. Part I presents a global perspective on women in business and reviews women managers in Europe and female entrepreneurs in New Zealand, the United States and Norway. Part II concentrates on the career development issues for women managers, with particular emphasis on highflying businesswomen who represent important, successful role models. Here, the issues relating to networking, leadership and overseas assignments are discussed in relation to success in climbing the corporate ladder and shattering the glass ceiling. Part III groups together two important issues in the area of women in management – occupational stress (in both employed and unemployed managers) and race and gender issues for black and ethnic minority women managers in the USA and the UK. Finally, Part IV looks ahead to the future organizational and governmental initiatives and their impact and influence on ensuring equality of opportunity for women in management careers. This section includes chapters on the future of the glass ceiling, a review of the management of diversity approach combined with the business case arguments, issues concerning masculinity of management, the effects of Australian affirmative action policy and the implications of long- and short-term contracts in the workplace.

What is evident from the international research material reviewed in this book is that there have been some positive changes in the global position of women in management since our 1994 publication *Women in Management: Current Research*

Issues, while some issues have remained very much the same. In the European Union countries fewer than 5 per cent of women are in senior management roles and this percentage has barely changed since the early 1990s. However, over the past decade there has been an increasing trend for women to start their own businesses. In the USA women-owned small businesses increased from 5 per cent in 1970 to 33 per cent in 1996 (*The Economist*, 1996). In the UK, with a quarter of all self-employed being women, this is a figure which has doubled since 1980 (Equal Opportunities Commission, 1998). While many of these businesses are small, they are undoubtedly growing in size and number. In the US for example, the number of employees in women-owned businesses that have 100 or more workers is rising more than twice as fast as average for all such American firms (*The Economist*, 1996). Moreover, it has been suggested that the flexibility and control provided by owning one's own business are often a greater attraction to working women, particularly those with children, than is employment in a hierarchy-driven, male-dominated corporate culture.

Since 1994, there has also been a gradual increase in the percentage of women in the workforce in almost all countries in the western hemisphere. In the UK women now outnumber men and constitute just over 50 per cent of the total workforce (although unlike men, the majority work part-time) (Equal Opportunities Commission, 1998). There has also been a slight increase in the percentage of women entering various management levels in British organizations (see Table 1.1). Since 1994 the proportion of women managers in the UK has increased from 9.5 per cent in 1994 to 18 per cent in 1998. The 1998 survey also confirmed that the average profile of the British female manager compared to her male counterpart has hardly changed over the past decade. She earns less, even at director level, and on average females are younger at each responsibility level. There is still continued managerial segregation by gender, with the most popular jobs for women managers being in marketing and personnel, in both of which females make up around 35 per cent of managers. The least popular jobs are in research and development, physical distribution, manufacturing and production, and purchasing and contracting; where fewer than 6 per cent of managers are women (Institute of Management and Remuneration Economics, 1998).

TABLE 1.1 *Female – Sample size by responsibility level (%)*

	1974	1983	1991	1993	1994	1995	1996	1997	1998
Directors	0.6	0.3	2.6	2.8	2.8	3.0	3.3	4.5	3.6
Function heads	0.4	1.5	6.1	6.8	6.1	5.8	6.5	8.3	10.7
Department heads	2.1	1.9	8.1	9.0	8.7	9.7	12.2	14.0	16.2
Section leaders	2.4	5.3	11.6	13.2	12.0	14.2	14.4	18.2	21.9
Whole sample	1.8	3.3	8.6	10.2	9.5	10.7	12.3	15.2	18.0

Source: Institute of Management and Remuneration Economics (1998)

Women in top jobs

What is also evident in Table 1.1 is that the glass ceiling still exists, with the majority of women concentrated in the lower levels of management. Indeed, the percentage of women directors actually dipped to 3.6 per cent in 1998 compared to 4.5 per cent in 1997. Since 1994, the increase in the overall percentage of women directors has been less than 1 per cent (Institute of Management and Remuneration Economics, 1998).

While the British government continues not to introduce affirmative action legislation, the new Labour government has recently introduced more 'family friendly' employment legislation. Paid maternity leave has increased from 14 to 18 weeks, and after one year's service, can extend up to 40 weeks (unpaid). In addition, there are new provisions for unpaid parental and crisis leave.

In America despite affirmative action legislation, the glass ceiling still persists at corporate executive level. For example, Catalyst (1996) published a census of women corporate officers and top earners based on 1996 and 1995 US data. The census determined how many women hold these important positions in Fortune 500 companies, based on data from the companies' annual reports and proxy statements. Catalyst concluded that the representation of women among corporate officers and top earners may be increasing. The absolute number is still small, however. The census showed that women represented 10 per cent of corporate officers (1,302 out of 13,013) in 1995. This was an increase of 323 women (979 out of 11,241: 8.7 per cent) from 1994. Seventy-eight per cent of Fortune 500 companies (N = 394) had one or more women in 1995, an increase of nine companies over 1994. Twenty-one per cent of these companies in 1995, and 23 per cent in 1994, had no women corporate officers. Women accounted for 1.9 per cent of top earners in 1995 and 1.2 per cent of the top 2,500 earners in 1994.

Similar scenarios persist in Canada and it is of interest to describe in depth the findings of a recent Canadian study of senior female executives (Catalyst, 1997). The Conference Board of Canada and Catalyst undertook a study in the spring of 1997 of senior women and chief executives in top Canadian corporations and professional service firms. Male and female executives agreed that business reasons should motivate organizations to increase the representation of women in senior positions. The most common reasons endorsed by these women and men were that women form a large part of the available talent pool, women have valuable leadership skills which complement those of men, and also have a unique perspective to contribute to decision-making and problem-solving, and the fact that women form a significant consumer base whose buying power is increasing. Sixty per cent of chief executives considered women's advancement to be critical or very important for their organizations. This figure was higher among chief executives in corporations than chief executives in professional firms.

More chief executives than senior women believed that women's opportunities to advance had improved greatly or somewhat (74 per cent vs. 57 per cent). Chief executives also estimated a slightly higher percentage of women in senior management positions (13 per cent vs. 9 per cent) and a greater percentage in the next five years (24 per cent vs. 14 per cent).

Canada's employment equity policies received a mixed review. The largest percentage of senior women and chief executives indicated that these programmes had both positive and negative impacts on women's equity (50 per cent and 42 per cent respectively). A positive effect involved opening doors once closed to women, while negative effects included increases in backlash and negative reactions to hiring women using quota systems.

Chief executives and senior women agreed that there were several obstacles to women's advancement to senior levels (commitment to family responsibilities, lack of mentoring, failure of senior leadership to be accountable for women's advancement). There were large differences between these two groups on other factors, however. Women rated male stereotyping and preconceptions of women's roles and abilities, and exclusion from informal networks of communication, as more significant barriers than chief executives did. On the other hand, chief executives rated lack of significant general management or line experience, and lack of time in the pipeline, as greater barriers than did senior women. Not surprisingly, more senior women than chief executives believed that family responsibilities hindered women's advancement.

Sixty-two per cent of senior women in the study had considered leaving their organization. Chief executives and senior women agreed that greater compensation and greater advancement opportunities were important factors in women's decisions to leave their current employers. They differed on most others. Chief executives rated family responsibilities as more important and increased intellectual stimulation and compatible organizational values as less important.

The strategies which the senior women cited as being most important for their career success were: consistently exceeding performance expectations, developing a style that male managers found comfortable and seeking out difficult or high-visibility job assignments. Large numbers of women also identified networking and mentoring, developing and adhering to their own career goals and gaining line management experience as important to their advancement.

Senior women also believed that personal qualities influenced advancement. In particular, individual qualities such as capacity for hard work (76 per cent), integrity (74 per cent), desire for responsibility (69 per cent) and concern for financial results (53 per cent) were critical for advancement. The three most important organizational strategies women believed to be most beneficial to their careers were: identifying and developing high-potential women, providing women with high-visibility assignments and/or clients and cross-functional or developmental job rotation.

Interestingly, chief executives typically rated each strategy as more important than did senior women. In addition, chief executives considered in-house leadership training as second most important (behind identifying and developing high-potential women).

Both senior women and chief executives were somewhat optimistic about the representation of women at senior levels in the future. Fifty-nine per cent of senior women aspired to higher positions in their organizations and 68 per cent expected to obtain these positions within three years.

Chief executives identified the three most important areas of skill and experience required of senior executives and those areas in which they thought women lacked skills. Women were seen as having substantial interpersonal skills (team players, good communicators, business development abilities). Fifty-eight per cent of chief executives wanted general management skills and experiences (leadership, networking, demonstrating results) and 36 per cent felt women lacked these skills. About 75 per cent of chief executives cited experience in particular functions, as well as experience in both staff and line positions, as important. But 44 per cent saw women as lacking in these areas.

These data suggested that women will require both opportunities and experiences to develop skills in particular areas, as well as job rotation and training to obtain breadth.

The senior women worked 55 hours per week on average and found it difficult to achieve balance between work and personal life. A majority of these women gave up personal interests (e.g. hobbies, fitness, community involvement) to obtain a better balance. They were helped in many cases by supportive spouses. Few used flexible work arrangements to achieve work–family balance.

We believe that these findings have implications for furthering the career aspirations of ambitious, talented women. First, both performance as well as non-performance factors (a style men found comfortable) were important. Second, a perception gap exists between chief executives and senior women. Men see women as lacking in critical skills; women see the work environment and male attitudes as difficult. Third, there was considerable agreement on ways organizations can support women's advancement. These included: implementing specific career planning and development strategies, giving access for both women and men to high-visibility jobs, career coaching and mentoring, cross-functional job rotation and executive training and education. Fourth, the perception that family responsibilities affect women's job performance must be directly challenged. In this regard, senior women's use of flexible work options must be supported.

These findings reflect a common theme running throughout the research material presented in this book. Whilst there has been some progress in the position of women in management, this tends to be slow. There are still relatively few women in line positions, few women among the highest corporate ranks, and few women in industrial as opposed to service companies.

Conclusion

What is evident from the current women in management research issues outlined in the following chapters is that the following obstacles exist:

1 While there has been progress in the number of women entering managerial positions, progress is slow (particularly in senior corporate positions). Continuing attention to developing women's careers will be necessary to maintain momentum. One step is to continue counting their numbers.

2 Managerial job segregation by gender persists, with women managers dominating certain managerial jobs such as human resources, public affairs,

communications and the law. These routes rarely reach the executive level. Line experience in major business units in jobs having bottom-line impact, is what is required.

3   The percentage of black and ethnic minority women managers is still small and they continue to face the double bind of sexual and racial discrimination. The white old boys' network is alive and well at senior management levels.

4   Elimination of affirmative action in employment equity legislation in both Canada and the US, as well as a reduction in the application of such legislation in Australia, may severely restrict the future advancement of women in management in these countries. Though useful, these efforts have had their own burdens (e.g. backlash, tokenism).

5   Downsizing and restructuring efforts may create unique challenges for women in that the emphasis on lean and mean may conflict with their values. In addition, since women typically have less seniority than men, women may be more expendable during these transitional times.

6   The introduction of work–family initiatives which end up being superficial attempts to make a workaholic culture offer limited help to both women and men. Women who use these initiatives may limit their career prospects; men rarely use them. Instead fundamental changes must be made to the way work gets done to the benefit of both company productivity and quality of life.

7   Women's continuing responsibility for second shift duties limits the amount of time they can devote to work. Until organizations place less emphasis on 'face time', women will be disadvantaged.

8   The continuation of predominantly male cultures, particularly in the industrial sector, makes the workplace unfriendly to women. This places an additional burden on women.

9   The business case and the management of diversity model need to be more fully utilized by organizations. Full utilization of the talents of all employees is the 'smart thing to do' to remain competitive in an increasingly demanding global marketplace.

According to Wajcman

> If affirmation action was the policy of the 1980s, 'diversity management' is replacing it as the policy of the 1990s. In North America, and increasingly in Britain and Australia, the intention of equality initiatives is to value or manage 'diversity', which purports to be a positive valuing of differences between people. (1998: 20)

We hope that, as we enter the next millennium, this book (like its predecessor) will serve to interest more organizational researchers to consider the issues of women in management. We also hope that it will encourage organizations and governments to develop positive and effective equal opportunity programmes that will have value to the individuals whose work and life experiences we are attempting to better understand – namely women and men (from all ethnic backgrounds) in managerial jobs.

References

Catalyst (1996) *Women in Corporate Leadership: Progress and Prospects*, Catalyst, New York.
Catalyst (1997) *Closing the Gap: Women's Advancement in Corporate and Professional Canada*, Catalyst, New York.
Davidson, M.J. and Burke, R.J. (eds) (1994) *Women in Management: Current Research Issues*, Paul Chapman, London.
The Economist (1996) 'Breaking the glass ceiling', 10 August: 15.
Equal Opportunities Commission (1998) *Facts about Women and Men in Great Britain 1998*, EOC, Manchester.
Institute of Management and Remuneration Economics (1998) *UK National Management Survey*, Institute of Management, London.
Wajcman, J. (1998) *Managing Like a Man – Women and Men in Corporate Management*, Polity Press, Cambridge.

PART I

WOMEN MANAGERS AND ENTREPRENEURS – A GLOBAL PERSPECTIVE

2

The Position of Women in Management in Europe

Susan Vinnicombe

> *The biggest change in the nature of the European labour force is the tremendous increase in women's participation within the past decade, and the permanence of that change.*
>
> (European Study, *Women Setting New Priorities*,
> Whirlpool Foundation, 1996)

Twenty years after the EU adopted equal opportunity laws, European management is still a man's enclave. Women constitute 41 per cent of the European workforce, yet occupy only 10 per cent of management positions and make up a mere 1 per cent of board members (Pillinger, 1992). The higher the level in management the more glaring is the gender gap. Even where women managers rise to the top jobs, they nearly always earn less than men. 'Almost universally women have failed to reach leading positions in major corporations and private sector organizations, irrespective of their abilities,' says an ILO labour expert and author of the 1996 ILO report, 'Breaking through the glass ceiling: Women in Management' (Commission of the European Communities, 1993). This chapter aims to review the position of women in management in general in small and medium-sized enterprises, in public administration and most specifically at board level across

Europe. The explanation of women's poor representation at managerial and especially at board level can be viewed from a number of perspectives:

- equal pay
- education and qualifications
- career paths
- marriage and children

Ascertaining the exact number of women in management in Europe is difficult, firstly because different countries may have different definitions of 'manager', and secondly, because in many countries there is no regular system of gathering statistics in this area. For international comparisons of women in management the ILO data (see Table 2.1) constitute the most complete data set. But even this does not cover all European countries and moreover the data include administrative workers as managers, thus giving the impression that more women hold management jobs than is actually the case.

The UK has the highest number of women 'managers' in Europe, at 33 per cent (see Table 2.1) compared to Switzerland at 28 per cent and Turkey at 10 per cent. However, internationally the UK is still some way behind the United States and Australia, both at 43 per cent.

A survey carried out by Grant Thornton, into over 5,000 small and medium-sized enterprises (SMEs) in the 15 EU member states as well as Switzerland and Malta, revealed that few women held senior posts and in 50 per cent of companies there are no women at all in management positions. The UK and Spain are the 'best performers', with 37 per cent and 38 per cent of companies respectively having no women in management, compared to the 'worst performers', the Netherlands and Sweden where a full 70 per cent and 64 per cent of companies respectively have no women in these positions (see Figure 2.1). The report concluded that the results were the reverse of what had been predicted. Countries with the highest overall labour market participation of women and enlightened legislation, surprisingly had the lowest number of women in administration and management. Two explanations were provided for this. Firstly, the number of women in the top team related to the size of the team – the larger the team the more likely the presence of women members. Secondly, the high costs associated with long periods of maternity leave or the provision of childcare may act as a disincentive to SMEs to employ women at management level.

TABLE 2.1 *Women's share of administrative and managerial jobs and share in total employment, 1994–95 (%)*

Countries	Admin. and managerial jobs	Total employment
Austria	22	43
Finland	25	47
Israel	25	47
Norway	32	46
Switzerland	28	40
United Kingdom	33	45

Source: ILO (1998: 8)

A National Management Survey by the Institute of Management/Remuneration Economics in June 1998 surveyed 25,952 individual managers employed by 584 organizations to reveal that in the United Kingdom in 1998 18 per cent of all managers were women as opposed to 7.9 per cent in 1990. The same survey revealed that in 1998 3.6 per cent of all directors were women as opposed to 1.6 per cent in 1990.

One might assume that female managers would have the greatest chance of achieving success in the Scandinavian countries, where some of the highest numbers of women in the workforce are recorded, and family policies and equal opportunities programmes are strongly enforced by legislation. Yet the number of women managers is not significantly higher in Scandinavian countries than elsewhere in Europe. In Denmark, for example, it is estimated that only 10 per cent of women in both the private and public sectors hold middle management jobs. A 1991 survey showed that only 4 per cent of 755 company directors were women

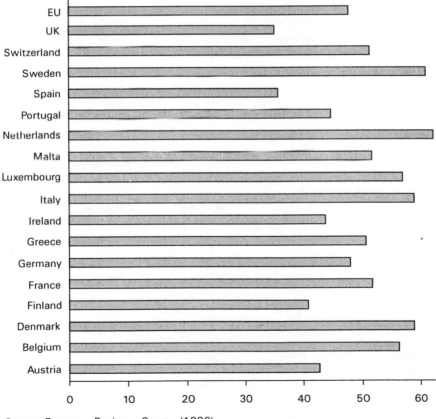

Source: European Business Survey (1996)

FIGURE 2.1   Proportion of firms with no women in management (%)

(Albertsen and Christensen, 1993). In Finland, the figures appear to be somewhat higher: Hanninen-Salmelin and Petajaniemi claim that in 1990, 21 per cent of 'senior officials and executives' were women. Still, even here women managers are concentrated in areas such as banking and the public sector; they continue to be poorly represented in most private sector organizations (Hanninen-Salmelin and Petajaniemi, 1994).

In southern Europe the situation for women managers is more complex. While women have traditionally been less career oriented in many south European countries, there are now signs that there is strong growth in the number of women in the workforce and the number of women managers. In Italy and Spain younger women in particular appear to have a different attitude to work and are embarking upon management careers. Their numbers, however, remain low. In Italy, women hold 3 per cent of upper management positions, and in Spain 5 per cent of private sector management jobs are filled by women (Davidson and Cooper, 1993). As elsewhere in Europe, women managers in the south tend to be concentrated in jobs in the service and public sectors.

Women ministers from 13 EU member states signed a second European charter in 1996, calling for the equal participation of women and men in all spheres of society. In the charter the ministers committed themselves to develop incentives, laws and regulatory measures to achieve equal participation of women and men in all positions of power, influence and decision-making (see Table 2.2). Women's equal participation in decision-making is a question of social justice, a requirement of democracy and a component essential to achieve maximum use of human resources – the so called 'business case' for increasing the number of women in management. A conference was held in Rome prior to the European Women's Summit in 1996 and the outcome of the discussions was presented

TABLE 2.2   *Participation of women in public administration at national level in the EU member states*

EU member states	Date	Total public administration (%)	Management level (%)	Highest level (%)
Belgium	1991	27.1	13.6	25.2
Denmark	1992	64.1	18.2	6.4
Germany	1993	28.0	7.4	4.4
Greece	1989–92	34.8	No data available	5.4
Spain	1994	42.0	17.0	16.3
France	1991	51.6	4.0	0.0
Ireland	1989	60.0	2.2	0.0
Italy	1991	46.5	14.1	0.0
Luxembourg	1991	24.7	6.8	2.0
The Netherlands	1993	30.4	1.0	0.2
Austria	No data available			
Portugal	1988	65.2	32.0	13.2
Finland	1994	63.0	34.0	16.0
Sweden	No data available			
United Kingdom	1991	36.8	9.6	5.3
European Commission	1994	9.9	10.1	2.9

Source: CREW (1996)

in the form of a four-year European Action Plan (1996–2000) for equal participation of women and men in decision-making (CREW, 1996).

Closing the gap on equal pay

Equal pay for women is as important an issue as participation itself. Whilst men are perceived to be the main breadwinners across Europe, a 1996 study shows that 60 per cent of working women provide at least half their family's income. The study, conducted in five countries (France, Germany, Britain, Italy and Spain) indicated that women have assumed a much stronger economic role over the last decade, but only about 15 per cent of the men and women surveyed recognized that women are making a substantial contribution. According to the study's results, 28 per cent of European working women provide all their household income, 10 per cent provide more than half and 22 per cent provide about half. There were significant variations by country: 38 per cent of working German women and 36 per cent of working French women said they were the sole breadwinner, while 12 per cent of working British women provided all household money. By comparison 18 per cent of working women in the United States provided all household income. European women describe a successful woman as one who has a good job and is satisfied with her life (www.nando.net, 1996).

Just as their entry into the workforce has not guaranteed European women access to top jobs, so it has not guaranteed equal pay. In the UK, for example, women employees working full time in 1997 earned 80 per cent of men's average hourly wage and women working part time earned only 58 per cent of the pay of male full-timers. Average gross weekly earnings of full-time employees in 1997 was £347 for women and £536 for men in the managers and administrators category, according to the Labour Force Survey quarterly bulletin in March 1998. Women managers are gaining ground when it comes to increasing their pay packets. While male managers' pay rose by 6.8 per cent in 1998, women managers have seen their salaries increase by 7.7 per cent. However, the average female manager is 37 years old and earns £31,622. Her male colleague is aged 43 – six years older – and earns £37,235. (Labour Force quarterly bulletin, March 1998). The gap between male and female managers is similar to this in France (Serdjanian, 1994). In the Netherlands, it is as high as 40 per cent. In Germany, however, while women earn about one-third less than men do overall, the earnings gap between male and female managers is smaller, with women being paid approximately 20 per cent less than their male colleagues (Antal and Krebsbach-Gnath, 1993).

It is debatable whether the pay inequalities between men and women are shrinking. What is clear is that there is a new growing gender polarization in the jobs market between part-timers – mainly women – and full-timers, men and women. Over 80 per cent of those working part time in Europe are women. A Department for Education and Employment working paper published in England in 1996 analysed the pattern of pay for a large group of 32-year-olds in 1978 and 33-year-olds in 1991 (*The Independent*, 1996). Between those two years women's participation in work, especially part time, increased dramatically. In 1978 nearly one in five women worked full time and nearly as many part time. In 1991,

23 per cent worked full time and 58 per cent worked part time. Men in the 1978 group had a pay lead of 64 per cent on women, and 35 per cent on full-time women. Full-time women's pay was 40 per cent higher than for part-time women. By 1991 these gaps had changed to 40 per cent, 20 per cent and 52 per cent respectively. The significant figure here is the increasing gap between full-time women's pay and part-time women's pay.

In the boardrooms of Britain the news is not so good. Women directors' pay rose by 7.4 per cent, behind that of their male counterparts, who received an average increase of 10.3 per cent. Today's average female director is 41 years old and earns £66,711. Her male colleague is 48 years old and earns £94,742. 'Looking at the earnings of women directors, the real issue would seem to be position,' said Ms Chapman, the Director General of Institute of Management. 'Chief executives and finance directors are the real heavy hitters in terms of boardroom pay and women are as yet largely absent from these roles, which partly explains the earnings gap' (National Management Salary Survey, Institute of Management 1998).

Improved educational standards provide part of the explanation for the changing wage gaps, although full-time women are now better qualified than full-time men but still get paid less. A second explanation is that women and men have different kinds of jobs. This is particularly the case for part-timers, who are more likely to work for small firms. A further explanation is motherhood. A number of women have worked their way into management in large organizations over a period of years, then take several years off to bring up their children and return to the same organizations, where they are forced to start again at the bottom. While bosses often reward male employees who become parents, with pay rises and, in international management, with increased opportunities for attractive expatriate assignments, mothers suffer. It is primarily the women who leave their jobs and return after a break who suffer, not the women who just take maternity leave. However, where these women renegotiate their full-time jobs into part-time jobs, which is becoming increasingly popular, many report putting in many more hours than formally negotiated for no extra money. Unfortunately, this increasing polarization of full-time and part-time pay is not slowing down. Governments need to encourage companies to enhance their man and woman power rather than exploit it (*The Independent*, 1996).

Education and qualifications

Qualifications for women are on an upward curve across Europe. The evidence is that women are now as well educated as their male counterparts, if not better. In the UK in 1994–95, around 60 per cent of further education students were female, double the number 21 years ago (Central Statistical Office, 1994). The number of female undergraduates exceeded the number of male undergraduates in 1995–96 (683,500 against 625,300). (Higher Education Statistics Agency). In a provocative Panorama documentary television programme entitled 'The Future is Female' (1994) the BBC exploded the myth that males, as they develop physically, catch up in education, both in GCSEs and A levels. Females have opened up a commanding and increasing lead over their male counterparts in all subject areas except science and maths, where their results are comparable. In England and Wales in 1995–96 49 per cent of girls and 40 per cent of boys aged 16 gained five or more GCSEs at Grades A–C and 24 per cent of girls and 21 per cent of boys gained one or more GCE A/As levels at school by age 19 (Welsh Office, 1995–96). In France 46 per cent of girls and 36 per cent of boys pass the baccalaureate, and over half the university students are female. In Italy, women constitute half of all those studying at university.

It seems that 'personal belief' rather than 'objective qualifications' is at the core of job discrimination against women. Men are convinced that they are more intelligent than women, even rating their fathers as brighter than their mothers, according to Halla Beloff's research in the *Psychologist* (1992). So strong are these cultural beliefs that women students also underestimate their own intelligence and believe that their fathers are cleverer than their mothers. Such beliefs damage women's professional prospects by lowering their self-confidence. According to a study by Valerie Walkerdine, Professor of Psychology at Goldsmiths' College, London, girls cannot escape fear of failure, no matter how talented they are (*The Sunday Times*, 1997). In a 1997 study girls were found to suffer anxiety and low confidence even though they had overtaken boys in academic achievement. The irony is that girls who get better results than boys still think boys are more confident. 'Women managers tend to rate themselves lower than their male colleagues, and they have a lot of resistance to accepting they are perceived as more competent by others,' says Professor Beverly Alimo-Metcalfe of Leeds University (*The Sunday Times*, 1997). This lack of self-esteem among women can lead to the so called 'impostor syndrome' where women fear they will be 'found out' or unmasked as unworthy of the success they have attained or the positions they have won (Harvey and Katz, 1983).

Women still appear to lag behind their male counterparts when it comes to studying for business qualifications in most European countries. While France claims that 50 per cent of its business school students are female, in Italy just 26 per cent of those obtaining graduate degrees from management and business schools are women (Serdjanian, 1994). In the UK, the Association of MBAs estimates that the proportion of women MBA graduates now stands at around 25 per cent – much lower than the North American figure. According to the European Commission, by the year 2000 women will make up 75 per cent of Europe's new workers and will hold half the graduate slots in Europe's business schools (*Business Week*, 1996). Victoria Griffith disputes this prediction on women's enrolment on MBA programmes. She maintains that female enrolment has stagnated. Further, the women who do MBAs concentrate in the fields that would tend to get them staff not leadership positions when they graduate (*Financial Times*, 1998). 'Inequality on the MBA programmes is perpetuating inequality in the work place,' says Mary Mattis of Catalyst, a women's rights watchdog organization based in New York. Catalyst considers the situation a threat to the progress of women in business and has launched the first major study of the issue. Several hypotheses have been put forward for the low attendance of women:

- Lack of payback for an MBA in the business world. There are few senior women in business. The macho culture in certain industries like finance and engineering also puts women off.
- Work–family concerns. The timing of business school often conflicts with the timing of children.
- The cost of the MBA seems to worry women much more than men.
- A male-oriented culture in the business school means that often women are seen as commodities to be divided up across study groups. Also they can be stereotyped as the secretaries, facilitators and organizers of the groups.
- Lack of female role models within business schools. There are few women professors and this has quite a negative impact on female students.

Maybe this new study will challenge business schools to look at the ways they work and how they could become more female friendly.

Career paths

The nature of women's career paths often blocks their progress to the top of organizations. At the junior management levels women are often in staff functions such as personnel or training, rather than in operating or commercial functions. Top jobs require strategic experience, thereby excluding many women. In Finland the proportion of female personnel managers rose dramatically from 17 per cent in 1970 to 70 per cent in 1990. Once women perform well in these support roles it is often difficult for them to negotiate moves into a commercial function. These barriers are referred to as the 'glass walls'. Compounding this structure of careers is the fact that it is extremely difficult for women managers to network and forge important political connections at work. It is difficult because most of the networks are almost exclusively male, and because the whole practice of networking and self-promotion often runs counter to most women's beliefs. Most women managers work hard, want to perform well and expect their good work to be noticed. This does not reflect the reality of most organizations.

The whole situation has worsened recently with the onset of downsizing and corporate restructuring. More women than men are leaving their organizations, either voluntarily or involuntarily. Unemployment rates among women across Europe continue at a level significantly above that of men, except in Austria, Finland and the UK (Tomlinson, 1998). Many women leave to set up their own businesses. Three times as many women as men are going solo in the UK. One-third of all German start-ups are now woman-owned, up from 10 per cent in 1975. According to Julie Hay, who left British Airways to set up her own business, 'It's about doing a job the way you want to do it. There is often a tough culture that people want to move out of and the pioneers are women' (*Observer*, March 1995). Life then for the remaining female (and male) managers is even tougher – harder targets, longer working hours.

Marriage and children

Long working hours make it very difficult for women to combine careers with family responsibilities. Survey after survey shows that women tend to take the lion's share of child rearing and running a household. Combining work with child rearing is very stressful for most women and it is clear that some organizations have compounded this problem by operating a double standard for marriage: they view the married male manager as an asset, with a stable support network at home allowing him to give his undivided attention to his work, but the married female manager as a liability, likely to neglect her career at the expense of her family at every possible opportunity. 'Professional women today are being caught between a rock and a hard place,' says Professor Ethel Roskies. 'They're told, "If you want to get ahead for success, you better not get married and have kids". Yet the stereotype of the old maid is still with us – "you can only be happy if you're married and have kids"' (*The Times*, 1992).

It is not surprising, therefore, that many women managers have had little choice but to take this double standard for marriage into account in their career strategies, avoiding the responsibility of family commitments wherever possible. Research carried out in the UK by the British Institute of Management showed that only 58 per cent of women managers are married, compared with 93 per cent of male managers. Of the married women, half have children, compared with nearly 90 per cent of their married male counterparts. In other words, male managers are three times more likely to have children than their female colleagues. One in five women in Britain can now expect to die without bearing a child. The startling statistic – a childlessness rate that has doubled in a generation – is to be investigated by the Family Policy Studies Centre. One of the study's main aims is to find out whether infertility amongst women is a voluntary social choice or an imposition dictated by new social and economic pressures (*The Independent*, 1995). Other research (Alban-Metcalfe and Nicholson, 1984) showed that married women were highly likely to have spouses in full-time employment, whereas married men surveyed were likely to have spouses based at home. If organizations want to attract more women into management, then there needs to be a fundamental change of attitude, one that adapts to the reality of women's lives.

The situation appears to be much the same for women managers elsewhere in Europe. In the former West Germany, only 40 per cent of women managers are mothers, and they usually have only one child. In contrast, almost all their male colleagues are married and have an average of two children (Antal and Krebsbach-Gnath, 1993). The whole social structure in Germany is still so oriented around the woman as homemaker that it is difficult for women to take paid employment. Elementary schools send children home for lunch. Few companies provide day-care facilities. Shops by law must be closed in the evenings, and by early afternoon on Saturdays. In a survey carried out in a large computer company in France (Serdjanian, 1994) the women managers were more likely to be unmarried and not to have children. Of those who did have children, the vast majority had only one or two.

It is agreed that a key problem for women pursuing a career is finding a supportive partner, not only one who is prepared to share family and household responsibilities but one who will not feel threatened by a woman earning more and being more successful than he is. Anita Roddick of the Body Shop, million-airess and mother, has gone on record as saying 'Of course you can have it all – it's all down to the partner you choose. We need better editing of partners in life' (*Financial Times*, 1991). Research has shown that women managers are much more likely to be divorced or separated than men; even in Catholic countries divorce rates for women managers appear to be on the increase: according to CRORA's research the Italian women managers they surveyed were twice as likely to be divorced or separated in 1987 than they were in 1975.

While it has now become the norm for many educated men to espouse the belief that they should share household duties with their partners, their behaviour falls short of the ideal. In the UK, 73 per cent of women still do 'nearly all the housework' and men with working partners have an average of six hours more spare time at weekends than their partners do (Cooper and Lewis, 1993). While childcare responsibility tends to be more evenly shared, men are likely to be involved in the more pleasurable aspects of it, for example taking the children to the cinema or theatre. In the Netherlands, women spend 15 per cent of every working day on housework, whereas men spend only 4 per cent (Tijdens, 1993). In France, employed mothers devote 48 out of every 100 hours to domestic work and 52 to professional activities, while men devote 28 to domestic work and 72 to professional activities (Laufer, 1993).

Throughout Europe, the main responsibility for household tasks still lies with women. This poses a particular problem for women managers in that managerial jobs have traditionally been structured to suit a man who has a wife at home pro-viding him with a full-time support system. Even if women managers do not have children, they still have to contend with other family responsibilities which many of their male colleagues do not share. Women managers who do wish to combine a career with raising a family must arrange childcare, which is difficult to do. Some writers believe that lack of childcare facilities is the key block to women achieving managerial jobs.

Women directors

In 1993, two economists used data about 20,000 senior managers working in around 400 British companies to evaluate the progress women were making in management. They wished to test the view that the increasing entry of women into lower levels of management would, in time, ensure their progress to senior positions. Tracking the promotions and remuneration levels of both men and women from 1989 to 1992, Gregg and Machlin (1993) found no evidence to sup-port the view that *it is simply a matter of time* before women work their way up the corporate hierarchy. Instead, they report that, allowing for a range of personal and organizational characteristics, women senior executives are less likely than their male colleagues to be promoted; among the latter, *young* men are the most likely to advance quickly. European organizations are some way behind their American counterparts, where 50 per cent of the workforce are women and

10 per cent of board members are women. Even Britain, considered Europe's most positive working women environment, has only one female board member on 41 per cent of the 100 largest British companies, compared with 95 per cent of the 100 largest American companies (*Business Week*, 1996). In 1996 the first female managing director of a company listed in the London Stock Exchange's top 100 was appointed: Marjorie Scardino – and she was brought in from the USA! Until recently, when Stella Rimmington was made a non-executive director, Marks and Spencer plc had no females amongst its 17 board members, despite the fact that women constitute 85 per cent of the 53,000 employees. 'There are very few women in positions of line authority. It's not going up or down, it's just nudging along the bottom,' says Yve Newbold, chief executive of board recruiters Pro Ned Ltd and herself ex-board member of Hanson plc and British Telecom plc (*Business Week*, 1996).

In France a quarter of the top 200 companies have a female director – but only two of those companies have executive female board members, i.e. internal directors: Patricia Barbizet-Dussart at retailer Pinault-Printemps-Redoute and Veronique Morali of the property company Fimalac. 'The women who manage to slip into the system (as non-executive board members) are usually the wife or the daughter of the owner,' says Jean-Michel Quatrepoint, who edits a newsletter about French management (*Business Week*, 1996). A survey of 22,000 French businesses in 1996 found that those headed by a woman are twice as profitable and grow twice as fast. Medium-sized companies run by women do even better, with three times the growth and profitability. The women bosses say their strengths are pragmatism, intuition and an ability to smooth over rows. They say that they work harder than men, initially to reach the top and then through pride and fear of criticism. This rubs off on their staff because they will not tolerate laziness or negligence. They favour consensus rather than bullying and are good at communicating and anticipating market changes. On the negative side, they are more prone to stress, made worse by a drive for perfectionism or by suffering from the 'impostor syndrome' (Hussell, 1996).

Women still have a long way to go to make their presence felt at the top of Europe's management structures. The case of Susan Wilson serves to emphasize the difficulties. Susan Wilson was made Director of Quality, Head of Personnel and the first female board member of Vickers Defence Systems in 1990 at the age of 38. In December 1994 in a cost-cutting move Vickers claimed they no longer needed a quality and personnel director. Her boss also admitted that he and Wilson had a personality clash. Susan Wilson filed for an unfair dismissal case, saying she was pushed out because she was a woman. She was pregnant at the time with her second child. Vickers denied that Wilson's gender or pregnancy played a role in the case. A week before the case was due to be heard Vickers settled out of court for a sum estimated at £100,000 (*Business Week*, 1996).

Government initiatives in Europe to help women in management

In many European countries there have been initiatives to try to increase the number of women managers working in the public sector, so that the government itself is seen to set a good example. In Denmark an equal opportunities action plan within government departments led to an increase in women's share of management positions from 9 per cent to 11 per cent between 1989 and 1990. There was a similar programme in Germany.

There have also been a number of attempts to influence private sector employers to improve the position of women managers, but these have usually been on a voluntary basis – Brewster and Hegewisch (1994) estimated that only 43 per cent of organizations monitored women's progress in terms of promotions.

Launched in 1991, NOW (New Opportunities for Women) was the first European Community initiative aiming to promote equal employment opportunities for women. It formed an integral part of the third Medium-term Action Programme for Equal Opportunities (1991–95) and became a respected instrument for promoting equal opportunities within the framework of the Structural Funds. The NOW initiative was set up to help women enter the job market and to help redress their position, particularly where they were excluded from the regular labour force or obliged to accept jobs where they lacked any security. NOW also aimed to upgrade and promote women's skills and to help change attitudes in the business world, making it easier for women to set up their own businesses (*Employment NOW*, 1996).

The initiative was funded mainly by the European Social Fund, with supplementary funding from the European Regional Development Fund. The budget of 153 million ECUs with additional funding from member states created a European programme of more than 800 projects during 1991–93. With a total budget of more than 670 million ECUs for the period 1994–99, NOW is by far the largest programme in Europe for conceiving, testing and implementing new ideas for women's training and employment. Its actions now focus on priority areas identified by the Fourth Community Action Programme on Equal Opportunities between Women and Men: reconciliation of working and family life; desegregation of the labour market; access to education and training; and a balanced representation of women and men in decision-making. A critical objective of NOW is the integration of successful outcomes of projects into national systems of training and employment.

NOW has eight characteristic features:

1 It provides an opportunity to try out new methods and to explore innovative ideas for women's training and employment.
2 It has provided clear evidence of the effectiveness of an individualistic holistic approach, linking social and psychological support with training, work experience and job search.
3 Especially at a local and regional level, NOW forges solid coalitions with key actors such as public administrations, employment services, social partners, voluntary organizations and private sector companies. Such partnerships greatly help the process of mainstreaming by involving key actors in the projects themselves. Private companies, for instance, provide work placements for project beneficiaries.
4 NOW contributes to significant policy changes at European and national level. During the second reform of the European Structural Funds in 1993,

NOW played a crucial role in the introduction of equal opportunities as a transversal objective for all parts of the Structural Funds. This also resulted in changes to the range of actions that projects could undertake. NOW also contributed to the definition and integration of new occupational profiles into national systems of occupational classification.

5 An important contribution of NOW concerns the reconciliation of professional and family life. NOW shows that a lack of supportive infrastructure is often the most serious barrier to women entering the job market. It therefore creates a framework of accompanying measures to address this need.

6 NOW highlighted the evolution of the care services sector as an important aspect of job creation for women. As with many predominantly female sectors, however, most jobs were poorly paid and demanded minimal professional qualifications. An important characteristic of NOW projects is to develop training that upgrades and adds value to such work.

7 With more than 800 projects, NOW's actions focus on the specific needs of women in their different situations, including newcomers to the labour market; women with shared or sole responsibility for children; women with disabilities; older women; migrants; and women from ethnic minorities. Previously such people were hardly visible as target groups of the Community Structural Fund and/or national programmes for fighting unemployment.

8 For most participants, NOW provided the first opportunity to work with people in other member states. Project managers, trainers and the participants themselves benefited from an exchange of knowledge, experience and know-how concerning the training and employment policies and systems of other countries. Such multifaceted co-operation resulted in a greater appreciation of 'European citizenship' and often led to the creation of common outputs, like training and teaching materials. This transnational aspect generated higher visibility as the media were stimulated by the European dimension of projects. Finally, transnational co-operation provided job enrichment for project managers and trainers and was an asset for participants, who could highlight their transnational experience in their curricula vitae.

The priorities set for the NOW programme are:

- Redressing the horizontal and vertical segregation of the labour market. Access will be widened to sectors and managerial levels where women are under-represented and which have potential for the future.
- Promoting entrepreneurship and job creation by women. This is one way of enhancing their social and economic independence and releasing their economic potential, particularly where it contributes to local development.
- Improving the reconciliation of employment and family responsibilities. This will be achieved through the development of new patterns of work organization for women and men and the provision of sufficient accessible support for the care of children and other dependants.
- Stimulating employers, training organizations, trade unions and other relevant actors. Key actors will be encouraged to review their training and employment

policies to ensure that they do not discriminate against women (*Employment NOW*, 1996).

In October 1991, 61 employers in the United Kingdom signed up to a new campaign whose main aim was to increase 'the quality and quantity of women's employment opportunities in private and public sector organizations'. Opportunity 2000 was to be very different from previous attempts at helping working women. It was to be business-led and business-driven. Employers were invited to sign up to the campaign for the competitive and performance advantages it would bring, rather than for any social or moral reason. A strategic approach was needed to help organizations rebuild an entirely new organizational culture.

When organizations join Opportunity 2000 they must make several commitments:

- Top management must endorse their commitment to the campaign.
- They must audit their own organizations in terms of the position of their female employees, and must then set realistic goals for recruiting, retaining and developing able women.
- They must monitor their progress regularly and share their results with Opportunity 2000.

In 1996 the campaign had over 300 members who employ over 25 per cent of the UK workforce. Private and public sector employers are equally well represented. Perhaps the most persuasive evidence of members' progress is the data recording women's improved representation in management. In 1996 women in Opportunity 2000 organizations accounted for 17 per cent of senior managers, 31 per cent of middle managers, 41 per cent of junior managers and 11 per cent of directors. Overall women make up 31 per cent of managers in member organizations, against 12.3 per cent of managers in industry in general. This indicates that women in the member organizations are likely to fare better than those in organizations outside the campaign (see Table 2.3).

In December 1996 more than 100 participants, mainly women, attended a tripartite meeting held by the ILO. Twenty countries were invited to be represented. Observers from additional governments, as well as intergovernmental and non-governmental international organizations were also represented. Austria, Finland, Norway, Switzerland, Turkey and the United Kingdom represented Europe at the meeting. The discussion was wide ranging, from national initiatives taken to advance gender equality and promote women in management to obstacles to women's career development. Participants emphasized the importance of a tripartite approach and the strategic issue of ensuring that more women gained decision-making positions in the structures of organizations.

The participants at the tripartite meeting on 'Breaking through the Glass Ceiling: Women in Management' recommended several strategies to promote women in management, including:

- regulatory mechanisms and legal frameworks to eliminate discrimination on grounds of sex;
- affirmative action and guidelines to genuinely change attitudes, while taking existing diversities into account;

- the adoption of appropriate steps by enterprises, institutions and governments to ensure that employees are aware of obligations and rights, including those stemming from equal employment laws where applicable;
- positive action and equal opportunities policies to level the playing field and ensure equal opportunities and treatment for women in recruitment and promotion;
- the development of ways, which can include more flexible working hours, reduced hours of work and adequate child- and elder-care facilities, to enable both women and men to combine the building of a career and the raising of a family;
- mentoring for women to provide advice and develop their professional skills;
- the appointment of corporate officers in the personnel departments of enterprises with responsibility for monitoring and promoting equal opportunities throughout the enterprise; and
- access of women to business skills training and entrepreneurship development to help them run their own businesses.

The participants also emphasized the importance of employers' and workers' organizations appointing women to top positions in their own structures and the significant role of national tripartite commissions, where they exist, in promoting equal opportunities for women and men (ILO, 1998).

Some problems are under researched. This is not the case for European women's poor representation in management. The problems are well known (and

TABLE 2.3   *Improved policies and practices**

	1992 %	1996 %
Flexible working		
Job-sharing	24	62
School term contracts	14	25
Maternity and paternity		
Enhanced maternity arrangements	466	5
Paternity leave	42	70
Career breaks	34	46
Family care		
Advice on childcare	24	56
Workplace nursery	4	22
Holiday play schemes	16	30
Leave for care of elderly/disabled	34	57
Training and development		
Ongoing training for part-time staff	6	88
Training with family care support	5	21
Developing career paths for secretaries and clerical staff	16	34
Women-only training	13	22
Sexual harassment training	9	41

Note: *Figures showing the proportion of Opportunity 2000 members offering various family-friendly training policies and options in 1996 compared with members' provision in 1992.
Source: The Independent (1996)

supported by statistical evidence), the solutions are clear and multifaceted. The political will to address the problems has been partial and irresolute because all of the various government initiatives to redress gender imbalance in management are voluntary. As a consequence only a minority of progressive organizations get involved. Although these organizations tend to be large they are not numerous enough to create the critical mass needed for change. Until the European Union take the issue of women in management seriously, by compelling all organizations to set targets and measure progress against them, no real progress will be made. Implementing strategies for increasing the number of women in management remains both the greatest challenge and the richest opportunity for the new European Community as it approaches monetary union.

References

Albertsen, J. and Christensen, B. (1993) 'Denmark' in M. Davidson and C. Cooper (eds), *European Women in Business and Management*, Paul Chapman, London.

Alban-Metcalfe, B. and Nicholson, N. (1984) *The Career Development of British Managers*, British Institute of Management Foundation, London.

Antal, A.B. and Krebsbach-Gnath, C. (1993) 'Germany', in M. Davidson and C. Cooper (eds), *European Women in Business and Management*, Paul Chapman, London.

Beloff, H. (1992) 'Mother, father and me: our IQ', *Psychologist*, 5: 309–311.

Brewster, C. and Hegewisch, A. (1994) *Policy and Practice in European Human Resource Management*, Routledge, London.

Business Week (1996) 'Europe's corporate women' International Edition, 15 April.

Central Statistical Office (1994) *Social Trends*, CSO, London.

Commission of the European Communities, (1993) *Employment in Europe*, Directorate-General, Employment, Industrial Relations and Social Affairs, Brussels.

Cooper, C. and Lewis, S. (1993) *The Workplace Revolution: Managing Today's Dual Career Families*, Kogan Page, London.

Coyle, D. (1996) 'The Wage gap leaves women in part-time ghettos', *The Independent* (Business Section), 21 March: 24.

Coyles, M. (1995) 'Women on Top', *Sunday Observer* (Business Section), 19 March: 10.

CREW (1996) 'Women in Decision-making', 4th edn, (Report 6–7).

Davidson, M. and Cooper, C. (eds) (1993) *European Women in Business and Management*, Paul Chapman, London.

European Business Survey (1996) *Proportion of SMEs with No Women in Management*.

European Employment Initiative (1996) *Employment NOW*.

Financial Times, (1991) 23 June.

Griffith, V. (1998) *Financial Times*, 20 April.

Hanninen-Salmelin, E. and Petajaniemi, T. (1994) 'Women managers: the case of Finland', in N. Adler and D. Izraeli (eds), *Competitive Frontiers: Women Managers in a Global Economy*, Blackwell, Cambridge, MA.

Harvey, J.C. and Katz, C. (1983) *If I'm So Successful, Why Do I Feel Like a Fake: Impostor Phenomenon*, St Martins Press, New York.

Hussell, L. (1996) 'Why the perfect boss is a woman', *Daily Mail*, 31 October: 15.

The Independent (1995) 'The declining appeal of motherhood', 11 April: 13.

International Labour Organization (1998) *World of Work*, 23: 8. ILO, Switzerland.

Labour Force Survey Quarterly Bulletin, March 1998.

Laufer, J. (1993) 'France', in M. Davidson and C. Cooper (eds), *European Women in Business and Management*, Paul Chapman, London.

National Management Salary Survey, Institute of Management (IM) and Remuneration Economics, Press Release, 5 November 1998.

Office of National Statistics (1996) *New Earnings Survey*, ONS, London.
Office of National Statistics (1998) *National Management Salary Survey*, ONS, London.
Panorama documentary (1994) 'The Future is Female'.
Pillinger, J. (1992) *Feminising the Market: Women's Pay and Employment in the European Community*, Macmillan, London.
Pope, N. and Woods, R. (1997) 'Clever girls racked by imposter syndrome', *The Sunday Times*, 30 March: 11.
Serdjanian, E. (1994) Women managers in France, in N. Adler and D. Izraeli (eds), *Competitive Frontiers*, Blackwell, Cambridge, MA.
Tijdens, K. (1993) 'The Netherlands', in M. Davidson and C. Cooper (eds), *European Women in Business and Management*, Paul Chapman, London.
The Times (1992) 21 November: 15a.
Tomlinson, J. (1998) *Women at Work*, MEP European Report, March.
Welsh Office, Department for Education and Employment, 1995/96 GCSE and GCE A/As examination results.
Whirlpool Foundation (1996) *Women Setting New Priorities*, European Study, Whirlpool Foundation.
www.nando.net (1996) Nearly 60 per cent of European working women are major breadwinners.

3

French Women Managers: A Search for Equality but Enduring Differences

Jacqueline Laufer

Women managers have increased in France during the last 15 years in noticeable proportion. They now represent around 30 per cent of the total category of managers. However, in spite of the increase in the rate of activity of women in the workforce, their spectacular progress in the educational sphere and in qualified and professional jobs (including management), women's access to top-level jobs and senior staff positions within firms and in the economic sphere appears to progress relatively slowly.

Various explanations can be given for this unequal access to top-level jobs. While women's achievements in the academic sphere might be still too recent to secure them power positions in organizational hierarchies, processes linked with unequal opportunities can be observed within organizational cultures and hierarchies where women are still confronted by 'glass ceiling' effects of various natures.

Women's own professional and personal strategies can also lead some of them to have what could be considered an ambivalent attitude towards a 'masculine' model of career progression. On the basis of recent research findings on female managers' career processes, a conflict between 'time' and 'power' for some women managers can be identified (Laufer and Fouquet, 1997). Not that French women managers do not want to have careers or to exert power, but compared to their male counterparts, they face more tension between careers and the demands of reconciliation with family responsibilities, especially in the case of dual career couples (CEREQ, 1997).

While voluntary and positive actions could be implemented by French organizations to facilitate women's access to top jobs, analysis of existing equal opportunity schemes negotiated under the 1983 law on professionnal equality indicates that they gave little attention to the issue of women managers' access to top-level jobs. Another trend for change can be found in the debate now taking place in France, as elsewhere, concerning flexibility of working time to satisfy both the demands of the firm and the aspiration of employees to accommodate professional and family responsibilities.

Women in management

In 1994, women represented 44 per cent of the active working population in France. Employment in France is characterized by a high concentration of women in typically female jobs and by a high level of professional and social inequalities between women with and without qualifications (Maruani, 1998). In 1990, out of 455 listed professions, 20 covered 47 per cent of employed women, and in 316 women comprised less than 10 per cent of the workforce. Less qualified women are restricted, by and large, to childcare, cleaning jobs, routine administration jobs and sales. Women also constitute the vast majority of primary school teachers and nurses (INSEE, Service des Droits des Femmes, 1995).

It is in administrative, managerial and professional occupations in both the public and private sectors that feminization has been evident. Women now represent 54 per cent of professors and members of scientific professions, 33 per cent of professionals but only 29 per cent of managers within private firms (27 per cent in public service). However, their participation as managers has greatly increased during the last 15 years and has more than doubled since 1982, from 125,000 to 300,000 in 1994. While administrative and commercial jobs are now largely feminized – the proportion of women has grown from 19 per cent to 29 per cent since 1982 – the technical jobs remain largely masculine. In spite of a large increase (women were 6 per cent of engineers in 1982), women represented only 13 per cent of engineers and technical managers by 1994 (Laufer and Fouquet, 1997).

Advertising and public relations, administration and finance, recruitment, training and personnel administration are among the more feminized occupational categories. For example, women represent up to 48 per cent of the managers in public relations. They are less well represented among sales and commercial managers, at around 15 per cent. However, it is among top executives and senior staff that women are the least represented, constituting only 7 per cent of the total (Laufer and Fouquet, 1997). Among the CEOs of the 200 largest French firms, there is not one woman (Bauer and Bertin-Mourot, 1996), and among the top executives of these firms, women form only 5 per cent of top executive team members. Moreover, public firms appear to be no more 'open' to appointing women to top executive positions (Bertin-Mourot, 1998).

A 1996 sample of 5,000 leading firms in France, and their 26,700 top executives, showed that the share of women among top executives decreases as the size of the firms increases. While in the smaller firms (less than 50 employees) women represent 8.7 per cent of the top executives, in those firms employing 500 and more, only 4.8 per cent of executives are women. However, some economic sectors are more favourable to women. In the hotel and catering business, for example, women represent 16 per cent of the top executives; in luxury goods and clothings, 13 per cent; in cosmetics and pharmacy, 12 per cent, and in the media, 12 per cent.[1]

In other sectors women represent between 12 per cent and 6 per cent of the senior executives: computer industries, retailing, food industries and transportation. Nevertheless, it is still difficult for women to reach senior positions in industries such as plane manufacturing, building and public works, where only 4 per cent of the top positions are filled by women (Laufer and Fouquet, 1997).

The increase in women among managers and in professional categories in France, as in other European countries, can be largely related to the progress of girls in the educational system. There has been a large increase in the number of students reaching the baccalaureate level at the end of secondary school, and within this growth, a rise in the representation of women. By 1994, girls represented 53 per cent of the students in the last year of secondary school. After an increase of 56 per cent in the number of university students between 1982 and 1992, girls constitute 55 per cent of the student population. The representation of women has increased across all disciplines: they represent 71 per cent in humanities, 66 per cent in pharmacy, 60 per cent in law, 50 per cent in economies and in medicine. However, the proportion is only 36.4 per cent in sciences. In the French system of *grandes écoles* (business and engineering schools), women are also well represented: close to 50 per cent in business schools and 22 per cent in engineering schools (INSEE, Service des Droits des Femmes, 1995).

Another factor in the progress of women among the managerial ranks is the increasing trend for a continuous pattern of employment for working women in France, and especially for qualified women. In the past, French women would interrupt their working lives to have children but this is no longer the case. In 1994, 77 per cent of working women between the ages of 30 and 40 were economically active, against 79 per cent in the age ranges 25–29 and 40–44 (INSEE, Service des Droits des Femmes, 1995).

Furthermore, France, like many other European countries such as Denmark, Portugal and Belgium, has seen the rate of activity of mothers increasing with the level of education. It is among those with university diplomas that we find the highest employment rates for mothers (CCE, 1995). In France, 75 per cent of university-educated women with three children were in employment in 1990, compared with 45 per cent of mothers of three without qualifications (Chaudron, 1991).

Women managers and careers

Women managers have not always been able to compete on a level playing field with men, especially in terms of formal education. It was only in the 1970s that the leading *grandes écoles* were opened to women both in the engineering and in the business management field.

In a study conducted in 1982 in various sectors and types of firms including department stores, a bank, a computer firm and a communication agency, while a third of the 40 women sampled had become 'cadre' (middle manager or manager) on the basis of internal promotion, other women had a university diploma and a few had graduated from engineering or business schools (Laufer, 1982).

This study went on to reveal that in the computer industry a few women had broken the glass ceiling by obtaining 'masculine' jobs in sales or marketing functions. In the communication agency, they were well represented in the 'creative function'. However, the dominant pattern for women managers was one of specific career paths and 'feminine careers': staff jobs within administrative or accounting functions, 'assistance' jobs on the basis of legal or human resource expertise, jobs which would be 'peripheral' to men's decision-making or operational jobs, jobs which were considered compatible with 'feminine qualities': loyalty, stability or such qualities as 'taste for the product' in the case of purchasing jobs.

In all these jobs, women were still supposed to use 'feminine qualities' or 'feminine motivations', which would make them 'complementary' to men, while their career paths were not supposed to be identical to those of men in terms of decision-making power.

As for women themselves, they defined their motivations in terms of interest for a job where they could use their specific expertise: accounting, law, personnel management issues, etc. – and in terms of stability. They often mentioned that they were not interested in 'management' or in 'power' this motivation often being related to the fact that it allowed those particular women managers to reconcile the demands between work and family. Only a small group of women managers, generally single and without children, could then keep up with a 'masculine' career model (Laufer, 1982).In other words, the situation of women managers remained characterized by a traditional articulation between feminine and masculine roles, and by such key features as 'subordination' of feminine roles to masculine roles or by 'complementarity' between these roles, leading women managers to limit their career aspirations.

In many ways, access of women managers to the same formal educational status as men tends to 'homogenize' the career prospects of men and women managers. As a consequence of their achievements in the educational sphere, the graduate female population now has access to much more similar jobs to those occupied by their male counterparts in managerial and professional ranks. During the last 10 years, the best-qualified women have therefore been able to share with men the benefits of the rapid increase in managerial and professional jobs (CEREQ, 1997).

A recent study of women managers also indicates that a characteristic feature of the present evolution is the more proactive orientation of many women managers toward career achievements (Laufer and Fouquet, 1997). Far from defining their careers only in terms of 'interest for the job', many young female managers now want to have a diversified profile of career and not to be stuck in a specialist profile. To this extent, functional mobility is sought, together with the development of a diversified set of competences including management skills, and the will to experience both staff and operational functions.

Beyond the desire to discover a diversity of jobs and acquire new competences, these young women managers do not want only to be guided by the opportunities offered by the firm but also want to bring them about. The main issue for them is to become visible in their professional environment through capitalizing on their own successes, and to take their own destiny in hand.

Another feature of this proactive orientation can be described as a 'taste for performance'. This is often linked to the performance evaluation systems found now in an increasing number of firms. Women managers know that they can benefit from such performance appraisal systems, which often contribute to the eradication of traditional and stereotyped attitudes towards women's managerial roles. While a taste for 'power' was not supposed to exist on the part of women managers in the past, younger women managers emphasize that power in its various forms is needed if they are to make something of their working lives. These women managers also express a clear awareness of the need to manage the balance between family and career. While for some time, women managers justified their own restrictive attitude towards having a career because of their family responsibilities, younger women managers emphasize that they want to manage this tension without sacrificing either dimension of their lives. Finally, functional and external mobility are considered as obvious ingredients of an ascending career. Geographical mobility – national and international – is of course another issue, especially for dual career couples (Laufer and Fouquet, 1998a).

While in some firms the choice of an international career is made quite early in the career process and concerns *de facto* only men or single women managers, in other firms, international – European or worldwide – assignments are considered a necessary step for a fully fledged career leading to senior staff roles. While these firms are concerned by the need to accommodate as best they can – for their own interest and for the interest of the managers – the dual career situation of their most promising young women and men managers, international mobility can be seen as a key issue and obstacle to women managers' access to senior staff jobs (Laufer and Fouquet, 1997).

A facilitating factor for women's careers is the increasing concern of many firms for the career development of younger managers. This leads these firms to offer young women managers similar career paths to those of men with the same qualifications (engineering or business) and career paths which are grounded in the same diversity of job experiences, for example in marketing or more technical functions. This evolution cannot be generalized to all firms but it illustrates a general concern within organizations to make the best use of available human resources at all levels for the global performance of the firm (Laufer and Fouquet, 1997, 1998a).

However, in spite of identical diplomas and more proactive career orientations, some noticeable differences can still be found between men and women managers in terms of salaries and careers.

A recent study of the graduates of one of the top French engineering schools indicated that, while two-thirds of women graduates had managerial and personnel responsibilities and 25 per cent of them managed teams of more than 10 people, they had less access to leading positions: director, head of department, chief engineer, etc. (Marry, 1995). In 1994 a study of the graduates of top French management schools reached similar conclusions. While the women graduates did have access to a wide variety of managerial functions, they were less well represented among the chief executives and had responsibility for fewer people, only 4 per cent of junior managers and 13 per cent of senior managers (HEC Junior Conseil, 1994). These differences in managerial responsibilities have, among other factors, an impact on remuneration. Indeed, the differential of salary between men and women managers in France is roughly 15 per cent (INSEE, Service des Droits des Femmes, 1995; Silvera, 1996).

Glass ceiling effects

Various types of explanation can be found in the literature to account for the glass ceiling effects which characterize French women managers.

The first type of explanation has to do with what we could call a situation of historical delay. When few women graduated from university or gained engineering and business school degrees, they were obviously unable to compete on an equal footing with men for the top-level jobs.

A second type of explanation now established by some studies in France, and even more in the Anglo-Saxon literature, has to do with the multidimensional organizational processes which tend to produce glass ceiling effects and still limit the career development of women managers and therefore their access to top management positions. Among processes which tend to discriminate explicitly or implicitly against women we find such phenomena as the negative effects of masculine organizational cultures, persistent stereotypes related to career paths or jobs 'suited' to women, and implicit co-optation processes which determine access to top jobs and which tend to favour men (Laufer, 1982, 1996; Laufer and Fouquet, 1997). It is also evident that women have to be more mobile to gain access to top-level jobs. While in France, top leaders are generally recruited from outside the firm, this is even more the case for women, which means that to get access to top level jobs, women have to display an even more proactive attitude than men. This is all the more significant given the traditional image that women managers are less mobile than their male counterparts (Bertin-Mourot, 1998). Indeed, it appears – as only 7 per cent of top executives are women – that neither women managers nor firms have yet overcome the obstacles facing women in their access to the top-level jobs. In these situations where – as one woman manager puts it – 'the game is no longer competence-based but power-based', the top power structures of firms do tend to remain 'masculine clubs' (Laufer and Fouquet, 1997).

However, some significant evolution could take place through the development of mentorship. Indeed, in some firms mentorship appears to be an essential ingredient in French women managers' access to top jobs (Laufer and Fouquet, 1997) as it is in other cultures and countries (Ibarra and Smith-Lovin, 1997; Schor, 1998). More awareness of these key processes among French firms – and French researchers – should lead to a more systematic evaluation of how they could be developed to facilitate women's careers. As to women managers' networks, only French-based American firms provide examples of such strategies and can testify to their usefulness, but up to now these have not taken root in French firms (Laufer and Fouquet, 1997).

A third type of explanation of the factors which impede women managers' access to top-level jobs has to do with women's own career strategies and ambivalent attitude towards a 'masculine' type of career orientation which could be characterized by competition for power (Marry, 1995; Laufer, 1997). In fact, it does appear that this ambivalent attitude has much to do with the tensions felt by women managers, endeavouring to maintain a balance between professional and family responsibilities.

While many women managers no longer want to have to choose between career and family aspirations, the unequal sharing of family responsibilities continues to determine their career development. In 1994 while only 9 per cent of business school graduates felt that they had given up their career ambitions for family reasons, the issue of home/work time organization remained a difficulty for a large share of them (HEC Junior Conseil, 1994). In the case of engineering school graduates, the majority of female graduates were married, had children, and were part of a dual career couple. This situation had an impact on the working hours of the managers, both male and female. Half of the male graduates worked more than 50 hours a week and worked evenings and weekends, while this was the case for only a quarter of the women graduates (Marry, 1995). Given the fact that most women – and men – managers assert that 'availability' is a major element in career success, this situation brings about some specific difficulties for women (Laufer and Fouquet, 1997). Another study of 40 university graduates (men and women) showed that after eight years of professional activity, it is only when young women managers liberate themselves from family constraints that they have the same career expectations as men (CEREQ, 1997).

While this has to be put into the context of the dominant model of working hours for managers in France, which is one of very long hours (Bouffartigues, 1996; Boulin and Plasman, 1997), it does have a negative impact on women managers' access to careers and to top-level jobs. While women managers in the most advanced firms do not face as many of the risks of specific career tracks, the balance between career and family life remains a major source of tension, in a context where globalization and a search for competitiveness leads to very demanding models of managerial job functions. Women managers are very much aware that availability has been a key factor in their career achievement, but at one point – usually after the birth of a first or second child – the tension between conflicting demands, and especially time demands, comes to the forefront.

Equal opportunities and positive actions

French women managers have benefited little from the French legal attempts to promote positive action devised by the 1983 law on professional equality and companies have on the whole been reluctant to be the main initiators in the implementation of equal opportunity programmes (Chalude et al., 1994).[2] In general firms have shown little concern to integrate corrective positive measures into employment practices. Only around 30 French firms have implemented positive action schemes, which means that most companies have not felt it necessary to include equal opportunities among their strategic objectives; or, if they have, they have seen no reason to publicize their commitment to gender equality (Laufer, 1998a). Whenever adopted, these positive action schemes have covered such areas as recruitment, career development, training and the reconciliation of work and family life (Laufer, 1991). While training has been at the centre of most equality plans, training schemes have mainly been directed towards factory workers with few qualifications.

These schemes could have been considered productive experiments on the basis of which some expertise on positive action strategies could have been developed, but this has not been the case and positive action strategies have not, up to now, gained legitimacy among French firms. There are several possible reasons why so few firms have regarded positive action strategies as legitimate or economically useful. One reason is the lack of political will on the part of the French state, reflected in the limited public resources allocated to implementation of the initiative of the 1983 law (Mazur, 1995). The legislation had emphasized a voluntary approach to positive action and did not specify the scope of negotiation between social partners. To make such a decentralized and permissive approach work, a vigorous communication strategy involving publicity, advice and support structures was required. In reality these were offered on a limited scale and barely sustained (Laufer, 1998a).

While a determined attitude characterized the first years after the enactment of the law, as in particular public employers were called upon to experiment and to innovate in the field of equal opportunity strategies, other priorities took precedence as unemployment grew and began to dominate public discourse about the French labour market. Indeed, only four public sector employers have negotiated *plans d'égalité*, and in these organizations the situation of women continued to be characterized by strong inequality of access to some traditionally male jobs, and to higher-level jobs in general (Grandin et al., 1989; Laufer, 1996).

A second reason relates to the behaviour and attitudes of French trade unions. With some exceptions, trade unions have done little to promote positive action, leaving this largely to management. In many cases it was clear that unions, lacking familiarity with the subject of professional equality, found it difficult to develop their own proposals.

A third explanation for the reluctance of firms and unions to negotiate specifically on equal oppotunities might be, paradoxically, the high degree of regulation of wage structures and employment contracts in France. French firms are already subject to minimum-wage laws, to compulsory negotiation on remuneration, to minimum amounts of funds which must be devoted to training, and to public policies in the social sphere (specifically training programmes to requalify unskilled workers or to develop new skills, etc.). Though these requirements are not explicitly geared to equal opportunities, firms have a tendency to assume that in meeting these requirements and calling on publicly funded training they are, in effect, fulfilling their institutional obligation to both men and women (Laufer, 1998a).

Reconciling professional and family responsibilities

French state family policies have long been geared towards the reconciliation of professional and family responsibilities by providing French women with public crèches, nursery schooling, financial support for child-minding, and tax deductions for employing help in the home when children are small (Hantrais and Letablier, 1996).[3]

Beyond maternity leave, parental leave has existed since 1977: this allows, under certain conditions, any salary earner to take unpaid leave for up to three years.[4] A parental allowance also allows mothers (or fathers) of two children to take a break from the labour market. However, the take-up of parental leave can be considered quite risky in terms of career progression since parental leave does guarantee a return to employment but not in the same job or in the same part of the firm. As for parental leave allowance, its low amount makes it more likely for women with low salaries to take advantage of it (Fagnani, 1998).[5]

As for part-time work, while it has been developing in France, it is predominantly located in low-level jobs in both public and private sectors in the form of 'imposed' part-time work rather than 'chosen' part-time work. While only 5 per cent of men work part time, this compares to 28 per cent of active working women. Except in the public sector, part-time jobs are concentrated in services for which qualifications are low – retail trade, catering and cleaning. Of women managers, only 9 per cent work part time (INSEE, Service des Droits des Femmes, 1995).

However, the right for managers to work part time – generally 80 per cent of the 'normal' time – does exist, especially the right to take part-time parental leave after the birth of a child. Nevertheless, the implicit or explicit norms, in terms of managerial implication in most firms, are that part-time working and full career development are generally incompatible, given the demands of the jobs. Consequently, it means that if a woman manager wants to work part time, she will have to look for or to accept those jobs perceived as compatible with part time, even if intrinsically these jobs are not the most favourable from the point of view of career development. Most French women managers who would like to work part time in private firms face the incompatibility of being part time and having a career. Only a limited number of firms offer an explicit family-friendly policy which incorporates part-time positions for managers. However, these policies seldom take into account the risks that exist for women working part time in terms of image and evaluation and their consequences on career and pay (Laufer, 1998b).

Women entrepreneurs

Women entrepreneurs in France constitute a minority: they represent only 15 per cent of the category. In recent years the number of female heads of firms employing more than 10 people has been increasing slightly. There were 16,000 in 1982, and in 1994 this had increased to 18,000, which represent 0.2 per cent of the female working population. However, their share in this category has slightly diminished since the number of men heading firms of more than 10 people has increased more rapidly (Laufer and Fouquet, 1997).

Recent research emphasized a diversified pattern concerning access to the status of entrepreneur in small and medium-sized firms in France. One study indicated that among women entrepreneurs, 46 per cent had started their own business, while 33 per cent had bought it and 27 per cent had inherited it. A similar type of distribution can be found among men entrepreneurs. It does not appear, therefore, that there is a feminine specificity as to the mode of access to the status of entrepreneurs in small and medium-sized firms (Duchenaud, 1996).[6] However, a survey on entrepreneurs who started their businesses in 1990–91 shows that while 0.63 per cent of the masculine population over 15 years old created a business, women entrepreneurs were only 0.23 per cent of the feminine population. The likelihood of women starting a business appears to be related – even more than in the case of men – to their level of education: 26 per cent of women entrepreneurs had studied beyond the baccalaureate against 10 per cent of the total female population over 15 years old (INSEE Service des Droits des Femmes, 1995).

Another study (Laufer and Fouquet, 1997), of a sample of 100 women heads of firms in the Paris region, tended to show that women entrepreneurs head rather small firms as only 13 per cent of the respondents were leading firms of over 200 persons.[7] Also, 60 per cent of the firms belonged to the service sector (consulting, training, but also cleaning, catering, etc.) and only 17 per cent to the industrial sector, with 23 per cent of the firms having commercial (retail and wholesale) activities. A majority of women in the sample – 83 per cent – had a university degree, 62 per cent were married and only a minority had no children, which indicates that they were able to reconcile professional and family responsibilities. Among the respondents, 44 per cent had started their own businesses, while the others either took over a family business or an existing firm, or became head of a firm through internal promotion (9 per cent). Only 34 per cent of the respondents had the intention to head a firm from the start of their professional life and 48 per cent of them had occupied between two and four jobs before becoming entrepreneur or head of a firm. For those who started their own business, the wish to develop an activity in relation to their present job or a new activity, association with the project of their husband, encountering potential associates or the loss of a job, appeared to be the most frequent triggering factors. Among those firms which were started by the respondents, only 20 per cent employed more than 50 people.

While the respondents indicated that they encountered difficulties when they became heads of firms (financial difficulties, 39 per cent; reconciliation of professional and family life, 33 per cent; commercial difficulties, 31 per cent; difficulties with the constitution of a team, 26 per cent), three-quarters of them thought that men would have encountered the same difficulties. The main motivations of those women entrepreneurs and heads of firms was to ensure the profitability of their businesses (65 per cent) and to ensure a basis for their professional and personal autonomy (57 per cent). Half of the respondents worked within the firm with one or several members of their family, usually their husbands. This was often the case for those women who had inherited their business or for those who had started their own business (Laufer and Fouquet, 1997).

While many recent studies raise the issue as to whether or not women entrepreneurs manage 'differently', i.e. with different values (Birley, 1989, Olson and Curie, 1992), the respondents tended to answer that on the various issues linked to managerial practices, they think they behaved similarly to men (Laufer and Fouquet, 1997).

Entrepreneurship does appear here as a true alternative to organizational careers for women. Through such ventures, women with various levels of educational qualifications can indeed gain access to power and decision-making, capitalizing both on educational qualifications and on prior professional experience. Available data indicate however that women who are already entrepreneurs or independent professionals are more likely to start their own business than wage earners (INSEE, 1995). Further research should reveal more information as to whether or not the obstacles women managers face in breaking the glass ceiling within large organizations could be a powerful motivation for women to start or to take over an independent business. It would also be worthwhile to investigate why the proportion of women entrepreneurs has not increased more in recent years.

Conclusion

French women managers have benefited from the development of managerial and professional jobs and enjoy a diversified set of careers. However, they have not greatly increased their representation among entrepreneurs, are absent from the CEOs of the 200 largest French organizations and are still quite under-represented among the top leaders of large firms. While there is little evidence that in the short term this situation can be tackled through positive action, the emerging concern for more parity between men and women in the sharing of power could benefit women managers' access to tops jobs. Indeed, the 'parity movement' has made a strong impact in France (Pisier, 1995; Sineau, 1995). It is viewed not only as an answer to the contrast between a well asserted principle of equality and of professional equality and the continuing scarcity of women in elected assemblies at both the national and regional level, but also in relation to power position and decision-making jobs, especially in the political sphere, a situation which puts France in a low ranking position among European countries (Mossuz-Lavau, 1998). As a consequence of this public debate, the issue of the difficult access for women to power positions in the business sector, which contrasts with their increasing access to careers could gain new visibility (Laufer and Fouquet, 1997).

Other changes, in the reduction of working hours and the more flexible organization of working time, could also help address important factors which hinder equal opportunity for men and women managers (Laufer, 1998b).[8] While there is much controversy as to how the reduction in working time could apply to the specificity of managerial work, it does create a new awareness of the dominating model of long working hours which characterizes French management (Bouffartigues and Bocchino, 1998). This model as a side effect has a negative impact on women managers' career expectations, given the unequal sharing of professional and family responsibilities between men and women.

Notes

1   This study includes a statistical analysis of the situation of French women managers based on the INSEE (National Institute of Economic and Statistical Studies) 1993 and 1994 employment surveys and the 1990 population census. To get a more detailed picture of top female executives, it also includes a secondary analysis of the 'Carnet du Nouvel

Economiste' (1996) which presents the '5,000 leading firms' in France and their 26,700 executives. A qualitative analysis on a sample of 40 women managers is also taken. The sample considered here is of 40 women from five large firms, three of which are multinational, and two French, with activities including computer activities, pharmaceutical industries and chemical products, banking, electrical and domestic appliances. These firms were chosen because their human resource policy was oriented towards the career development of women – and men – graduates, and because these firms were known to have some concern for equal opportunity and for an equal recruitment policy of young men and young women graduates.

The women managers we interviewed were identified by human resource managers. These were asked to identify 'successful' women who held top-level jobs within the firms. Their ages ranged from 27 to 45 years. All but two had a university diploma or had graduated from a *grande école*. Seventeen of them had one or several children and eleven had none (Laufer and Fouquet, 1997).

2 In France it is the 13 July 1983 law on professional equality which constitutes the legal basis for positive action in the private sector. Each year, companies must draw up a report on the comparative status of women and men in relation to recruitment, training, promotion, qualifications, working conditions and pay. This report must be discussed with the elected work council. Companies are also encouraged to negotiate positive action schemes with trade unions to improve the status of women in areas such as recruitment, training, promotion or working conditions. Financial aid can be granted by the state, if the proposed measures are judged to be 'exemplary'. If negotiation fails, the management of the firm can implement the scheme by themselves. Since 1987, another measure to promote gender equality and break down sex segregation is the 'contrat pour la mixité des emplois' a contract for the desegregation of jobs. Firms can sign contracts with the government concerning the training and promotion of individual women. These contracts are directed at small and medium-sized businesses which employ up to 600 people. They are designed to promote a greater number of women in positions traditionally occupied by men. More than 1,000 individual affirmative action contracts have been signed up to now. Financial aid from the state provides 50 per cent of the training costs and a 30 per cent wage subsidy during the length of training period. Some of these contracts could facilitate access for a number of women to middle management, but in general they have only marginally affected women managers as such.

3 Since 1986, the AGED (Allocation de Garde d'Enfants à Domicile) has provided support for families to employ a childminder in their homes in the form of social insurance cover until the child has reached the age of three; in the context of growing unemployment this was seen as much as job creation as a gender equality measure.

4 Parental leave and part-time parental leave are open to any parent having a child under three.

5 APE (parental allowance) can be claimed by parents who have two or three children, whose youngest child is less than three years old, and who have been professionally active for at least two of the past five years. The full allowance is about 3,000 francs a month. Half of the allowance can be combined with a part-time job. Between 1994 and 1998, 500,000 women took up the scheme, some of whom were previously unemployed (Fagnani, 1998).

6 The total here is greater than 100 due to some multiple answers. The study by B. Duchenaut covered 5,800 firms employing 10 to 499 people (Duchenaud, 1996).

7 The study was performed by random sampling on the basis of files held by the Chamber of Commerce of Paris. Four hundred questionnaires were sent out and the response rate was 25 per cent (Laufer and Fouquet, 1997).

8 A law was passed in France on 13 June 1998 aiming to reduce the length of work from 39 to 35 hours a week. On 1 January 2000 this will apply to all firms employing 20 persons or more and on January 2002, to all firms employing less than 20 persons. The 1998 law includes various measures to encourage social partners to anticipate and to negotiate over working time, job creation and flexible working time organization.

References

Bauer, M. and Bertin-Mourot, B. (1996) *Vers un Modèle européen de dirigeant?* CNRS – BOYDEN, Paris.

Bertin-Mourot, B. (1998) 'Toujours pas de dirigeantes à l'horizon', *Le Pouvoir au féminin, les femmes dirigeantes en entreprise, Les cahiers ENSPTT*, 8 (Avril): 50–53.

Birley, S. (1989) 'Female entrepreneurs. Are they really different?' *Journal of Small Business Management*, 30 (1) January: 32–37.

Bouffartigues, P. (1996) 'Le temps de travail des cadres: enjeux, potentialités, perplexités', *Stratégie et ressources humaines*, 16: 35–39.

Bouffartigues, P. and Bocchino, M. (1998) 'Travailler sans compter son temps? Les cadres et le temps de travail', *Travail et emploi*, 74 (01/98): 37–51.

Boulin, J.Y. and Plasman, R. (1997) 'Le temps de travail des cadres en Europe'. Symposium Eurocadres, Bruxelles.

CCE (Commission des Communautes Europeènnes) (1995) Bulletin sur les femmes et l'emploi, No. 6, Direction Generale Emploi et Affaines Sociales, Unité' Egalité des Chances, April.

CEREQ (1997) 'Insertion professionnelle et début de carrière – Les inégalités professionnelles entre hommes et femmes résistent-elles au diplôme?' *Cereq Bref* 135 (Octobre).

Chalude, M., De Jong, A. and Laufer, J. (1994) 'Implementing equal opportunity and affirmative action programmes', in M. Davidson and R. Burke (eds), *Women in Management: Current Research Issues*, Paul Chapman, London.

Chaudron, M. (1991) 'Vie de famille, vie de travail', in F. De Singly (ed.), *La Famille, l'état des savoirs*, La Découverte, Paris.

Duchenaud, B. (1996) *Les Dirigeants de PME, enquête, chiffres, analyse*, Editions Maxima, Paris.

Fagnani, J. (1998) 'Lacunes, contradictions et incohérences des mesures de conciliation travail/famille', *Droit social*, 6: 596–602.

Grandin, C., Maruani, M. and Meynaud, H. (1989) 'L'Inégalité professionnelle dans les entreprises publiques à statut règlementaire', GIP, *Mutations industrielles*, 34, Paris.

Hantrais, L. and Letablier, M.T. (1996) *Familles, travail et politiques familales eu Europe*, cahiers du Centre d'Etudes de l'Emploi, Service des Droits des Femmes, Paris.

HEC Junior Conseil (1994) L'evolution professionnelle des diplomés. Groupe HEC: Jouy en Josas.

Ibarra, H. and Smith-Lovin, L. (1997) 'New directions in social network research on gender and organizational careers', in C.L. Cooper and S.E. Jackson (eds), *Creating Tomorrow's Research Organizations*, Wiley, Chichester.

INSEE – Service des Droits des Femmes (1995) *Les femmes, contours et caractères*, INSEE, Paris.

Laufer, J. (1982) *La Féminité neutralisée – Les femmes cadres dans l'entreprise*, Editions Flammarion, Paris.

Laufer, J. (1998a) 'Equal opportunity between men and women: the case of France', *Feminist Economics*, 4 (1): 53–69.

Laufer, J. (1998b) 'Les Femmes cadres entre le pouvoir et le temps?' *Revue française des affaires sociales*, 3 (Juillet–Septembre): 55–70.

Laufer, J. (1991) *L'entreprise et l'égalité des chances: enjeux et démarches*, La Documentation Française, Paris.

Laufer, J. (1996) 'Les Carrières féminines à EDF–GDF: regards d'hier, regards d'aujourd'hui', in H.Y. Meynaud (ed.), *Les Sciences sociales et l'entreprise: 50 ans de recherches à EDF*, La Découverte, Paris.

Laufer, J. (1997) 'L'accès des femmes à la décision économique', in F. Gaspard (ed.), *Les Femmes dans la prise de décision en France et en Europe*, L'Harmattan, Paris.

Laufer, J. and Fouquet, A. (1997) *Effet de plafonnement de carrière des femmes cadres et accès des femmes à la décision économique*, Groupe HEC, Centre d'Etudes de l'Emploi, Service des Droits des Femmes, Paris.

Laufer, J. and Fouquet, A. (1998a) 'La nouvelle donne pour les femmes en entreprise', *Le Pouvoir au féminin, les femmes dirigeantes en entreprise, Les cahiers ENSPTT*, 8 (Avril): 17–24.

Laufer, J. and Fouquet, A. (1998b) 'Les Femmes dans l'entreprise: le plafond de verre est toujours là', *Revue Française de gestion*, 119 (Juin–Juillet–Août): 143–144.

Marry, C. (1995) 'Polytechniciennes = polytechniciens?' *Les Cahiers du Mage*, 3/4, CNRS–IRESCO, Paris.

Maruani, M. (ed.) (1998) *Les Nouvelles frontières de l'inégalité, hommes et femmes sur le marché du travail*, La Découverte, Paris.

Mazur, A. (1995) *Gender Bias and the State. Symbolic Reform at Work in the Fifth Republic of France*, University of Pittsburgh Press, Pittsburgh.

Mossuz-Lavau, J. (1998) *Femmes/hommes pour la parité*, Presse de Sciences Po., Paris.

Olson, S.F. and Curie, H.M. (1992) 'Female entrepreneurs: personal values and business strategies in a male dominated industry', *Journal of Small Business Management*, 30 (1): 49–57.

Pisier, E. (1995) 'Egalité ou parité?' in *EPHESIA: La Place des femmes, les enjeux de l'identité et de l'egalité au regard des sciences sociales*, La Découverte, Paris.

Schor, S.M. (1998) 'Femmes, hommes: deux routes vers le sommet', *L'Expansion Management Review*, 88 (Mars): 37–44. (Translated from *Business Horizons*, 40 (5) September–October 1997.)

Silvera, R. (1996) *Le Salaire des femmes, toutes choses inégales*, La Documentation Française, Paris.

Sineau, M. (1995) 'Parité et principe d'égalité: le débat français', in *EPHESIA La Place des femmes, les enjeux de l'identité et de l'égalité au regard des sciences sociales*, La Découverte, Paris.

4

Women Managers and Business Owners in New Zealand

Judy McGregor and David Tweed

New Zealand has been falsely comforting itself that it is uniquely progressive in terms of women's equality ever since the nation was the first to grant women the vote in 1893. A century later the nation celebrated progress in eliminating discrimination against women with an emphasis on women achievers at work, particularly one or two exceptional and visible senior managers and a series of high-flying female entrepreneurs who had started their own businesses. A year-long series of sponsored television advertisements, for example, profiled success stories amongst women-owned businesses, concentrating on the glamorous aspects of self-employment without at the same time acknowledging any of the barriers specific to female self-employment, such as the domestic division of labour. The Suffrage Year Centennial celebrations, which achieved international attention, were a worthwhile consciousness-raising activity and a fitting acknowledgement of the strengths of individual women. But the hoopla diverted attention from New Zealand's inability to sustain the reputation it won for being the first nation state to deliver women's suffrage.

As predicted (McGregor, 1994), life after the year-long celebration has been a continuation for women at work of the struggle against fundamental and historical inequalities inherent in our society. Perhaps nowhere is this better reflected than in the status of New Zealand women in management. Women have persistently failed to reach leading positions in both private sector corporations and in the public sector in any numbers. Additionally, the higher the management position, the more glaring the gender gap in terms of numbers and salary difference (McGregor et al., 1994).

Comparative research shows, in fact, that many of the features of women's economic development in terms of achieving management positions and setting up their own businesses are similar to other countries. For example, the remarkable explosion of women's participation in small business ownership in New Zealand, is part of a worldwide phenomenon. It follows international trends in other Western developed nations such as rising education levels for women, increasing female labour force participation through new entry jobs, re-entry and part-time work.

But there are some unique features of the status of managerial women and the state of female entrepreneurship in New Zealand which have prompted debate and are subjects of research attention. It is these features, which highlight both similarities with and differences from other countries, which are addressed in this chapter. First it is important when examining the status of women in management in New Zealand and the role of female entrepreneurship to address the relevant cultural, social and economic environments in which these women in business are situated.

Environmental factors

New Zealand has a dominant view of itself which influences the cultural environment of women's progress at work. The country has only 3.6 million people, and is geographically isolated at the bottom of the globe with Australia as its nearest neighbour. It has unique difficulties associated with its size and isolation in competing in the global marketplace and in the processes of internationalization. The country's scale, physical insularity and ethnocentrism have also, though, underpinned New Zealand's sense of identity as ingeniously self-sufficient. More recently the position of women at the top, whether it be in management positions, on corporate boards, in self-employment or as leaders, has been spotlighted by the elevation of New Zealand's first female Prime Minister, Jenny Shipley, who heads the National Party and leads the Coalition Government. For the first time this pitted two female political leaders against each other at the top, with Labour's Helen Clark leading the main opposition party. In an important signal, Mrs Shipley retained for a short time the women's portfolio as Minister of Women's Affairs, which introduced a new gender dynamic into caucus deliberations. Much of Mrs Shipley's efforts have gone into strategy associated with the *Platform for Action* which was adopted by the Fourth World Conference on Women, Beijing, September 1995. At the conference the Minister announced she planned to:

> use the actions outlined in the *Platform* as the basis for developing a strategy for New Zealand women in terms of the areas of legislative, administrative and attitudinal change that still need attention. (Status of New Zealand Women Report, 1998)

As a consequence the New Zealand government is addressing several themes which are of relevance to this chapter. These are mainstreaming a gender perspective in the development of all policies and programmes, women's unremunerated work, the gender pay gap, an emphasis on indigenous (Maori) women, and enhancing women's role in decision-making.

Previous research in New Zealand shows that progress for women in business generally differs in a number of important ways according to whether women work in the public or private sectors (McGregor et al., 1994, 1997; Shilton et al., 1996; Pajo et al., 1997). This is partly because equal employment opportunities legislation is compulsory in the public sector but voluntary in the private sector. The research shows, however, that the private sector in New Zealand is more conservative about women in the executive suite and that elevating women within managerial ranks remains a fundamental challenge for corporations in the new millennium.

Research opportunities and limitations

New Zealand's smallness provides both strengths and limitations for researchers interested in women in management and in self-employment. Obvious difficulties stem from its absence of a research tradition and the small number of people engaged in examining the role, status and experience of women in these fields. As the American researcher Sekaran (1990) notes, women in management as a field of research endeavour is relatively new, 'at best in its adulthood stage'. In the New Zealand context, though, it is still in its puberty. Many of the studies are benchmarking the status and situation of women with an eye to future longitudinal, comparative and contextual analysis. Much of the research compares and contrasts New Zealand with its larger neighbour, Australia, reflecting networks and alliances between researchers (McGregor et al., 1996). The need for more and better data collection on all aspects of women at work has been acknowledged by the government (Status of New Zealand Women Report, 1998).

The country's scale, equally, provides an important research opportunity to gather nationwide samples, whereas overseas researchers must often rely on regional or sectoral samples. In two major studies, one of women in management (McGregor et al., 1994) and the other of women in self-employment (McGregor and Tweed, 1998), nationwide samples were utilized. Additionally, these studies made it possible to address Australian criticism (Still and Chia, 1995) of the absence of comparative studies of the experiences of men and women, particularly when establishing whether there was a gender difference in barriers to progress.

Women in management

Women in New Zealand comprise 51.2 per cent of the working age population and 44.7 per cent of the labour force. While figures specific to female managers are hard to find, a partial picture emerges from official statistics which show that over the past six years there has been an increase in the proportion of women working in a combined category of legislators, administrators and managers (from 8.1 per cent in 1991 to 9.3 per cent in 1997, Status of New Zealand Women Report, 1998). Perhaps the most reliable picture of the status of managerial women in New Zealand came from a study which surveyed the top 663 organizations in New Zealand by number of employees and examined both public and private sectors (McGregor et al., 1994). The 188 organizations which responded (a response rate of 28.4 per cent) employed a total of 70,411 employees; 46,424 men and 23,987 women. Of the men employed, a total of 6,637 (14.3 per cent) held management positions. They also represented 84.3 per cent of the total management group. Of the 23,987 women employed, a total of 1,236 (5.2 per cent) held management positions. Women represented 15.7 per cent of the total management group. New Zealand, then, neatly fits into the ILO analysis of women in management which shows that according to national surveys, women's overall share of management jobs rarely exceeds 20 per cent (ILO, 1998).

Two other features of this study confirmed previous international scholarship as it relates to women in management (Still, 1990; Davidson and Cooper, 1992; Still et al., 1992). First, the study looked at the management composition of participating organizations and discovered that over half the women in the managerial sample were located at junior management levels and less than 8 per cent were in the top jobs. By comparison 20 per cent of male managers were in senior management. Furthermore the median remuneration packages of male and female managers showed that women earned substantially less than men, with the gender pay gap increasing at the top (see Table 4.1).

The study reported that 'at every level of management women are substantially under-represented, under-paid and there is little incentive for women to press on to senior management' (McGregor et al., 1994: 14). The findings were similar to those of a comparable study undertaken in Australia using a similar questionnaire to gather data (Still et al., 1994). The benchmark research, the first to examine women in management nationwide in New Zealand, was undertaken during a time of profound change in the country's organizational life. Since 1987 New Zealand has witnessed a dramatic embracing of *laissez-faire* economic policies which has resulted in a fundamental shift from public ownership to either corporatization or private ownership. Coupled with this organizational upheaval are the effects of the deregulation of New Zealand's labour market and its subsequent impact on women at work. The survey indicated that male managers were the bigger losers from restructuring, with a net loss of 62 managers from redundancy and other factors compared with a net gain of 243 female managers. The finding provides tentative support for the suggestion that older male managers rather than female managers were the casualties of organizational downsizing and economic restructuring (McGregor et al., 1994).

In the New Zealand research the educational attainment of women was generally equivalent to that of men, which undermines arguments that differences in education contribute to the gender pay gap. There appears to be no short-term solution to the issue of managerial pay relativity. A report by the New Zealand Institute of Economic Research (Cook and Briggs, 1997) conducted for the Ministry of Women's Affairs, indicates that the gender pay gap in general is unlikely to narrow over the next five years, if recent industry trends continue. This reflects the historical concentration of women in industries such as business

TABLE 4.1 *Management composition of participating organizations and median remuneration packages by gender*

	Men		Women	
	%	Median remuneration package	%	Median remuneration package
Junior managers	32.5	NZ $40,000	53.6	NZ $36,000
Middle managers	47.5	NZ $51,000	38.6	NZ $46,500
Senior managers	20.0	NZ $80,000	7.8	NZ $68,000

Source: McGregor et al. (1994)

and financial services where the gender earnings gap is predicted to grow, and above average wage growth in industries where women are under-represented. Managerial women at all levels appear destined to be both underpaid and under-valued for some years to come.

The undervaluing of female managers is revealed in a number of ways. For example, there is nothing in the findings to suggest organizational support for the business case for more women in management. The business case (Cassell, 1997) focuses on the business benefits that employers accrue through making the most of the skills and potential of women employees. A little over a quarter of organizations in the New Zealand study (28 per cent), said they had a policy of identifying female employees who showed management potential, while at the same time insisting that they did not discriminate on gender grounds in recruiting or promoting managers. (McGregor et al., 1994). This suggests that while companies regard themselves as not discriminatory and therefore as complying with the tenets of equal opportunities, they do not proactively seek women for the executive suite on the basis of economic benefits and competitive advantage to their organizations.

Female managers, themselves, may well undersell their economic value, largely because they are very often the only woman in the executive suite of an organization and are not privy to male networks which discuss and disclose the 'going rates'. A study of 10 top female managers in New Zealand, which examined the way they negotiated their own contracts, was revealing because it showed that the majority were relatively passive in the process (McGregor and Tremaine, 1995). The research followed the deregulation of New Zealand's labour market and sought to test the assumption that the Employment Contracts Act 1991, which moved from collective to individual systems of bargaining, offered women more flexibility in negotiating wages and conditions. The research showed that eight of the 10 women were offered pro forma or draft contracts by their CEOs, while none of the senior managerial women had prepared comprehensively for their contract negotiations. There was a perception by half of the women interviewed that a fundamental difference existed between men and women in negotiating style. This tends to support the view that salary allocation processes in the executive chambers of firms can be a covert form of bias in organizations against women. The results imply an interesting tension between the so-called feminine style of management focusing on collaboration, co-operation, motivation and information sharing and the competitive individualism senior women managers must demonstrate when bargaining for themselves.

All of the scholarship and statistics surrounding managerial women in the New Zealand environment point to the fallibility of the pipeline argument which suggests that the executive suite will eventually fill with female candidates given the numbers of women currently entering managerial ranks. The optimistic pipeline approach is flawed because it assumes a level managerial playing field and that women need only passively wait their turn.

For their part, managerial women are upskilling themselves in readiness for senior positions. A total of 66 per cent of participants were women on Institute of Management residential courses in 1997, a 100 per cent increase on 1995 (Matheson, 1998). The upskilling trend is confirmed by the nationwide study

(McGregor et al., 1994) which showed that a greater proportion of women managers (54 per cent) attended formal training courses than male managers (39.3 per cent) both within their organizations and externally (31.5 per cent of female managers compared with 20.8 per cent of male managers).

So why hasn't a significant breakthrough occurred in the number of women in the executive suites of New Zealand companies? Prime Minister Jenny Shipley tends to support the gender-centred approach to women's under-representation by suggesting that women's innate modesty prevents them from aggressively competing for senior jobs. She urges women to be more confident and assertive in seeking top positions. In reality, though, the marginalization of women at the top is more likely to stem from a complex interplay of systemic barriers in the labour market, sex-role stereotyping, and male-norm organizational practices sustained by a media world view which reinforces a macho corporate culture. Hede's (1995) longitudinal analysis of managerial inequity in the Australian workforce shows that the improvement in women's managerial representation since the mid-1980s is simply a result of their increasing participation in the workforce and that there has been no real improvement in representativeness. This somewhat depressing finding could have application in New Zealand too.

Women business owners

While there is ample evidence of blocked progress in managerial ranks there has been a spectacular increase in the number of women business owners in New Zealand. At least some of the growth has come from female fallout from managerial ranks. When mid-career women could not meet their needs for challenge, flexibility, career advancement and a compatible organizational culture, many opted for self-employment. The authors' nationwide study of small businesses in New Zealand also shows that more younger women are owning businesses than men (19.6 per cent under 34 years of age compared with 10.7 per cent of men under 34 years of age), which indicates a heightened awareness of self-employment as a vocational choice by younger women. In the New Zealand context small and medium-sized enterprises are of increasing economic and social significance both in terms of the number of companies and the numbers employed. The explosion of micro enterprises, employing five people or less, has profound gender implications in New Zealand in terms of business start-ups and the development of cohesive networking. The numbers of women going into self-employment is increasing at a rate of 20 per working day (Status of New Zealand Women Report, 1998). A total of 40 per cent of new businesses are started up by women, compared with 35 per cent in Australia, and this is predicted to increase to 50 per cent within the next four to five years (Status of New Zealand Women Report, 1998). New high-profile female networks are reconfiguring the notion of the old boys' network. Launched in 1992, the Women into Self-Employment (WISE) Network has expanded from one branch to 36 branch networks nationwide with more than 12,000 members in six years. The objectives of the network are to:

- provide skills for women to succeed in business;
- provide informal mentoring and networking;

- provide a means for women to promote their business;
- encourage women to trade with one another; and
- overcome business isolation. (Status of New Zealand Women Report, 1998)

Perhaps for the first time, reliable nationwide data about women business owners has come from a survey of small and medium enterprises undertaken in 1997 by Massey University researchers (McGregor and Tweed, 1998) which used a modified version of a Western Australian questionnaire designed by Professor L.V. Still and Cathy Cupitt in 1995. The study, which surveyed men and women, selected its sample of businesses from the Telecom Yellow Pages listings database. The majority of companies responding had been in existence for at least a year. Enterprises at risk of business failure in the first 12 months, regarded as a critical danger period, were mostly excluded. The nationwide study provides a rich source of information about both male and female business owners and allows for inter-gender comparisons as the sampling frame was appropriately randomized. A response rate of 43.1 per cent was achieved with 1,514 responses from an effective nationwide sample of 3,510. There was a total of 337 female respondents in the sample of 1,514, representing 22.3 per cent.

The nationwide study was supplemented with a second sample from the WISE women network, which resulted in two sets of data about women owning small and medium-sized enterprises and allowed a comparison between members of a strong women's network and those women in the national study. A response rate of 43.9 per cent was achieved from the WISE sample with 290 respondents from an effective sample of 660. A combined total of 627 female business owners provided data for this research: 290 from WISE and 337 from the nationwide study.

In a series of structured and unstructured questions the study asked respondents for demographic data, descriptive information about their businesses, financial data and plans for future business expansion. In the nationwide study, women-owned businesses tended to be smaller (see Table 4.2), with 63.2 per cent employing fewer than five and just 9.8 per cent employing more than 10 persons. More than two-thirds (68.8 per cent) of the WISE businesses have less than five employees.

Women had owned their own businesses for less time than men; 28.3 per cent of businesses owned by women were less than two years old (37.1 per cent of the WISE businesses). Half of the males had owned their businesses for eight years or more compared to 27.5 per cent of the females and just 18.8 per cent of the WISE sample.

When considering location, women in the nationwide study were more likely to run their businesses in rented premises outside the home (59.3 per cent) whereas the WISE were largely home based (45.1 per cent). Men were more likely to have started a business from full-time employment (74.7 per cent) whereas women were more likely than men to start from part-time employment (13.2 per cent) or from no work at all (18.0 per cent). Just 24.8 per cent of the businesses owned by men had a turnover of less than $100,000 compared to 41.1 per cent of the women-owned businesses and the majority (59.1 per cent) of WISE businesses.

Attitudes to self-employment

The attitudes of the self-employed were also explored including their motivation for starting their own businesses, the importance of particular goals, and the degree of satisfaction experienced. The difficulties of starting a new business and how the owners of small and medium-sized enterprises saw their own needs and skills were also canvassed.

Exploring the attitudes of men and women who own their own businesses revealed a number of gender differences both in the nationwide sample and when this data was compared with the stand-alone sample from the WISE network. For example, when asked what were the difficulties associated with start-up, more women (50.3 per cent) identified gaining the necessary confidence than men (38.7 per cent), and more women (26.5 per cent) reported difficulties in locating the necessary information and advice than men (15.5 per cent) (see Table 4.3).

TABLE 4.2   *Comparison of male- and female-owned businesses by relevant demographics[1]*

	Nationwide study				WISE	
	Overall	Male	Female	Gap[2]		Gap[3]
Demographic	%	%	%	%	%	%
Business size						
0–5 people employed	57.3	55.6	63.2	7.6	68.8	5.6
5–9 people employed	27.2	27.3	27.0	− 0.3	23.2	− 3.8
10 or more people	15.5	17.1	9.8	− 7.3	8.0	− 1.8
Years owned						
0–2 years	21.0	18.8	28.3	9.5	37.1	8.8
3–7 years	34.0	31.1	44.2	13.1	44.1	− 0.1
8 or more years	45.0	50.1	27.5	− 22.6	18.8	− 8.7
Location						
Home based	17.5	17.9	16.4	− 1.5	45.1	28.7
Owned premises outside home	21.1	23.5	12.8	− 10.7	5.3	− 7.5
Rented premises outside home	51.4	49.1	59.3	10.2	38.3	− 21.0
Other	10.0	9.5	11.5	2.0	11.3	− 0.2
Employment status at start-up						
Employed full time	70.6	74.7	56.3	− 18.4	48.0	− 8.3
Employed part time	5.1	2.7	13.2	10.5	16.4	3.2
Not in workforce/homemaker	8.1	5.2	18.0	12.8	17.1	− 0.9
Other	16.2	17.4	12.5	− 4.9	18.5	6.0
Turnover ($NZ)						
Less than $30,000	7.0	6.2	10.4	4.2	32.4	22.0
$30,000 to $100,000	21.2	18.6	30.7	12.1	26.7	− 4.0
$100,000 to $500,000	40.0	39.4	42.2	2.8	30.5	− 11.7
More than $500,000	31.8	35.8	16.7	− 19.1	10.4	− 6.3
n[1] =	1352	1047	305		261	

[1] This table was compiled from several demographic questions in the survey. The reported number of respondents is derived from the question which received the lowest response rate.

[2] This gap is the gender response differential and equals the female minus the male percentage.

[3] This column compares the WISE women with the women in the nationwide study and equals the WISE minus the female percentage.

It is interesting that the findings suggest that women perceive they lacked both 'soft' attributes, such as initial confidence, and 'hard' skills such as business plan writing when they began. The results have clear policy implications for the government departments which are expected to provide infrastructural support for economic growth and for business development training programmes in local communities (McGregor and Tweed, 1998).

Motivation

The motivation for starting a business can be analysed against 'push' and 'pull' factors. 'Push' and 'pull' factors have been identified as catalysts for people becoming self-employed (Bollard, 1989). In the New Zealand experience these factors have been associated with periods of unemployment, organizational restructuring which has resulted in managerial redundancy, and labour market change. Push factors provide rather negative but nonetheless powerful reasons for starting a small business (Bollard, 1989). Pull factors, on the other hand, though equally powerful, are more positive reasons for business ownership which relate to the sense of intrinsic benefits attached to entrepreneurship and self-employment.

Respondents to the two surveys were asked why they started their business against 14 categories (see Table 4.4). The sample of WISE women placed the desire for 'greater independence and flexibility' (a pull factor) ahead of 'more opportunity to be creative through work' (pull) and 'to earn a living' (push). Men in the nationwide sample listed financial considerations such as 'to earn a living' (push), followed by 'to make a profit' (push and pull) with 'greater independence and flexibility' (pull) as the third most commonly cited reason for starting a business. Women in the nationwide sample listed earning a living, a desire for greater independence and flexibility, and making a profit, in that order.

TABLE 4.3 *Difficulties associated with business start up (%)*

Item	Nationwide study				WISE
	Overall[1]	Male[1]	Female[1]	Gap[2]	Gap[3]
Writing/developing a business plan	18.5	15.6	28.1	12.5	38.9	10.8
Gaining the necessary confidence	41.4	38.7	50.3	11.6	56.1	5.8
Locating information and advice on starting a business	17.9	15.5	26.5	11.0	27.1	0.6
Obtaining the money necessary to start	26.8	26.6	27.4	0.8	19.8	−7.6
Selling to people/organizations	24.1	24.0	24.5	0.5	43.5	19.0
Gaining support from family/partner	13.5	13.7	12.9	−0.8	13.4	0.5
Identifying a viable idea/opportunity	13.9	14.1	12.9	−1.2	18.3	5.4
Finding a suitable location	25.6	26.2	23.5	−2.7	18.7	−4.8
Other	13.8	14.6	11.0	−3.6	21.0	10.0
n =	1371	1061	310		262	

[1] In each case the number is the percentage of respondents indicating that the item had been a difficulty.

[2] This gap is the gender response differential and equals the female minus the male percentage.

[3] This column compares the WISE women with the women in the nationwide study and equals the WISE minus the female percentage.

Women seemed to place more emphasis on the 'opportunity to be creative through work' (45.4 per cent) and this was particularly so for the WISE women (59.8 per cent). Linked to this was a greater desire to meet a particular service need (women 21.5 per cent; WISE women 34.4 per cent). While identifying a gap in the market did not distinguish men (24.1 per cent) and women (23.3 per cent) in the national study, it was an important start-up reason for the WISE women (45.7 per cent). Women placed higher importance on the need to be at home (10.7 per cent) than men (4.6 per cent) and this was even more so for WISE women (16.7 per cent). To work with a business partner was mentioned more often by women (9.6 per cent) than men (4.8 per cent). On the other hand, men placed more emphasis on earning more money and making a profit than women.

The results suggest that the motivation for owning a business combines the pragmatics of profit generation with perceived intrinsic benefits and that for many women in particular money may be less important for a variety of reasons than notions of creativity and personal freedom. In part, this reflects the pathways to self-employment. Our study showed only half of the women (56.3 per cent) were in full-time employment before they started their own businesses and a further 13.2 per cent were in part-time work (see Table 4.2, p. 47). This suggests that about a third of women were not in the workforce and may not necessarily be in the position of replacing a wage as a salary earner with a wage from self-employment. This

TABLE 4.4 *Reasons for starting an enterprise (%)*

Item	Nationwide study				WISE	
	Overall[1]	Male[1]	Female[1]	Gap[2]		Gap[3]
More opportunity to be creative through work	36.1	33.3	45.4	12.1	59.8	14.4
To be at home with children or dependent adults	6.0	4.6	10.7	6.1	16.7	6.0
To meet a particular service or need in my area	17.4	16.2	21.5	5.3	34.4	12.9
To work with a business partner	5.9	4.8	9.6	4.8	10.9	1.3
To earn a living	55.9	55.2	58.5	3.3	49.3	− 9.2
Tired of working for someone else	37.2	36.4	39.7	3.3	36.6	− 3.1
Other	8.3	7.5	10.7	3.2	15.2	4.5
Wanted greater independence and flexibility	51.8	51.1	54.0	2.9	65.6	11.6
To work with or employ family members	10.8	10.5	11.6	1.1	12.3	0.7
Because I could not find a job	3.9	3.9	4.2	0.3	9.1	4.9
Identified a gap in the market	23.9	24.1	23.3	− 0.8	45.7	22.4
Made redundant	7.7	8.4	5.4	− 3.0	6.9	1.5
To make a profit	53.2	54.2	49.6	− 4.6	42.0	− 7.6
To earn more money than I could working for someone else	42.9	45.0	35.8	− 9.2	32.6	− 3.2
n =	1475	1140	335		276	

[1] In each case the number is the percentage of respondents indicating that the item was a reason.
[2] This gap is the gender response differential and equals the female minus the male percentage.
[3] This column compares the WISE women with the women in the nationwide study and equals the WISE minus the female percentage.

compares with 75 per cent of men in full-time employment in the three years before starting their own businesses.

Financial considerations aside, the findings reveal that independence and personal growth underpin the attitudes of women who start their own businesses. Women are seeking self-employment to satisfy their own personal needs as well as to answer financial imperatives. It is these areas of motivation and satisfaction which need to be further explored by researchers seeking to link female self-employment and economic and employment growth. There has been debate in Australasia about the desirability of turning 'satisficers' into 'expansionists' in keeping with government wishes to see small business expand its employment growth potential (Still and Chia, 1995). Still and Timms (1998: 2) state it is easy to see 'why the contribution of women-owned business to the economy, and their relative lack of growth and expansion trajectories in comparison to businesses owned by men, is of vital interest to Government'. They suggest the need for a new paradigm for women business owners to highlight and acknowledge the diverse reasons which compel women to self-employment. It may be that some are escapees from corporate management, or that women start up businesses to buy themselves a job or that they seek from self-employment creativity, flexibility and autonomy which is not available to them in the paid workforce. Still and Timms (1998) make the point that overall there is little understanding from either policy-makers or economic analysts about the expansion of female-owned business and its linkage to other intrinsic aspects and life experiences of women. They state that 'while this point is gender-inclusive' it is especially applicable to women given that their multiple roles sometimes prevent them from following the anticipated business and work paths (1998: 9). The barriers they identify as particular difficulties for women in business are the domestic division of labour, time poverty and the 'culture of advantage' from which women are excluded.

The notion that women in small business pursue growth less than men is challenged somewhat by empirical findings in the New Zealand context. A larger number of WISE survey respondents indicated that they had expanded since start-up (57.2 per cent) than either the male (50.3 per cent) or the women (48.3 per cent) in the nationwide general survey. And again, the networked women indicated that they were thinking of expanding further (69.1 per cent) in greater numbers than either the men (50.7 per cent) or women (43.9 per cent) in the general study. This suggests a positive linkage between expansion and the proactive alliances and connections which come from organized women's networking. Given that WISE's aims include the provision of a means to promote their business, avoidance of business isolation, and encouraging women to trade with one another, this suggestion is intuitively reasonable. The expansionist profile of many WISE respondents indicates also that micro businesses, often sole operators who are home-based, are maturing because they have been able to accumulate working capital, secure markets and increase in business confidence.

If further research confirms a nexus between aggressive networking by women and expansion, this has clear policy implications. It suggests, for example, a pathway towards the generation of employment opportunities and the possible relocation from home residences as the business base.

Conclusion

Overall in New Zealand the picture of women in management confirms the static position of females in the executive suites of corporate companies, despite the country's unique view of itself as self-reliant and progressive about women's issues. The Prime Minister has committed herself to better representation for women. But political influence, which is significant in terms of public sector representation, has limited impact on the culture of corporate companies, some of which are multinationals. While there is some evidence that managerial women have not been the casualties of job loss and restructuring that has accompanied organizational change in the same way as men, this may merely affirm the low numbers of women and their marginal status in managerial ranks in the first place. Women certainly have not been the beneficiaries of a tide change in corporate thinking about either equal opportunities imperatives or the business case for managerial diversity. Those managerial women who do make it tend to under-value themselves in the executive suite and need to adopt new negotiating styles in an age when individualism is the dominant employment norm (McGregor and Tremaine, 1995). It would be a bitter irony indeed if women at the top also continued to perpetuate the gender pay gap, simply because they did not insist on being paid what they were worth.

The negative picture of the status of women as managers is tempered somewhat in the New Zealand context by the profile of self-employed women who are exhibiting independence and entrepreneurship in small and medium-sized enterprises. A host of 'push' and 'pull' factors lie behind the extraordinary growth of women business owners. Owning their own businesses may be forced upon women wanting to enter the labour force, it may represent women buying themselves a job, or it may represent an alternative to blocked progress within the corporate sector. Owning a business may equally represent a deliberate and thoughtful choice by women about the intrinsic benefits of working for themselves. Whatever their motivations, the number of women who establish or buy into businesses represents an increasing level of awareness by women of the array of choices they have for career and professional development. Women as business owners and the networking relationships they are aggressively pursuing with each other are new dynamics, demanding greater research scrutiny and policy analysis. Female business owners also represent a reservoir of creativity and of economic and social value whose significance is only just being realized.

References

Bollard, A. (1989) *Small Business in New Zealand*, Allen & Unwin/Port Nicholson Press, Wellington.

Cassell, C. (1997) 'The business case for equal opportunities: implications for women in management', *Women in Management Review*, 12 (1 & 2): 11–16.

Cook, D. and Briggs, P. (1997) *Gender Wage Gap: Scenarios of the Gender Wage Gap: Report*, NZ Institute of Economic Research, Wellington.

Davidson, M.J. and Cooper, C.L. (1992) *Shattering the Glass Ceiling: The Woman Manager*, Paul Chapman, London.

Hede, A. (1995) 'Longitudinal analysis of managerial inequity in the Australian workforce', *International Review of Women and Leadership*, (1): 11–21.

ILO (1998) 'Women in management: lonely at the top', *World of Work: The Magazine of the ILO*, 23, February.

McGregor, J. (1994) 'Breaching the convention: New Zealand's international obligations', in J. Sayers, and M. Tremaine (eds), *The Vision and the Reality: Equal Opportunities in the New Zealand Workplace*, Dunmore Press, Palmerston North, pp. 99–112.

McGregor, J. and Tremaine, M. (1995) 'Negotiating the package: the managerial woman's experience in New Zealand's deregulated labour market', *Women in Management Review*, 10 (44): 17–24.

McGregor, J. and Tweed, D. (1998) 'Unemployment to self-employment: the long and winding road', *Social Policy Journal of New Zealand*, 10: 190–202.

McGregor, J., Thomson, M. and Dewe, P. (1994) *Women in Management in New Zealand: A Benchmark Survey*, Women in Management Series, working paper 19, University of Western Sydney.

McGregor, J., Still, L. and Dewe, P. (1996) 'The earnings gap and the managerial woman in transition', *Equal Opportunities International*, 15 (2): 25–35.

McGregor, J., Pajo, K., Cleland, J. and Burke, R. (1997) 'Equal opportunities and the boardroom: the challenge of corporatisation', *Equal Opportunities International*, 16 (8): 1–7.

Matheson, D. (1998) 'More women upskilling for senior management roles', *Central Link*, Feb./March: 1.

Pajo, K., McGregor, J. and Cleland, J. (1997) 'Profiling the pioneers: women directors on New Zealand's corporate boards', *Women in Management Review*, 12 (5): 174–181.

Sekaran, U. (1990) 'Frontiers and new vistas in women and management research', *Journal of Business Ethics*, 9 (4–5): 247–256.

Shilton, J., McGregor, J. and Tremaine, M. (1996) 'Feminizing the boardroom: a study of the effects of corporatization on the number and status of women directors in New Zealand companies', *Women in Management Review*, 11 (3): 20–26.

Status of New Zealand Women Report (1998) 'The combined third and fourth reports on New Zealand's progress on implementing the convention on the elimination of all forms of discrimination against women', Ministry of Women's Affairs, Wellington.

Still, L.V. (1990) *Enterprising Women: Australian Women Managers and Entrepreneurs*, Allen & Unwin, Sydney.

Still, L.V. and Chia, B. (1995) *Self-employed Women: Four Years On*, Women and Leadership series, paper 1, Edith Cowan University, Western Australia.

Still, L. and Timms, W. (1998) *Women's Business: The Need for a New Paradigm of Women in Small Business*, Discussion Paper series, University of Western Australia.

Still, L.V., Guerin, C.D. and Chia, W. (1992) *Women in Management Revisited: Progress, Regression or Status Quo?* Women in Management working paper 16, Faculty of Commerce, University of Western Sydney, Nepean.

Still, L., McGregor, J. and Dewe, P. (1994) 'Room at the top? A comparison of the employment status of women in management in Australia and New Zealand', *International Journal of Employment Studies*, 2 (2): 267–287.

5

Women Entrepreneurs in the United States

Mary C. Mattis

For the last three decades women have succeeded in entering careers in corporate America in unprecedented numbers. Today, women make up a growing segment of the talent pool from which American business organizations draw entry-level professional and management employees. In most business organizations, women also represent a sizeable percentage of more seasoned employees: in 1997, women held 49 per cent of managerial and professional specialty occupations in the United States (US Bureau of Labor, 1999). However, research by Catalyst and other organizations shows that for the vast majority of female managers, advancement stops there (Brenner et al., 1989; Adler, 1993; Federal Glass Ceiling Commission, 1995; Catalyst, 1998b). While women have increasingly prepared themselves for careers in business, companies have not dismantled the barriers that prevent them from effectively developing and advancing female talent.

So it is not surprising that, from the mid-1980s on, articles began to appear in prominent business publications noting a dramatic rise in women's entrepreneurship. These articles cited a number of reasons for this increase: pay inequities, the stifling of women's upward mobility within corporations, and the fact that women were able to manage dependant-care responsibilities more effectively with the greater flexibility entrepreneurship affords (Foderaro, 1997; Alva, 1997; Petzinger, 1997; Hamm, 1997).

A review of the literature shows that before 1978, virtually nothing was known about female entrepreneurs (Stevenson, 1986). Then, between 1975 and 1990, the number of self-employed women more than doubled. The female self-employment rate increased by 63 per cent as women started businesses twice as frequently as men (Murphy, 1992). By 1990, one out of every 10 women over the age of 35 was involved in an entrepreneurial venture (Divine, 1994). Moreover, these businesses also have grown dramatically in economic strength. Employment has tripled, and sales have more than tripled between 1987 and 1996. Women-owned businesses now employ one in four US company workers, and contribute nearly $2.3 trillion annually to the economy (National Foundation for Women Business Owners, 1997).

In 1999, the number of systematic, scholarly studies on the female entrepreneur still is not large. However, directories of female entrepreneurs have begun to appear and a number of organizations are expanding the body of information on this group, most notably the National Foundation for Women Business Owners (NFWBO).

What research that has been carried out on women entrepreneurs suggests that, prior to the 1980s, women had limited access to capital, business and technical education and management experience (Moore and Buttner, 1997). The typical pre-1980s female entrepreneurs were most likely to be persons with liberal arts background (Scott, 1986; Stevenson, 1986) and unlikely to start businesses in male-dominated industries (Bowen and Hisrich, 1986; Buttner and Rosen, 1988b). As Moore and Buttner (1997) described this early group of women entrepreneurs they fit a single profile, 'primarily sole proprietors with similar educational backgrounds and a basic interest in extending home skills into the marketplace'– self-employed but not necessarily entrepreneurs according to the narrow definition of an entrepreneur advanced by Drucker (1985): 'one who drastically upgrades the yield of resources and creates a new market and a new customer'.

A new style of female entrepreneur began appearing in the 1980s whom researchers referred to as a 'Second Generation' (Gregg, 1985). Many were women who had left corporations to be their own bosses, to exercise their educational and technical skills, and to increase their income (Scott, 1986; Fried, 1989; Rosener, 1989). These are the women in whom Catalyst was especially interested as it contemplated this research.

Unlike their predecessors, this second generation of female entrepreneurs is not monolithic in background or choice of industry. They have entered a wide variety of occupations, many in traditionally male business arenas such as finance, insurance, manufacturing, and construction (Hisrich and O'Brien, 1981, 1982). For example, data from the Small Business Administration documented that in the 1980s, in the major industry divisions of agricultural services, forestry and fishing, mining, construction and manufacturing, the growth rate of female-operated businesses exceeded that of the industry as a whole (US Department of Commerce, Bureau of the Census, 1986).

This newer generation of female entrepreneurs, many of them expatriates from corporate careers, had management and communications skills and networks that provided them with greater access to capital and customers/clients than their predecessors. Concomitantly, the success rate of organizations headed by these women has been comparable to that of male business owners (Hisrich and Brush, 1987; Birley, 1989; Kalleberg and Leicht, 1991).

Entrepreneurship was not always the initial career choice of women in this second generation of women business owners; rather, it was a response to the limited opportunities and barriers to advancement many of them encountered in corporate careers (Rosener, 1989). Their reasons for leaving, documented in a number of earlier studies (Catalyst, 1986; Taylor, 1986; Birley, 1989; Adler, 1993; Fischer et al., 1993; Noble, 1993; Hood and Koberg, 1994) were systematic attitudinal and organizational barriers to women's advancement and a hostile corporate culture.

In 1997 Catalyst, the Committee of 200 and the National Foundation for Women Business Owners joined forces in a landmark study, funded by Salomon Smith Barney, Inc., to expand and clarify data about women's motivations for undertaking entrepreneurship and the paths they have taken in that direction. Data for three cohorts of women entrepreneurs were examined in this study: first generation women entrepreneurs – who have owned businesses for 20 or more years; second generation women who have owned businesses for 10–19 years; and, the most recent crop of women entrepreneurs, who have owned businesses for less than 10 years.

The aim of this chapter is to present the findings of this study along with the recommendations designed by Catalyst to assist companies to retain, develop and advance entrepreneurial women currently within their professional and managerial ranks.

Catalyst is the non-profit research and advisory services organization that works with business and the professions to advance women. Its dual mission is to enable women to achieve their full potential and to help employers capitalize on women's talent. The Committee of 200 (C200) is a professional organization of pre-eminent businesswomen who exemplify and promote entrepreneurship and corporate leadership among women of this generation and the next. C200 currently comprises more than 375 US and international members from 70 industries. The National Foundation for Women Business Owners (NFWBO) is recognized as the premier source of information on women business owners and their enterprises worldwide. NFWBO's mission is to strengthen women business owners and their enterprises through research and sharing information.

Specific questions addressed by the research described in this chapter include:

- What motivates women to start their own businesses?
- What work experiences pre-date women's entrepreneurial ventures?
- Have the paths and motivations for women's entrepreneurship changed over time?
- How, if at all, do these motivations and work experiences differ for men?
- What has been the influence of the 'glass ceiling' and corporate downsizing on women choosing to start businesses?
- What, if anything, would attract women business owners back to careers in corporations?

Catalyst's unique interest in this research was to understand experiences and motivations of women who had worked in the private sector prior to starting or acquiring their own businesses. Since women's entrepreneurship has generally been regarded as a positive trend, few studies have examined the downside of this phenomenon; that is, the view that assesses the cost of losing female talent in which business organizations have made considerable investment.

The most obvious costs to corporations of losing high performing and high potential women professionals and managers is failure to leverage the investment companies have made in their recruitment and training, along with the cost of recruiting and training their replacements. Other less visible costs include reduced productivity and morale, damage done to relationships with clients/customers, the loss of intellectual capital, and the very real possibility that former employees turned entrepreneurs can become future competitors. Recently, the Saratoga Institute (1997) examined the costs of turnover of seasoned professionals and managers and put the figure at 100 per cent to 200 per cent of annual salary. It is not surprising then, that, increasingly, companies include the cost of turnover of women and people of colour in their business case for diversity.

Methodology

Researchers have not always agreed on the definition of an entrepreneur, with the result that data are inconsistent across government and other sources of statistics on women-owned businesses. The United States government, for example, until 1996 grouped all business owners under the category of 'sole proprietor'. The US Small Business Administration's Office of Women's Business Ownership defines women-owned as '51 per cent owned, operated and controlled by a woman or women' (US Department of Commerce, 1986: 17). The US Bureau of Labor Statistics computes its total of women entrepreneurs from the number of women reporting themselves as self-employed. Recently, the NFWBO changed its definition of a business owner to include women owners with a plurality, rather than 51 per cent or more of their businesses' shares, due to the increasing costs of capitalizing business start-ups, especially technology and bio-medical companies.

For this research, a nationally representative, randomly drawn sample of 800 US business owners was selected – 650 women and 150 men, all of whom were interviewed by telephone in September 1997, using a structured interview protocol. The sample was drawn from a directory of business owners developed by Dun & Bradstreet Information Services (a commercial provider of business listings) using the National Foundation of Women Business Owners selection criteria. The sample was stratified, so that the employee size distribution of businesses selected would be representative of that of the total population of small businesses. Firms with 500 + employees were over-sampled due to the fact that they represent less than 1 per cent of all entrepreneurial ventures in the US.

In the spring of 1998, two focus groups of 12 women each, from Washington, DC and Maryland, were conducted prior to the development of the survey instrument. The women were selected to represent a wide range of industries/occupations and different-sized businesses re: number of employees and annual sales volume. The results of the content analysis of materials collected during these focus groups enabled the researchers to formulate the protocol to be used in interviews with a stratified, randomly selected sample of 800 female and male entrepreneurs in the United States. A letter describing the study was sent to each of the prospective respondents. Shortly thereafter an interviewer called to schedule an appointment to administer the questionnaire by telephone.

For purposes of this analysis, we will focus on findings from the research that were of particular interest to Catalyst in undertaking the study: (1) the expectations, experiences and perceptions of women whose work experiences pre-dating their entrepreneurship were in the private sector; and (2) differences between cohorts or 'generations' of women entrepreneurs, i.e., those who had owned businesses for 20 or more years, 10–19 years, and less than 10 years, respectively.

Profiles of women entrepreneurs

Personal characteristics

The median age of women business owners in the study was 49 years. The majority (59 per cent) had an educational attainment level of four years or less of college or technical training, 19 per cent had attended graduate school, 7 per cent had an MBA degree, and 22 per cent had a high school education or less. In comparison, the educational attainment of a sample of women executives surveyed by Catalyst in 1996 was considerably higher: 36 per cent had four years or less of college, close to a third (31 per cent) had an MBA, and one-third had other advanced degrees i.e. Juris Doctor; Master of Arts/Science/PhD (Catalyst, 1996). Interestingly, in focus group discussions several women reported that one reason they had started their own business was their feeling that they could not compete against younger employees who, though they had less on-the-job experience, had earned MBAs. Further research is needed to understand how educational credentials, or lack thereof, played into the decisions of private sector professionals to become entrepreneurs as opposed to pursuing advancement in corporate careers, especially first generation women business owners.

The majority of the respondents – 93 per cent – identified themselves as Caucasian. Yet, in 1996, one in eight woman-owned companies in the United States was owned by a woman of colour (NFWBO, 1997). It is not clear whether under-representation of women of colour in this research is a function of sampling or respondent bias. The businesses of entrepreneurs who are women of colour could have been on average newer and, therefore, not listed in Dun & Bradstreet, or women of colour might have been sampled in proportion to their representation among business owners, but a disproportionate number may have declined to be interviewed for the study.

Background data on the women and men businesses owners surveyed for this study suggest that they are similar to each other in several respects, and they are generally representative of the business population at large (US Department of Commerce, Bureau of the Census, 1986). Most respondents were in their forties and fifties, married with children. However, male business owners in our survey were more likely to be married than their female counterparts, who are more likely to be single, divorced or widowed.

Professional characteristics

Women arrive at entrepreneurship from a variety of prior work experiences. Over half of the women surveyed (58 per cent) had been working in the private sector for five or more years before starting their own businesses. These were the women in whom Catalyst had the most interest. What could not be corrected through over-sampling was the reality that most women in this group had worked in small to mid-size companies – 83 per cent compared to 73 per cent of male respondents; or non-profit organizations – 4 per cent vs. 0 per cent of the men; not large public companies which have been the primary focus of Catalyst's research. Another 13 per cent of women business owners came to entrepreneurship from the public sector (including the fields of education and health), 11 per cent were out of the labour force for an extended period before starting businesses,

9 per cent were self-employed before opening their own business, and 4 per cent came from a non-profit organization.

The phenomenon of women entrepreneurs gaining business experience in corporations before striking out on their own has been aptly referred to by Moore and Buttner (1997) as the 'corporate incubator'. That is, women use the time they spend in companies to gain needed business skills and technical competencies that will be used to establish their own business ventures, rather than to climb the corporate ladder. Although we did not ask the question in the phone interviews, focus group participants said they personally had benefited from their previous corporate experience and would recommend spending the early years of their careers getting corporate experience to women considering entrepreneurship. However, they would caution women about remaining in corporate careers.

The positions held by women business owners just prior to starting their businesses were also quite diverse. Prior to starting their businesses 26 per cent had been employed in a professional position (such as attorney or certified public accountant), 16 per cent were in senior manager or executive positions in corporations; 14 per cent held clerical positions; and another 14 per cent described themselves as middle managers. Of the remainder, 5 per cent were nurses/doctors/other health care workers; 5 per cent were teachers; 5 per cent held technical positions; and 5 per cent owned another business. Women who had been employed in large companies prior to becoming business owners were significantly more likely to have been in managerial positions than were women from smaller companies (less than 500 employees) and were twice as likely to have earned an MBA (11 per cent vs. 5 per cent).

By segmenting the sample by years of business ownership, we were able to identify some differences in experiences of different 'generations' of women entrepreneurs. One finding of the segmentation analysis was that the types of position held by women prior to becoming business owners have changed over time, no doubt because educational and employment opportunities were more restricted for women starting businesses 20 or more years ago. Only 11 per cent of women who had owned their businesses for 20 or more years were in senior management or executive positions when they left their jobs in the private sector, compared to 22 per cent who were business owners for less than 10 years. Twenty-nine per cent of the longer-tenured women reported having held clerical positions compared to just 8 per cent of those in business for themselves for less than 10 years.

Because of increasing career opportunities for women, the functional areas where women have worked have also changed over time. In this sample, women who had owned businesses for the longest period of time were more likely to have been employed in accounting and finance departments of the companies they left – 29 per cent vs. 12 per cent of newer women business owners – and less likely to have been in management or sales – 17 per cent vs. 33 per cent of newer owners.

Interestingly, when women decide to start or purchase their own business, they do not seem to limit their choices to past employment experience. Women are just as likely to own a business that is totally unrelated to a previous job (42 per cent) as they are to own one that is closely related to what they were doing just prior to entrepreneurship (41 per cent); whereas male business owners were more likely to be engaged in a business that was closely related to a previous career experience (59 per cent).

Motivations for becoming a business owner

More than one-third (37 per cent) of the women who were interviewed for the study became business owners as a result of the family situation, such as the death of a spouse or other family member. Other reasons for acquiring or starting a business given by women included: 'to be my own boss' (25 per cent), 'took over/inherited a business' (16 per cent), 'a partnership with a family member' (12 per cent), 'more income' (11 per cent), 'the opportunity arose' (10 per cent), and 'independence' (10 per cent).

Typically, for both women and men, acquiring or starting up a business was a gradual process. More than half (55 per cent) of women business owners reported that they became a business owner through a gradual process, as did 65 per cent of men. Compared with men, women were somewhat more likely to start their business as a result of an event or series of events: 42 per cent of women and 35 per cent of men reported that the road to entrepreneurship was, for them, event-driven.

Twenty-one per cent of those 'event-driven' women reported a job loss as the event, 15 per cent just got tired, fed up or felt they needed a change, 11 per cent mentioned an illness or death in the family, for another 11 per cent becoming business owners was stimulated by a geographical relocation.

Although job loss, relocation and getting fed up were the three most frequently cited events for women and men, there are some interesting gender differences with regard to other events. Women were more likely than men to cite either a divorce (5 per cent vs. 0 per cent respectively) or illness or death in the family (11 per cent vs. 3 per cent respectively), while men (8 per cent) were more likely than women (2 per cent) to point to their own or another family member's retirement.

A key objective for Catalyst in undertaking this research was to understand what motivates women to leave corporate careers to start their own businesses, especially the newest group of women entrepreneurs, and what, if anything, could corporations do to retain these women? In particular, we wanted to examine whether an inevitable and perhaps growing percentage of corporate women will leave their jobs to start businesses in order to fulfil a lifelong goal – the women we characterize as 'born to be' entrepreneurs. Or, are there actions companies could take to channel the entrepreneurial qualities of such women in ways that would ensure their retention and capitalize on the value they could bring to their organizations.

In reality, data from this study show that very few business owners, regardless of gender, see themselves as 'born to be' entrepreneurs – just 2 per cent of women business owners and 4 per cent of male business owners described themselves in this manner. The largest share of women in this sample could be described as having evolved into entrepreneurs, people who had an idea for a service or product that they believed they could develop on their own: 44 per cent of the women in our sample fell into this category. These women started their businesses because they were positively drawn to entrepreneurship rather than as a response to a negative prior job- or family-related experience (divorce, death of a spouse).

Looking specifically at women who left the private sector to start their own businesses, we found that a substantial number did so in response to negative factors in their work environment. The four top reasons for leaving private sector jobs given by this group were: the need for more flexibility (51 per cent), glass ceiling (29 per cent), unhappy with work environment (28 per cent) and feeling unchallenged by the job (22 per cent). Women with private sector experience mentioned each of these factors with a higher frequency than did women with other kinds of prior job experience.

Desire for flexibility

Focusing on women who had left the private sector to become entrepreneurs, we found that 51 per cent had done so because they wanted more flexibility related to childcare obligations; desire for greater participation in community/civic affairs; personal health concerns; and elder care or other dependant care responsibilities. Childcare was the most frequently mentioned reason, cited by 30 per cent of the women who had left private sector jobs. Given that starting a business is a time-intensive process, these women were not so much seeking reduced work hours as they were seeking greater control over when and where they worked.

Glass ceiling

The term 'glass ceiling' was coined in 1986 by two *Wall Street Journal* reporters to describe the invisible barrier that blocks women from the most senior positions in corporate America. Catalyst and other researchers have documented the persistence of the glass ceiling in limiting women's advancement (Catalyst, 1990, 1996; Morrison et al., 1994; Federal Glass Ceiling Commission, 1995).

Nearly one-third (29 per cent) of the women previously employed in the private sector cited the glass ceiling as a reason they left their former employers to start their own businesses, for example:

> I worked for a corporation in the area and I just got tired of people coming in, especially male counterparts, who were being promoted above me.

> I spent about six years at a Fortune 500 company...and eventually I topped out in my pay grade and there were always management changes. So you were always proving yourself over again to another team and that got pretty old. The option was to spread my own wings and try it.

Components of the glass ceiling most frequently cited by respondents were: failure to have their contributions recognized (47 per cent of women out of the private sector); and not being taken seriously (27 per cent). Women also mentioned feeling isolated in their organizations (29 per cent) and seeing others promoted ahead of them (27 per cent). These findings are consistent with Moore and Buttner's (1997) research – 27 per cent of their sample reported a desire for increased responsibility and recognition as a reason for leaving the corporate environment.

Another dimension of the glass ceiling is what might be characterized as a work environment that is inhospitable to women professionals (as well as other minority and non-traditional employee populations). Twenty-eight per cent of the women formerly employed in the private sector reported that they were not happy or comfortable with the work environment of their previous job. In Catalyst's 1996 report, *Women in Corporate Leadership: Progress and Prospects*, 35 per cent of women executives said that an inhospitable corporate culture was a key barrier to women's advancement. In addition, 22 per cent of women business owners in this study who had left the private sector, along with 19 per cent of respondents with other employment backgrounds, characterized themselves as unchallenged in their previous positions.

Looking at other responses of this group of ex-corporate-sector women, we found that what they liked best about owning their own businesses was independence, being in control, and setting their own hours. However, while this group gave 'being my own boss' as one of three top reasons for becoming entrepreneurs, it was not one of the top three things they liked best about actually being a business owner. In contrast, 'being my own boss' was among the top three satisfactions of entrepreneurship given by women who described themselves as 'born to be' entrepreneurs.

What would attract women back to private sector careers?

Over half (58 per cent) of the formerly private sector women said that nothing would attract them back to a corporate job. Of those who said they might consider going back, 24 per cent reported that more money would be an incentive; 11 per cent said they might return if they were offered greater flexibility. One woman described the kind of work environment that would attract her back as follows:

> I think that if I was in an environment where it was a given, not a token but a given, that I had autonomy, made decisions, and my talents were part of the company, I could be a team member.

Another answered a follow-up question in this fashion:

> *Q* : Was there anything your firm could have done to keep you?
> *A* : They could have made me a partner.

As would be expected, women who had owned businesses the longest (20 or more years) were more likely to say that nothing would attract them back to a corporate position (64 per cent).

Differences among three generations of women business owners

Interest in flexibility/glass ceiling
Half of the women who had left the private sector to start their own businesses (51 per cent) reported that they wanted more flexibility and gave this as a reason for leaving their companies. Newer entrepreneurs (less than 10 years in business)

were significantly more likely to cite flexibility as a motivator than women who had been in business 20 or more years (55 per cent vs. 28 per cent).

More and more, American women and men are expecting and receiving work-place flexibility from employers. Catalyst's research on dual career couples, undertaken in the early 1980s and again in 1998, shows that women in dual career marriages are much more likely today to expect their companies to provide solutions for work/life flexibility than was the case in the 1980s when members of dual career couples assumed it was their personal responsibility to manage work/life obligations (Catalyst, 1981, 1998c). The 1997 study also found that dual career couples most wanted informal discretion over their time rather than formal flexibility programmes such as part-time, job-sharing or full-time telecommuting arrangements. Both men and women wanted freedom to control their hours, the ability to leave work for dependant care commitments such as school meetings, and the option to work from home on a temporary basis (Catalyst, 1998c).

Perception of a glass ceiling

What is evident from the above discussion is that the percentage of women who reported leaving their salaried positions in response to a glass ceiling has more than doubled over the past two entrepreneurial generations. Just 9 per cent of the women who started their businesses 20 or more years ago stated that the glass ceiling was a factor in their decision compared to 15 per cent of women who started their businesses 10–19 years ago and 22 per cent of the newest women business owners.

Lack of challenge in previous jobs

The share of women business owners reporting that they were unchallenged in their previous job situation has also doubled over time: 28 per cent of the newer women business owners said that they were unchallenged compared to 14 per cent of women who had owned their businesses for over 20 years. As would be expected, newer entrepreneurs are younger, on average, than women who have owned businesses for 20 years or more.

These findings derived from segmenting our sample of women business owners suggest that newer owners, representing younger career women, have greater awareness of issues related to women's advancement (flexibility, work environment, glass ceiling) and/or higher expectations of employers than did women employed outside the home 20 years ago. This should not be surprising, considering the extensive coverage given to these issues in business publications and the media. We would expect that this generation of women entered business careers assuming that more progress toward levelling the playing field for women had been made. If this is the case, retaining the most talented of these younger women represents a unique challenge for business organizations for they have experienced what social theorists have referred to as the revolution of rising expectations – they expected more, therefore they are less likely to settle for less than women of earlier generations who had no such expectations.

Furthermore, many of these women are part of a dual career couple. Half of the women (51 per cent) in our sample said a second income was 'critically' or 'somewhat' important for covering household expenses when they were starting their businesses. Catalyst found a similar trend in our study of dual career couples (Catalyst, 1998c). Fifty-five per cent of the survey respondents in that research said they had more freedom to make career choices because their spouses worked full time. In fact, the finding from that research showed that both men and women in dual career couples felt increased freedom to take risks, particularly career risks, such as changing jobs, stepping into and out of the fast lane, and starting their own businesses.

Recommendations to corporations

Based on the results of this study and previous research on entrepreneurs, we propose specific recommendations to corporations in order to stem the tide of women leaving the public sector to start their own businesses. These include recommendations to (1) increase the availability to professionals and managers of flexible work arrangements, especially informal arrangements; (2) identify and address stereotypes and preconceptions that keep women from succeeding and advancing in sales and other entrepreneurial functions within companies; (3) provide for early identification and development of entrepreneurial female talent; (4) create more intrapreneurial opportunities within companies and ensure that women have equal access to these opportunities; (5) consider recruiting successful women entrepreneurs from outside the company and from related industries to fill key senior management and governance roles in companies.

Increased flexibility

Catalyst's most recent research on flexibility (Catalyst, 1997) and on dual career couples (Catalyst, 1998c) shows that:

- flexibility, including part-time arrangements and informal flexible options, is a critical issue for employees;
- persistent and formidable barriers limit the availability and effective use of flexibility in many business organizations, even in those companies that have formal policies supportive of alternative work schedules and work-at-home options.

Women business owners interviewed for this research expressed their dissatisfaction with the rigidity they experienced in corporate careers by voting with their feet. Employees today want a more nuanced approach to flexibility; one that recognizes their professionalism and the value they place on reciprocity between themselves and their employers, i.e. the obligation to return flexibility for flexibility.

In benchmarking corporate approaches to flexibility, Catalyst has identified the following success criteria: clear and consistent communication of leadership commitment and vision; articulation of a business rationale for flexibility; a focus on continuous learning and improvement; guidance and support for professionals with flexible arrangements and their supervisors; establishment of explicit expectations and monitoring of the commitment of managers as well as that of employees to fulfilling those expectations; providing policies, systems and structures that support flexibility; and focusing on work productivity (as opposed to hours spent in the office, i.e. 'face-time').

Early identification of professionals and managers with entrepreneurial inclinations

Companies need to be as aggressive about recruiting from their internal ranks as they are about external recruiting. The emphasis in this recommendation is on early identification of women whose skills might be developed for intrapreneurial business opportunities in companies. Research (Catalyst, 1992, 1996; Morrison et al., 1994; Federal Glass Ceiling Commission, 1995) shows that women are concentrated in positions that support line activities like sales (e.g. customer service). Increasing female professionals' access to line positions is critical to providing the challenging assignments entrepreneurial women are seeking. Research also shows that female professionals frequently stay 'in grade' longer than their male counterparts due to male managers' reluctance to take what they perceive as 'risks' promoting female candidates for key assignments (Berndtson and Cornell University, 1994). It follows that companies that fail to communicate their commitment to women early in their careers and do not hold managers accountable for developing and promoting female talent, will fail to retain high-potential women, especially those with entrepreneurial interests/skills.

Increase women's access to intrapreneurial positions

Increasingly companies are realizing that they need individuals with entrepreneurial skills to succeed in today's business environment. These activities are frequently called 'intrapreneurial' because they involve the same risk-taking, innovation and leadership that starting a business demands, only they are employed inside a corporation.

One obvious way that companies can address this issue is by ensuring that women are adequately represented among their sales representatives and senior sales leadership. Catalyst's (1995a) study of women in sales documented a number of barriers to recruiting, retaining and advancing women in sales, including

- male stereotypes of the 'sales personality' that create barriers to recruiting women into sales;
- compensation inequities that arise out of gender differentials in starting salaries, and assignments of territories/customer accounts;
- exclusion of women from key networks and informal channels of communication that lead to better training, business development and advancement opportunities;
- lack of attention to and accountability for providing a work environment that is both safe and free of sexual harassment; and
- stereotyping about women's leadership abilities and assumptions about their career commitment and flexibility to travel/relocate that prevent women from advancing to managerial roles in sales.

Since sales is one of the most visible intrapreneurial areas within companies, these barriers to women's success need to be dismantled.

There are other areas of business activity that could be considered intrapreneurial. Start-ups, turn-arounds, business and new product development, and international assignments all offer challenges to employees with entrepreneurial inclinations. Companies need to do more to profile the rewards involved in such assignments and to mitigate the fear that many women (and some men) have that they are too 'risky' and could be career breakers. Providing support for women to accept high-risk assignments is critical, as is challenging male managers' perceptions that it would be too risky for them or for the company to recruit/promote women to such positions. Finally, companies need to examine the way work is currently organized to ascertain whether employees are empowered to make decisions and exercise independence in their day-to-day work activities. Leading companies have begun to recognize this need and to articulate to managers the business case for reconceptualizing work to retain a talent pool that has increased expectations of employers and more leverage to explore other options if those expectations are not met.

Recruit female entrepreneurs to corporate boards and senior management positions

Successful women business owners should be targeted by companies seeking to fill key strategic positions in their organizations. Chief executive officers (CEOs) frequently identify the lack of qualified women as a key factor in the low representation of women on corporate boards (Catalyst, 1995b). Female entrepreneurs bring proven business experience to corporate boards and should be seen as suitable replacements for the traditional corporate director – a male CEO or former CEO of a large public company.

This research shows limited openness among female business owners for returning to careers in corporations. However, that, too, may change. Recently we have seen examples of successful entrepreneurs moving back into corporate positions. One such woman is Judy Estrin, profiled in the 12 March 1998 issue of the *Wall Street Journal.* In the early 1980s, Ms Estrin and her husband, William Carrico, founded two successful technology companies. One of these companies, Bridge Communications Inc., was among the first companies to develop and market networking hardware, now one of the fastest-growing fields in the computer industry.

In 1986, 3Com bought Bridge for over $200 million and Estrin and Carrico became 3Com executives. During their tenure at 3Com, they urged the company to shift its focus from software to hardware. When 3Com rejected their advice, they left to start up another business, Precept Software Inc. 3Com eventually went on to adopt their business strategy, a move that turned the company's fortunes around. In March 1998, CISCO Systems Inc. acquired Precept Software Inc. for $84 million, naming Ms Estrin their chief technology officer (Gomes, 1998). In describing her motivations for moving back into a corporate environment, Ms Estrin said, 'It intrigued me right away, but I had to think it through, because it was such a big change.' Other factors cited by Estrin were 'Cisco's dominant market position', and 'the fact that, in the mature technology business, it isn't getting any easier to launch a successful start-up'.

Ms Estrin's experience may signal a new generation of female entrepreneurs who will migrate in and out of companies based on their assessment of competing opportunity structures. These talented women will not be faced with a forced choice between a corporate career or entrepreneurship. As attitudinal and organizational barriers to women's advancement fall, entrepreneurial women will join or leave corporations for the right reasons, i.e. a decision based on where they will be most likely to fulfil their potential and contribute to the bottom line.

Conclusion

In today's labour market, large corporations cannot afford to lose seasoned, high-potential women because of lack of flexibility and failure to dismantle glass ceilings and glass walls. Increasingly such women have meaningful options and the resources to act on them.

Corporate decision-makers may be operating under the false assumption that there is nothing they can do to retain one segment of the female talent pool – women with entrepreneurial proclivities. This research shows that, in reality, most women who leave corporations to start their own businesses do not think of themselves as 'born to be' entrepreneurs. They are as much running away from something as running to something else.

The findings from this study show that the youngest cohort of women entrepreneurs entered corporate careers with expectations of a playing field that would be fair and flexible. Compared to earlier generations of women in corporate careers, these women are likely to have a combination of traits – greater educational attainment and technical skills, solid operations and general management experience, and substantial financial resources provided by a dual career marriage – that are predictive of a higher rate of turnover should the corporations they work for fail to measure up to their expectations.

Catalyst has more than 30 years of experience working with major US companies and firms which demonstrate that addressing glass ceiling issues and providing greater flexibility to high-performing women can positively impact on retention rates for this group (Catalyst, 1998a). Consistent with this experiential base, the findings from this research show that companies could retain a larger proportion of women with entrepreneurial interests and abilities by offering them greater flexibility in work scheduling and sites, especially informal flexibility; by dismantling attitudinal and organizational barriers commonly referred to as the glass ceiling and by increasing the financial rewards they receive for their contributions.

In addition, Catalyst has identified strategies that companies could use to address the unique opportunities and challenges related to retention of entrepreneurial women in their professional and managerial ranks, outlined above.

References

Adler, N.J. (1993) 'Competitive frontiers: women managers in the triad', *International Studies of Management and Organization*, 23 (2): 3–23.

Alva, M. (1997) 'One idea hard to franchise: women as units' owners', *Crains New York Business*, 25 August.

Berndtson, P.R. and Cornell University (1994) 'Time in grade of corporate executives', *Wall Street Journal*, March 8.

Birley, S. (1989) 'Female entrepreneurs: are they really any different?' *Journal of Small Business Management*, 27 (1): 32–37.

Bowen, D.D. and Hisrich, R.D. (1986) 'The female entrepreneur: a career development perspective', *Academy of Management Review*, 11 (2): 393–407.

Brenner, O., Tomkiewicz, J. and Schein, V. (1989) 'The relationship between sex role stereotypes and requisite management characteristics revisited', *Academy of Management Journal*, 32: 662–669.

Buttner, E.H. and Rosen, B. (1988b) 'The influence of entrepreneur's gender and type of business on decisions to provide venture capital', in D.F. Ray (ed.), *Southern Management Association Proceedings, Atlanta*, Mississippi State University, University, MS, pp. 314–317.

Catalyst (1981) *Corporations and Two-career Families: Directions for the Future*, Catalyst Career and Family Center, Catalyst, New York.

Catalyst (1986) 'Why women are bailing out: a study of women's departure from corporate life to entrepreneurship', unpublished.

Catalyst (1990) *Women in Corporate Management: Results of a Survey*, Catalyst, New York.

Catalyst (1992) *On the Line: Women's Career Advancement*, Catalyst, New York.

Catalyst (1995a) *Knowing the Territory: Women in Sales*, Catalyst, New York.

Catalyst (1995b) *The CEO View: Women on Corporate Boards*, Catalyst, New York.

Catalyst (1996) *Women in Corporate Leadership: Progress and Prospects*, Catalyst, New York.

Catalyst (1997) *A New Approach to Flexibility: Managing the Work/Time Equation*, Catalyst, New York.

Catalyst (1998a) *Advancing Women in Business: The Catalyst Guide: Best Practices from the Corporate Leaders*, Jossey-Bass, San Francisco, CA.

Catalyst (1998b) *1998 Census of Women Corporate Officers and Top Earners*, Catalyst, New York.

Catalyst (1998c) *Two Careers, One Marriage: Making it Work in the Workplace*, Catalyst, New York.

Divine, T.J. (1994) 'Characteristics of self-employed women in the United States', *Monthly Labor Review*, 117 (3): 20–34.

Drucker, P.F. (1985) *Innovation and Entrepreneurship*, Harper & Row, New York.

Federal Glass Ceiling Commission (1995) *Good for Business: Making Full Use of the Nation's Human Capital*, Federal Glass Ceiling Commission, Washington, DC, March.

Fischer, E.M. et al. (1993) 'A theoretical overview and extension of research on sex, gender, and entrepreneurship', *Journal of Business Venturing*, 4: 429–442.

Foderaro, L.W. (1997) 'Women-owned businesses', *New York Times*, 27 March.

Fried, L. (1989) 'A new breed of entrepreneur – women', *Management Review*, 78 (12): 18–25.

Gomes, L. (1998) 'Cisco systems taps pioneer for company's top tech post', *Wall Street Journal Interactive Edition*, 12 March.

Gregg, G. (1985) 'Women entrepreneurs: the second generation', *Across the Board*, 22 (1): 10–18.

Hamm, S. (1997) 'Why women are so invisible', *Business Week*, 25 August.

Hisrich, R.D. and Brush, C.G. (1987) 'Women entrepreneurs: a longitudinal study', in N.C. Churchill, *Entrepreneurship Research*, Center for Entrepreneurial Studies, Babson College, Wellesley, MA, pp.187–199.

Hisrich, R.D. and O'Brien, M. (1981) 'The woman entrepreneur from a business and sociological perspective', in K. Vesper (ed.), *Frontiers of Entrepreneurship Research*, Center for Entrepreneurial Studies, Babson College, Wellesley, MA, pp. 21–29.

Hisrich, R.D. and O'Brien, M. (1982) 'The woman entrepreneur as a reflection of the type of business', in K. Vesper (ed.), *Frontiers of Entrepreneurship Research*, Center for Entrepreneurial Studies, Babson College, Wellesley, MA, pp. 54–67.

Hood, J.N. and Koberg, C.S. (1994) 'Patterns of differential assimilation and acculturation for women in business organizations', *Human Relations*, 47 (2): 159–181.

Kalleberg, A.L. and Leicht, K.T. (1991) 'Gender and organizational performance: determinants of small business survival and success', *Academy of Management Journal*, 34 (1): 131–161.

Moore, D.P. and Buttner, E.H. (1997) *Women Entrepreneurs: Moving beyond the Glass Ceiling*, Sage Publications, Thousand Oaks, CA.

Morrison, A. White, R.P. and Van Veslor, E. (1994) *Breaking the Glass Ceiling: Can Women Reach the Top of America's Largest Corporations?* Addison-Wesley, Reading, MA.

Murphy, A. (1992) 'The start-up of the '90s', *Inc.*, 14 (3): 32–40.

National Foundation for Women Business Owners, and Dun & Bradstreet Information Services (1995) *Women-owned Businesses: Breaking the Boundaries – The Progress and Achievement of Women-owned Enterprises*, NFWBO, Silver Springs, MD, April.

National Foundation for Women Business Owners (1997) 'Minority women-owned firms thriving', press release, NFWBO, 25 June.

Noble, B.P. (1993) 'Reforming the talk on labor reform', *New York Times*, 17 October: F25.

Petzinger, Thomas Jr (1997) 'Entrepreneur finds success in the failure of her business', *Wall Street Journal Interactive Edition*, 31 October.

Rosener, J. (1989) '"Corporate flight" and female entrepreneurs: is there a connection?' Paper presented at the Annual Meeting of the Academy of Management, Washington, DC.

Saratoga Institute (1997) *1997 Human Resources Report*, Saratoga Institute, Santa Clara CA.

Scott, C. (1986) 'Why more women are becoming entrepreneurs', *Journal of Small Business Management*, 24 (4): 37–44.

Stevenson, L. (1986) 'Against all odds: the entrepreneurship of women', *Journal of Small Business Management*, 24 (3): 30–36.

Taylor, A. (1986) 'Why women managers are bailing out', *Fortune*, 18 August: 16–23.

US Bureau of Labor (1999) Labor force statistics from the Current Population Survey; Annual average tables from the January 1999 issue, *Employment and Earnings*, January.

US Department of Commerce (1986) *Women and Business Ownership, an Annotated Bibliography*, Government Printing Office, Washington, DC.

US Department of Commerce, Bureau of the Census (1986) *Current Population Reports* (Series p–23, No.146), Government Printing Office, Washington, DC.

6

Women Entrepreneurs and Small Business Owners in Norway and Canada

Astrid M. Richardsen and Ronald J. Burke

The global trend in the workforce over the past 20 years or so has been a tremendous increase in the number of women who are gainfully employed. It is estimated that by the year 2000, women will compose almost half of all people employed in the United States and Canada (Moore and Buttner, 1997). In Norway, the number of women who entered the workforce between 1962 and 1995 almost doubled, and the increase of women represents nearly 90 per cent of the total increase in the labour force (Statistics Norway, 1996). By 1997, 57 per cent of all women were employed, comprising 45.8 per cent of the total labour force (Norwegian Gender Equity Council, 1997).

The number of women-owned businesses in North America seems to increase at two to three times the rate of businesses owned by men (Scott, 1986; Stevenson, 1986; Neider, 1987; Moore and Buttner, 1997). In fact, Brush (1992) reported that by 1990, 30 per cent of small businesses were owned by women, and it is estimated that by 2000, nearly half of all American companies will be owned by women (Moore and Buttner, 1997). There are indications that the development of women-owned businesses are similar in Scandinavia (Vangsnes, 1993; Kirkeng and Ørbeck, 1997). The long-term trend in both Sweden and Norway is that the number of female entrepreneurs is increasing, despite a general decrease in self-employment in both countries since 1950 (Norwegian Gender Equity Council, 1986, 1997).

The increase in women-owned businesses may also reflect another trend. Research on women entrepreneurs indicates that since the 1980s the typical demographic picture of women who become business owners may have changed (Moore and Buttner, 1997). The 'traditional' entrepreneur, whose background, domestic orientation, and limited access to capital led her into sole proprietor service businesses, that tended to have low income and to be small and slow growing, has given way to the 'modern' entrepreneur, who has left corporations to become her own boss, to exercise her educational and technical skills, and to make money. Such developmental trends create important changes in the labour market, and suggest avenues for further research on women business owners.

Small business in Norway represents 96 per cent of all firms, and employs 40 per cent of the private sector workforce. This parallels the situation in Canada, where small business represents 96 per cent of all firms and employs 34 per cent of the private sector work-force. It is likely that the economic performance of both Norway and Canada in the next few decades will depend highly on entrepreneurship, and with the increasing number of women entrepreneurs in the workforce, it is important to understand the characteristics of this group in a cross-national perspective. This chapter will review data on female entrepreneurs and small business owners in Norway and Canada, and analyse similarities and differences.

Research on women entrepreneurs is scarce and studies often have serious methodological limitations. There are discrepancies in definitions, interpretation of terms and availability of data on female business creators and owners (Brush, 1992; Moore and Buttner, 1997), which makes comparison between studies difficult. In addition, it is almost impossible to accurately identify the exact number of women entrepreneurs and women-led firms (Holmquist, 1996). Data sources concerning female entrepreneurs are few all over the world, because most databases do not provide the gender of the business owner (Brush, 1992; Moore and Buttner, 1997). Data on small businesses are often inconsistent across public sources of information, which also creates difficulties in making cross-national comparisons. Finally, studies on female entrepreneurs have often used 'male-based' models of entrepreneurship, which makes interpretation of findings on women entrepreneurs tenuous and contributes to keeping women entrepreneurs 'invisible' (Holmquist, 1996). Consequently little theoretical development has occurred which might lend itself to explaining female entrepreneurship (Stevenson, 1986). Stevenson (1990) has stressed the need to feminize research on women entrepreneurs, so that new models can emerge from women's experiences as entrepreneurs.

The aim of this chapter is therefore to review the existing data on the situation for women entrepreneurs in Norway and in Canada, and to compare the two countries in terms of demographic and descriptive characteristics, motivations and goals, success and survival, challenges and obstacles, joys and benefits, and future prospects. Data on country support for women entrepreneurs will be presented, and we will consider a future research agenda and relevance to women in management issue, before some concluding remarks.

The situation in Norway

Since 1950, self-employment has been decreasing in Norway. Between 1950 and 1980 the number of self-employed people decreased by almost 60 per cent and continued to decrease in the decade after 1980 (Vangsnes, 1993). However, the number of self-employed women increased by 22 per cent between 1980 and 1990, whereas there was a 10 per cent decrease in the number of self-employed men. In 1990 women represented 24 per cent of the total number of self-employed, and an even higher percentage of self-employed over 35 years of age (Spilling, 1998). Between 1990 and 1996, the total number of self-employed people continued to decrease, mostly among men (approximately 10 per cent), while there was a 6 per cent increase in self-employed women (Statistics Norway, 1996).

According to Norway's most recent labour market statistics (1997), the total number of people in Norway who are self-employed is 169,000, which constitutes 7.7 per cent of the total labour force. Of these, approximately 74 per cent (125,000) were men and 26 per cent (44,000) were women. In terms of registered sole proprietorships, data show that 25 per cent of sole owners of companies are women. Between 1993 and 1997 there was a general increase of about 5 per cent in sole proprietorships. The largest increase (14 per cent) was among women sole proprietors, while the increase among men was under 3 per cent. In addition, 21 per cent of women and 79 per cent of men indicated that they work as a manager or director of a company or organization, whereas the national registry of commercial enterprises shows that among the companies that record data on leadership and gender, general managers consist of 16 per cent women and 84 per cent men. A study of 1,500 small and medium-sized businesses in Norway indicated that only 15 per cent of the firms had women leaders (Spilling, 1997). Thus, despite some inconsistencies in the data sources, a picture of Norwegian women entrepreneurs and business owners emerges when data from a variety of sources are combined (Spilling, 1998).

Demographic and descriptive picture

A little over half of all self-employed women (53 per cent) indicate that they are working full time (37 or more hours per week), as compared to 85 per cent of the men (Statistics Norway, 1997). Approximately 36 per cent of the women work under 30 hours per week (8 per cent for men entrepreneurs), and 25 per cent worked 45 hours or more (57 per cent for men). Eighty-three per cent of self-employed women earned less than NKr 150,000 per annum (approximately US $20,000) in 1990, as compared to 60 per cent of the men, which is lower than the average salaries for the total employed population (Spilling, 1998). Only 3 per cent of the self-employed men and 0.8 per cent of the women earned over NKr 400,000. At the same time, almost 64 per cent of self-employed men earned the main income in the family as compared to 29 per cent of the women.

There are few differences between men and women entrepreneurs in terms of age, although there has been a shift towards younger age groups. In 1980, the median age for all self-employed people was 47 years, whereas in 1990 it was 44 years (Vangsnes, 1993). The age range of 40–49 years had a higher concentration of self-employed women. The data on sole proprietorships show that for both sexes, the largest number of proprietors were in the age group of 26–35 years (about 33 per cent), and 83 per cent of the total number of owners were between 26 and 55 years of age.

There has also been a shift towards more self-employed women being single or separated/divorced (Vangsnes, 1993), which may be a result of the shift in age. Still the great majority of both men and women are married (73 per cent and 77 per cent respectively), and the proportion of single entrepreneurs is 21 per cent among the men and 12 per cent among the women.

Vangsnes (1993) reported that the level of education has increased among all self-employed in the past decades, and that in general, the level of education is higher among women. In the survey of small and medium-sized businesses in Norway (Spilling, 1997), it was found that the proportion of men and women with university education was almost equal. A larger proportion of men had specific vocational training, most often in trade and technology (35 per cent) and agriculture (30 per cent), whereas more women had higher education in the humanities (34 per cent) and in health and service professions (29 per cent). However, the level of education among the self-employed was generally lower than the employed population at large. Most women seem to have education and previous work experience in the same industry as they start a business (Milje 1995; Kirkeng and Ørbeck, 1997).

Thirty-four per cent of all self-employed workers in Norway are found in agriculture and the primary industries (hunting, forestry and fishing), and of these, 82 per cent are self-employed men, and only 18 per cent are women (Statistics Norway, 1997). However, women constitute 62 per cent of 'family workers' (as part of a family business) in agriculture. The largest proportion of self-employed women is found in the wholesale and resale trade (42 per cent) and in community and social services (56 per cent). There are no self-employed women registered in the construction industry, and women are under-represented in transport and telecommunications (8 per cent). The number of self-employed women in manufacturing (25 per cent) as well as in finance, insurance, real estate and business services (25 per cent) has increased by almost 50 per cent since 1990. The increase in manufacturing has mainly been in the textile industry and food production, graphic design and publishing.

Nevertheless, data indicate that women's enterprises in Norway tend to be small with one or two employees, and tend to be concentrated in two commercial sectors: the wholesale and retail trade, and community and social services (Bolkesjø, 1992; Spilling, 1997). In addition, over 60 per cent of women leaders are concentrated in retail sales (20 per cent), childcare centres (18 per cent) and hairdressing and beauty care (14 per cent). As a rule, therefore, women-led enterprises are often operating in a local market economy and have only local competition. Women-led businesses are also more often sole proprietorships than businesses led by men, which more often tend to be limited companies.

Motivations, aspirations and goals

It has been claimed that women often start their own enterprise as a result of wanting more flexibility to balance work and family (Brush, 1992), and may be motivated by a desire for increased independence and for new challenges (Berg, 1991; Alsos and Ljunggren, 1995). In a study of women entrepreneurs in Oslo (Kirkeng and Ørbeck, 1997), the women indicated that the most important motive for starting their businesses was the wish to have more control over their own work situation and working hours, followed by the need to use their own resources and skills, support from family and friends, good potential for sales and profits, and the wish to start their own businesses. Balancing work and family was not a major motivation. A high proportion of women entrepreneurs indicated that they had a near relative or friend who also was an entrepreneur (Spilling, 1997). Other studies of small communities in Norway suggest that there is a lot of diversity in terms of motivating factors, type of business venture, and background among women entrepreneurs, and conclude that there is no such thing as the 'typical' woman entrepreneur (Alsos and Ljunggren, 1995; Milje, 1995).

Research on new business ventures is most often carried out by men, for men and is adapted to men (Alsos and Ljunggren, 1997). It is often assumed that women operate according to the same criteria for success, have the same goals in mind and act according to the same motivations as do men. Several Norwegian studies have indicated that women entrepreneurs may not be primarily interested in growth (Alsos and Ljunggren, 1995; Milje, 1995; Kirkeng and Ørbeck, 1997). Since women tend to be over-represented in certain trades, they start businesses which grow at a slower rate, have fewer employees, and have lower sales and profits than businesses started by men, their goals and aspirations may be to create work for themselves, to gain personal development, to work fewer hours, and to do things they are really interested in, rather than to achieve profit and growth.

Success and survival

There is little gender information available in terms of new registrations and deregistrations every year (Spilling, 1997). Some data on success and survival of business ventures come from follow-up studies of various educational programmes for women wanting to start a new business. Bolkesjø (1992) studied women who completed business venture education between 1985 and 1988, and found that the survival rates of those who established their own businesses was about 70 per cent of businesses after five years. However, few businesses had grown, only 4 per cent had more than 10 employees, and salaries were on the whole quite low. Evaluations of the Enterprise School for Women, which has offered programmes all around the country (Sandvig, 1998), indicate that of the 2,400 businesses started by women since 1980, there is an 80 per cent survival rate. Most of these had 2–12 employees.

Challenges and obstacles

A critical factor in establishing one's own business is the availablity of financial support, and research has indicated that women meet more barriers than men in seeking business loans (Riding and Swift, 1990; Fay and Williams, 1993). There is anecdotal evidence that women entrepreneurs in small communities in Norway find the economic support for enterprises insufficient (Alsos and Ljunggren, 1995; Milje, 1995), whereas women in larger communities reported no such barriers (Kirkeng and Ørbeck, 1997). However, many women start so low key that their projects may be assessed as being too small to receive financial support.

In both these studies, there was great diversity in the women's needs and what they considered barriers. Milje (1995) found that many women had need of assistance in discussing their business idea and getting advice on various aspects of the process, but this type of regional government support seemed to be limited and varied greatly from community to community. Other barriers reported were negative attitudes from friends, colleagues, regional advisors and customers;

conflicts between personal life and work; lack of experience in finance and marketing; and limited help and supervision after start-up (Alsos and Ljunggren, 1995; Kirkeng and Ørbeck, 1997). However, these studies were based on interviews with a few women, and the data are too limited to generalize.

In terms of network, i.e. partners, contractors, customers, bank and loan officers, distributors, other branch offices and family members, male business owners are often better integrated in their environment. This means that women have less support in areas of need when establishing a business. Therefore communal support in terms of supervision and advice may be more important than financial support (Milje, 1995).

Joys and benefits

Most women entrepreneurs emphasize the satisfaction of being able to make their own decisions, be completely independent and able to organize their time (Kirkeng and Ørbeck, 1997). Other studies (e.g., Milje, 1995) report that women are generally satisfied with having started a business, but no data are available on job and career satisfaction.

Future prospects and predictions

The descriptive evidence from Norway indicates that trends in the general workforce as well as in small business parallel global trends. Women entrepreneurship is increasing, and the demographic and descriptive picture looks similar to what is found in other countries. However, in terms of motivating factors and obstacles and satisfaction, the research is mostly anecdotal and based on interviews with local convenience samples of women entrepreneurs. Thus, little is known about the specific factors that may help and hinder women who want to start a business in Norway, as well as the factors that promote survival and growth once established. Until research is conducted that includes representative samples and considers longitudinal evidence, it is impossible to generalize findings.

The situation in Canada

In Canada, unlike Norway, self-employment, or entrepreneurship, has been growing. More than 25 per cent of all employment growth from 1976 to 1994 has been in the form of self-employment (Baldwin and Picot, 1994). Women accounted for one in three entrepreneurs in 1994, an increase from the one in four found in 1976. The number of self-employed women tripled from 197,000 in 1976 to 598,000 in 1994. The corresponding numbers for men were 614,000 to 1.2 million. Women accounted for 40 per cent of the rise in self-employment during this period. Two-thirds of women entrepreneurs work full time (Cohen, 1996). Twenty-five per cent of self-employed women were employers in 1976; 28 per cent in 1994. Women made up 22 per cent of all employers in 1994 and 12 per cent in 1976.

A study sponsored by the Bank of Montreal's Institute for Small Business, in collaboration with Dun & Bradstreet and *Canadian Business* magazine, was released in 1996 and provides the most comprehensive description of women-led firms in Canada so far. Women held the position of president, owner, co-owner, CEO, chair, or partner in almost one-third of all firms in Canada, more than 700,000 firms in total. These firms exist in every region of Canada and employ 1.7 million Canadians, more than *Canadian Business's* Top 100 companies. Comparing 1991 and 1994, the number of woman-led firms increased at twice the national average (19.7 per cent vs. 8.7 per cent), and created jobs at four times the average rate (13.0 per cent vs. 3.1 per cent). Women were also moving away from fields in which they were previously found (retail) into male-dominated fields, such as high tech and resources. Woman-led firms were younger than the average Canadian firm (66 per cent vs. 73 per cent have been in business nine or more years; 4.6 per cent vs. 57 per cent have been in business 12 or more years), but were found to be as creditworthy, viable and stable as the average business in Canada. It was found that 49 per cent of all woman-owned businesses were still in business after five years, compared to 25 per cent for men.

Demographic and descriptive picture

Demographic information indicates that self-employment rises with age for both women and men (Baldwin and Picot, 1994). Self-employed women were more likely to be married than were paid workers (72 per cent vs. 64 per cent), partially reflecting their greater age. Women entrepreneurs worked either few or many hours in their main job. Thus, 37 per cent worked less than 30 hours per week (12 per cent for male entrepreneurs); 21 per cent worked 50 or more hours per week (44 per cent for men entrepreneurs). Self-employed women (in 1993) earned less than female paid workers and self-employed men ($18,000, $25,000 and $30,000, respectively).

Self-employed women tend to be concentrated in a few service industries, as do employed women (Baldwin and Picot, 1994). However, the growth in women's self-employment came from business in health and social services, comparing growth between 1989 and 1996 (MacNedie, 1997). During this period, the growth in women's self-employment was almost equal to men's. For women, about 20 per cent of this increase was in business services (accountants, bookkeepers, management consultants, other business services). Another 17 per cent was in other services (beauty shops, service to private households). New businesses in wholesale and retail accounted for a further 14 per cent of the overall growth.

However, several studies of entrepreneurship among women in Quebec and New Brunswick (Colerette and Aubry, 1990; Lee-Gosselin and Grise, 1990; Grondin and Grondin, 1994), indicate that many women entrepreneurs may still fit the traditional picture. These studies found that the businesses were for the most part small, were relatively new, had few employees, low annual sales, and provided modest revenues. They had low initial investment costs and low overhead expenses. These women wanted to create small and stable businesses, i.e. they chose to remain small in size. This situation emerged as a workable adaptation to the business, family, social and personal demands they were experiencing.

Belcourt et al. (1991) undertook a study of more than 200 women business owners across Canada. Slightly over half the participants had businesses in the retail sector (52 per cent) followed by services businesses (25 per cent). Sixty per cent founded their company while an additional 29 per cent bought theirs. A majority (60 per cent) were solo owners. Almost half started their businesses between the ages of 25 and 35. The majority were both wives and mothers when they began their businesses, and currently. Interestingly, many of these women (40 per cent) started businesses in sectors where they had no experience. In addition, 55 per cent of the women had no managerial experience when they began their businesses. Lawyers, bankers and suppliers were the most common source of help (advice, information) when these women started their businesses. Little use was made of government programmes designed to help entrepreneurs.

Motivations, aspirations and goals

In terms of motivations, Belcourt (1990) studied factors contributing to the decision to become an entrepreneur. She conducted extensive interviews with 36 of Canada's most successful women entrepreneurs. Their firms had model sales of $2–5 million; 11 to 20 employees; had been 6 to 10 years in business; and the women had yearly incomes of $51–80,000 in salary. About one-third were in retail and manufacturing. The majority (about 60 per cent) were sole owners. There was an emphasis on self-reliance (independence, control of their own lives) as women's key motivation for opening their businesses. In addition, these women were likely to report unreliable husbands, as well as difficulties fitting into the corporate world. In another study, women reported that motivations for entrepreneurship included the desire to be their own boss, financial independence and increased self-esteem (Colerette and Aubry, 1990).

Challenges and obstacles

Canadian women entrepreneurs also meet challenges and obstacles in their business ventures. Some researchers have suggested that credit terms differ between women and men business owners to the disadvantage of women (Belcourt et al., 1991; Orser and Foster, 1994), while others report no differences (Riding and Swift, 1990; Wynant and Hatch, 1991). Fabowale et al. (1995) reported that women and men business owners differed in a number of ways, but when these differences were controlled for, no differences in bank credit were present. This area remains contentious and inconclusive. However, women business owners indicated that they were treated disrespectfully by bank lending officers to a significantly greater degree than did men business owners.

Belcourt et al. (1991) found that most women financed their businesses through their own savings (72 per cent). Banks were the second most common source of financing, with 49 per cent of women using them. About half of the women requesting funds from the banks received the funds they asked for. A surprisingly small percentage (10 per cent) prepared business plans or financial statements. However, only 20 per cent of these women were earning more than $50,000 a year.

Other obstacles have been addressed by Stevenson (1990), who discussed the finding that women entrepreneurs seem less interested in growth than are male entrepreneurs. Women may have less access to capital, borrowed money, information, technical and business training, may have younger firms, and have greater responsibilities for home and family, which would interfere with business growth. Stevenson found many women entrepreneurs to be frustrated by the difficulties experienced in developing their firms. These women, particularly those with children, make compromises and settle for less.

In a study by Colerette and Aubry (1990), female entrepreneurs in Quebec reported two major problems with owning and running a business: work and family problems and difficulties obtaining funds for the business. More than half worked over 40 hours per week. Two-thirds devoted more time than 10 hours a week to household responsibilities. In a national study it was found that almost one-quarter of the women were working more than 70 hours per week (Belcourt et al., 1991), and many of the women also shouldered family and home responsibilities. Spouses were of very limited help in providing family care, and hiring external help was not often done. Most of the women entrepreneurs saw their paid work and family roles as complementary, followed by compensatory, i.e., success in one role compensates for disappointment in another. Few women saw the two roles as conflicting.

The roles of entrepreneur, spouse/partner and parent were all important to these women's self-identity. The women reported significant demands placed on them by the three roles, but rated themselves as having considerable competence in dealing with these roles. Not surprisingly, these women were also highly satisfied with their performance in these roles (Belcourt et al., 1991).

Canada vs. Norway – similarities and differences

What is clear from the material presented so far in this chapter, is that there are many similarities between Canada and Norway. First, the number of women entrepreneurs seems to be increasing in both countries. Second, the demographic and descriptive picture of these entrepreneurs is much the same. Women entrepreneurs in both countries tend to be concentrated in a few service industries, the firms are small, operating in the local marketplace, and bringing in modest revenues. Interestingly, there are indications in both countries that an increasing number of women are establishing enterprises in traditionally male-dominated fields, especially manufacturing and business services, which require high levels of skill. This suggests a new development giving rise to the modern woman entrepreneur.

Despite many similarities, the overall trends of entrepreneurship in the two countries are different. Since 1950, there has been a decrease in the number of self-employed people in Norway, and this trend continues. In Canada, entrepreneurship has been growing steadily over the past decades. The increase in self-employment in Canada reflects, in part, the shift to a service economy. It also reflects the effects of company downsizing and restructuring and the greater use of contracting out. In Norway, the decrease in self-employment reflects various structural changes within industries after World War II, along with a rapid increase in the use of technology and a shift towards larger companies (Vangsnes, 1993). The decrease was largest in agriculture and the primary industries. Given that small business makes up such a large part of trade and employment in both

Canada and Norway, it is likely that entrepreneurship will continue to grow in other fields.

The amount of research data available on women entrepreneurs differs in the two countries. In the past decade, several large studies of women entrepreneurs in Canada have been published, whereas the work in this area in Norway has been largely unpublished. The gender aspect of entrepreneurship has only recently been addressed (Spilling, 1998), and few published research findings are available (Kolvereid et al., 1993). Like most of the early work on Canadian women entrepreneurs, the work on Norwegian women entrepreneurs is necessarily descriptive. In addition, small locally based samples are typically considered. Despite these limitations, pictures of the nature of women-owned businesses and women owners have emerged, identifying problems women face in starting and managing their firms. There are still no theories of female entrepreneurship, however.

National support for these women

Since 1980 the Norwegian government has made efforts and taken initiatives to stimulate new business ventures in order to promote economic growth and increase employment, especially in small communities. Although not all of these initiatives are developed only for women, female entrepreneurs are a high-priority group.

Venture capital in the form of grants of up to NKr 200,000, is available from both national and regional funding sources. In addition, there are several regional industrial funds, which may award grants for businesses with small start-up costs. Evaluations of these initiatives indicate that women generally apply for less money than men. However, women who receive grants follow through on their business plan to a greater extent than men. A majority of women who received grants believed this was an important factor when starting up their businesses (Bolkesjø, 1992), although some felt more follow-up support could have been given. Nevertheless, even if women are a high-priority group, the proportion of grants awarded to women is decreasing (Milje, 1995).

Network Credit, a women's banking institution which is modelled on Grameen Bank, a community bank concept from Bangladesh, was established in 1992 in northern Norway. The bank is for women and run by women, and offers venture loans for business projects of up to NKr 50,000 without collateral at a lower interest rate than regular banks. The model also involves establishing networks among women in the community, which is a development that has been encouraged both nationally and regionally. Today almost 80 self-governing groups exist with a total investment capital of NKr 8.5 million. An evaluation of the project (Thomassen, 1995) indicated that the group participants were satisfied with the bank, that the groups worked well together, and that a network of support and follow-up of projects had been established.

Since the early 1980s, several enterprise training programmes have been developed for women. The scope and content of these are quite similar and include development of a business plan, finance/accounting, marketing, some management training, and self-efficacy training (Spilling and Sæter, 1993). Data indicate that female entrepreneurs who have participated, reported increased self-esteem and greater motivation to start a business (Haukaa, 1985; Milje, 1995), felt better prepared for the process of entrepreneurship, particularly financial control (Bolkesjø, 1992), and felt that the programme had been instrumental in getting their business idea into action (Haukaa, 1985). In addition, approximately 70 per cent of participants actually have established their own businesses. However, evaluations of the enterprise training programmes vary greatly in terms of content, measures and analyses, which makes it difficult to compare and generalize the success of projects.

Several sources of support also exist in Canada for women entrepreneurs. Courses in entrepreneurship and management are widely available through community colleges, universities, private companies, cable television, and all levels of government. Women entrepreneurs also receive advice and support for their ventures through a number of professional associations. Chartered banks and other financial institutions have become increasingly sensitized to the way they treat women business owners (Wynant and Hatch, 1991; Fabowale et al., 1995).

Future research agenda

From a research perspective, there seems to be a reduced interest in women entrepreneurs as subjects for study in the past few years. Stevenson (1990) listed several research topics on women entrepreneurs in 1990. These topics remain relatively unchanged as we approach the millennium.

First, she advocates the development of a database of women entrepreneurs which would make research studies easier. She then offers the following list of topics for attention (1990: 444):

- in-depth research on motivations of women entrepreneurs;
- influences on the start-up rate of women owners;
- growth strategies of women owners;
- how women compromise the business and personal aspects of their lives;
- comparative studies between women entrepreneurs and women executives;
- women entrepreneurs and women who want to start a business;
- women entrepreneurs in developed countries and women in developing countries;
- existing women entrepreneurs and women who are no longer in business;
- women and men as entrepreneurs;
- impact of women entrepreneurs on economic development;
- success/survival of woman-owned firms;
- management styles of women entrepreneurs;
- longitudinal studies on the development of woman-owned firms, e.g. strategies developed by women as the business develops, problems at each stage, the process of development and the accompanying impact on their lives;
- women in home-based businesses;
- role of women in family businesses;
- taking over a family business;
- wives contributing to family businesses.

Belcourt et al. (1991) suggest other topics. These include: why do businesses owned by women start small and stay small? do women entrepreneurs manage differently than men entrepreneurs? does entrepreneurial training lead to business growth and projects? why do women seek self-employment in the first place? are more women becoming entrepreneurs because of career frustrations within medium and large organizations? and are women entrepreneurs in the 1990s different (e.g. more educated) than women entrepreneurs of the 1970s and do they have different motivations and aspirations?

Relevance to the women in management issue

Many women become entrepreneurs because of a desire for increased autonomy. Not only do women want to control their work environment and working time, they also want to decide for themselves how to manage a business. Women are increasingly dissatisfied with the opportunities for advancement in many organizations, and even if they reach management positions, the traditional structure of the company may put restrictions on leadership style and management practices. Entrepreneurship represents an opportunity for women to choose their own leadership style.

Conclusion

Research on women entrepreneurs indicates that on the whole they are satisfied and like what they do. They quite often create viable businesses, but stay small, clustering in business sectors with low financial payoff. They tend to work hard, yet make modest amounts of money, and some blend work and family. Yet there is evidence to suggest that the work enhances their self-esteem, despite the fact that many women entrepreneurs face some unique challenges and obstacles (Belcourt et al., 1991).

Evidence from both Canada and Norway indicates that women entrepreneurs may face discrimination from several sources, including customers and colleagues. Other obstacles include difficulties in getting finance; limited relevant work experience and management training and experience; shortage of peer support networks and limited time and money to develop and maintain them; and limited time and money to find and attend training courses. Conflicting demands of managing a business, a home and children are also a challenge, especially since many women have little concrete help from spouses/partners.

The issue of business growth has been addressed in some Scandinavian studies (Sundin and Holmquist, 1989). Women-owned businesses often have low financial return, and are not considered successful according to traditional measures. Critical voices in Norway have claimed that women's enterprises are too small, and that they are hobby activities that should not be supported by public financing. However, some authors (Alsos and Ljunggren, 1997) maintain that other measures of success need to be considered, such as offering a product or service otherwise not available, 'new' or 'untraditional' ventures in a community bound by tradition, developing products or services in which preservation of resources is a focus, creating a social network in the community, contributing to turning around a negative development, preserving culture and history, and creating employment in small communities.

In order to ensure the continued growth of women-owned businesses and increased survival of new business ventures, proposals for change include an information clearing house on courses in entrepreneurship and management (short duration, low cost, taught by experienced entrepreneurs); financial incentives to support women's attendance at courses and the hiring of replacement workers in their absence; creating networks or associations for entrepreneurs and small business owners; educating financial institutions in how to cultivate business with women entrepreneurs; and subsidizing women's attendance at educational courses.

The Bank of Montreal's study (1996) laid to rest the following four myths about women-led firms in Canada:

Myth 1   : They have no real economic significance.
Reality   : Women-led firms are a significant and growing force in the economy.
Myth 2   : They are financially unsophisticated.
Reality   : Women-led firms are as financially strong as the average firm.
Myth 3   : They don't have what it takes to succeed.
Reality   : Women-led firms have staying power.
Myth 4   : They are clustered in retail and personal services.
Reality   : Women-led firms are diversifying into non-traditional sectors.

An examination of the contributions of women entrepreneurs and small business owners in Norway and Canada suggests that the economic power of woman-led firms is an important area of research world wide.

Note

Preparation of this manuscript was supported in part by the Department of Psychology, University of Tromsø, Norway and the Schulich School of Business, York University, Toronto.

References

Alsos, G.A. and Ljunggren, G.A. (1995) *Kari Askeladd og de gode hjelperne. Om forholdet mellom kvinnelige etablerere og kommunale næringsetater i Lofoten.* (The relationship between women entrepreneurs and regional agencies for business services in Lofoten). NF-report no. 11, Nordland Research Institute, Bodø.

Alsos, G.A. and Ljunggren, E. (1997) 'Kvinnelige etablerere – suksess etter hvem sin målestokk?' (Female enterprises – success according to whose definition?). Paper presented at the conference 'Women's Lives in the North', Tromsø.

Baldwin, J. and Picot, G. (1994) *Employment Generation by Small Producers in the Canadian Manufacturing Sector*, Statistics Canada, Ottawa.

Bank of Montreal (1996) *Myths and Realities*, Bank of Montreal's Institute for Small Business, Toronto.

Belcourt, M. (1990) 'A family portrait of Canada's most successful female entrepreneurs', *Journal of Business Ethics*, 9: 435–438.

Belcourt, M., Burke, R.J. and Lee-Gosselin, H. (1991) *The Glass Box: Women Business Owners in Canada*, Canadian Advisory Council on the Status of Women, Ottawa.

Berg, N.G. (1991) *Kjønnsperspektiv på entrepreneurskap i distriktene* (Gender perspective on entrepreneurship), SFS Allforsk, Norwegian University of Science and Technology, Trondheim.

Bolkesjø, T. (1992) *Virkemidler overfor nyetablerere: Oppnådde resultater og vurdering av fremtidig bruk* (Help to entrepreneurs: results and evaluation for future use), report series, Telemarksforskning, Norway.

Brush, C.G. (1992) 'Research on women business owners: past trends, a new perspective and future directions', *Entrepreneurship: Theory and Practice*, 16: 5–30.

Cohen, G.L. (1996) 'Women entrepreneurs', *Perspectives*, Statistics Canada, Ottawa, pp. 23–28.

Colerette, P. and Aubry, P. (1990) 'Socio-economic evolution of women business owners in Quebec', *Journal of Business Ethics*, 9: 435–438.

Fabowale, L., Orser, B. and Riding, A. (1995) 'Gender, structural factors, and credit terms between Canadian small business and financial institutions', *Entrepreneurship, Theory and Practice*, 19: 41–63.

Fay, M. and Williams, L. (1993) 'Gender bias and the availability of business loans', *Journal of Business Venturing*, 8: 363–376.

Grondin, D. and Grondin, C. (1994) 'The export orientation of female entrepreneurs in New Brunswick', *Women in Management Review*, 9: 20–30.

Haukaa, R. (1985) *Kvinner med eget firma. Hvem er de? Hva vil de? Hvor går de?* (Women business owners. Who are they? What do they want? Where are they going?), Report series, Technological Institute, Oslo.

Holmquist, C. (1996) 'Women have always been entrepreneurs', in Nordic Council of Ministers, *Conference on Women's Enterprising*, TemaNord, Stockholm, p. 593.

Kirkeng, K. and Ørbeck, B. (1997) 'Kvinnelige entrprenører i Oslo og Akershus' (Female entrepreneurs in Oslo and Akershus), unpublished dissertation, Norwegian School of Management BI, Sandvika.

Kolvereid, L., Shane, S. and Westhead, P. (1993) 'Is it equally difficult for female entrepreneurs to start businesses in all countries?' *Journal of Small Business Management*, 31: 42–51.

Lee-Gosselin, H. and Grise, J. (1990) 'Are women owner-managers challenging our definitions of entrepreneurship? An in-depth survey', *Journal of Business Ethics*, 9: 423–433.

MacNedie, I. (1997) 'Key labor and income facts', *Perspectives*, Statistics Canada, Ottawa, pp. 65–68.

Milje, H. (1995) 'Kvinnelige etablerere og kommunale støtteordninger' (Female entrepreneurs and local support), unpublished thesis, Bodø Graduate School of Business, Norway.

Moore, D.P. and Buttner, E.H. (1997) *Women Entrepreneurs. Moving beyond the Glass Ceiling*, Sage Publications, Thousand Oaks, CA.

Neider, L. (1987) 'A preliminary investigation of female entrepreneurs in Florida', *Journal of Small Business Management*, 25: 22–29.

Norwegian Gender Equity Council (1986) *Kvinner som selvstendig næringsdrivende: Utviklingen fra 1950–1980* (Women and self-employment: the development from 1950–1980), report, Oslo.

Norwegian Gender Equity Council (1997) *Minifacts on Gender Equality*, Summary of official statistics, 1993–96, Oslo.

Orser, B.J. and Foster, M.K. (1994) 'Lending practices and Canadian women in micro-based businesses', *Women in Management Review*, 9: 11–19.

Riding, A. and Swift, C. (1990) 'Women business owners and terms of credit: some empirical findings of the Canadian experience', *Journal of Business Venturing*, 5: 327–340.

Sandvig, A.M. (1998) 'Etablererskolen for kvinner i Norge' (The Enterprise School for Women in Norway), unpublished report, Oslo.

Scott, C. (1986) 'Why more women are becoming entrepreneurs', *Journal of Small Business Management*, 24: 37–44.

Spilling, O.R. (1997) *SMB 97 – fakta om små og mellomstore bedrifter i Norge* (Facts about small and medium-sized businesses in Norway), Fagbokforlaget, Bergen.

Spilling, O.R. (1998) 'Kjønn og ledelse i SMB' (Gender and leadership in SMB), in O.R. Spilling (ed.), *SMB 98*, Fagbokforlaget, Bergen.

Spilling, O.R. and Sæter, J.A. (1993) *Etablererservice – et ambisiøst prosjekt i et vanskelig terreng* (Enterprise education – an ambitious project in difficult terrain), report, Østlandsforskning, Lillehammer.

Statistics Norway (1996) *Labour Market Statistics 1995*, Report on official statistics of Norway, Statistics Norway, Oslo.

Statistics Norway (1997) *Labour Market Statistics 1996*, Report on official statistics of Norway, Statistics Norway, Oslo.

Stevenson, L. (1986) 'Against all odds: the entrepreneurship of women', *Journal of Small Business Management*, 24: 30–36.

Stevenson, L. (1990) 'Some methodological problems associated with researching women entrepreneurs', *Journal of Business Ethics*, 9: 439–446.

Sundin, E. and Holmquist, C. (1989) *Kvinner som företagare – osynlighet, mångfald, och anpasning* (Women as entrepreneurs – invisibility, diversity and adaptation), Liber, Malmö, Sweden.

Thomassen, B. (1995) *Nettverkskreditt – banken for kvinner i Flakstad og Moskenes* (Network Credit – the Women's Bank in Lofoten), Report 12/95, NORUT Research, Tromsø.

Vangsnes, K. (1993) 'Kvinner som selvstendig næringsdrivende 1980–1990' (Women and self-employment 1980–1990), Report, Norwegian Gender Equity Council, Oslo.

Wynant, L. and Hatch, J. (1991) *Banks and Small Business Borrowers*, The Western Business School, University of Western Ontario, London, Ontario.

PART II

CAREER DEVELOPMENT
AND HIGH FLIERS

7

Think Career Global, but Act Local:
Understanding Networking as a
Culturally Differentiated Career Skill

Cheryl Travers and Carole Pemberton

> Networking... 'Talking to anyone who might be useful to you in your work and who might benefit from your expertise. It is making use of your contacts as a resource for help and advice. It gives you a collective backing where you might have struggled on alone and it also gives you a pool of experienced people at your disposal. Networking covers all kinds of mutual help...'
>
> (Bird, 1996: 67)

Networking has long been considered a crucial ingredient for success in any professional career due to the many advantages to be gained by its practice, including information exchange, collaboration, career planning and strategy making, professional support and encouragement, and access to visibility and upward mobility (e.g. Stern, 1981; Welsh, 1981; Green, 1982). Networking may be formal or informal, between or within organizations, or by individuals inside or outside their work organizations. A key principle of networking is that of trust – as networking is based on mutually beneficial exchanges between similar or dissimilar people or organizations.

The importance of networking as a career management tool for women in particular has been claimed and, given the recognized strength of networks for male career development, it is remarkable that women have only begun to realize the potential of networks in recent years. Due to this, the research in this area is rather sparse, and in the main has been largely anecdotal in nature.

This chapter presents a review of some of the current research into women's networking behaviour and focuses mainly on the issue of cross-cultural networking based on the authors' own research findings from a study of an international sample of women from the UK, USA and Spain. First though, the nature and role of networks and networking will be presented by examining other research and literature in this area.

Networks and networking

Numerous attempts have been made to capture the nature and essence of networks and networking. Warner Burke (1995: 346) describes networking as 'the process of contacting and being contacted by people in our social network and maintaining these linkages and relationships,' and a network as 'a set of relations, linkages, or ties among people'. On a more instrumental level Kanter (1977) defines networks as collections of individuals who regularly exchange information, support and favours within the organizations in which they work. However, researchers commonly agree that networks are most vital when people value them without expecting benefits (Sonnenberg, 1990). Also, Smart (1991) states that because effective networks evolve over time, the soundest advice is to build a network and have it well in place before you need to use it for assistance.

Evidently, a network relies on some form of connection between people which may consist of both content (type of connection, e.g. information exchange or simply friendship ties) and form (strength of the connection, such as the number of contacts made between people over time, or degree of intensity, i.e. how long contact is maintained). Within organizations Olson (1994) has found that the most frequently referenced and perhaps ideal number of people in a network (the network density) is six to eight.

Other definitions emphasize the importance of a certain amount of homogeneity within networks: for example Vinnicombe and Colwill (1996: 88) define networking as 'the banding together of like-minded people for the purposes of contact and friendship and support'. More specifically, they explain that networking, in the context of women's networks, 'is women's attempts to create for themselves the support generated for men by their informal same-sex grouping'.

When talking about networking, it is essential to talk about kinds of networks and networking not only as a behaviour, but also as a skill that is increasingly crucial to an individual's career development. Much that is written about networking is designed to help the reader develop networking in order to aid their career development. More and more books now that are designed to help women, and indeed men, develop business and management skills have sections devoted to this topic. There have been many claims for the merits of networking for career success (e.g. Brass, 1985; Cannings and Montmarquette, 1991; Peluchette, 1993).

Types of interaction networks within organizations:
formal and informal networks

Networking is not confined to talking to your colleagues or opposite numbers in other related companies or businesses. Everyone you meet is a potential part of your network.

Your contacts can be friends, neighbours, colleagues, bosses, subordinates, fellow professionals or trade members, people you meet when you go to the shops or to the doctor, friends, friends of friends or your children or your partner, relatives, friends of your relatives, strangers you meet when you travel – the list is endless. (Bird, 1996: 68)

Within organizational research a distinction is usually made between prescribed and emergent networks, or simply formal and informal structures (Ibarra, 1993). Both types have their uses, are clearly not mutually exclusive but there may be overlaps between the two. When referring to a formal network what is described is a 'set' of individuals with formally specified relationships, between superiors and their subordinates and among those who have to interact with others outside of their usual functional groups in order to accomplish certain tasks.

By contrast informal networks involve interactive behaviours between individuals whose relationships are more likely to be the result of their own choice, and which may be formed to accomplish work related tasks or to provide social benefits, or both.

These kinds of relationships emerge out of 'the purposive action of social actors who seek to realize their self interests, and…negotiate routinized patterns or relationships that enhance these interests' (Golaskiewicz, 1979: 16).

The culture and climate of an organization cannot be viewed in isolation from organizational power structures, which in turn determine access to the opportunity to use informal organizational networks. Coe (1992) has identified the 'men's club' as one of the main barriers encountered by women in their managerial careers and informal organizational networks are essential to the effective performance of managerial roles. Kilduff and Krackhardt (1994) suggest that an individual's reputation for performance within an organization depends on both the actual performance and on his or her association with prominent friends. Tjosvold and Weicker (1993) found that co-operative goals and interaction contribute substantially to successful networking.

The informal aspect of organizational life is increasingly important. Marshall (1985) has listed the following functions provided by informal organizational mechanisms: transmitting information; socialization of new recruits; coping with uncertainty; assessing the intangible elements of managerial effectiveness and potential; achieving organizational visibility; problem-solving through exchanges involving influence, reciprocity and conflict; providing prompt and frank feedback about individuals' performance, acceptability and prospects. Looking at all of these functions it is hard to see how anyone can be effective as a manager without networks. It can also be seen why these can be detrimental to outsiders – especially women.

One of the most frequently reported problems by women in organizational settings is the fact that they experience limited or indeed no access to informal interaction networks (Miller et al., 1975; Kanter, 1977; Lincoln and Miller, 1979; Lipman-Blumen, 1980; O'Leary and Ickovics, 1992). An effect of this exclusion is limited access to the instrumental resources critical to one's job effectiveness and career advancement that are allocated by these networks. In addition, friendship and social support are often provided by this medium (Tichy, 1981). So for anyone experiencing difficulty in gaining access to these networks multiple disadvantages may result, including restricted knowledge of what is going on within the organization, and difficulty forming alliances – these in turn may be linked to career advancement issues such as limited mobility and 'glass ceiling' effects.

In addition, Brass (1984, 1985) found that women were not well integrated into male networks, and vice versa. Burke et al. (1995) concluded that managerial and professional women are still less integrated into important organizational 'male' networks, composed of individuals who hold power in the organization (Hennig and Jardim, 1977; Kanter, 1977; Fagenson, 1986). Exclusion from the old boys' network can also perpetuate male customs, traditions and negative attitudes towards women within organizations. Though it may not necessarily be favourable to keep men and women separate in networks, we need to gain a better understanding of what women want from networks, so that more effective integration can take place.

Women's exclusion from the formal network structure in organizations has negatively affected their advancement within the corporate environment and participation on corporate boards (Haberfeld, 1992; Bilimoria and Piderit, 1994; Ohlott et al., 1994). As women are also often excluded from informal networks, they consequently lack access to real time information via the grapevine (Handley, 1994).

Women and networking

Due to the exclusion of women from this informal system over the last 20 years or so, an increasing number of women's networks has been established, both inside and outside of work, to meet the needs of the growing number of women in paid employment and to encourage women to form networking groups. Originating in the USA, these female networks help combat the isolation often experienced by women managers in particular, and help women to form the type of social support network usually associated with men (Davidson and Cooper, 1992).

Women can be encouraged to join and form a variety of networks, though there does tend to be much 'mystique, opprobrium and disapproval surrounding the operation of women's networks' (Woodall and Winstanley, 1998: 232). Women's networks appear to be an antidote to the men's club and, as Segerman-Peck (1991) points out, they provide a range of benefits from the more instrumental information on job opportunities and business contacts to access to role models, mentors, training expertise, support and confidence-building. There is now a variety of networks for women, both general business and more specific, needs and these tend to fall into three main types (Vinnicombe and Colwill, 1996: 88):

> Professional and occupational networks bringing together women who have similar professional qualifications (e.g. Women in Management) in order to provide information and career guidance, and a way of learning about what is going on in their profession, occupation or industry. As long ago as 1984, the Brussels-based European Foundation for Management Development sponsored a cross-cultural network to address issues pertaining to women in business.
>
> In-company networks which are formal or informal female groupings within a particular organization, some of which are only open to women at a certain level, and others for the shared concerns of all women.

Training networks that are in effect support groups, with a specific, general or professional training focus.

Networks do appear to satisfy very specific needs for certain kinds of women. Moore and Buttner (1997) suggest from their work with female entrepreneurs that one of the chief reasons why women become involved in networking is to overcome a number of organizational contextual factors that they have witnessed, both inside organizations and later as business owners. The research in this area in particular suggests that informal networks are more important than formal ones (Birley, 1985; Brass, 1985; Burt, 1992; Baucus and Human, 1994). Foss (1993) found that the most important kinds of support for starting one's own business were resources obtained through social networks (material support), emotional support for the idea of starting a business (affective support), and advice on finance, production and other matters (information support).

Despite the claims for the benefits of women's networks, there appears to be little research that explores whether they are actually achieving what they set out to do, i.e. are satisfying the needs of their members and achieving the payoffs which are associated with male networks. Much of the research on networking is really literature of the old boys' networks; networks that have traditionally excluded women. Much research on social networks has demonstrated their influence in diverse areas of social life (Moore, 1990) but there have been relatively few studies on women's networks within and outside work organizations. This was the main driver and rationale for the authors' research outlined in this chapter.

Network relationships: instrumental and expressive

An important area addressed by the literature explaining women and networking is the identification of the kinds of relationships that women networkers seek. A distinction has been made between the more instrumental network ties and those developed for friendship and social support (Tichy et al., 1974; Fombrum, 1982).

Instrumental ties are those which result from carrying out a particular work role. These involve the exchange between individuals of certain job-related resources, e.g. information and expertise, professional advice, political access and sometimes material resources (Pettigrew, 1973; Tichy et al., 1974; Lincoln and Miller, 1979; Fombrum, 1982; Kanter, 1983). Such ties may also be providing developmental opportunities, for example career direction and advice, exposure to senior management, aid in obtaining projects that are visible and challenging and also support for promotion (Kram, 1988; Thomas, 1990).

On the other hand, friendship and social support is what is exchanged between expressive ties. These are usually typified by a higher degree of trust and closeness than that which is observed in more instrumental relationships. (Krackhardt, 1992). Of course individuals have more freedom in choosing their friends than their colleagues, and so expressive relationships tend to be less closely related to the formal structure in which they operate and the work roles that they carry out, though they can be just as useful for decision-making, resource mobilization and information exchange (Ibarra, 1993).

It is important to distinguish between these two kinds of network relationships because their very nature identifies the resources to be exchanged – especially as conflicting types of relationship and personal networks provide access to instrumental versus expressive benefits (Ibarra, 1993). From a research perspective, it is very important to explore both aspects when examining networks.

The nature of the networking relationship was of particular interest to the research study outlined in this chapter.

The strength of ties between individuals

Being a member of a personal network does not automatically ensure access to resources as this is contingent upon, among other things, the nature and strength of the relationship held with others. This is why 'tie strength' is another important concept dealt with in the literature. This varies with 'the amount of time, emotional intensity, the intimacy (mutual confiding) and reciprocal services that characterize the tie' (Granovetter, 1973: 1361).

Ibarra (1993) says that at an aggregate level, the strength of ties between individuals refers to the actual balance of personal network relationships that are close, stable, and binding, relative to weaker, more superficial links lacking in emotional investment.

Another concept related to this is that of 'multiplicity', which refers to the number of dimensions present within a network relationship (Monge and Eisenberg, 1987). If a person has a 'multiplex tie' with another, this means that they exchange a variety of resources (e.g. they may share career related advice but also provide social support). Evidence reveals that the greater the number of these links between individuals the stronger the experienced tie will be (Granovetter, 1973; Tichy, 1981).

Though tie strength is valued, the benefits of weak ties have been recognized, as in an instrumental sense, these can provide the channels through which individuals can obtain ideas, influences or information to which they may otherwise not have access (Granovetter, 1973). Otherwise disconnected parts of a social system may be connected via weak ties hence creating a more diverse base of information and contact. Strong ties on the other hand are more likely to be among similar people, so they may actually be less effective in terms of what resources they can provide access to.

The strength of a tie is characterized by frequency of contact, level of closeness and degree of reciprocity between individuals (Marsden, 1990), so in order to maintain strong ties with others an individual needs to expend a great amount of effort (Granovetter, 1973). This means that there are limits to the number of strong ties that can be sustained (Aldrich, 1989). The literature generally agrees that both weak and strong ties can add value, and any network, to be successful, needs to include a variety of the two (Granovetter, 1982; Brass, 1992).

The issue of whether a tie is strong or weak is crucial when networking as we need to be clear about the kinds of ties that we want to develop, so that these match the expectations of others with whom we choose to network.

Men and women networking – the differences

Research has suggested that, while men include more co-workers in their networks, women have been found to have fewer non-kin ties (Fischer and Oliker,

1983; Wellman, 1985; Marsden, 1987). There are clear disadvantages in terms of career advancement of women including fewer co-workers in their networks, as developmental benefits from networks external to the organization are more likely to be psychosocial in nature and less likely to involve the organization-specific assistance gained from internal networks (Burke et al., 1995). However, increasing membership of women's networks suggests that the above argument may well no longer apply. Members of women's networks come from a range of occupational levels, from junior clerks to experienced middle managers, directors and independent company directors and cover all ages and races (Coleman, 1991). The important thing, if we consider the earlier-presented definition of Vinnicombe and Colwill, is that the individuals are like-minded.

Segerman-Peck (1991) has argued that, by using networks to share information with others, women empower themselves and gain support and respect from others. Although this chapter is not concerned with comparing male and female attitudes towards, and experiences of, networking, some of the literature in this area is relevant. Networking may serve different functions. Vinnicombe and Colwill (1996) suggest that it is more 'utilitarian' for men and more 'social' for women. Though some evidence reveals that male networkers are more likely to use networking in an instrumental way (i.e. to obtain jobs) than women (Zoltie and Clarke, 1993), networking does serve other socializing purposes, and the social needs of women may differ from those of men. The paradox is that, although research hints that women may place greater importance on the social-izing aspects of networking (e.g. Persaud et al., 1990), they are often excluded from many of the social events and workplace interactions in which men engage. Ibarra (1993) reveals that women often find themselves straddling both a male-dominated network for work orientation issues and a women's network to pro-vide more comfortable social ties. This indicates that women may benefit from seeking social support from other women outside the workplace.

Vinnicombe and Colwill (1996: 90) state that

> to see networks from a utilitarian perspective is to see the instrumental value of every interaction. To see networks from a social perspective is to receive another very different kind of gift – that of friendship and support.

The literature shows that women tend to be particularly adept at giving and receiving these gifts in the context of networking. Men, seeing networks as utili-tarian, are more likely to gain their utilitarian benefits. Women, seeing them as social, may reap mainly social rewards.

The composition of networks

Yet another important area for examination is the composition of networks. The opportunities made available to us through networking obviously are dependent upon the kinds of people with whom we are networking. To a large extent com-munication, predictability of others' behaviour, and relationships based on trust and reciprocity (essential to networking) are more likely to result from interpersonal similarity with others (Kanter, 1977; Lincoln and Miller, 1979). Homophily refers to the degree of similarity in identity of organizational group affiliations between interacting individuals (Rogers and Kincaid, 1981; Marsden, 1988).

Instrumental and expressive benefits are more likely to be gained from sharing certain demographic characteristics in common with network contacts (South et al., 1982; Kaplan, 1984; Tsui and O'Reilly, 1989).

It is especially the case that when a task environment is uncertain or turbulent, individuals will display a preference for networking with similar types to themselves (Kanter, 1977; Golaskiewicz and Shatin, 1981).

The desire for homophily, or the interaction with others of the same race or sex, has been used to explain women's exclusion or restricted access to traditional networks. For women in an organization, or indeed working outside of their usual culture, there will be a more limited set of similar others with which to network and develop professional relationships that are based on homophily, for example entrepreneurial networks which contain more men than women (Aldrich, 1989). This means that the desire to network with same sex individuals is often not an option for women due to a lack of availability.

More recent research in the area of networking – cross-cultural networking

This section presents recent research into the networking attitudes and behaviours of women in and out of networks, with a particular area of interest in the area of cross-cultural networking. Previous research outlined in this chapter reveals that there may be barriers for women attempting to network in organizations or with men. But what of the experience of women attempting to network with other women – especially overseas or in cross-cultural networks? Can we assume that all women want the same things from networking? As more and more women work in cross-cultural settings, and rely on networks for socialization and career development, as well as business contacts, it is increasingly important to understand how these networks can be made more effective.

Background to the research

The research was originated by one major women's professional network, the European Women's Management Development network (EWMD). Frequently held discussions within the network centred on what purposes the network actually served for its members. There was a lack of clarity among the Executive Committee as to why women joined, and much conjecture as to whether the network was primarily valued for its association with women in other countries, its ability to provide career development opportunities or its psychosocial support. The agenda for the research outlined here was fairly exploratory in the first instance, starting from an issue which was concerning many other women's networks at the time – what is it that our members want from us, and how do we get women who are resistant to networking to see the potential value?

In 1994 the authors, as committee members, carried out a survey of those who were either network members or who had shown an interest in the network, to assist the committee to understand more about how networks operate as a tool for career development. Using the limited previous literature and the experience of EWMD committee members, a questionnaire comprising closed and open-ended questions was devised. The key areas of interest were: how people came to join networks; why they joined; how far their expectations were met; what stopped people joining and what encouraged them to become members; how people networked; networking skills; the need for development of those skills and the important characteristics of networking.

A sample of 328 was achieved, of which 93 per cent were female, with 21 per cent being between the ages of 41 and 45. Sixty-eight per cent were currently members of a network, and 29 per cent were EWMD members. Seventy-seven per cent were located in the UK, 22 per cent in continental Europe and 1 per cent in the US.

In brief, the findings of this initial study indicated that women joined networks to help their personal skills development, to meet others who could help their careers, and for social contacts (i.e. a mix of instrumental and expressive ties). In general these expectations were met. Findings revealed that women rated the psychosocial benefits as greater than career support. The skills necessary for successful networking were identified as the ability to project oneself to new contacts, knowing how to work within a network, and knowing how to use the network effectively.

Examining the responses and comments of a sample of EWMD members from Europe and the USA, as compared to the UK, suggested potential differences dependent upon geographical location. It appeared that the UK women had gained more career support from colleagues and senior managers within the networks than those in Europe and the USA. They also seemed more interested in the self-development activities of networks. These differences suggested that there was more interesting work to be done in examining the issue of women networking in different cultures and hence across international boundaries. In addition, this was felt to be important as an area of study because of the increase in numbers of women travelling to work abroad, and also from talking with network members.

Women travelling and networking overseas

On the whole, the business world is opening up for women who work today. The removal of barriers to trade throughout the EU was instigated by the creation of the single market in 1992 which has increased business travel opportunities for UK business people, not least British women. As business in the global context has expanded, the number of expatriates – employees sent from a firms' home country to work in a foreign location – has grown. For women who choose to have a career above a family this may become increasingly attractive as a career option. It raises some interesting issues with regard to women working on expatriate assignments where traditionally the expatriates or business travellers have been male. It is most likely that the business networks in place are male orientated and women working overseas may find themselves excluded, as they are from men's networks in their home country.

In America for example most expatriate managers are males in their forties and fifties who are accompanied by one or more of their family members (Guzzo et al., 1994). This means that if women choose to take on expatriate assignments, especially longer-term rather than short-term project-based relocations, then they may well need to network with others in the new culture where they find themselves in order to learn about the culture and to fit in. It is not necessarily the case that women only want to network with other women, but many who join networks want to, simply because so much of the working life of successful professional women is shaped by contact with men.

So it is very important that women use networks and their networking skills to make contact with others who may help their acculturation both socially and from a business perspective. There are many reasons why women, like men, may have to go abroad to work: to make new business contacts; to seek new markets; to consolidate business contacts; to check progress of business; to sign and finalize business contracts; and to sort out problems. All these needs can be helped if the individual has a network in the country that is being visited. It may also be that the woman has moved abroad to follow her husband's or partner's work, and a network may be helpful here, though its composition may be very different.

Research into expatriate adjustment and adaptation has revealed the relevance of social support from one's close ties (Adelman, 1988). Adelman also cites the importance of social support from weak ties or 'fringe' relationships, such as one might have with locals (e.g. neighbours). The support from non-intimate acquaintances in the local culture can be very instrumental in a journey to a new culture, by providing explicit assistance in coping with daily life and by providing insights into culture. These weak ties can be especially powerful early on in the process. Women expatriates may not travel with family and so these weak ties are even more crucial, and what better way to gain them than by joining local businesswomen's networks? But of course this research suggests that some consideration of cross-cultural differences needs to be taken into account. We must not assume that 'a network is a network is a network' – i.e. that any professional network to which a woman belongs will operate according to the same norms and values.

A recent study conducted at McGill University in Montreal surveying approximately 700 major US and Canadian companies found that about 6 per cent of their international management positions had been taken up by women (cited in Bourne, 1996). Bourne has found that women are just as successful as men in these foreign assignments and predicts that the 6 per cent will be surpassed in years to come. These findings relate to a selection of the following recommendations made by Wah (1998: 27) for 'smoother sailing for overseas assignments' and what women expatriates, their bosses and human relations departments should do to ensure that expatriate acculturation takes place:

- Women should: 'build solid foreign language skills and understand the political and cultural backgrounds of the host countries; follow the local customs for business behaviour'.
- Bosses should: 'provide clear directions and information about the local culture; provide appropriate mentoring'.

- HR departments should 'before women executives leave for assignments, give them the opportunity to talk to other women expats in [the] company or to others.'

These needs or suggestions may be met more easily if the woman uses relevant networks effectively.

Of particular relevance to this chapter are the comments made by Polly Bird in *The Working Woman's Handbook* (1996), where she outlines some tips for travelling in Spain and the USA (as well as in other countries):

In Spain:

> Business and social behaviour is very informal. You will be on first name terms quickly.... With the exception of large companies, there is a marked absence of correspondence, memos and other written communications. Communication is predominantly face-to-face. Procrastination and delay are endemic and the traditional function of meetings, if they occur at all, is to communicate instructions. Lunches and dinners are a vital part of business life and are used to establish a personal working relationship. Discuss anything except business until coffee is served then wait for your host to bring up the specific subject of the meeting. (1996: 149)

As for the USA:

> To do business in the USA you need to demonstrate competence and professionalism by taking a numerate, analytical approach to problem-solving. Modesty is not a virtue here – you will gain more respect by knowing your worth and showing motivation and commitment. Bluntness is preferred to subtlety. Companies operate a rigorously defined hierarchy. Status in the US business world is equated to power so be sure to use your business title. Planning is detailed and taken very seriously; meetings are primarily for imparting and gathering information. A joke is obligatory as a warm-up to speeches and presentations. Long working hours are common in certain business industries and cities, especially New York, and you should expect to be accessible in the evenings and at weekends. Business relationships are tempered by a great deal of informal socialising and friendliness but at social events business is often the main topic of conversation. You will find that strangers at a cocktail party (including yourself) will be introduced by employer and business title as well as by name. (1996: 150)

These observations are fascinating when one looks at the results of the research presented in the remainder of this chapter.

The cross-cultural networking survey

Following in-depth factor analysis and content analysis of quantitative and qualitative data gathered, the original questionnaire designed by the authors was modified and distributed to women's networks within the UK, USA and Spain. The aim was to look more closely at the issue of cross-cultural differences in networking. While the issue of cross-cultural differences in management has received much attention research-wise (Hofstede, 1980; Trompenaars, 1993), differences in networking behaviours have not been a particular focus of study – perhaps due in part to the fact that networking in itself is rather a new area.

The investigation set out to explore differences between cultures in a wide variety of areas along the lines of the EWMD study, and so explored the following research questions. Do women in the three countries differ in terms of: (a) why they join networks and to what extent their expectations are met; (b) what would make non-network members join, what would deter them from joining; (c) why they might leave the network; (d) what they see as important networking skills; and (e) what skills they need to develop?

The Networking Attitudes Questionnaire (NAQ)

A 191-item questionnaire was designed which examined eight main areas:

- why women join networks (e.g. to make contacts that would help my career or business);
- whether women's networking expectations are met (e.g. to what extent has networking enabled you to learn more about issues related to your work?);
- what would encourage non-network members to join (e.g. how important is the exclusiveness of the network?);
- what factors deter women from membership (e.g. how far has having to travel to meetings stopped you from joining?);
- network exit (e.g. how important was lack of communication from the network a factor in your leaving?);
- networking skills (e.g. how important when dealing with others is your ability to project yourself?);
- job recommendations (e.g. have you ever been recommended for a job owing to your links with the network?);
- the strengths and weaknesses of networks (how far do you agree with the benefits of career contacts, social contacts, etc.?).

A number of demographic variables were also included (age, gender, dependants, employment status, job category, career stage, education and qualifications, and most importantly geographic location).

Apart from questions which were scored categorically, for example by answering 'yes' or 'no', all other attitudinal questions were rated on Likert-type scales (from 'strongly disagree' to 'strongly agree', or 'to a great extent' to 'not at all'), depending on type of the reply given.

The sample   The questionnaire, which was administered via a postal survey, yielded 117 responses that were felt to be suitable to use for comparative analysis. Of respondents, 86 per cent were current network members. Of these, 30 per cent were from the UK, 31 per cent from the USA, and 39 per cent from Spain. They were drawn from seven networks, their age range was 36–40 years, and 44 per cent had dependants. The distribution of demographics was very similar, on most variables, though the US women were younger on average (i.e. early to mid-thirties compared with early to mid-forties for the UK and Spain). The sample was more highly educated than the general population, with 47 per cent having reached Master's degree level or higher and including 41 per cent having obtained a first degree. Looking at their employment status, 74 per cent were employed and 16 per cent were self-employed. The most common job categories were professional/specialist (21 per cent), senior manager (16 per cent) and consultant (11 per cent). Respondents most often described their career as being established to their satisfaction (24 per cent), building a second or third career (22 per cent), and wanting to broaden their reputation more widely than their organization (14 per cent); 66 per cent of the sample had a professional qualification.

Findings – are there any cultural differences? In an attempt to answer the research questions posed, the data were treated to a series of one-way analyses of variance statistics in order to compare the mean scores on aspects of the questionnaire. Though there were many attitudes towards networking in common across the three groups, a number of significant differences were found that could have implications for women attempting to network effectively across different cultures. At a time when international networking is increasing, and there are more opportunities for women to increase their presence on overseas assignments, the authors feel that these results are very interesting and informative. All differences outlined achieved 'f' values significant at or below the $p <= .05$ level and differences outlined are obtained by using the post-hoc test Tukey b.

The findings suggest that with regard to networking needs, expectations, membership activity and skills, we are looking at three rather distinct approaches to networking which highlight cross-cultural differences. In analysing the data the authors chose the labels provided here for each of the three groups as they seemed best to fit the overriding patterns of attitudes and behaviours observed.

The USA – the instrumentalists (assertive Americans) US respondents differed from the other two groups in their greater focus on active learning, and in their use of a network as an arena for self-projection. They were noticeably more confident in their networking skills than were UK women.

In particular the US respondents differed from both other groups in that they:

- had a greater expectation that networking should give them useful experiences to add to their CV;
- placed more emphasis on the use of a network for learning;
- were more likely not to join a network because of conflicts with family demands;
- would leave a network if it failed to provide them with what they wanted.

They differed from Spanish respondents in that they:

- were less interested in the social aspects of networking;
- were more likely to have learned about work-related issues, and to have gained experiences to add to their CV;
- were more concerned about developing their skills than enjoying meeting new people.

They particularly differed from British women in that they placed more importance on self-projection as a networking skill.

The UK – the developers (bashful Brits)   The UK respondents were noticeably different in the greater emphasis they placed on the use of networks as an arena for developing self-confidence and networking skills. They were more concerned that the network should be outside their organization, and focused more on establishing the power sources within a network. The UK women saw their network as a place to learn, rather than a place to do business.

They differed from the other two groups in that they:

- were more likely to be persuaded to join a network which was outside their organization;
- stated a stronger need to develop the skills of self-confidence, to establish areas of common interest with new people, to keep the purpose of being there in mind, to judge the appropriate time to offer a business card, and to enjoy meeting new people.
- had a tendency to leave a network when they got what they wanted (i.e. training).

They differed from their Spanish counterparts in that they:

- placed less importance on meeting others with shared interests;
- were more interested in increasing their personal power;
- placed more importance on identifying the person who has the power to help, and judging the relevance of events as networking skills.

In comparing British women to women from the USA they:

- were more likely to say that not having enough information about the network was a powerful disincentive towards joining that network;
- were more concerned to follow up on new contacts, and to establish who has the power or information to help them; and,
- were more likely to prefer a single-sex network.

Spain – the socialites (social Spaniards)   The Spanish respondents placed a noticeably higher level of importance on the social aspects of networking than did the other two groups. Business and learning outcomes were less visibly sought, and the opportunity to spend enjoyable time with other women was a more explicit part of their agenda.

They differed from the other two groups in that Spanish women:

- were less interested in making career contacts;
- placed less emphasis on the use of informal networking for career management and business contacts;
- focused less on judging the appropriate time to offer a business card;
- were less concerned about asking for help;
- believed it was more important that any network they join should have more international links;
- believed that self-development was less crucial as a potential network strength;
- were more likely to leave a network if they found it boring!

They differed from UK women particularly in that they:

- were more likely to have found suppliers to their business as a result of the network membership;
- thought that the cost of membership in time and monetary terms was less of a potential weakness.

They especially differed from women from the USA in that they:

- were less concerned over the demands that network membership placed on them;
- were less concerned about keeping the purpose of network membership in mind.

These findings and the subsequent profiles have been presented and explored with women from a variety of different cultures including the UK, the USA and Spain, at a number of international conferences and workshops (e.g. EWMD USA, 1995 and the Annual Occupational Psychology Conference, British Psychological Society – Pemberton et al., 1996). Drawing upon personal experience and anecdotal evidence, it was suggested by delegates that these three 'cultural networking types' identified via quantitative methods also had 'face validity'. Indeed, the behaviours were amusingly evident at the US conference, with UK women revealing a reticence to hand over their business cards too soon to enthusiastic US fellow networkers, and the Spanish women wondering what all the fuss was about – 'let's just enjoy ourselves!'

Conclusions

This study suggests that there are cross-cultural differences in women's approaches to networking that further develop the theme of cross-cultural differences in how work is managed. The assumption that networking fulfils a similar need across cultures because it is overtly related to career development or social support needs to be explored more fully, especially as the growth of international management assignments implies both greater cross-cultural networking and the use of networks outside one's own country as a mechanism of social integration. These findings suggest that expectations, benefits and networking skills differ across cultures, and that individuals may have to adjust their behaviours and expectations in moving outside their own culture.

The findings point to potential difficulties and barriers to effective networking across cultures but 'cross-cultural networkers' may prevent problems if they avoid falling victim to a number of assumptions. Women – and indeed, we would hypothesize, men too – must not assume that the members of a network will be like them, when the network has a very different demographic profile from their own. They must also not assume that the needs of the members are similar to theirs when, as the results show, they may have very different agendas. One other issue that the research has raised is that women cannot expect that the time dimension of the network is the same as theirs: they should not rush into developing business contacts out of synchrony with the rhythm of network members who may not accept such instrumental behaviour. Also, the assumption that the network is unable to meet our needs may in part be due to the differing social norms of the culture in which the network resides.

In order to network effectively women may need to adjust their expectations of a network when they move outside their own culture, and alongside this should acquire a broader range of networking skills. It is important to look for levers which will make networking across cultures more satisfying and effective. For example, at the basis of all three of the networking approaches outlined here is a fundamental belief that by networking with other women advantages can be gained in both social and career terms. If this belief is kept in mind and women are open about their needs and expectations, then it may be possible to work around these cultural differences for everyone's benefit. Although the research points to some key differences, there were many things in common. The survey instrument was very extensive in its coverage, and the majority of items gleaned no significant differences which means that the networking women have more in common than not.

This study has unearthed some interesting findings, but what is needed now is a larger and wider cross-cultural sample, which could further explore cultural differences and allow for more fruitful statistical exploration of the impact of culture and demographic variables. Some of the differences found in this study may be explained by the differing profiles of the samples in each of the three countries, (e.g., age profiles, employment categories and career stages). For example, attitudes towards networking may be a function of the particular career stage which a woman has reached, and this may well be age-linked.

A great deal of interest was shown in the research from a number of countries not assessed within the scope of the project and so these could be followed up in a larger-scale project.

Furthermore, male differences across cultures could also be examined. Males and females from the same culture may be more similar to each other than to their same-sex counterparts from another culture.

The implications for networking research overall are that previous findings from research need to be re-examined in terms of the culture from which the sample was selected. As in much research in the area of career management and the social sciences generally, we often report findings on topics without accounting for the fact that they may have a cultural bias and therefore cannot be generalized with confidence. With growing emphasis on cross-cultural work environment there needs to be more research in this area generally, coupled with an increased awareness of the differences that may impact on these findings.

The limitations of the scale of this particular study are acknowledged, but the authors believe that the findings open up a new area of enquiry in the arena of career management activity which has been largely ignored in empirical studies. In addition, it has generated a number of potential scales for measuring the concept and practice of networking behaviour further.

References

Adelman, M.A. (1988) 'Cross-cultural adjustment: a theoretical perspective on social support', *International Journal of Intercultural Relations*, 12: 183–204.

Aldrich, H. (1989) 'Networking among women entrepreneurs', in C. Rivchu O'Hagan and D. Sexton (eds), *Handbook of Organisational Behaviour*, Prentice Hall, Englewood Cliffs, NJ, pp. 190–222.

Baucus, D.A. and Human, S.E. (1994) 'Second-career entrepreneurs: a multiple case study analysis of entrepreneurial processes and antecedent variables', *Entrepreneurship Theory and Practice*, 19 (2): 41–71.

Bilimoria, D. and Piderit, S.K. (1994) 'Board committee membership: effects of sex-based bias', *Academy of Management Journal*, 37 (6): 1453–1477.

Bird, P. (1996) *The Working Woman's Handbook: The essential guide for every working woman*, Piatkus, London.

Birley, S. (1985) 'The role of networks in the entrepreneurial process', *Journal of Business Venturing*, 1 (2): 107–117.

Bourne, W. (1996) 'Old lessons, new perspectives: moving toward a global mindset', *Executive Speeches*, 10 (6), Dayton, June/July.

Brass, D.J. (1984) 'Being in the right place: a structural analysis of individual influence in an organisation', *Administrative Science Quarterly*, 29: 518–539.

Brass, D.J. (1985) 'Men's and women's networks: a study of interaction patterns and influence in an organisation', *Academy of Management Journal*, 28: 327–343.

Brass, D.J. (1992) 'Power in organisations: a social network perspective', in G. Moore and J. Whitt (eds), *Research in Politics & Society*, JAI Press, Greenwich, CT. pp. 295–323.

Burke, R.J., Rothstein, M.G. and Bristor, M. (1995) 'Interpersonal networks of managerial and professional women and men: descriptive characteristics', *Women in Management Review*, 10 (1): 21–27.

Burt, R.S. (1992) *Structural Holes: The Social Structure of Competition*, Harvard University Press, Cambridge, MA.

Cannings, K. and Montmarquette, C. (1991) 'Managerial momentum: a simultaneous model of the career progress of male and female managers', *Industrial Labour Relations Review*, 44 (2): 212–228.

Coe, T. (1992) *The Key to the Men's Club: Opening the Doors to Women in Management*, a British Institute of Management report, BIM, London.

Coleman, G. (1991) *Investigating Organizations: A Feminist Approach*, SAUS Publications.

Davidson, M.J. and Cooper, C.I. (1992) *Shattering the Glass Ceiling. The Woman Manager*, Paul Chapman, London.

Fagenson, E.A. (1986) 'Women's work orientation: something old, something new', *Group and Organisation Studies*, 11 (1): 75–100.

Fischer, C. and Oliker, S. (1983) 'A research note on friendship, gender and the life cycle', *Social Forces*, 62: 124–132.

Fombrum, C.J. (1982) 'Strategies for network research in organisations', *Academy of Management Review*, 7: 280–291.

Foss, L. (1993) 'Resources, networks and entrepreneurship: a survey of 153 starters and 84 non-starters in the cod farming industry in Norway', in N.C. Churchill, S. Birley, W.D. Bygrave, J. Doutriaux, E.J. Gatewood, F.S. Hoy and W.E. Wetzel Jr (eds), *Frontiers of Entrepreneurship Research*, Center for Entrepreneurial Studies, Babson College, Babson Park, MA, pp. 355–369.

Golaskiewicz, J. (1979) *Exchange Networks and Community Politics*, Sage Publications, Beverly Hills, CA.

Golaskiewicz, J. and Shatin, D. (1981) 'Leadership and networking among neighbourhood human service organisations', *Administrative Science Quarterly*, 26: 343–448.

Granovetter, M. (1973) 'The strength of weak ties', *American Journal of Society*, 78: 1360–1380.

Granovetter, M.S. (1982) 'Who gets ahead? A review', *Theory & Society*, 11: 239–262.

Green, M. (1982) 'A Washington perspective on women and networking: the power and the pitfalls', *Journal of NAWDAC*, 46: 17–21.

Guzzo, R.A., Noonan, K.A. and Elron, E. (1994) 'Expatriate managers and the psychological contract', *Journal of Applied Psychology*, 79: 617–626.

Haberfeld, Y. (1992) 'Employment discrimination: an organisational model', *Academy of Management Journal*, 35 (1): 161–180.

Handley, J. (1994) 'Women, decision-making and academia: an unholy alliance', *Women in Management Review*, 9 (3): 11–16.

Hennig, M. and Jardim, A. (1977) *The Managerial Woman*, Anchor/Doubleday, New York.

Hofstede, G. (1980) *Culture's Consequences – International Differences in Work Related Values*, Sage Publications, London.

Ibarra, H. (1993) 'Personal networks of women minorities in management: a conceptual framework', *Academy of Management Review*, 8 (1): 56–87.

Kanter, R.M. (1977) *Men and Women of the Corporation*, Basic Books, New York.

Kanter, R.M. (1983) *The Changemasters*, Simon & Schuster, New York.

Kaplan, R.E. (1984) 'Trade routes: the managers' networks of relationships', *Organisational Dynamics*, Spring: 37–52.

Kilduff, M. and Krackhardt, D. (1994) 'Bringing the individual back in: a structural analysis of the internal market for reputation in organisations', *Academy of Management Journal*, 37: 87–108.

Krackhardt, D. (1992) 'The strength of strong ties: the importance of philos in organisations', in N. Notiva and R.G. Eccles (eds), *Networks and Organisation Structure, Form and Action*, Harvard Business School Press, Cambridge, MA.

Kram, K.E. (1988) *'Mentoring at Work: Developmental Relationships in Organisational Life*, Scott Foresman, Glenview, IL.

Lincoln, J.R. and Miller, J. (1979) 'Work and friendship ties in organisations: a comparative analysis of relational networks', *Administrative Science Quarterly*, 24: 181–199.

Lipman-Blumen, J. (1980) 'Female leadership in formal organisations: must the female leader go formal?' in H. Leavitt, L. Brady and D. Boje (eds), *Readings in Managerial Psychology*, 3rd edn, University of Chicago Press, Chicago, pp. 341–362.

Marsden, P.V. (1987) 'Core discussion networks of Americans', *American Sociological Review*, 46: 393–405.

Marsden, P.V. (1988) 'Homogeneity in confiding relations', *Social Networks*, 10 (1): 57–76.

Marsden, P.V. (1990) 'Network data and measurement', *Annual Review of Sociology*, 16: 435–463.

Marshall, J. (1995) *Women Managers Moving On*, Routledge, London.

Miller, J., Labovitz, S. and Fry, L. (1975) 'Inequities in the organisational experiences of women and men: resources, vested interests and discrimination', *Social Forces*, 54: 365–381.

Monge, P.R. and Eisenberg, R.M. (1987) 'Emergent communication networks', in F.M. Jablin, L.L. Putnam, K.H. Roberts and L.W. Porter (eds), *Handbook of Organisational Communication: An Interdisciplinary Perspective*, Sage Publications, Beverly Hills, CA, pp. 304–342.

Moore, D.P. (1990) 'An examination of present research on the female entrepreneur-suggested research strategies for the 1990s', *Journal of Business Ethics*, 9 (4/5): 275–281.

Moore, D.P. and Buttner, E.H. (1997) *Women Entrepreneurs: Moving beyond the Glass Ceiling*, Sage Publications, Beverly Hills, CA.

Ohlott, P.J., Ruderman, M.N. and McCauley, C.D. (1994) 'Gender differences in managers' developmental job experiences', *Academy of Management Journal*, 37 (1): 46–67.

O'Leary, V.E. and Ickovics, J.R. (1992) 'Cracking the glass ceiling: overcoming isolation and alienation', in U. Sekeran and F. Leong (eds), *Womanpower: Managing in Times of Demographic Turbulence*, Sage, Beverly Hills, CA, pp. 7–30.

Olson, A.A. (1994) 'Long term networking: a strategy for career success', *Management Review*, April: 33–35.

Peluchette, J.V.E. (1993) 'Subjective career success: the influence of individual differences, family and organisational variables', *Journal of Vocational Behaviour*, 43: 198–208.

Pemberton, C., Stevens, S. and Travers, C. (1996) 'Women's networking across boundaries: recognising different cultural agendas', in *Book of Proceedings, The British Psychological Society, Annual Occupational Psychology Conference*, Eastbourne, 3–5 January, pp. 327–333.

Persaud, I., Sipley, B., Coutts, B. and Colwill, N.L. (1990) 'Gender differences in informal social groups: implications for integrating women into management'. Paper presented at the 1990 ASAC Conference, Whistler, BC, June.

Pettigrew, A. (1973) *The Politics of Organisational Decision-making*, Tavistock Institute, London.

Rogers, E.M. and Kincaid, D.L. (1981) *Communication Networks*, Free Press, New York.

Segerman-Peck, L.M. (1991) *Networking and Mentoring: A Woman's Guide*, Piatkus, London.

Smart, G.M. Jr (1991) 'Building a chain of contacts', *Training and Development Journal*, January: 21–27.

Sonnenberg, F.K. (1990) 'How to reap the benefits of networking', *Journal of Business Strategy*, January/February: 59–62.

South, S.J., Bonjean, C.M., Markham, W.T. and Corder, J. (1982) 'Social structure and intergroup interaction: men and women of the federal bureaucracy', *American Sociological Review*, 47: 587–599.

Stern, B. (1981) *Is Networking For You?* Prentice-Hall, Englewood Cliffs, NJ.

Thomas, D.A. (1990) 'The impact of race on managers' experience of developmental relationships (mentoring and sponsorship): an intra-organisational study', *Journal of Organisational Behaviour*, 2: 479–492.

Tichy, N.M. (1981) 'Networks in organisations', in P.C. Nystrom and W.H. Starbuck (eds), *Handbook of Organisational Design*, Oxford University Press, New York, pp. 225–249.

Tichy, N.M., Tushman, M.L. and Fombrum, C. (1974) 'Social network analysis for organisations', *Academy of Management Review*, 4: 507–519.

Tjosvold, D. and Weicker, D. (1993) 'Co-operative and competitive networking by entrepreneurs: a critical incident study', *Journal of Small Business Management*, 31 (1): 11–21.

Trompenaars, F. (1993) *Riding the Waves of Culture*, Brealey Publishing, London.

Tsui, A.S. and O'Reilly, L.A. III (1989) 'Beyond simple demographic effects: the importance of relational demography in superior–subordinate dyads', *Academy of Management Journal*, 32: 402–423.

Vinnicombe, S. and Colwill, N.L. (1996) *The Essence of Women in Management*, Prentice-Hall, Englewood Cliffs, NJ.

Wah, L. (1998) 'Smoother sailing for overseas assignments', *Management Review*, (New York) 87 (8): 27.

Warner Burke, W. (1995) 'Networking', in N. Nicholson (ed.), *Encyclopaedic Dictionary of Organisational Behaviour*, Blackwell Business, Oxford.

Wellman, B. (1985) 'Domestic work, paid work and net work', in S. Duck and D. Perlman (eds), *Understanding Personal Relationships*, Sage Publications, London, pp. 159–191.

Welsh, M.S. (1981) *Networking: The Great New Way for Women to Get Ahead*, Warner Books, New York.

Woodall, J. and Winstanley, D. (1998) *Management Strategy and Practice*, Blackwell Business, Oxford.

Zoltie, D. and Clarke, S. (1993) 'News and views', *Women in Management Review*, 8 (1): 31–33.

8

Women and Expatriation: Revisiting Adler's Findings

Linda K. Stroh, Arup Varma and Stacey J. Valy-Durbin

Women have made great inroads in domestic US management, yet they are still significantly under-represented in the international arena (Adler, 1997; Black et al., 1998). As several researchers have asked, the obvious question is why?

From the employees' perspective, international assignments are becoming an increasingly critical element of their professional experience and for advancement up the corporate ladder (Harris, 1995; Adler, 1997). It's not surprising, therefore, that many managers – men and women – see offers to relocate internationally as plum opportunities.

Women currently make up almost 50 per cent of the American workforce (Adler and Izraeli, 1994) and now comprise large percentages of the graduates of both MBA and other professional programmes (Adler, 1997). Yet the percentage of women expatriates is still considerably lower than the percentage of men (Westwood and Leung, 1994; Harvey, 1996).

This chapter examines some of the explanations as to why so few women are selected for international assignments and offers suggestions for future academic and practitioner-oriented research. Addressing these issues may enable us to identify the root of some of the misconceptions about women on international assignments and thus help companies better educate their employees, help employees reconcile perceptual differences, and improve overall communication between management and potential candidates for positions overseas.

The findings reported in this chapter are based on a survey that solicited female employees' opinions about their experiences as expatriates and their supervisors' perceptions about such matters as the degree of fairness in selecting candidates for international assignments and prejudices against women in foreign countries. The goal of our research was to affirm and/or contradict past research findings and assumptions, especially the myths Nancy Adler identified as to why women are so rarely offered assignments abroad.

According to a 1995 survey conducted by Windam International and the National Trade Council, by the year 2000, 20 per cent of all expatriates will be women. As of a few years ago, however, women comprised only 5–12 per cent of the expatriate population (Adler, 1984b; Moran et al., 1988; Tung, 1997; Black et al., 1998). Given the increasing amount of international business corporations are conducting and the ever larger percentage of the managerial workforce represented by women, these are surprisingly small percentages.

Nancy Adler was the first researcher to conduct an in-depth study investigating why companies appeared to be so reluctant to send women overseas. Her landmark research revealed evidence of several pervasive myths (Adler, 1984b).

Myth 1 : Women are not interested in going on international assignments.
Myth 2 : Companies are hesitant to send or resistant about sending women on international assignments.
Myth 3 : Prejudices against women in foreign cultures prevent them from being effective while on international assignments.

Myth 1

To test the validity of this myth, Adler (1984b) questioned male and female MBA students from two Canadian, three US, and two international schools about their interest in pursuing international assignments. She found that among both the men and the women, 84 per cent were interested in such opportunities.

A more recent study (Hill and Tillery, 1992) focused on interest among undergraduate business students. In this case, the women actually showed greater interest than the men. Reasons given for wanting to go abroad included the opportunity to gain knowledge about different cultures, as well as the chance to enhance their interpersonal skills. A study by Chusmir and Frontczak (1990) supports Adler's findings that women are as interested in international assignments as men. Specifically, the female respondents in Chusmir and Frontczak's study believed more strongly than the male respondents that many qualified women would accept an international assignment if offered one.

Myth 2

Of the three myths Adler identified in her research, this one was the most strongly supported by empirical data gathered from a survey of human resource professionals from 60 multinational companies. Of these professionals, 70 per cent reported that they were hesitant to send women on international assignments (Adler, 1984a). The most commonly cited reasons for their reluctance were that the women were in dual career relationships that would make it difficult or impossible for them to accept such assignments and that gender prejudice would be a serious problem in the countries to which they would be sent. Both these issues are discussed in greater detail later in this literature review. Among the other reasons companies have cited are loneliness, isolation, and concerns about sexual harassment (Izraeli et al., 1980).

Adler's breakthrough research and subsequent studies (Chusmir and Frontczak, 1990) suggest that gender bias in the workplace is the greatest obstacle women face in their efforts to achieve equal consideration for international assignments. Adler's respondents indicated that those who were responsible for selecting candidates often had problems separating the myths from the reality (1984a). Chusmir and Frontczak note that, given that most decisions about international assignments are made by men, many of whom hold traditional perceptions and attitudes about women in positions of international management, qualified female employees may be getting overlooked. Further, sensing these attitudes, qualified women are likely to form their own negative attitudes about the likelihood of being selected and, as a result, will not actively pursue international positions (Chusmir and Frontczak, 1990).

Myth 3

The third myth Adler identified – that prejudices against women in foreign cultures prevent them from being effective managers – is also one of the primary reasons companies give for being hesitant to relocate women overseas. To test the pervasiveness of this myth, Adler (1987) interviewed 52 female expatriates about their international experiences in several countries in Asia. Her research showed that, contrary to the myth, the women did not experience prejudice. Specifically, nationals did not behave toward the female expatriates as they would toward local women. In most cases, the female expatriates were seen first as representatives of their companies, second as Americans, and third as women (Adler, 1987).

Other research supports Adler's findings. In a study of female expatriates working in Hong Kong, Westwood and Leung (1994) found that most of the women felt that as long as they were professional and competent in their jobs as managers, gender was not an inhibiting factor in their efficiency and productivity. In some studies (Adler and Izraeli, 1994; Taylor and Napier, 1996), female expatriates have mentioned that being a woman was an advantage, because it gave them higher visibility, enabled them to build stronger interpersonal relationships with clients, and enabled them to adapt better to life as an outsider.

It should be noted, however, that the research devised to test this myth was fraught with methodological weaknesses (Adler, 1984a, 1984b, 1987; Westwood and Leung, 1994). Not only were the samples small, but they were limited in scope. One might assume that surveying women in a region (i.e. Asia) known for its biases against women in the workplace would have put this myth to its strongest test. Research (Frontczak and Cateora, 1988) indicates, however, that the research findings would have been more reliable if the sample of women had been more representative.

Results of a study by Stone (1991) suggest that women do experience discrimination on international assignments. What was especially surprising in this study was that the source of the discrimination was not natives in the foreign culture, but the women's male counterparts and peers (Stone, 1991; Westwood and Leung, 1994). A similar study found that the level of prejudice by foreign nationals varied from country to country (Frontczak and Cateora, 1988). These findings provide justification for researchers to conduct a more in-depth, country-specific look at Adler's findings before considering them to be true of all cultures.

Summary

Without minimizing Adler's research, it is important to recognize that it was conducted from the mid-1970s to the mid-1980s and was in some cases based on limited sample populations (albeit, making major contributions to the field at that time). These factors alone may limit the degree to which Adler's findings are still generalizable. It was from this perspective that we began our data-collection effort.

Background to our study

We began the data-collection process by administering a survey to the membership of the International Personnel Association (IPA). The IPA is a professional organization consisting of the top 60 multinational organizations in the United States and Canada. The member companies are in a variety of industries, but all participate widely in the global arena.

Of the 60 companies surveyed, 44 responded, yielding a response rate of 73 per cent. The participating companies had anywhere from 10 to 1,723 international assignees, of which the number of women ranged from 0 to 123. The average number of male expatriates was 230, the average number of females was 21. All the respondents were employed in one of the following eight industries: telecommunications, food and beverage, consumer products, financial services, pharmaceutical, chemical, petroleum, or hotel and entertainment (see Table 8.1).

Data were collected through two surveys administered at one point in time. The respondents included female international assignees (defined as current expatriates, inpatriates, and repatriates who had returned from an international assignment

TABLE 8.1   *Expatriate demographics and policies for IPA member companies (n = 44)*

Demographic variable	Mean
Average number of current international assignees (expatriates and inpatriates)	
Male	229.66
Female	21.02
Average number of current repatriates	
Male	41.23
Female	7.62
Percentages of employees accepting offers for international assignments (within past 3 years)	
Males	91.83%
Females	89.17%
Percentages of women accepting offers for international assignments who	
Were single	52.41%
Were in dual career relationships	41.23%
Had children between the ages of 0–18 years	24.29%
Did not have children	51.79%
Top three reasons given by women for rejecting offers of international assignments	
Dual career conflicts	25.13%
Impact on children	19.70%
Family conflicts	16.80%

within the past three years) and their supervisors. Each sample group completed a different survey. Many questions were similar, but questions about the respondents' backgrounds and about the experience of being a female expatriate were different for the two groups.

Ensuring confidentiality was of utmost importance. For each group of respondents, the researchers used a coding system that replaced the names of individuals with random numbers. Companies were assured that their company names would not appear anywhere in the report on the study.

Sample selection

Two sample populations were identified for this study: female international assignees/expatriates and their supervisors.

Female international assignees

Included in this group were women who were currently on international assignments, as well as women who had returned within the past three years (n = 261). The respondents had been relocated to 38 countries and originated in 31 home countries. More than half (64 per cent) were from the United States. Almost half the women were single (47 per cent) and Caucasian (77 per cent), and they were an average of 38 years old. On average, they had worked for their companies for 11 years. More than a third (38 per cent) had a college degree; 36 per cent had a Master's degree, and 10 per cent had an advanced professional degree.

A total of 567 surveys were sent to the female expatriates. Of these, 261 surveys were completed and received, yielding a response rate of 46 per cent (see Table 8.2).

Supervisors

The group of supervisors (n = 78) consisted primarily of Caucasian (80 per cent) men (88 per cent), most of whom (75 per cent) reported having some previous international experience. The average age of the respondents in this group was 45 years old. Specific demographic data for this population can be found in Table 8.3. Seventy-six completed surveys were received from the supervisors, for a response rate of 31 per cent (see Table 8.3).

Methodology

Survey of IPA members

Before collecting any information from the expatriates or their supervisors, we faxed a representative of each International Personnel Association (IPA) member company a two-page survey that asked for general information about the size of the company's expatriate population and the company's practices concerning such matters as how candidates for overseas assignments were selected. In addition, we requested the names of all current female international assignees (defined as current expatriates, inpatriates, and repatriates who had returned to the

TABLE 8.2 *Female international assignee demographics (n = 261) (%)*

Marital status		Caucasian/white	76.6
First marriage	41	Hispanic/Latino/Latin	9.5
Second marriage or more	8	Other	1.5
Separated/divorced	11		
Partner	4	**Education**	
Single	36	High school	0.4
		Some college	5.6
Partner employed on assignment		College graduate	38
(those in dual career relationships)		Some Postgrad work	10
At the same level prior to assignment	16	Master's degree	36
Above level prior to assignment	6	MD, JD, PhD or	
Below level prior to assignment	5	other professional degree	10
Was not able to secure employment	14	**Age (average, in years)**	37.59
Did not want to work	1	**Years current company (average)**	10.94
Not in dual career relationship	43		
Other	15	**Industry of organization**	
		Financial services/consulting	20.34
Number of children under 18		Consumer products/manufacturing	19.49
while on assignment		IT/communications	17.37
No children	76	Food/beverage and hospitality	11.86
One	11	Pharmaceutical	8.48
Two	10	Chemicals	5.09
Three	1.2	Gas/power/oil	4.66
Four	0.4	Electronics	3.81
Five	0.4	Personal care/beauty	2.97
Mean	0.41	Apparel	2.97
		Tobacco	1.69
Ethnicity		Aluminium	1.27
African American/black	1.7		
Asian/Asia Indian	10.7		

company within the past three years), as well as their addresses, phone/fax numbers, or email addresses.

Companies were encouraged to contact their female international assignees before providing their names, in order to ensure that these employees were informed about the purpose and the voluntary nature of the study. To help in this effort, we provided a sample form letter to the companies. In approximately 60 per cent of the cases, follow-up calls were made and email messages were sent to remind the representatives of these companies to complete and return the materials.

Survey of female expatriates/inpatriates/repatriates

Each female international assignee who agreed to participate in the study was mailed a seven-page survey that solicited her opinions on her expatriate experience, female expatriates in general, and her direct supervisor's perception of the female expatriate experience.

Survey of supervisors

Included in the mailing to each female expatriate was a separate envelope that she was to give to her direct supervisor. Enclosed was a three-page survey that asked

TABLE 8.3   *Supervisor demographics*

Demographic variable	Mean
International assignment experience (total number of assignments)	
Zero	25%
One	28%
Two	30%
Three	7%
Four	7%
Five or More	3%
Percentage of time spouse accompanied assignee on assignment (for those married)	
Yes	87%
How many assignments did spouse accompany on international assignment?	
Zero	1.9%
One	40.4%
Two	34.6%
Three	13.5%
Four	5.8%
Five or More	3.8%
Gender	
Male	88%
Female	12%
Age (average in years)	45
Ethnicity	
African American/black	3.8%
Asian/Asia Indian	3.8%
Caucasian/white	80.0%
Hispanic/Latino/Latin	5.0%
Native American	0.5%
Other	6.9%

Supervisor: n = 78

many of the same questions as the survey of the female expatriates asked. It was up to the discretion of the female employee whether she passed the survey along to her supervisor.

Both the female expatriates and their supervisors were given approximately three weeks to complete and return the surveys from the time they were mailed. Envelopes were provided to both groups in which to return completed surveys. Respondents were also given the option of faxing their surveys to us. As was done for the IPA company representatives, follow-up letters and email messages were sent to the female expatriates reminding them to complete and return the surveys.

Confidentiality issues and survey administration

To ensure confidentiality, a random number was assigned to each survey we received from a female expatriate. The same number was assigned to the survey from her supervisor to enable us to compare their responses. A cover letter to both the international assignees and to their supervisors reinforced the confidential and voluntary nature of the study.

Measures

The survey of the female expatriates consisted of 62 questions and was divided into six sections: selection, background information, perceptions of the supervisor's attitudes, supervisor/female expatriate relationship, personal experience, and demographic data.

One of the purposes of our study was to test whether there was still support for the three myths Adler identified in her research. Thus, both the female expatriates and their supervisors were asked how strongly they agreed or disagreed with a series of statements that addressed the three myths she identified. A five-point Likert scale was used (5 = strongly agree, 1 = strongly disagree) for this purpose (see Table 8.4).

Myth 1

Three statements were used to test myth 1. The first was: 'Women are not interested in going on international assignments.' Our data showed that both the female expatriates and their supervisors strongly disagreed with this statement, corroborating Adler's (1984b) research.

Both the female expatriates and their supervisors were also asked to assess the likelihood that women would accept international positions if they were in dual career relationships and given other family considerations. There were no significant statistical differences in responses. Respondents in both groups said that women in dual career relationships accepted slightly fewer international assignments than single women or women who lived with non-working partners.

Another question addressed whether women with children accepted fewer international assignments than women who did not have children. In this case there was a significant difference between the responses of the female expatriates and their supervisors. Specifically, the female expatriates expressed stronger agreement with the statement than their supervisors. Company data confirmed these women's perceptions; only 24 per cent of the female expatriates reported that they had children (see Table 8.1).

Myth 2

We asked several questions of both the female expatriates and their supervisors to determine whether there is still support for myth 2: that companies are hesitant to send women on international assignments. In her research, Adler showed that companies were hesitant to send women on international assignments, grounding this statement in reality rather than simply mythology (the reader is reminded of the limited scope of Adler's sample).

In our data, the responses of the female expatriates to the questions dealing with whether their companies were hesitant to send women on international assignments indicated that the female expatriates responding neither agreed nor disagreed that their companies generally favour males over females for international assignments. The supervisors, however, more strongly disagreed with the statement that their companies were hesitant to send women on these assignments.

TABLE 8.4   *Comparisons of female international assignees' perceptions and the perceptions of their supervisors on key variables (a)*

Issue	Female Perceptions (n = 261)		Supervisors Own Perceptions (n = 78)		t-test (b)
	Mean	SD	Mean	SD	
In general, women aren't interested in going on international assignments.	1.67	0.91	1.76	0.83	− 0.80
Women who are in dual career relationships ACCEPT fewer international assignments than women who are single or living with non-working partners.	3.78	1.09	3.59	0.90	1.42
Women who have children ACCEPT fewer international assignments than women who do not have children.	3.60	0.96	3.27	0.90	2.30*
My company generally favours males over females when considering an appropriate candidate for an international assignment.	2.99	1.13	2.23	1.09	4.76*
In general, companies are hesitant to send women on international assignments.	2.99	1.09	2.39	0.93	3.83*
Women who are in dual career relationships are OFFERED fewer international assignments than women who are single or living with non-working partners.	3.27	1.14	2.79	1.06	2.97*
Being in a dual career relationship more negatively affects a woman's ability to be CHOSEN for an international assignment relative to her male counterparts.	3.23	1.17	2.42	0.93	5.37*
Women who have children are OFFERED fewer international assignments than women who do not have children.	3.22	1.07	2.49	0.97	4.89*
Being female negatively affects my PERFORMANCE on the international assignment.	1.71	0.98	1.56	0.66	0.99
Being female positively affected my SELECTION for my most recent international assignment.	2.45	1.05	2.46	0.72	− 0.94
In general, host country nationals both inside and outside of the company are prejudiced against female expatriates.	2.25	1.13	2.19	0.81	0.42
Local cultural norms based on 'typical female' expatriate behaviour limit my ability to be effective on my current international assignment.	2.01	0.93	2.47	0.88	− 03.19*
The host country's culture has not prevented me from being successful on my most recent international assignment.	4.10	1.03	3.29	0.94	4.99*

(Contd.)

(Contd.)

Issue	Female Perceptions (n = 261)		Supervisors Own Perceptions (n = 78)		
	Mean	SD	Mean	SD	t-test (b)
Being female has made it very difficult to adapt to the host country's culture.	1.93	1.05	2.17	0.92	− 2.10*
The country of the international assignment impacts the company's decision to OFFER a woman an international assignment.	3.83	1.22	3.34	1.10	2.71*
The amount of notice given prior to an international assignment impacts a woman's decision to ACCEPT an international assignment.	3.43	1.03	3.86	0.85	− 3.17*
The country of the international assignment impacts a woman's decision to ACCEPT an international assignment.	4.22	0.80	4.21	0.71	0.10

(a) Wording of issues and corresponding numbers based on female international assignee surveys.
(b) T-test analyses relationship between female perceptions and supervisors' own perceptions.
* Indicates $p \leq .05$

In each case, the responses of the female expatriates differed significantly from those of their supervisors. The women expressed neither strong agreement nor disagreement with the statements that their companies were hesitant to send women on international assignments or that their companies favoured males over females when considering candidates. This distinction in responses shows some reservation on the part of the female expatriates to feel support from their companies for potential international assignments.

Respondents were also asked whether women in dual career relationships were offered fewer international assignments than single women, or women living with non-working partners. The supervisors disagreed with this statement, whereas the female expatriates expressed reluctance to agree or disagree. A comparison of the responses of the two samples indicates a significant statistical difference in perception – namely, the supervisors thought their companies were not hesitant to send women in dual career relationships on international assignments, whereas the female expatriates were less convinced of this.

We also asked the survey participants to assess the likelihood that women in dual career relationships would be chosen for international assignments relative to their male counterparts. Again, the supervisors did not think that being in a dual career relationship negatively affected a woman's chances of being chosen for an international position. Their female expatriate subordinates did not share this view. They neither agreed nor disagreed, again suggesting uncertainty on this point.

The supervisors also disagreed that women with children were offered fewer international assignments than women without children. In line with other responses, the female expatriates neither supported nor refuted this statement, once again indicating some uncertainty concerning the company's support on this issue.

Two additional questions were used to determine whether respondents believed that being female negatively affected performance on international assignments and whether being female positively affected whether a candidate was selected for international assignments. A comparison of the responses from each group of participants indicates no significant difference in perception. Both the female international assignees and their supervisors reported that being female did not negatively affect performance. Further, the members of both groups agreed that being female did not positively affect whether a candidate was selected for an international assignment.

In this case, our findings contradict Adler's. From the supervisors' perspective at least, companies are not hesitant to send women on international assignments, under both general and specific conditions. This is an especially valuable finding given that the literature claims that women are often reluctant to accept such assignments if a husband or significant other is also committed to a career. These findings may demonstrate some degree of progress since Adler conducted her research.

The female assignees, however, refrained from reporting any level of agreement or disagreement with the statement that women in dual career relationships are often reluctant to accept international assignments. The women's responses are puzzling and suggest that perhaps women suspect, but are not certain, that companies are still reluctant to send women overseas. If women on international assignments are unclear whether their companies are hesitant to send women on these assignments, we can reasonably assume that women might be hesitant even to pursue such positions. Further, if the women's supervisors claim their companies are not reluctant to send females on international assignments but behave in ways that are inconsistent with this belief (i.e. choose women less often), it is not unreasonable to assume that these supervisors also discourage women, however tacitly, from pursuing international assignments.

Myth 3

To test the third myth Adler identified, that prejudice prevents women from being successful on international assignments, we asked six questions that focused on prejudice against women on foreign assignments. Respondents were asked to agree or disagree that nationals from the host country were prejudiced against female expatriates. Both the female expatriates and their supervisors disagreed with this statement.

These results may lead one to believe that prejudice is not a problem for women in foreign countries. Other results, however, indicate that the picture is not necessarily so rosy – namely, two questions specifically focused on whether the culture and norms of their host countries inhibited the women from being effective. When asked if local norms about what constituted typical female behaviour limited the women's ability to be effective, the female international assignees answered with a resounding 'no'. The supervisors also disagreed with the statement, but much less strongly.

We also asked about the extent to which the host country's culture prevented the women from being successful on international assignments. Whereas, in this case, the supervisors' responses reflected a neutral viewpoint, the women expatriates indicated that the local culture definitely did not prevent the women from being successful. Again, the difference in the responses is statistically significant.

We also assessed whether the respondents believed being female made adapting to the host country more difficult. Both the women expatriates and their supervisors indicated that being female did not make adapting more difficult, although the women disagreed more strongly than the supervisors. Again, the relationship was statistically significant.

Another issue that interested us was the extent to which the specific country to which the company was sending an employee affected the company's decision to offer the assignment to a woman and her willingness to accept the position. The supervisors took a relatively neutral approach, indicating that the country did not greatly affect whether the company offered the assignment to a man or a woman. The female expatriates felt that the country had greater relevance in this decision. The difference in perceptions on this issue was statistically significant.

By contrast, both the supervisors and the female expatriates believed that where the assignment was located had a significant bearing on whether a woman would accept or turn down an international assignment. It is important to note, however, that the literature claims this is also true for men (Hill and Tillery, 1992).

Overall, the findings from our study support the claim reported in the literature that it is often the perceptions of home country managers and supervisors about host country prejudices and cultural challenges that prevent women from obtaining international assignments. In general, the supervisors believed this claim more strongly than the international assignees.

It is important that women who are interested in going on international assignments remember that supervisors often assume that cultural obstacles will hinder women's effectiveness. Women should be encouraged to speak directly to expatriates who have first-hand experience in working in the country to which other women employees will be sent. These expatriates can provide the most realistic picture of the limitations other women will face.

Discussion

It appears from these findings that the differences in the perceptions of female international assignees and their supervisors may contribute to why so few women make up the expatriate population. Specifically, when it comes to their perceptions of the female expatriate's international experience, female international assignees and their supervisors share few views. For example, when asked to assess the impact of a host country's culture on a woman's ability to be effective as an international manager, the female expatriates felt strongly that the cultural norms of the host country were not a consideration. Their supervisors were less convinced. The obvious question is, 'Why are there patterns of significant differences in responses?' Similarly, the female expatriates and their supervisors expressed different views on whether companies were hesitant to send women on international assignments. Contradicting Adler's research (1984a), the supervisors reported that companies were not hesitant. The female expatriates were less sure.

The female expatriates were also reluctant either to acknowledge or deny that being in a dual career relationship, and having children, affected a woman's chances of being selected for an international assignment or of accepting an offer once it was made. Their supervisors thought these family considerations were of little or no relevance in whether a woman would be selected for an international position. Finally, both the women and their supervisors differed in their views of the elements of support they believed companies provided and those that companies should provide for women on international assignments.

Implications

What are the implications for global human resource professionals and female international assignees if these differences in perceptions continue? At the most basic level, we can assume that qualified women will continue to be left out of the pool of candidates being considered for international assignments. As a result, the probability of choosing the best candidate may be diminished. This, in turn, could lead to ongoing unsuccessful or only modestly successful international assignments.

At the same time, if women do not understand their companies' policies and practices regarding international assignees, they may be discouraged from making their interest and willingness known. As Harris (1993) has noted, whether a woman is sent on an international assignment largely depends on the opinions and beliefs of the woman's supervisor about the expatriate experience.

Overall, companies need to improve their communication strategies concerning international assignments. Although this sounds like a general guideline, in fact, several specific action strategies are necessary.

Given that our findings indicate that, in general, women in management are eager to be selected for international assignments, companies need to ensure that their recruitment and selection policies encompass women as potential candidates for such assignments. Although the respondents in the companies that participated in this study reported that they were not hesitant to send women on international assignments, the female international assignees in our study do not necessarily share this opinion. To reconcile the differences in perception, companies need to communicate their positions better.

Female international assignees strongly believe that the cultural norms of host countries do not prevent women from succeeding on international assignments; their supervisors believe this less strongly, however. Companies need to examine these differences so as to prevent supervisors from basing selection or recruitment decisions on preconceived and perhaps false notions.

Whereas the supervisors reported that international assignments contribute to women's career advancement, the female assignees believed this less strongly. This suggests that women may not be adequately informed about the elements that contribute to their advancement within their companies. Companies need to communicate the value placed on international assignments in the company, so that those women interested in climbing the ladder will understand the steps necessary to get there.

Companies need to encourage communication in order to bridge the gaps in perceptions between supervisors and female international assignees regarding the extent to which being in a dual career relationship or having children affects whether one is offered or selected for global assignments. Likewise companies need to ensure that all qualified candidates for international assignments are considered in the selection process.

Companies may need to rethink ways to reconcile these differences in perceptions through formal mechanisms, such as scheduled feedback sessions and performance appraisals. As companies groom and select employees for international assignments, they should be encouraged to work closely in educating both supervisors who select candidates for international assignments and women being considered for such assignments. The focus should be on reconciling differences in the myths and the realities.

Companies should also be encouraged to use the data we gathered as reference points for evaluating their policies and practices pertaining to the selection of candidates for expatriation. The hope is that companies will then create strategies in order to do things better. The responses of both the supervisors and their subordinates should be extremely helpful in developing the combination of policy elements that will best meet the needs of current and prospective expatriate employees.

Women themselves also have to take some responsibility for improving their chances of being selected for international assignments. As a first step, they have to clearly communicate their interest in being considered for these assignments as well as why they are well qualified to undertake them. Second, women need to be forthright in asking about the criteria that are used to make selection decisions.

Third, in communicating with their supervisors, women should openly discuss the areas that often represent differences in perceptions between them. The findings of this study indicate that although companies appear to be overcoming some of their resistance to sending women overseas, supervisors still harbour many prejudices against sending women. It can be assumed, therefore, that much of the improvement women are making can be attributed to their own active attempts to reverse patterns of discrimination and express an interest in pursuing international opportunities.

Conclusion: areas for future research

Additional research needs to track the progress women make in the international business arena, especially as expatriates. Specifically, figures provided by research groups such as Windam International and the National Trade Council, which have projected that by the year 2000 women will represent 20 per cent of the total expatriate population, may be seriously inflated. Clearly, future studies need to determine whether significant improvement has occurred in the representation of women on international assignments. Similarly, the impact of dual career relationships should be monitored to determine whether, as predicted in the current literature, career-related issues become an increasing concern for men considering international assignments.

A follow-up study to this research would be beneficial, especially one that focused on changes in the perceptions of female international assignees and their supervisors. Such a study could also address the following unanswered questions:

- What role, if any, does the gender of a prospective international assignee or his/her supervisor play in how expatriation is perceived and in who is selected for expatriation?
- How do the perceptions of female international assignees regarding the experience of being a female expatriate differ from those of women who have not gone on international assignments?

Answers to the above questions could contribute immensely to the research that has been done so far. Additional research will also help both men and women better understand the factors that affect the decision to accept an international assignment. Finally, companies will find this additional research useful in helping them to determine changes they need to make to ensure that female candidates for international assignments are treated equally and fairly.

Acknowledgments

The authors would like to thank the International Personnel Association, in particular Glen Anderson, Matt Ashe, Bill Edgley, Michael Gordon, Sven Grasshoff, Bob Maheu, Robert Nalewajek, Ed Nunez, Larry Olufsen, Jim Pilarski, Raj Tatta, Linda Watson and Bill Yadlosky for their support and contributions to this study. We would also like to thank the female participants and their supervisors who gave their time and consideration. Lastly, thanks to Ms Tamara Birch for her technical advice and expertise.

References

Adler, N.J. (1984a) 'Expecting international success: female managers overseas', *Columbia Journal of World Business*, 19: 79–85.

Adler, N.J. (1984b) 'Women do not want international careers: and other myths about international management', *Organizational Dynamics*, 13: 66–79.

Adler, N.J. (1987) 'Pacific basin managers: a gajin, not a woman', *Human Resource Management*, 26: 169–191.

Adler, N.J. (1997) *International Dimensions of Organizational Behavior*, 3rd edn, South-Western College Publishing, Cincinnati, OH.

Adler, N.J. and Izraeli, D.N. (1994) *Competitive Frontiers: Women Managers in a Global Economy*, Blackwell, Cambridge, MA.

Black, J.S., Gregersen, H.B., Mendenhall, M.E. and Stroh, L.K. (1998) *Global Assignments*, Addison-Wesley, Reading, MA.

Chusmir, L.H. and Frontczak, N.T. (1990) 'International management opportunities for women: women and men paint different pictures', *International Journal of Management*, 7 (3): 295–301.

Frontczak, N.T. and Cateora, P.R. (1988) 'Opportunities for women in international business: an update', in F.L. Patrone (ed.), *Mountain Plain Management Conference: Abstract of Proceedings*.

Harris, H. (1993) 'Women in management: opportunity or threat?' *Women in Management Review*, 8: 9–14.

Harris, H. (1995) 'Organizational influences on women's career opportunities in international management', *Women in Management Review*, 10: 26–31.

Harvey, M. (1996) 'Addressing the dual career expatriation dilemma', *Human Resource Planning*, 19: 18–39.

Hill, C.J. and Tillery, K.R. (1992) 'What do male/female perceptions of an international business career suggest about recruitment policies?' *SAM Advanced Management Journal*, Autumn: 10–14.

Izraeli, D.N., Banai, M. and Zeira,Y. (1980) 'Women executives in MNC subsidiaries', *California Management Review*, 22: 53–63.

Moran, Stahl and Boyer (1988) *Status of American Female Expatriate Employees: Survey Results*, Westview, Boulder, CO.

Stone, R.J. (1991) 'Expatriate selection and failure', *Human Resource Planning*, 14: 9–18.

Taylor, S. and Napier, N. (1996) 'Working in Japan: lessons from women expatriates', *Sloan Management Review*, 37: 76–84.

Tung, R.L. (1997) 'Canadian expatriates in Asia-Pacific: an analysis of their attitude toward and experience in international assignments'. Paper presented at the meeting of the Society for Industrial and Organizational Psychology, St Louis, MO.

Westwood, R.I. and Leung, S.M. (1994) 'The female expatriate manager experience: coping with gender and culture', *International Studies of Management and Organizations*, 24: 64–85.

9

Feminine Leadership – A Review of Gender Differences in Managerial Behaviour and Effectiveness

Claartje J. Vinkenburg, Paul G.W. Jansen and Paul L. Koopman

Introduction

More and more organizations are actively looking for women to join their top management ranks. There are two important reasons to hire, promote and retain talented women: demographic changes due to a continuously dropping birth rate and the growing need for diversity. Furthermore, women are currently being called 'the managers of the 21st century' (Rosen et al., 1989; Schwartz, 1992; Fisher, 1998). This chapter contains a literature review to further our understanding of real or supposed gender differences in managerial behaviour, managerial effectiveness and the personal determinants of both behaviour and effectiveness. The chapter draws on a doctoral thesis by Vinkenburg (1997), and the review includes some results from an empirical study on gender differences in management in the Netherlands conducted by the author. The introduction deals with current views on effective management, the feminization of management, the advancement of women into management positions and explanations for this paucity, focusing on the 'individual differences' explanation. Next, the review looks at studies on gender differences in personal factors, managerial behaviour and effectiveness. The final section integrates the general conclusions of the materials reviewed throughout the chapter with the issues discussed in the introduction.

Effective management and the feminization of management

As organizations and their environments change at a seemingly ever-greater speed, the need to find a way to select, train and develop people who will contribute to attaining organizational goals becomes increasingly important. Managers, by leading subordinates, can have such an impact. Traditional managerial roles and requirements for effective managerial behaviour change along with the organization. As organizational structures and cultures change, directive, task-oriented and hierarchical leadership of subordinates has to make way for managing high-involvement work teams with an emphasis on consensus decision-making and learning instead of control (Bohl et al., 1996). With or without open acknowledgement, management is described more and more in traditionally feminine terms (Fondas, 1997) such as sharing responsibility, helping and developing others and building a connected network of relationships. Both academics and people in organizations have uncovered this phenomenon, which Fondas (1997) calls 'the feminization of management'.

Effective managerial behaviour, requirements for successful leaders, and feminine management have been the topics of various articles in both professional and popular media, ranging from the *Harvard Business Review* and the *New York Times* to *Business Topics* (Presley Noble, 1993; Bass and Avolio, 1994; Metze, 1994; Peters, 1996). Most of these sources, however, rely on commonly held stereotypes and untested notions of what managers do and how women are different from men. Furthermore, determinants of managerial advancement have not been well established (Tharenou et al., 1994), as only a few studies have examined a broad range of personal and situational variables. The question remains whether the 'feminization of management' will lead to a larger proportion of women in management positions.

The advancement of women into management

Gender differences in the level and type of formal education and in participation in the labour force are rapidly disappearing; but the rate of advancement of women into higher positions in organizations is relatively slow. The position of women in managerial jobs worldwide in the last decade has been described as improving but women are still at a disadvantage when compared to men's position (Adler and Izraeli, 1993; Davidson and Burke, 1994). Generally speaking, a growing number of women occupy management positions, but at top levels still very few women are present. Some sources even indicate that the number of women in top positions is currently declining, a trend observed in both the United States and Europe, including the Netherlands (Dwyer, 1996; Vossen, 1998).

Women's slow movement into management positions can be explained in three different ways (Morrison and von Glinow, 1990; Van Vianen and Keizer, 1992; Gutek, 1993):

- structural barriers or discrimination;
- gender roles and stereotypes;
- individual differences or deficiencies.

None of these explanations stands alone; there are obvious and complex inter-relationships between them.

The structural barriers approach (Kanter, 1977) emphasizes that minority group members encounter difficulties in adjusting to and fitting in with the majority culture. When group membership is related to occupational status, it is harder for minority members to cross boundaries between occupational status groups. Minority members become 'tokens'; their behaviour is taken as an example of their entire group's behaviour and they are always in the spotlight. The dual labour market, with jobs that are primary and secondary in terms of value and status, exists also within management levels with women often holding secondary jobs in staff departments with little chance for upward mobility.

Gender role stereotypes have a major impact on selection and promotion procedures as well as on evaluation of managerial performance. The typical good manager is (still) described in traditionally masculine terms (Frank, 1988; Hellman et al., 1989; Schein and Mueller, 1992; Perry et al., 1994). This bias ('think manager, think male') can lead to differential treatment of women in more than one way: because they are expected to be less effective managers anyhow, because they are expected to want a family and therefore will drop out of the career path; and because gender role incongruent behaviour is generally evaluated more negatively than gender role congruent behaviour (Statham, 1987; Rojahn and Willemsen, 1994).

   The final explanation, individual differences as the main reason for the paucity of the advancement of women into management, looks into the question of whether the stereotypes illustrated above are for real. Are women different from men in terms of personality, motivation or behaviour? If women and men are essentially similar, they should have equal rights to organizational roles. If women and men are essentially different, women can make a complementary contribution to organizations (Adler, 1987). This final explanation, of individual differences, will be further explored in this chapter because it fits well with the 'feminization of management' idea.

Individual differences

Regarding gender differences in management, authors generally start from one of three basic viewpoints (Tavris, 1991):

'Women are opposite and deficient.'
'Women are just like men.'
'Women are opposite and superior.'

Taking the first point of view, the slow advancement of women into management is explained by the fact that women are thought to be less capable as managers. Women may indeed seem deficient if gender differences are expected or found and men are taken as the norm. Traditionally, data from research on gender differences were presented phrased in terms such as: 'women have less self-esteem'. However, if one presents the same data taking women as the norm, the results could be phrased as: 'men overestimate their own capacities'.

The second viewpoint regarding gender differences in management, 'women are just like men', claims there are in fact very few differences. This viewpoint, based on empirical research, generally serves to illustrate that there are few legitimate reasons to deny women who are qualified and want a career access to (higher) management positions. Powell (1988, 1990) is one of the advocates of the 'no differences' view. His review contains many relevant studies to prove this point.

The third viewpoint, in line with the 'feminization of management' phenomenon, takes differences as women's strengths, and claims that 'women are opposite and superior' as managers. Rosener (1990) in an article entitled 'Ways women lead' describes a more feminine leadership style that is said to be optimal for recent developments in organizations. Despite criticism of her research method, her viewpoints do appeal to many people as the gender distinction is a very relevant and common social category; and gender differences are intuitively expected. As women are expected to be more relation-oriented, nurturing and caring, organizations that become flatter and more team-structured may learn to appreciate these qualities in managers and promote more women into management positions (Grant, 1988; Helgesen, 1990; Rosener, 1991; Thooft, 1994). Mintzberg finds that female managers bring nursing qualities into management, which in his terms is just what organizations need (1994, 1996). Appelbaum and Shapiro (1993) even ask 'Why can't men lead like women?' and suggest that women should stop disregarding their 'natural instincts' and reconsider choosing to lead like men. Others agree that women managers do not have to 'act like men' and can benefit from using a more feminine or androgynous management style (Korabik and Ayman, 1989).

However, these sources rely mostly on interview studies and their arguments typically build on commonly held stereotypes and untested notions of how women are different from men. A first concern is to test these notions; a second concern is argued by Fierman (1990), who states that 'feminine leadership' is just another stereotype. Flatter organizations and teamwork represent the current most effective way to run a business; it is no more feminine than the more traditional way was masculine; and it is no less dominated by males. The 'nurturing' image may even result in more women being in people-oriented areas of business (dealing with human resources, dealing with customers); which often are dead-end career tracks (Ferrario, 1991; Nichols, 1993). Ferrario states that 'the emphasis on gender differences reinforces the male managerial model' (1991: 19). Additionally, Calás and Smircich (1993) suggest there may be dangers associated with 'such feminine-in-management positions'. They write:

> Although these positions are presented as a call for change in organizational thinking, they do in fact little more than restate existing management approaches under a different name. The dangers are very real...insofar as their apparent valuing of some essential women's qualities maintains an illusion of opportunity and equality for women in the managerial world while obstructing critical examination of the pervasive theoretical assumptions sustaining that world. (Calás and Smircich, 1993: 72)

Some authors claim that current management and organization theory is indeed filled with adjectives and characteristics traditionally considered feminine (Fondas, 1997); and unveiling this feminization shows that gender is (becoming) a part of the conceptualization of management. Fondas recognizes the need for further research into the extent to which feminized management ideas have been put into practice by actual managers. In particular, she emphasizes the need to study how managers do things, rather than what managers do, in order to be able to pinpoint feminine qualities in both men and women.

On the one hand, the concerns voiced above clearly signify a need for further empirical research into gender differences in management and the feminization phenomenon. Even authors who persist in claiming 'the female advantage' say the fact that few actual gender differences show up in research has more to do with the research methods than the study object (Plesch, 1994). Differences between men and women in brain structure (Moir and Jessel, 1990), cognitive and verbal abilities have been proven; why shouldn't differences in leadership style be just as real? Advocates of further research on gender differences note that studying differences between groups (or genders) does not mean neglecting similarities between groups or neglecting differences within groups. Neither does studying gender differences automatically mean that women are not expected to live up to a male standard (Eagly, 1995). Results from such studies may prove widely held stereotypes wrong and might therefore lift structural barriers for women in organizations.

On the other hand, further research into gender differences may not be able to settle the debate between the different viewpoints, as results are never fully generalizable to different organizations or cultures. Results from such studies may also prove widely held stereotypes right, but as argued above, this does not necessarily mean that a future emphasis on feminine qualities in management will make more room for women in management positions. Results may even be used to show that women are less capable as managers or less interested in such positions.

In an effort to give an up-to-date and empirically based answer to the question of whether there are indeed differences between male and female managers, the next section of this chapter contains a review of studies that have looked into differences between female and male managers in personal factors, behaviour and effectiveness.

Gender differences and determinants of managerial behaviour and effectiveness

The literature review in this section is organized according to a model of the determinants of managerial behaviour and effectiveness presented by Vinkenburg (1997) (see Figure 9.1). This model is based on various models from literature on managerial behaviour and effectiveness, advancement and career success (Campbell, et al., 1970; Blumberg and Pringle, 1982; Ronen, 1986; Gattiker and Larwood, 1988, 1990; O'Reilly and Chatman, 1994; Tharenou et al., 1994; Chen, 1995; Melamed, 1996).

The contextual determinants (the general organizational context) and situational determinants (characteristics of the specific work situation) of managerial behaviour and effectiveness will not be discussed because the focus is on individual (gender) differences. The review starts with a number of studies on gender differences in personal factors, distinguishing between personality, demographics and person–job factors. Second, studies on gender differences in managerial behaviour and management styles are discussed. Finally, gender differences in various measures of managerial effectiveness or success are described. Of course, not all possible determinants, dimensions of behaviour or criteria for effectiveness will be discussed in this literature review. However, those most relevant to the subject matter are included.

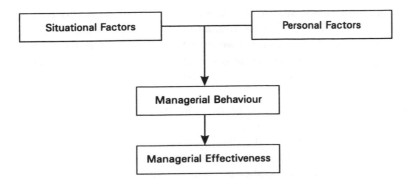

FIGURE 9.1   *A model of managerial behaviour and effectiveness*

Personality

It is relevant to discuss studies on gender differences in five types of personality factors: the 'Big Five' personality characteristics, motivation, commitment, self-efficacy and self-monitoring.

The 'Big Five' personality characteristics refer to five broad factors that consistently appear in personality research. The factors are labelled agreeableness, conscientiousness, extraversion, openness to experience and (emotional) stability or low neuroticism (Barrick and Mount, 1991; McCrae and John, 1992). The Myers-Briggs Type Indicator (MBTI) measures similar personality dimensions to the five-factor model (except for neuroticism) (Furnham and Stringfield, 1993a, 1993b). Studies indicate that female managers display greater communal (interpersonal) qualities; men display more agentic (task-oriented) qualities (Pratch, 1996); i.e. women are more oriented towards establishing and maintaining relationships. Also, women score somewhat higher than men on the 'intuition' and 'feeling' dimensions of the Myers-Briggs Type Indicator (Vinnicombe, 1988), the latter of which is sometimes equated with agreeableness (Nordvik, 1997). Moreover, Furnham and Stringfield (1993b) found that women scored higher on the MBTI extraversion, intuition and feeling dimensions. However, in the study by Vinkenburg (1997) there were no gender differences in any of the five factors.

There are two main lines of work on managerial motivation, one carried out by McClelland (McClelland and Boyatzis, 1982) and the other by Miner (1993). Managers generally have moderate to high needs for achievement, power and for routine administrative functions; and a low need for affiliation. Gender differences in achievement motivation, with fear of success and competitiveness in women, are often found (Lipman-Blumen et al., 1983; Gattiker and Larwood, 1990; Ruf and Chusmir, 1991). Female managers are, however, likely to be what Schwartz (1989) calls 'career-primary oriented' as opposed to 'career-family oriented' (Burke and McKeen, 1993); they put their career first. Therefore their levels of need for achievement and need for power generally do not differ from men's (Chusmir, 1985; Sutherland and Veroff, 1985; Stevens and Brenner, 1990; Ferrario, 1994). A meta-analysis on 'motivation to manage' has shown a greater need for routine administrative functions in female managers (Eagly et al., 1994), which is explained by the fact that women are expected to be more conscientious, patient and painstaking. Because of women's relation orientation, female managers were expected to have a higher need for affiliation in the study by Vinkenburg (1997). This expectation was not confirmed, nor were any other differences in motivation found.

In studies of managerial commitment, a distinction is often made between commitment to the organization (affective commitment), team commitment and career commitment (Blau et al., 1993; Meyer et al., 1993; Aryee et al., 1994; Becker et al., 1996). Results from various studies show few gender differences in commitment (sometimes operationalized as the intention to leave), with women sometimes being less, sometimes equally and sometimes more committed than men (Chusmir, 1987; Wazienski, 1987; Rosin and Korabik, 1991; Giacobbe Miller and Wheeler, 1992; Aven et al., 1993; Burke and McKeen, 1993; Marsden et al., 1993; Ellemers et al., 1996; Schneer and Reitman, 1996). Although a higher level of team commitment (and equal levels of career and organizational commitment) were expected of women in the Vinkenburg study (1997), no differences were found.

Self-efficacy describes an individual's belief in his or her capability to mobilize the motivation, cognitive resources and courses of action needed to meet given situational demands; to perform a certain task, to control events and achieve goals. Individuals with high personal efficacy have higher aspirations, will exert more effort and persist longer in mastering a challenge; self-efficacy affects one's choice of settings and activities, and promotes skill acquisition (Bandura and Schunk, 1981; Gist and Mitchell, 1992; Tsui and Ashford, 1994). Various studies have shown lower or equal levels of perceived task-related self-efficacy in women compared to men in organizational settings or career matters (Betz and Hackett, 1981; Hackett et al., 1990; Vasil, 1992; Gardner et al., 1994; Stone, 1994). The findings of lower self-efficacy may either indicate a 'real' difference, or can be explained by women being realistic and men being over-confident as far as their own capabilities are concerned (Grant, 1988; Chusmir and Koberg, 1992; Tuckman and Sexton, 1992; Stone, 1994); or by the finding that women are less likely to attribute their own successes to their abilities (Gerike, 1983; Rosenthal et al., 1996). Vinkenburg (1997) did find no gender differences in managerial self-efficacy.

Finally, it is also relevant to discuss the notion of self-monitoring. This refers to the ability to observe and control one's expressive behaviour and self-presentation. Self-monitoring has a significant role in displaying behaviour that is appropriate according to situational and interpersonal cues. High self-monitors are sensitive to such cues and requirements, and are motivated and able to regulate their behaviour to fit the situation (Snyder and Gangestad, 1986; Jenkins, 1993; Kilduff and Day, 1994; Tsui and Ashford, 1994). As women are thought to be more sensitive to social situations and situational cues, they are often found to score higher on self-monitoring. This holds especially for women in higher management positions because self-monitoring abilities facilitate career movements into occupational roles that are not traditional to one's gender (Anderson, 1987; Gardner et al., 1994; Riordan et al., 1994). No gender differences in self- monitoring were found by Vinkenburg (1997).

Demographics

When studying gender differences in personality or behaviour, most studies control for differences in age, tenure, level of education, management experience and level, as these might 'overrule' the gender effect (Lefkowitz, 1994). In most samples, gender differences in demographics are small or non-existent because researchers make sure they have demographically comparable respondents. However, being 'career-primary oriented' as female managers often are, as opposed to 'career-family oriented', may require that they remain single or at least childless; or if they do have children, that they let others take care of them (Gerike, 1983). Male managers can have both orientations as well, but this does not mean they have to make a choice because they are more likely to have a partner who works fewer hours outside the home than they do. Women have (or take) more housework and childcare responsibilities than men; women's partners have fewer such responsibilities as opposed to men's partners (ESB, 1992; Burke and McKeen, 1993; Schneer and Reitman, 1993; Kirchmeyer, 1996; Tharenou, 1996; Snabilié, 1997). These differences were confirmed in Vinkenburg's study (1997).

Person–job factors

'Person–job factors' refers to those personal factors which are related to the job of the manager. In studies of managerial behaviour and effectiveness, typical person–job factors include: tenure at the organization and in the current job or position; type of contract (full- versus part-time); number of hours worked per week; management experience; and finally mentoring. As with demographics, often such variables are used as covariates (Lefkowitz, 1994). Women are more likely to work part time, even in management positions (Eurostat, 1996). However, when they do work full time, women work the same amount of hours per week as men do (Burke and McKeen, 1993; Burke, 1995). Working part time may have a negative impact on perceived effectiveness, as commitment to one's career, the team and the organization may seem lower. Having a mentor has a positive effect on women's career success (Noe, 1988; McKeen and Burke, 1989; Burke and McKeen, 1992; Wentling, 1992), but there are a number of studies that describe barriers for women in gaining a mentor; i.e. women are less likely to have a mentor. Barriers vary from a lack of access to networks and information to norms against cross-gender relationships at work (Noe, 1988; Ragins, 1989; Ragins and Cotton, 1991, 1993; Shellenbarger, 1995). Some organizations try to break down these barriers and make an effort to assign (if necessary male) mentors to women (Anonymous, 1993). Women are just as likely to be mentors as their male counterparts; but they are more likely to have and prefer a female protégée (Ragins and Scandura, 1994; Turban and Dougherty, 1994; Burke and McKeen, 1995; Vinkenburg, 1997).

Gender differences in managerial behaviour and management styles

Surprisingly, there are very few empirical studies of gender differences in actual managerial behaviour. Reviews that do include studies of behavioural differences mostly summarize the results as inconsistent (Leavitt, 1982; Powell, 1988, 1990); i.e. mostly there are no differences, sometimes there are 'stereotypical' differences (women behave in ways that conform with gender role stereotypes); and sometimes there are non-stereotypical differences.

One of the differences found by Dobbins (1986) was that women, in responding to poor performance of a subordinate, are more likely to use a combined standard of equality and equity rather than equity alone. Gerike (1983) revealed, in a matched sample of male and female managers, that women were less involved in informal interactions with colleagues (i.e. networking) and had somewhat lower levels of risk-taking behaviours. Some differences in communication abilities were found, indicating that female managers felt greater apprehension and thought they were less skilled in communicating (Penley et al., 1991). Fisher (1998) describes a number of studies that show gender differences in communication, again related to the argument that women are more relation oriented, and have more communal, interpersonal qualities. No gender differences were found in other studies (Donnell and Hall, 1980; Noordegraaf, 1994). Furthermore, Vinkenburg (1997) studied managerial behaviour operationalized as self-reported reactions to work situations and found few gender differences.

Other researchers have shown that female managers, although in similar middle management positions and with the same credentials in terms of education and general management experience, lack experience in dealing with specific difficult and complex situations (labelled 'developmental job components'; for example dealing with an impossible supervisor) which may serve as a reason for not promoting them to higher management positions (Ruderman et al., 1990; McCauley et al., 1994; Ohlott et al., 1994). Examining such possible gender differences in the frequency of having had such experiences, may explain more than looking for gender differences using more general behavioural measures.

As far as gender differences in management styles are concerned, somewhat more studies have been conducted. Powell (1990) and Ferrario (1991) give an overview of such studies, again indicating inconsistent results. Women use more interaction facilitation (Gibson, 1995); have a more supportive style (Nebenzahl et al., 1993) and are both more task- and more relation-oriented than men, who appear image-engrossed and autonomy-invested (Statham, 1987). Women have in some studies been shown to be more transformational leaders (Bass and Avolio, 1994; Urch Druskat, 1994; Bass et al., 1996); and in some studies women are less relation-oriented (Winther and Green, 1987). Finally, women seem to be more participative and considerate (Watson, 1988). No gender differences in management style were found by other authors (Dobbins and Platz, 1986; De Jong and van Doorne-Huiskes, 1989; Ruijs, 1990). Morevoer, a meta-analysis was performed on 162 studies of gender differences in management styles, using two aspects: task- versus relation-orientation and participative (or democratic) versus directive (or autocratic) leadership (Eagly and Johnson, 1990). Results from this study indicated that the type of study (organizational, laboratory or assessment) had an impact on the kind of results found. In actual organizational studies, there are no gender differences on the task–relation dimension; women are however somewhat more participative and less directive compared to men. Since more differences were found in the other two types of studies, Eagly and Johnson (1990) argue that existing ('real') gender differences get overruled by selection and socialization processes in organizations.

Gender differences in managerial effectiveness

The final part of this review on gender differences in management deals with differences in effectiveness and other criteria for managerial advancement and performance. In terms of perceived effectiveness, according to their peers and subordinates, women managers outperformed men on six out of seven dimensions of managerial behaviour in a study recently published on the Internet (Perrault and Irwin, 1996), not only on the interpersonal factors but especially in 'controlling'. In a meta-analysis of studies on gender differences in leader effectiveness, no significant differences were found aggregated across all studies (Eagly et al., 1995). However, managers of both genders were considered more effective when they acted in a way which conformed with their stereotypical gender role in jobs that required task abilities (for men) versus interpersonal abilities (for women). In another meta-analysis, male managers were found to be more effective than female managers, but this difference was only significant in laboratory studies (Dobbins and Platz, 1986). Some differences were also found in perceived effectiveness of conflict management behaviours (Korabik et al., 1993); women needed to be more obliging and less dominating than males in order to be considered effective.

Gender-specific models of career progression (Stroh et al., 1992; Goffee and Nicholson, 1994; Powell and Butterfield, 1994; Kirchmeyer, 1996; Melamed, 1996) show that women advance more slowly, and that factors influencing success in terms of hierarchical growth differ for the genders. As shown by Stroh et al. (1992), even if women managers have done 'all the right stuff' (i.e. have a similar education, do not move out of the workforce, bring in a large portion of their families' income), their salary progression and number of promotions lagged behind men's. Indeed, a very consistent difference between male and female managers is that men receive higher pay or salary in similar positions; and that their annual salary grows at a higher rate (Gerike, 1983; Jacobs, 1992; Barnum et al., 1995; Shellenbarger, 1995; Brouns and de Bruijn, 1996).

Vinkenburg (1997) looked at a number of different criteria for managerial effectiveness and found no gender differences in salary, salary progression, performance appraisals, potential ratings or hierarchical progression. There was no gender difference in this study either in the degree to which individual managers deviated from an organizational's expert profile of effective managerial behaviour.

Conclusion

In this chapter, studies on gender differences in managerial behaviour, effectiveness and its determinants were reviewed. Despite recent 'feminization' of organization and management theory, a call for 'feminine' leadership qualities, and the impact that these developments may have on the advancement of women in management positions, the review shows that few actual gender differences in personal factors and behaviour have been consistently and empirically confirmed.

This may be due to the fact that both men and women currently in management positions resemble a similar management prototype. The findings on gender differences may indicate that out of the general population, managers fit a typical personality and demographic prototype, and both men and women managers are more like the prototype (thus similar) than different from each other. Furthermore, selection and socialization may have reduced any possible difference (whether gender specific or not). Perhaps only women who conform to the 'male' norm of the organization are selected for management positions. However, it should be taken into consideration that most of the managers in these studies started their career at least 15 to 20 years ago, when society was different and gender-stereotypical expectations more profound. Women with an orientation towards combining a career and a family left the organization or the career track either by choice, by force or (most likely) a combination of the two. Women (and men) who are only just starting their career at this time may be able to make other choices, have more flexible care arrangements or other possibilities for making choices about having both a family and a top management job. Therefore, the sample of women managers in these studies may be a more select group than a younger sample.

Another explanation for the lack of empirical proof of consistent gender differences, as opposed to popular opinion and stereotypes, may be that different types of personal factors, behaviour or management style dimensions or effectiveness criteria than the ones described here, should be studied. Some authors suggest looking at the adaption–innovation orientation of managers, as a possible source for differences (Tullett, 1995; Kaufmann et al., 1996). Other authors suggest a shift away from looking for actual gender differences towards studying the perception or evaluation of managers by relevant others. Several authors report the existence of an evaluation bias (Nye and Forsyth, 1991; Hoffman and Watson, 1996), indicating that identical behaviour when performed by a female manager is evaluated more or less positively than when performed by a male manager. This bias is often related to the fact that gender role congruent behaviours are evaluated more positively than incongruent behaviours (Statham, 1987; Russel et al., 1988; Gattiker and Larwood, 1990; Williams and Levy, 1992; Nichols, 1993; Rojahn and Willemsen, 1994; Eagly et al., 1995). According to these authors, managers displaying traditionally gender-stereotyped behaviours (masculine for men, feminine for women) are considered more effective.

However, the general conclusion that there are few consistent gender differences in personality, managerial behaviour and effectiveness can also be interpreted as indicative of the idea that despite persistent stereotypes about gender differences, there are in fact no reasons not to promote women who are both motivated and capable of performing as a manager into top management positions. This indicates that, according to this review of recent studies, the 'women are just like men' viewpoint should be favoured over the 'women are opposite and superior' viewpoint. Hopefully, this viewpoint has potentially the same positive impact on the advancement of women into management positions as the feminization of management phenomenon.

References

Adler, N.J. (1987) 'Women in management worldwide', *International Studies of Management & Organization*, 16 (3–4): 3–32.
Adler, N.J. and Izraeli, D.N. (1993) 'Competitive frontiers: women managers in the triad', *International Studies of Management & Organization*, 23 (2): 3–23.
Anderson, L.R. (1987) 'Self-monitoring and performance in nontraditional occupations', *Basic and Applied Social Psychology*, 8 (1 & 2): 85–96.
Anonymous (1993) 'Breaking glass at Penney's', *Personnel Journal*, December: 54.
Appelbaum, S.H. and Shapiro, B.T. (1993) 'Why can't men lead like women?' *Leadership & Organization Development Journal*, 14 (7): 28–34.
Aryee, S., Chay, Y.W. and Chew, J. (1994) 'An investigation of the predictors and outcomes of career commitment in three career stages', *Journal of Vocational Behaviour*, 44 (1): 1–16.
Aven, F.F., Jr, Parker, B. and McEvoy, G.M. (1993) 'Gender and attitudinal commitment to organizations: a meta-analysis', *Journal of Business Research*, 26 (1): 63–73.
Bandura, A. and Schunk, D.H. (1981) 'Cultivating competence, self-efficacy, and intrinsic interest through proximal self-motivation', *Journal of Personality and Social Psychology*, 41 (3): 586–598.
Barnum, P., Liden, R.C. and Ditomaso, N. (1995) 'Double jeopardy for women and minorities: pay differences with age', *Academy of Management Journal*, 38 (3): 863–880.
Barrick, M.R. and Mount, M.K. (1991) 'The Big Five personality dimensions and job-performance: a meta-analysis', *Personnel Psychology*, 44: 1–26.
Bass, B.M. and Avolio, B.J. (1994) 'Shatter the glass ceiling: women may make better managers', *Human Resource Management*, 33 (4): 549–560.
Bass, B.M., Avolio, B.J. and Atwater, L. (1996) 'The transformational and transactional leadership of men and women', *Applied Psychology: an International Review*, 45 (1): 5–34.
Becker, T.E., Billings, R.S., Eveleth, D.M. and Gilbert, N.L. (1996) 'Foci and bases of employee commitment: implications for job performance', *Academy of Management Journal*, 39 (2): 464–482.
Betz, N.E. and Hackett, G. (1981) 'The relationship of career related self-efficacy expectations to perceived career options in college women and men', *Journal of Counseling Psychology*, 28 (5): 399–410.
Blau, G., Paul, A. and St John, N. (1993) 'On developing a general index of work commitment', *Journal of Vocational Behaviour*, 42: 298–314.
Blumberg, M. and Pringle, C.D. (1982) 'The missing opportunity in organizational research: some implications for a theory of work performance', *Academy of Management Review*, 7 (4): 560–569.
Bohl, D.L., Luthans, F., Slocum, J.W. Jr and Hodgetts, R.M. (1996) 'Ideas that will shape the future of management practice', *Organizational Dynamics*, 25 (1): 7–14.
Brouns, M. and de Bruijn, J. (1996) 'Functiewaardering en het beloningsverschil tussen mannen en vrouwen', in *Radar 96: stand van zaken in de wetenschap*, Aramith, Amsterdam.
Burke, R.J. (1995) Guest editorial: 'The sounds of shattering glass: corporate initiatives for advancing managerial women', *Women in Management Review*, 10 (7): 1–53.
Burke, R.J. and McKeen, C.A. (1992) 'Women in management', in C.L. Cooper and I.T. Robertson (eds), *International Review of Industrial and Organizational Psychology*, Wiley, New York.

Burke, R.J. and McKeen, C.A. (1993) 'Career priority patterns among managerial and professional women', *Applied Psychology: an International Review*, 42 (4): 341–352.

Burke, R.J. and McKeen, C.A. (1995) 'Do managerial women prefer women mentors?' *Psychological Reports*, 76: 688–690.

Calás, M.B. and Smircich, L. (1993) 'Dangerous liaisons: the "feminine-in-management" meets "globalization"', *Business Horizons*, 36 (2): 71–81.

Campbell, J.P., Dunnette, M.D., Lawler, E.E., III and Weick, K.E. Jr (1970) *Managerial Behavior, Performance and Effectiveness*, McGraw-Hill, New York.

Chen, M. (1995) *Asian Management Systems*, Routledge, London and New York.

Chusmir, L.H. (1985) 'Motivation of managers: is gender a factor?' *Psychology of Women Quarterly*, 9 (1): 153–159.

Chusmir, L.H. (1987) 'Gender differences in variables affecting job commitment among working men and women', *Journal of Social Psychology*, 126 (1): 87–94.

Chusmir, L.H. and Koberg, C.S. (1992) 'Relationship between self-confidence and sex role identity among managerial women and men', *Journal of Social Psychology*, 131 (6): 781–790.

Davidson, M.J. and Burke, R.J. (1994) *Women in Management. Current Research Issues*, Paul Chapman, London.

De Jong, A. and van Doorne-Huiskes, A. (1989) *Stijl van leidinggeven van vrouwen en mannen*, Rapport Bureau Voorlichting no. 33, Ministerie van Sociale Zaken en Werkgelegenheid.

Dobbins, G.H. (1986) 'Equity vs equality: sex differences in leadership', *Sex Roles*, 15 (9/10): 513–525.

Dobbins, G.H. and Platz, S.J. (1986) 'Sex differences in leadership: how real are they?' *Academy of Management Review*, 11 (1): 118–127.

Donnell, S.M. and Hall, J. (1980) 'Men and women as managers: a significant case of no significant difference', *Organizational Dynamics*, Spring: 60–77.

Dwyer, P. (1996) 'Europe's corporate women. Struggling to get ahead', *Business Week*, April 15: 40–46.

Eagly, A.H. (1995) 'The science and politics of comparing women and men', *American Psychologist*, 50 (3): 145–158.

Eagly, A.H. and Johnson, B.T. (1990) 'Gender and leadership style: a meta-analysis', *Psychological Bulletin*, 108 (2): 233–256.

Eagly, A.H., Karau, S.J., Miner, J.B. and Johnson, B.T. (1994) 'Gender and the motivation to manage in hierarchic organizations: a meta-analysis', *Leadership Quarterly*, 5 (2): 135–159.

Eagly, A.H., Karau, S.J. and Makhijani, M.G. (1995) 'Gender and the effectiveness of leaders: a meta-analysis', *Psychological Bulletin*, 117 (1): 125–145.

Ellemers, N., van den Heuvel, H. and de Gilder, D. (1996) 'Career-oriented versus team-oriented commitment as determinants of work effort and job turnover', unpublished paper, Vrije Universiteit Amsterdam.

ESB (1992) 'Statistiek. De verdeling van formele en informele arbeid', *Economisch Statistische Berichten*, 19 (2): 185–187.

Eurostat (1996) *Labour Force Survey Results 1995*, no. 3c, Eurostat, Luxembourg.

Ferrario, M. (1991) 'Sex differences in leadership style: myth or reality?' *Women in Management Review & Abstracts*, 6 (3): 16–21.

Ferrario, M. (1994) 'Women as managerial leaders', in M.J. Davidson and R.J. Burke (eds), *Women in Management. Current Research Issues*, Paul Chapman, London.

Fierman, J. (1990) 'Do women manage differently?' *Fortune*, 17 December: 115–117.

Fisher, A.H. (1998) 'De top (m/v): de paradox van emoties', *Gedrag en Organisatie*, 11 (4): 203–214.

Fondas, N. (1997) 'Feminization unveiled: management qualities in contemporary writings', *Academy of Management Review*, 22 (1): 257–282.

Frank, E.J. (1988) 'Business students' perceptions of women in management', *Sex Roles*, 19 (1/2): 107–118.

Furnham, A. and Stringfield, P. (1993a) 'Personality and occupational behaviour: Myers-Briggs Type Indicator correlates of managerial practices in two cultures', *Human Relations*, 46 (7): 827–848.

Furnham, A. and Stringfield, P. (1993b) 'Personality and work performance: Myers-Briggs Type Indicator correlates of managerial performance in two cultures', *Personality and Individual Differences*, 14 (1): 145–153.

Gardner, W.L., III, Van Eck Peluchette, J. and Clinebell, S.K. (1994) 'Valuing women in management. An impression management perspective of gender diversity', *Management Communication Quarterly*, 8 (2): 115–164.

Gattiker, U.E. and Larwood, L. (1988) 'Predictors for managers' career mobility, success, and satisfaction', *Human Relations*, 41 (8): 569–591.

Gattiker, U.E. and Larwood, L. (1990) 'Predictors for career achievement in the corporate hierarchy', *Human Relations*, 43 (8): 703–726.

Gerike, A.E. (1983) 'Women in upper-level and middle-level management: a study of salary and status, job-related behaviours, and other factors in comparison with those of male counterparts', Ph.D. thesis, University of Nebraska-Lincoln.

Giacobbe Miller, J. and Wheeler, K.G. (1992) 'Unraveling the mysteries of gender differences in intentions to leave the organization', *Journal of Organizational Behaviour*, 13: 465–478.

Gibson, C.B. (1995) 'An investigation of gender differences in leadership across four countries', *Journal of International Business Studies*, 26 (2): 255–279.

Gist, M.E. and Mitchell, T.R. (1992) 'Self-efficacy: a theoretical analysis of its determinants and malleability', *Academy of Management Review*, 17 (2): 183–211.

Goffee, R. and Nicholson, N. (1994) 'Career development in male and female managers – convergence or collapse?' in M.J. Davidson and R.J. Burke (eds), *Women in Management. Current Research Issues*, Paul Chapman, London.

Grant, J. (1988) 'Women as managers: what they can offer organizations', *Organizational Dynamics*, 16 (3): 56–63.

Gutek, B.A. (1993) 'Changing the status of women in management', *Applied Psychology: an International Review*, 42 (4): 301–311.

Hackett, G., Betz, N.E., O'Halloran, M.S. and Romac, D.S. (1990) 'Effects of verbal and mathematics task performance on task and career self-efficacy and interest', *Journal of Counseling Psychology*, 37 (2): 169–177.

Helgesen, S. (1990) *The Female Advantage: Women's Ways of Leadership*, Doubleday Currency, New York.

Hellman, M.E., Block, C.J., Martell, R.F. and Simon, M.C. (1989) 'Has anything changed? Current characterizations of men, women and managers', *Journal of Applied Psychology*, 74 (6): 935–942.

Hoffman, L.R. and Watson, C. (1996) 'The dilemma of the informed woman'. Paper presented at the 1996 Academy of Management Meetings, Rutgers University.

Jacobs, J.A. (1992) 'Women's entry into management: trends in earnings, authority and values among salaried managers', *Administrative Science Quarterly*, 37 (June): 282–301.

Jenkins, J.M. (1993) 'Self-monitoring and turnover: the impact of personality on the intent to leave', *Journal of Organizational Behaviour*, 14: 83–91.

Kanter, R.M. (1977) *Men and Women of the Corporation*, Basic Books, New York.

Kaufmann, G., Isaksen, S.G. and Lauer, K. (1996) 'Testing the glass ceiling effect on gender differences in upper level management: the case of innovator orientation', *European Journal of Work and Organizational Psychology*, 5 (1): 29–41.

Kilduff, M. and Day, D.V. (1994) 'Do chameleons get ahead? The effects of self-monitoring on managerial careers', *Academy of Management Journal*, 37 (4): 1047–1060.

Kirchmeyer, C. (1996) 'Determinants of managerial career success, firm evidence and explanation of male/female differences'. Paper presented at the 1996 Academy of Management Meetings, Wayne State University.

Korabik, K. and Ayman, R. (1989) 'Should women managers have to act like men?' *Journal of Management Development*, 8 (6): 23–32.

Korabik, K., Baril, G.L. and Watson, C. (1993) 'Managers' conflict management style and leadership effectiveness: the moderating effects of gender', *Sex Roles*, 29 (5/6): 405–420.

Leavitt, J.A. (1982) 'Comparisons of men and women managers', in *Women in Management: an Annotated Bibliography and Source List*, Oryx Press, Phoenix, AZ.

Lefkowitz, J. (1994) 'Sex-related differences in job attitudes and dispositional variables: now you see them...', *Academy of Management Journal*, 37 (2): 323–349.

Lipman-Blumen, J., Handley-Laken, A. and Leavitt, H.J. (1983) 'Achieving styles in men and women: a model, an instrument and some findings', in J.T. Spence (ed.), *Achievement and Achievement Motives. Psychological and Sociological Approaches*, W.H. Freeman, San Francisco.

Marsden, P.V., Kalleberg, A.L. and Cook, C.R. (1993) 'Gender differences in organizational commitment. Influences of work positions and family roles', *Work and Occupations*, 20 (3): 368–390.

McCauley, C.D., Ruderman, M.N., Ohlott, P.J. and Morrow, J.E. (1994) 'Assessing the developmental components of managerial jobs', *Journal of Applied Psychology*, 79 (4): 544–560.

McClelland, D.C. and Boyatzis, R.E. (1982) 'Leadership motive pattern and long-term success in management', *Journal of Applied Psychology*, 67 (6): 737–743.

McCrae, R.R. and John, O.P. (1992) 'An introduction to the Five-Factor model and its applications', *Journal of Personality*, 60 (2): 175–215.

McKeen, C.A. and Burke, R.J. (1989) 'Mentor relationships in organisations: issues, strategies and prospects for women', *Journal of Management Development*, 8 (6): 33–42.

Melamed, T. (1996) 'Career success: an assessment of a gender-specific model', *Journal of Occupational and Organizational Psychology*, 69: 217–242.

Metze, M. (1994) 'Zoek de leider. De consequenties van moderne management-stijlen', *Business Topics*, 1 (1): 10–21.

Meyer, J.P., Allen, N.J. and Smith, C.A. (1993) 'Commitment to organizations and occupations: extension and test of a three-component conceptualization', *Journal of Applied Psychology*, 78 (4): 538–551.

Miner, J.B. (1993) *Role Motivation Theories*, Routledge, London.

Mintzberg, H. (1994) 'Rounding out the manager's job', *Sloan Management Review*, Fall: 11–26.

Mintzberg, H. (1996) 'Musings on management', *Harvard Business Review*, July–August: 61–67.

Moir, A. and Jessel, D. (1990) *Het grote verschil tussen man en vrouw: waarom de hersenstructuur mannen en vrouwen zo verschillend maakt*, Zomer & Keuning, Ede.

Morrison, A.M. and von Glinow, M.A. (1990) 'Women and minorities in management', *American Psychologist*, 45 (2): 200–208.

Nebenzahl, I.D., Jaffe, E.D. and Gotesdyner, H. (1993) 'Perceptions of Israeli male and female managerial behaviour in small group interactions', *International Studies of Management & Organization*, 23 (3): 97–111.

Nichols, N.A. (1993) 'Whatever happened to Rosie the Riveter?' *Harvard Business Review*, July–August: 54–62.

Noe, R.A. (1988) 'Women and mentoring: a review and research agenda', *Academy of Management Review*, 13 (1): 65–78.

Noordegraaf, M. (1994) 'Functioning of male and female managers in the public and private sector', unpublished explorative research report, Erasmus University, Rotterdam.

Nordvik, H. (1997) 'Personality dimensions and leadership tasks: interrelated variables or common concepts?' Poster presented at the 1997 Eighth European Congress of Work and Organizational Psychology, Verona, Italy.

Nye, J.L. and Forsyth, D.R. (1991) 'The effects of prototype-based biases on leadership appraisals: a test of leadership categorization theory', *Small Group Research*, 22 (3): 360–379.

Ohlott, P.J., Ruderman, M.N. and McCauley, C.D. (1994) 'Gender differences in managers' developmental job experiences', *Academy of Management Journal*, 37 (1): 46–67.

O'Reilly, C. and Chatman, J. (1994) 'Working smarter and harder: a longitudinal study', *Administrative Science Quarterly*, 39: 603–627.

Penley, L.E., Alexander, E.R., Jernigan, I.E. and Henwood, C.I. (1991) 'Communication abilities of managers: the relationship to performance', *Journal of Management*, 17 (1): 57–76.

Perrault, M.R. and Irwin, J.K. (1996) *Gender differences at work. Are men and women really that different? Analysis and findings from a study of women and men.* Published on the Internet; site address http://www.ateamware.com, Advanced Teamware Inc.

Perry, E.L., Davis-Blake, A. and Kulik, C.T. (1994) 'Explaining gender-based selection decisions: a synthesis of contextual and cognitive approaches', *Academy of Management Review*, 19 (4): 786–820.

Peters, T. (1996) 'We hold these truths to be self-evident (more or less)', *Organizational Dynamics*, 25 (1): 27–32.

Plesch, B.E.C. (1994) 'Vrouwelijke managers – de toekomst'. Paper presented at the 1994 NSC Conference on 'Women in Management', Den Haag, the Netherlands, Ministerie van Binnenlandse Zaken.

Powell, G.N. (1988) *Women and Men in Management*, Sage, Newbury Park, CA.

Powell, G.N. (1990) 'One more time: do female and male managers differ?' *Academy of Management Executive*, 4 (3): 68–75.

Powell, G.N. and Butterfield, D.A. (1994) 'Investigating the "glass ceiling" phenomenon: an empirical study of actual promotions to top management', *Academy of Management Journal*, 37 (1): 68–86.

Pratch, L. (1996) 'Active coping and leadership effectiveness: a structural psychological approach', ISSWOV Conference Proceedings/Montreal, pp. 351–360.

Presley Noble, B. (1993) 'Management. The debate over "la différence": Rosener vs. Powell', *New York Times*, section 3: 6.

Ragins, B.R. (1989) 'Barriers to mentoring: the female manager's dilemma', *Human Relations*, 42 (1): 1–22.

Ragins, B.R. and Cotton, J.L. (1991) 'Easier said than done: gender differences in perceived barriers to gaining a mentor', *Academy of Management Journal*, 34 (4): 939–951.

Ragins, B.R. and Cotton, J.L. (1993) 'Wanted: mentors for women', *Personnel Journal*, April: 20.

Ragins, B.R. and Scandura, T.A. (1994) 'Gender differences in expected outcomes of mentoring relationships', *Academy of Management Journal*, 37 (4): 957–971.

Riordan, C., Gross, T. and Maloney, C.C. (1994) 'Self-monitoring, gender, and the personal consequences of impression management', *American Behavioural Scientist*, 37 (5): 715–725.

Rojahn, K.M. and Willemsen, T. (1994) 'The evaluation of effectiveness and likability of gender-role congruent and gender-role incongruent leaders', *Sex Roles*, 30 (1/2): 109–119.

Ronen, S. (1986) *Comparative and Multinational Management*, Wiley, New York.

Rosen, B., Miguel, M. and Peirde, E. (1989) 'Stemming the exodus of women managers', *Human Resource Management*, 28 (4): 475–491.

Rosener, J.B. (1990) 'Ways women lead', *Harvard Business Review*, November–December: 119–125.

Rosener, J.B. (1991) 'The valued ways men and women lead', *HR Magazine*, 36 (June): 147–149.

Rosenthal, P., Guest, D. and Peccei, R. (1996) 'Gender differences in managers' causal explanations for their work performance: a study in two organizations', *Journal of Occupational and Organizational Psychology*, 69: 145–151.

Rosin, H.Z. and Korabik, K. (1991) 'Workplace variables, affective responses and intention to leave among women managers', *Journal of Occupational Psychology*, 64: 317–330.

Ruderman, M.N., Ohlott, P.J. and McCauley, C.D. (1990) 'Assessing opportunities for leadership development', in K.E. Clark and M.B. Clark (eds), *Measures of Leadership*, Leadership Library of America/Center for Creative Leadership, West Orange, NJ.

Ruf, B.M. and Chusmir, L.H. (1991) 'Dimensions of success and motivation needs among managers', *Journal of Psychology*, 125 (6): 631–640.

Ruijs, A. (1990) *Vrouwen en schoolmanagement*, Swets & Zeitlinger, Amsterdam.

Russel, J.E.A., Rush, M.C. and Herd, A.M. (1988) 'An exploration of women's expectations of effective male and female leadership', *Sex Roles*, 18 (5/6): 279–287.

Schein, V.E. and Mueller, R. (1992) 'Sex role stereotyping and requisite management characteristics: a cross-cultural look', *Journal of Organizational Behaviour*, 13: 439–447.

Schneer, J.A. and Reitman, F. (1993) 'Effects of alternate family structures on managerial career paths', *Academy of Management Journal*, 36 (4): 830–843.

Schneer, J.A. and Reitman, F. (1996) 'Do today's managers have a strong work ethic?' Paper presented at the Academy of Management Meetings, Cincinnati, OH.

Schwartz, F.N. (1989) 'Executives and organizations: management women and the new facts of life', *Harvard Business Review*, January–February: 65–76.

Schwartz, F.N. (1992) 'Women as a business imperative', *Harvard Business Review*, March–April: 105–113.

Shellenbarger, S. (1995) 'Sales offer women fairer pay, but bias lingers', *Wall Street Journal*, January 24: B1.

Snabilié, B. (1997) 'Carrière en kinderen: hoe is het mogelijk?!' *VVAO Mededelingen*, 63 (1): 5–6.

Snyder, M. and Gangestad, S. (1986) 'On the nature of self-monitoring: matters of assessment, matters of validity', *Journal of Personality and Social Psychology*, 51 (1): 125–139.

Statham, A. (1987) 'The gender model revisited: differences in the management styles of men and women', *Sex Roles*, 16 (7/8): 409–429.

Stevens, G.E. and Brenner, O.C. (1990) 'An empirical investigation of the motivation to manage among blacks and women in business schools', *Educational and Psychological Measurement*, 50 (4): 879–886.

Stone, D.N. (1994) 'Overconfidence in initial self-efficacy judgments: effects on decision processes and performance', *Organizational Behaviour and Human Decision Processes*, 59: 452–474.

Stroh, L.K., Brett, J.M. and Reilly, A.H. (1992) 'All the right stuff: a comparison of female and male managers' career progression', *Journal of Applied Psychology*, 77 (3): 251–260.

Sutherland, E. and Veroff, J. (1985) 'Achievement motivation and sex roles', in V.E. O'Leary, R.K. Unger and B.S. Wallston (eds), *Women, Gender and Social Psychology*, Lawrence Erlbaum, Hillsdale, NJ.

Tavris, C. (1991) 'The mismeasure of woman: paradoxes and perspectives in the study of gender', in J.D. Goodchilds (eds), *Psychological Perspectives on Human Diversity in America*, APA, Washington, DC.

Tharenou, P. (1996) 'Is there a link between family structures and women's and men's career advancement?' Paper presented at the Academy of Management Meetings, Cincinnati, OH.

Tharenou, P., Latimer, S. and Conroy, D. (1994) 'How do you make it to the top? An examination of influences on women's and men's managerial advancement', *Academy of Management Journal*, 37 (4): 899–931.

Thooft, L. (1994) 'De manager van de jaren '90 is een vrouw', *Marie Claire*, 3 (Maart): 77–82.

Tsui, A.S. and Ashford, S.J. (1994) 'Adaptive self-regulation: a process view of managerial effectiveness', *Journal of Management*, 20 (1): 93–121.

Tuckman, B.W. and Sexton, T.L. (1992) 'Self-believers are self-motivated; self-doubters are not', *Personality and Individual Differences*, 13 (4): 425–428.

Tullett, A.D. (1995) 'The adaptive-innovative (A-I) cognitive styles of male and female project managers: some implications for the management of change', *Journal of Occupational and Organizational Psychology*, 68 (4): 359–366.

Turban, D.B. and Dougherty, T.W. (1994) 'Role of protégée personality in receipt of mentoring and career success', *Academy of Management Journal*, 37 (3): 688–702.

Urch Druskat, V. (1994) 'Gender and leadership style: transformational and transactional leadership in the Roman Catholic Church', *Leadership Quarterly*, 5 (2): 99–119.

Van Vianen, A.E.M. and Keizer, W.A.J. (1992) 'De ambitie van mannen en vrouwen voor een leidinggevende functie in traditioneel door mannen beheerste werkomgevingen', *Gedrag en Organisatie*, 5 (6): 382–402.

Vasil, L. (1992) 'Self-efficacy expectations and causal attributions for achievement among male and female university faculty', *Journal of Vocational Behaviour*, 41: 259–269.

Vinkenburg, C.J. (1997) 'Managerial behaviour and effectiveness. Determinants, measurement issues and gender differences', PhD thesis, Vrije Universiteit Amsterdam, Tinbergen Instituut/Thesis Publishers.

Vinnicombe, S. (1988) 'What exactly are the differences in male and female working styles?' *Women in Management Review*, 3 (1): 13–21.

Vossen, M. (1998) 'Topvrouwen. Vrouwelijk managementtalent loopt stuk op mannencultuur', *Management Team*, 20 (8): 64–70.

Watson, C. (1988) 'When a woman is the boss. Dilemmas in taking charge', *Group & Organization Studies*, 13 (2): 163–181.

Wazienski, R.J. (1987) 'Structural and individual determinants of commitment to work', PhD thesis, University of Kansas.

Wentling, R.M. (1992) 'Women in middle management: their career development and aspirations', *Business Horizons*, January–February: 47–54.

Williams, J.R. and Levy, P.E. (1992) 'The effects of perceived system knowledge on the agreement between self-ratings and supervisor ratings', *Personnel Psychology*, 45 (4): 835–847.

Winther, D.A. and Green, S.B. (1987) 'Another look at gender-related differences in leadership behaviour', *Sex Roles*, 16 (1–2): 41–56.

10

Women Corporate Directors: Current Research and Future Directions

Diana Bilimoria and Jane V. Wheeler

While research on the subject of women corporate directors has become more popular in the past few years, overall the representation and status of women at the highest corporate levels has improved extremely slowly. Several years of empirical work have yielded a slew of survey statistics, experiential descriptions, profiles of successful women directors, as well as a few correlational studies, yet cumulatively these have resulted in few changes in the predominantly male-oriented upper echelons of the corporate structure. In this chapter, we review the overall patterns forwarded by existing research on women corporate directors and explore the nature of future research likely to render the insights most conducive for positive change in corporate behaviour and arrangements. Simply put, we seek to answer the question: Given limited research resources, what kinds of research are likely to spur improvement in the representation and status of women corporate directors?

In the first section of this chapter we systematically review the extant empirical literature on women corporate directors. In the second section, we outline directions for future research, describing the characteristics and content areas of impactful research on women corporate directors.

Current research on women corporate directors

Two streams of contemporary research on women at the corporate governance apex have begun to emerge: research on the representation of women on corporate boards, and research on the status of women corporate directors.

The representation of women on corporate boards

In the past decade or so, there has been a general upsurge in the amount of corporate interest evinced in women directors (see Ghiloni, 1984; *Nation's Business*, 1990; Romano, 1993; Lear, 1994; Tifft, 1994). Executive recruitment firms note increases in the numbers of corporate searches for women directoral candidates (e.g. Schwartz, 1980; *Business Week*, 1992; Evans, 1995; *Forbes*, 1995). For example, two-thirds of the searches to fill directors' seats at a prominent recruitment firm in 1993 were for female candidates (Evans, 1995), while another firm reported an increase from 11 per cent to 40 per cent since 1986, in officer-level searches that include women candidates (*Business Week*, 1992). Institutional investors and other shareholder associations have also begun to pressure corporate boards to increase the representation and use of women directors. Corporate governance reform campaigns by investors such as TIAA/CREF, US Trust Co., and church groups affiliated with the Interfaith Center on Corporate Responsibility have targeted specific companies for shareholder proposals aimed at increasing board diversity (see Browder, 1995; Dogar, 1997). The Investor Responsibility Research Center's (1993) survey on voting by institutional investors on corporate governance issues indicated that 39 per cent of respondents, up from 26 per cent in 1992, said that the lack of women and/or minority members on a board may affect their voting decisions, and 4 per cent of respondents noted that their guidelines require them to withhold their votes in such cases.

Empirical research in this area has been concerned with three major issues.

The contributions of women corporate directors Academic and popular writings indicate that positive business and political impact accrues from increased numbers of women at the top (Schwartz, 1980; Morrison, 1992; Fernandez, 1993; Mattis, 1993; Bilimoria, 1995; Cassell, 1997). Women directors help corporations gain competitive advantage by dealing more effectively with diversity in their product and labour markets (Morrison, 1992; Fernandez, 1993). Women corporate directors function as champions for change on women's issues, keeping issues of recruitment, retention and advancement of women high on the board's agenda and serving as role models, mentors and champions of high-performing women in the organization (Schwartz, 1980; Catalyst, 1993, 1995; Mattis, 1993; Burke, 1994a, 1994b; Tifft, 1994). In-depth interviews with 25 Fortune CEOs indicated that women directors bring strategic input to the boards on which they serve, and generate more productive discourse (Catalyst, 1995). Other writing suggests that, because the average female board member is younger than her male counterpart (Mattis 1993; Ibrahim and Angelides, 1994), boards benefit from the infusion of new ideas and approaches into business deliberations (Schwartz and Harrison, 1986; Burke, 1993, 1994b; Ibrahim and Angelides, 1994).

The presence of women corporate directors Despite these advantages, relatively few women serve on corporate boards (von Glinow and Mercer, 1988; *Directors & Boards*, 1992). Women occupy only 10.6 per cent of the seats at Fortune 500 board tables, up from 10.2 per cent in 1996 (Catalyst, 1997). While 84 per cent of these largest industrials have a woman director (Catalyst, 1997), up from 81 per cent in 1996 and 69 per cent in 1993 (Catalyst, 1993, 1996a, 1997), the majority of these firms have only one woman director (Collingwood, 1996; Catalyst, 1997), thereby furthering the likelihood of the tokenized treatment of women directors. Only one Fortune 500 company has achieved parity on its board with five women and five men directors (Catalyst, 1997). And only 1 per cent of inside directors on Fortune 500 boards (12 out of the 1,199 individuals drawn from a firm's top management) are women (Catalyst, 1997), signalling that the internal corporate board pipeline for qualified women top managers is still a fairly hollow conduit.

Despite being the most likely companies to have women directors on account of their size and visibility, more than 80 of the Fortune 500 companies do not have a single woman board member (Catalyst, 1997). Only 444 women occupy 643 of the 6,081 total seats on Fortune 500 boards (Catalyst, 1997), thereby continuing the conventional spread of a few prominent women over multiple corporate boards. Additionally, even those few women who reach the corporate governance apex tend to be utilized in sex-biased, stereotypical ways, serving to disproportionately staff the public affairs committee and under-proportionately staff committees such as the executive, compensation and finance committees of Fortune 300 boards (Bilimoria and Piderit, 1994). Clearly, these more detailed statistics and findings are in contrast to the popular media rhetoric suggesting that 'the fight is over. The battle is won. Women are now accepted as outside directors in the preponderance of American corporate boardrooms' (Lear, 1994:10; see also Romano, 1993).

Additionally, change has been slow to come. The rate of representation of women on the boards of the largest corporations increased only marginally (by 3 percentage points) over the five years from 1984 to 1988 (Catalyst, 1989). *Human Resources Magazine Update* (1992) reported that the number of women serving on the boards of Fortune industrial and service companies consistently remained slightly less than 400 during the period 1985–92. Catalyst (1997) identified 1993–95 as the years in which corporations undertook a big push to add women to their boards (an increase of about 6 per cent). Subsequently there has been stagnation in the growth rate (in 1997, the number of Fortune 500 board seats held by women increased by less than half a percentage point over the previous year). Most illustrative of the perceived superfluity of women corporate directors is the fact that while the number of Fortune 500/Service 500 directorships held by women increased from 721 in 1993 to 814 in 1994, the total number of directorships during this period increased from 11,715 to 11,790, suggesting that the bulk of the gains in women directorships came from the addition of new seats rather than the replacement of exiting men directors.

The overall picture is even more gloomy with regard to high-level insiders (corporate officers and directors). A 1990 report in Fortune identified a mere 19 women (one-half of 1 per cent) among the highest-paid officers and directors of the 1,000 largest US industrial and service companies (Fierman, 1990). Several years later this number had only marginally improved: 47 women were among the five most highly compensated officers in each company, amounting to less than 2 per cent of the 2,500 top earners in 1996 (Catalyst, 1996b) and to only about 1 per cent of inside directors in 1997 (Catalyst, 1997).

The expertise of women corporate directors   In contrast to the small gains in representation over the past several years, as a group women have vastly improved their qualifications for directorship (Catalyst, 1993; Mattis, 1993, 1997), making them considerably 'less likely to be window-dressing' (Burke, 1993: 8). In a recent comparison of the background characteristics of women directors between data obtained in 1977 (Burson-Marsteller, 1977) and data collected in 1990–91, Mattis (1993, 1997) noted a narrowing of the age difference between men and women directors. This research also found that contemporary women directors are more likely to have a focused, business-oriented career history as compared with earlier women directors. In a recent study, women were found to be equally, if not better, qualified than men on the director characteristics of type, occupation, business directorships, and non-business directorships, although their tenure on corporate boards was shorter than men's (Bilimoria and Piderit, 1994; see also Kesner, 1988).

The few women who gain entry to a corporate board continue to be seemingly so exceptionally qualified that they are highly sought after. In the Catalyst (1994) survey of the 1,000 largest firms, 570 women held 814 seats (1.42 firms per woman); in 1997, 444 women filled 643 Fortune 500 seats (1.45 firms per woman) (Catalyst, 1997). A 1992 survey of 496 companies in the Standard and Poor's 500 revealed that 282 (6.3 per cent) of the 4,473 individuals serving as directors were women, with approximately 20 per cent of these serving on four or more boards of public companies, and 5 per cent serving on at least six boards (Investor Responsibility Research Center, 1993).

Despite the positive trends in women's qualifications for directorship, CEOs continue to believe that the available pool of qualified women candidates is extremely limited (Mattis, 1993, 1997). In a recent survey, one third of the Canadian chief executives studied estimated the current size of the pool of potential women directors available to them at 50 or fewer women, and 80 per cent thought the pool was less than 250 women (Burke, 1994a). In another study, nearly half the US CEOs studied believed that the pool consisted of less than 250 women (Catalyst, 1993). These findings are particularly interesting in light of the more than 500 women currently serving on the boards of the largest business and service enterprises.

The status of women corporate directors

While women's boardroom representation is an overt issue requiring research attention, it is also important to address the less visible issues pertinent to their advance in corporate power circles, such as the status of women directors. Status issues pertain to the effective utilization of women on the board, and refer implicitly to the value placed on them by those holding power in the organization. The empirical research in this area has been concerned with three issues.

Role and identity issues Empirical research has indicated considerable role confusion and anxiety associated with and by women board members. While many women board members view themselves as directors, and not women directors (Burson-Marsteller, 1977; Collins, 1978; Sethi et al., 1981; Catalyst, 1993; Bilimoria and Huse, 1997), many believe that an important reason they were recruited is because they are women (Sethi et al., 1981; Mitchell, 1984). Despite the fear cited by many CEOs (that women will disrupt an otherwise co-operative boardroom climate by adversarially raising difficult women's issues) as the reason for not hiring women directors (cf. Dobrzynski, 1993; Briggs, 1994;

Burke, 1994a; Lear, 1994), and despite women directors' own consciousness of the dangers of being perceived as having a women's agenda or being a single-issue woman (Burson-Marsteller, 1977; Catalyst, 1993; Mattis, 1993), these women recognize their responsibility to address issues relating to women's recruitment, retention, development and advancement in organizations and see these as appropriate business issues for board discussion (Mattis, 1993; Burke, 1997a). This role confusion is furthered since 'whether women serving on corporate boards have, as part of their implicit mandate, responsibilities for leveling the playing field for women in these organizations...is not routinely specified in the job description of women directors. Some organizations would look on these initiatives favorably; others would not. Some women directors would feel comfortable with these activities; others would not' (Burke, 1993: 12).

Token treatment issues With regard to their effective performance as board members, the empirical literature indicates that women directors often face the additional burden of tokenism: being the only woman or one of a very small minority. Only 36 per cent (181 companies) of Fortune 500 companies had two or more women directors in 1997, up from 177 (35 per cent) in 1996 (Catalyst, 1997). Of the Fortune 1000 corporations, only 198 (19.8 per cent) had more than one woman (Catalyst, 1994). A 1995 survey of major corporations (in the manufacturing, service, high tech, financial, and utilities sectors) in nine countries indicated that 29 per cent of the responding firms had one woman director, 11 per cent had two women directors, and 2 per cent had three or more women on their boards (National Association of Corporate Directors, 1995). As Juanita Kreps, an early woman director who has served on numerous corporate boards notes, one woman on a board is not likely to change corporate policy (in her speech entitled, 'Help! There's a woman in the boardroom', cited in Mattis, 1993). Additionally, interviews of women directors reveal the loneliness and difficulties they experienced as the only woman on a board (Sethi et al., 1981; see also Tifft, 1994).

By virtue of being placed in groups in which they are significantly outnumbered by men, women become tokens and are faced with predictable treatment from others, which forces them into roles that limit their probabilities of success (Kanter, 1977). However qualified, token women are subject to excessive scrutiny, their differences from men become highlighted and polarized, and their attributes are distorted so that they become entrapped in stereotypical roles. Women directors, even though they are members of the innermost circles of corporate power, are subject to these phenomena influencing their effective performance as corporate directors.

Sex-biased utilization issues The empirical literature has examined the status of women directors as it relates to their appointment for the various tasks of corporate governance. A recent study has questioned the appropriate utilization of women corporate directors to staff the board's standing committees (Bilimoria and Piderit, 1994). After controlling for a number of relevant experience-based director characteristics, this study found significant sex differences in committee memberships, prompting the authors to conclude that even the few women who achieve the lofty status of corporate director are still not free from sex-based bias: their sex often keeps them off their boards' powerful committees (e.g., compensation, executive, and finance committees) and propels them toward less central ones such as the public affairs committee (Bilimoria and Piderit, 1994, 1995). Another study found that committees having women were generally larger than committees not having women; these authors concluded that committees were made larger by adding a woman rather than by replacing a man (Sethi et al., 1981).

Analysis of current research

Methodologically, existing empirical research on women corporate directors may be divided into two streams of work: descriptive reporting and correlational analyses. Table 10.1 highlights a sampling of descriptive reports, comprising (a) demographic descriptions of the gender composition of corporate boards, (b) surveys of attitudes and views held by CEOs towards women directors, and (c) surveys of women directors' attitudes, views, characteristics, and experiences and profiles of women directors. This stream of work is largely characterized by descriptive statistics (obtained from corporate surveys and analyses of corporate annual reports or other published materials) and anecdotal findings (from questionnaire and interview protocols administered to individual female or male board members).

A second stream of empirical work has utilized more analytic approaches. Many corporate governance studies routinely employ director gender (or diversity in board member composition) as one among a number of variables investigating a specific issue, such as acquisition decisions or corporate performance. Other studies have focused more directly on investigating women corporate directors' position and value on the board. These more focused analyses, summarized in Table 10.2, reveal gender-specific patterns in board composition and organization, director roles and functioning, and board performance.

Our analysis of the descriptive statistics and anecdotal evidence presented in Table 10.1, as well as the correlational studies reported in Table 10.2, yield some surprising insights. First, despite relevance to specific corporate governance areas investigated, overall there are simply too few theoretically rigorous studies to yield cumulatively powerful patterns and conclusions. At this time, women corporate directors remain an undertheorized and understudied domain of corporate governance and policy.

Second, despite continued difficulty and variation associated with even simple counting and reporting of the exact number of women on corporate boards, survey-type reports have succeeded in methodically documenting important facts about the representation and status of women directors. However, other than reporting the facts of current practice and phenomena, such descriptive statistics and survey findings generally do not advance the theoretical body of knowledge and fail to provide practitioners with constructive perspectives and tools for change. As Lawler (1985: 10) suggests regarding the production of facts through research, 'the justification for this endeavor is that facts are ultimately a useful product because they allow theory testing, theory construction, and of course, the improvement of practice. It is quite possible, however, that the best way to

TABLE 10.1 *Representative summary of survey-type studies on women directors*

Authors' names	Questions asked	Area of corporate governance studied	Methodology	Relevant results and conclusions
Burke (1994b)	Examined factors relating to the appointment of women to corporate boards: (1) criteria used in recruiting their first female directors; (2) how the names of these individuals were brought to the attention of the CEO; (3) important factors in recruiting a female director; (4) issues that might benefit from the perspective of a female director; (5) the impact of having a woman on the board on a variety of issues; (6) reasons why more women are not directors.	Board composition and impact of women directors.	Surveyed 66 male Canadian CEOs of private sector companies (obtained from the 1991 Financial Post *Directory of Directors*) having at least one woman on their boards. Various scales (e.g. 1 = Very important, 2 = Somewhat important, 3 = Not important) were used.	Business experience is the most important factor in finding and appointing female directors, followed by high visibility, previous corporate board experience, making a statement to customers/clients, making a statement to stockholders, and making a statement to management women. The most common ways that a female was brought to CEOs' attention were recommendations from other board members and they were known personally by the CEO. The most desirable profiles when recruiting a female director were: a woman who runs a successful small business; followed by a woman with high-level line experience in a major company; a woman who heads a division of a major company; and a woman with high-level international business experience. The strongest effects of having women on boards were reported in making female employees feel more positive about the company's commitment to advancing managerial women, making shareholders feel more positive about the company, and increasing board sensitivity to issues affecting female employees.
Burson-Marsteller (1977)	What are the backgrounds of women directors? What has been their experience to date	The experience of women directors.	Interviewed 31 women directors of the Fortune 500 industrials, the 50 largest	Women directors are strong-willed and highly competent individuals. A number expressed special interest in promoting the rights

(*Contd.*)

(Contd.)

Authors' names	Questions asked	Area of corporate governance studied	Methodology	Relevant results and conclusions
	on corporate boards? Does the fact that they are women change the way they approach their directorships? What has been the experience of the companies themselves? What advice do women directors offer to companies which are interested in recruiting women directors? What advice do women directors offer to younger career oriented women who would like-to get to the top and themselves serve as corporate directors?		banks and 50 largest retailers. Did not include those who had served for less than one year or were wives or daughters of company founders.	of women workers or bringing a more humanistic view to the boardroom. The women give little emphasis to a specific 'woman's viewpoint'. Few of the women have been placed on committees that might be considered traditional 'women's areas': consumer affairs, social responsibility, and contributions. Their heaviest representation is on the executive, compensation and audit committees, which usually are among the most important and powerful. Almost every woman said her first contact was with the chairman or president. The women serve an average of 2.5 directorships each. Average age was 53 years. The women show a level of educational success similar to that of male directors. Unlike men, their career fields are more diverse and less business-oriented. Tokenism is an issue. Some women believed being a woman is a specific asset as a corporate director, broadening the board's sensitivity and awareness. Equal numbers of women were emphatic that it was their specific career skills, not being female, which made them qualified.
Catalyst Annual Studies	Provide information about the numbers of women on corporate boards of Fortune 500 & Service 500 companies.	Board composition.	Survey information collected on the Fortune 500/Service 500 companies about the number and names of female board members and the total	In 1997, women held 10.6% of Fortune board seats, and 84% of Fortune companies had at least one woman director. The number of companies with at least one woman director increased for the fifth straight year although the rate of change has

(Contd.)

Authors' names	Questions asked	Area of corporate governance studied	Methodology	Relevant results and conclusions
				decreased. The actual number of women directors occupying board seats increased from 545 in 1994 to 643 in 1997. Women account for only 1% of inside corporate directors. More than one-third of the Fortune companies had two or more women corporate directors.
Catalyst (1993)	How can business leaders' awareness of the many women qualified for board service be increased? How can female directors help address the bottom-line needs of companies? How can women seeking directorships learn to best position themselves for these opportunities? Why is the process of increasing women's representation on corporate boards taking so long? How can the rate of change be increased?	Women directors of Fortune 500/Service 500 companies.	The study began with in-depth telephone interviews with 15 female directors, selected at random from a list of female directors of the Fortune 500/Service 500 companies. A 30-question survey was then sent to all female directors of Fortune 500/Service 500 companies for whom a mailing address could be identified (394). There was a 41% response rate. The survey included questions about the women's backgrounds, the boards on which they served, their expectations of the roles they play on boards, their experiences as corporate directors, and their relationships with other board members and	(1) The pool of current female directors is significantly bigger than it was in 1977, the date of the last known study of women on corporate boards. More women have significant business experience gained from leadership positions in corporations or in companies they have founded; (2) women indicate they are motivated to join boards because of interest in the company, or because they want to broaden their skills – not necessarily because they want to effect change for women. However, once women are on boards, they often address a range of non-traditional board issues, including equal opportunity for high-performing women and minorities and company policy on work/life balance. 85% or more of female directors believe that equal opportunity for high-performing women and minorities is an appropriate issue for boards to address; (3) female directors are only slightly younger (average age of 56) than their male counterparts (average age of 59). Female directors also are highly

Authors' names	Questions asked	Area of corporate governance studied	Methodology	Relevant results and conclusions
			with management women in the companies for which they are directors. Additional information on the background characteristics of 304 female directors for whom such data were available was gathered from corporations' annual reports and proxy statements. Following the analysis of the female directors' data, Catalyst piloted a survey for CEOs of Fortune 500/Service 500 companies about their recruitment of and experiences with female directors. An 8-question survey was distributed to CEOs by high-level women and female directors selected by Catalyst. Of the 130 questionnaires that were fielded, 46 were returned to Catalyst, for a response rate of 35 %. What is the background and experience of the current pool of female directors? What are the processes corporate boards use to identify outside directors? To what extent do these processes work for or against the recruitment of female directors? What are the expectations held by female directors and CEOs regarding female directors as advocates of women's workplace	educated, with 89% holding at least one degree and 25% holding three or more degrees. Interestingly, 25% of the female directors attended a women's college as either undergraduate or graduate students as compared to 2.5% in the general population of female college students; (4) 69% of female directors responding to Catalyst's survey are married; 15% are single, having never married; 9% are divorced and 6% are widowed. Almost three-quarters of the female directors have children; (5) CEOs generally look to their peers – other active or retired CEOs – to fill directorships.

Authors' names	Questions asked	Area of corporate governance studied	Methodology	Relevant results and conclusions
			issues? What role can female directors play in encouraging the recruitment, retention, development and advancement of women within the company's management ranks?	
Fierman (1990)	How many women are included as the highest-paid officers and directors of large corporations?	Board composition. Status of women directors.	Fortune examined 1990 proxy statements of the 799 public companies on its combined lists of the 1,000 largest US industrial and service companies.	Of the 4,012 people listed as the highest-paid officers and directors of their companies, 19 (less than half of 1%) were women.
Investor Responsibility Research Center (1993)	What are institutional investors issues? on corporate governance issues?	Board composition	Surveyed 496 companies in the Standard & Poor 500.	An increasing number of shareholders are considering board diversity when determining their vote for the board: 39% of the respondents, up from 26% in 1992, said that if a board lacks minority and/or women members, it may affect their voting decision. 4% of the respondents said their guidelines require them to withhold their votes in such a case. Two-hundred and eighty two, or 6.3%, of the 4,473 individuals serving as directors were women. Fifty-six of the female directors identified served on four or more boards of public companies, and 15 of those served on the boards of at least six public companies. Fifty-seven of the women, or 20% of the total were university professors or administrators. Twenty-six served as CEOs of either public or private companies, and another 25 were self-employed. For 15 of the directors, their

Authors' names	Questions asked	Area of corporate governance studied	Methodology	Relevant results and conclusions
				primary occupation was law, and for five others, government service.
Sethi, Swanson and Harrigan (1981)	Explored the extent of the presence of women directors on corporate boards, the degree and type of their involvement in the working of the board, and the personal experiences of women directors and their perception of how they might have influenced the workings of their boards.	The composition, structure and operating procedures of boards. The experiences of women directors.	Information derived from annual reports 10-K forms, proxy materials, and other published sources, supplemented by intensive interviews with a representative cross-section of women directors. The interviews focused on four areas: the process of nomination to the board, specific assignments to board committees, the functioning of a 'good' board, and the occupational and educational characteristics of women directors.	In general, industries with a service orientation or greater direct contact with consumers and the general public had better representation of women directors than companies in basic industries such as steel or mining. Companies headquartered in East Coast or West Coast metropolitan areas were found to have a higher per cent of women directors than corporations found elsewhere in the US. There is no strong evidence of tokenism in women directorships on the part of corporations. Women were appointed to the audit and nominating committees in the same proportion as their numbers in their database would indicate. Women were under-represented on the compensation committee and over-represented on the public policy social responsibility committees. When women members were added, the average committee size was greater, leading to the conclusion that when women were added the committee was enlarged, rather than a male member dropped. Reasons why women felt they were recruited: prominence, friendship, family ties, social relationships, public sector experience, tokenism, community leadership & corporate experience. Women accepted the positions because of a concern for women's rights, their careers, and their investments.

TABLE 10.2 *Summary of correlational studies of corporate women directors*

Authors' names	Questions asked	Area of corporate governance studied	Methodology	Relevant results and conclusions
Bilimoria and Piderit (1994)	Is there systematic sex-based bias in the appointment of directors to the board's committees? Do female directors lack the necessary experience-based characteristics for board committee membership?	The board's internal structure and composition.	Logistical regression analysis of 300 Fortune 500 companies. Independent variables were experience-based characteristics, director's sex, and interaction of these two variables. Experience-based characteristics included director type type, tenure, occupation, business directorships, and non-business directorships.	Sex-based bias limits women's access to committees, after controlling for directors' experience-based characteristics. Male directors are preferred over equally experienced female directors for membership in the compensation, executive and finance committees, while female directors are preferred for membership in the public affairs committee over equally experienced males. Membership odds for the audit and nominating committees do not differ for female and male directors. Women directors were equally if not better qualified for committee membership than their male counterparts on all director characteristics except board tenure.
Burke (1994a)	Examined views of male CEOs, each with women on their boards of directors, regarding benefits of having women as members of boards.	Board composition and impact of women directors.	Surveyed 66 male CEOs from Canadian corporations (obtained from the 1992 *Financial Post Directory of Directors*) having at least one woman on their boards of directors. Three multiple-item measures were used: Make a statement, Want women directors' perspectives, and Benefits. Pearson correlations were computed among the three measures.	All correlations were positive and significantly different from zero, ranging from 0.36 to 0.43. Male CEOs who stated that appointing women to their boards would make important statements to key constituencies also indicated more issues on which they wanted the perspectives of female directors and more benefits and greater influence of the women they had on their boards.
Burke (1997b)	What are the characteristics of women directors who	Characteristics of 'activist' women directors.	Survey findings from 278 women directors using	More activist women directors were older, had more experiences and

(Contd.)

(Contd.)

Authors' names	Questions asked	Area of corporate governance studied	Methodology	Relevant results and conclusions
	actively champion women's issues as part of the board's responsibilities?		a variety of questions to determine the correlates of women board members' activism (e.g. personal characteristics, perceived impacts, policy issues for board discussion, benefits of board membership, reasons for accepting directorships, availability of qualified women, comfort with women directors, interaction with company women).	business skills, had greater impact on their boards, indicated more reasons for accepting directorships and greater benefits from serving, were more critical about the current composition of corporate boards, and had more frequent contact with senior-level women in board companies.
Fryxell and Lerner (1989)	What contextual variables distinguish firms according to their responsiveness in incorporating women and minorities into top management or corporate governance? Are firm characteristics different when women are represented as officers than when women are represented as directors?	The factors influencing board composition.	111 firms from the food, health and personal care, appliance, home products, petroleum, airline, hotel and automobile industries provided information on the number of women on the board and in top management positions. Measures included women and minority representation as officers and directors, performance variables, environmental variables, and organizational variables. Discriminant analyses were employed to examine which variables are useful for classifying companies. A canonical discriminant procedure was then run to	Beyond the confirmation that the size of the firm increases the representation of women and minorities in corporate governance, three differences were observed: (1) those firms whose products involved women as the primary purchaser had more women represented on the board; (2) firms in traditional industries were characterized by high board representation of women but low officerial representation; (3) there was tentative evidence that minority representation varied by industry group.

(Contd.)

(Contd.)

Authors' names	Questions asked	Area of corporate governance studied	Methodology	Relevant results and conclusions
			obtain the standardized weightings of these variables.	
Fryxell and Lerner (unpublished)	Are HRM programmes promoting overall fairness more strongly related to the presence of women officers than to the presence of women directors? Are HRM programmes specifically geared toward women more strongly related to the presence of women directors than to the presence of women officers?	HRM policies and women in corporate governance.	Surveys concerning human resource programmes were sent to 222 firms which had earlier participated in a mailing to the 1,000 CEOs of the Fortune 500/ Industrials and the Service 500. The information on HRM programmes came from a follow-up survey yielding 131 usable responses (a response rate of 59%). Measures included: women in governance positions; HRM programmes promoting fairness to both sexes; and HRM programmes disproportionately benefiting women. There were three control variables: consumer-oriented industry; high levels of regulatory compliance; and size. Dependent variables were women officers and women directors. The study used a logit modelling approach to test the hypotheses.	Women in officerial positions are associated with HRM programmes which promote reward equity and career development regardless of gender. There is a weak but significant negative relationship between women officers and programmes intended to give women flexibility in managing role conflict. The number of women directors was related to reward equity programmes. The consumer orientation of the company was positively associated with the likelihood of women officers and women directors, regulatory compliance was positively associated with women directors, and size was negatively and marginally associated with women directors. The authors conclude that HRM programmes pertaining to overall fairness regardless of gender are associated with the presence of women officers. HRM programmes specifically targeted toward women are not associated with the presence of women directors.
Harrigan (1981)	What are the organizational factors influencing the likelihood of a woman director?	The factors influencing board composition.	Regression analysis of questionnaire data from 112 small publicly traded firms with sales volumes from $1 million to $1 billion and with census data showing employment of between 10 and 10,000 middle- and	Average probability of a firm electing at least one woman director was 20.54%. Likelihood of a woman director being elected was positively influenced by sales volume, positively influenced by the ratio of female to total managers and negatively influenced by the

(Contd.)

Authors' names	Questions asked	Area of corporate governance studied	Methodology	Relevant results and conclusions
			upper-level managers. Dependent variable was the probability that a corporate director will be female. Major independent variables were sales volume, total number of employees, and the ratio of female middle managers to total middle managers.	total number of employees.
Ibrahim and Angelides (1994)	Do directors' corporate social responsiveness orientation differ according to their sex?	The board's role.	Survey data from 398 corporate directors were analysed in two stages: (1) a multivariate analysis of variance procedure to explore differences between men and women on four indices (economic, legal, ethical, and discretionary responsibility); (2) univariate analyses of variance were conducted to understand the underlying contributions of the variables to the significant multivariate effects.	Female directors exhibit a stronger orientation toward corporate social responsibility while male board members showed stronger concern about economic performance. There were no significant differences between the two genders with respect to both legal and ethical dimensions. Women's younger average age was used to explain a possible 'generational gap': younger directors may hold certain values which are widely different from those of their older counterparts.
Izraeli and Talmud (1997)	What is the impact of prior firm ownership on the board's gender composition, mode of director recruitment, and director characteristics and attitudes?	Relationship between firm ownership and board dynamics and composition.	Questionnaire responses from 98 women and 129 men directors of publicly traded Israeli corporations were analysed using percentage counts and tests of differences.	A greater proportion of women than men came from previously family-owned firms, were inside directors, received their information about a board opening through family ties, consulted with family members, and had more dense consultation networks. Law was a relatively more important channel of mobility for women than for men. A greater proportion of men had formal business-related training than women. Men and

Authors' names	Questions asked	Area of corporate governance studied	Methodology	Relevant results and conclusions
				women also differed in their perceptions of the reasons for their appointment, their contributions to the board, and the benefits of directorship.
Kesner (1988)	Do the director characteristics of occupation, type, tenure and gender impact the membership of the board's key committees?	The board's internal structure and composition.	Data from proxy statements of 250 Fortune 500 companies from the year 1983 analysed. Chi-square analysis was used to test the differences between committee members and non-members on the director characteristics, and to test differences between men and women. Hierarchical log-linear modelling was used in follow-up analyses to determine the significant influences on the odds of committee membership.	Gender did not distinguish committee members from non-members. Examining committees separately, however, revealed that women serve less often than men in two cases – the nominating and executive committees. In the case of audit and compensation committees, women are proportionately represented. Follow-up analyses tended to support arguments that tokenism is not the underlying issue. First, there is some evidence to suggest that existing gender differences may actually be a function of the other factors under investigation. Female directors differ significantly in that they tend to come from outside organizations, to hold non-business positions, and to have shorter tenure than their male counterparts. Furthermore, in an examination of partial chi-squares, gender appeared to contribute less than tenure and type. Finally, with the exception of the compensation committee, examination of parameter estimates and antilogs indicated that odds that women directors will serve as members of one of these committees are substantially higher than those for men.
Stephenson and Rakow (1993)	What are the characteristics of the women who are overlapping directors?	Interlocking directorates.	The boards of the largest 100 industrial, 25 banking, 10 insurance, 25 service, 15 diversified finance, 30 retailing, 10 transport,	Women represent almost 10% of the population of overlapping directors, while they are only 7.6% of all

(Contd.)

Authors' names	Questions asked	Area of corporate governance studied	Methodology	Relevant results and conclusions
	Where do women fit into the network of overlapping directorships among large US companies?		and 25 utility from 1992 Fortune 500 list were examined to determine the overlapping directorships of men and women board members. *Standard & Poor's*, *Dun & Bradstreet*, and *Who's Who in America* were used to collect data.	directors. The probability that a woman who serves on a board of directors also serves on the board of another corporation (29.3%) is greater than that for a man (19.1%). The total network density is 0.041, while network density is 0.036 when only men are included. Women increase the network density by 14% while they comprise only 10% of overlapping directors. Female overlapping directors are far less likely than men to be currently employed as business executives. Female overlapping directors also have more formal education than their male counterparts. Women increase the network density of the whole face-to-face network by 21%, which is greater than their presence on corporate boards would indicate. However, women contribute relatively less to the financial sub-network, which is the centre of corporate co-ordination.

improve practice is not by producing facts but by producing frames, or ways of organizing and thinking about the world.'

Thus, while attitudinal studies and demographic composition reports are important in establishing a comparative database against which newer information may be evaluated, it may be preferable, from the point of view of limited research resources and the urgency of developing a substantive knowledge field, for academic researchers to desist from further investigations of a purely descriptive nature. Instead academic researchers should focus their attention on theory-driven qualitative and quantitative analyses that are likely to yield more complex insights into board-level phenomena affecting women. The continued generation of demographic and attitudinal surveys of women directors should be left to the well-established organizations observing and assisting corporate boards (e.g., Catalyst, Korn/Ferry International, Spencer Stuart, Heidrick and Struggles, Inc., and the Business Women's Network) or to credible business press sources such as Fortune, *Business Week*, and *Working Woman* which conduct pertinent and satisfactory annual and *ad hoc* descriptive studies. Unless there is a large-scale diminution in these descriptive reports, academic researchers would do better to concentrate on the conduct of empirical research that fulfils an analytic rather than a reportive function.

Third, based on our review of studies in Table 10.2, we find that overall there is a disturbing lack of theory driving the empirical work. The research questions and hypotheses investigated have generally been devoid of rigorous conceptual development and make little or no contribution to substantive knowledge creation. Few empirical studies shed light on the underlying causes, patterns and consequences of women's representation and status on corporate boards of directors.

Directions for future research on women corporate directors

Our conclusion from examining the empirical research is that cumulatively, the findings lack the explanatory power necessary to create an impetus for organizational change. Nor have these findings displayed the collective credibility that can raise the stakes for powerful organizational participants to improve the representation and status of women in corporate governance. Below we discuss the nature of the research that should be undertaken to generate such positive impact on corporate policy and practice.

Parameters of impactful research on women corporate directors

Research can have important organizational consequences (Lawler et al., 1985; Dunnette, 1992). Organizational science and organizational practice construct each other in a dynamic interplay of scholarship and practical interests (Benson, 1977, 1983). The organizational concerns of both participants and scholars provide the impetus for research. At the same time, knowledge generated through research guides organizational participants in better understanding and dealing with organizational phenomena. In this sense, organizational research constructs organizations as much as it studies them (Calás and Smircich, 1992).

For research on women corporate directors to have the greatest potential to catalyse organizational change, three requirements must be fulfilled. First, a critical mass of theory-driven empirical research must draw attention to women's issues as important organizational and boardroom concerns, providing the parameters for policy discussion at the highest corporate levels, and framing boardroom conversation in gender-attentive ways. Empirical research of sufficient quantity and rigour must generate a coherent and forceful framing of ideas, language and insights useful to board members in constructing their collective reality.

Second, research on women corporate directors must question and critically evaluate extant institutional conditions, exposing the hidden dynamics of boardrooms, and bringing to light the structures that underlie organizational arrangements affecting women. Research must reveal the often indiscernible and seemingly random patterns, flows and trends that influence board composition, structure, procedures and operations. Research must explicate the causes and consequences of board actions regarding organizational women including board members, spotlighting the embeddedness of institutional phenomena, the existing configurations of power and control, and the discreteness of leadership choices. And research must link society's treatment of women in general to corporate practices of women's boardroom representation and status.

Third, research must provide alternatives to limiting organizational arrangements. Research must produce both the generalizable and board-specific conclusions to spur generative organizational action about women directors. It must signal the pathways to positive action that board members might otherwise be blind to, or incapable of accessing. Research must proffer the knowledge structures, linguistic constructions and paradigmatic framing within which new boardroom actions regarding women directors are encouraged and justified. Presented as knowledge, research findings must be directed toward legitimizing the creation of new and vital boardroom structures and practices conducive to improved representation and status of women.

Content areas for future research on women corporate directors

Many corporate governance areas offer fertile ground for the empirical study of women corporate directors. Extant and developing knowledge about several organization science constructs and theories (e.g. mentoring, role models, social identity, leadership, group dynamics, communication, diversity, tokenism, institutionalism, and organizational demography) should be utilized in studying these areas, thereby infusing empirical research with rigour and meaning, and advancing substantive knowledge. The following are five major content areas that future empirical work should address.

The business case for women directors   In the context of realizing the competitive advantage represented by systematic recruitment to, and utilization of, women on corporate boards, Mattis (1993) has suggested three areas that need to be addressed by board chairs, CEOs and nominating committee members: the current business motivations for recruiting women directors, the desired background and qualifications sought in a woman director, and the critical roles that can be played by a woman director both on the board and in the larger organization. These three areas provide a starting point for rigorous research to establish the strategic importance of women directors.

For instance, research should empirically establish the relationship between the presence and effective usage of women directors and various board and firm outcomes. Preliminary evidence suggests that a positive relationship exists between the presence of women on the board and corporate profitability: an analysis of the 50 most profitable Fortune 500 companies indicated that 82 per cent have at least one woman director (all of the top 10 do) as compared to 48.6 per cent of the companies in the overall list (Catalyst, 1993). More recently, the top 100 Fortune 500 firms by revenue were found to be more than twice as likely to have multiple women directors as the bottom 100 (Catalyst, 1997).

Financial performance and other firm-level variables pertinent to corporate governance (e.g. corporate strategy, corporate illegal behaviours, and corporate social responsibility) also need to be rigorously investigated in the context of the presence and use of women directors. Additionally, board performance processes and outcomes such as top management monitoring and compensation, CEO succession, and merger and acquisition decisions need to be examined.

Further, research should more specifically address the relationship between women corporate directors and women in the corporate hierarchy. How do women directors facilitate the recruitment, retention, development and advancement of women in corporate management? In what ways are senior women managers benefited by the presence of women corporate directors? Do organizations with women directors have more women in senior management than organizations that have no women directors? What are the overt and covert mandates for women directors with regard to other women in the organization, and how are these played out in boardroom dealings? Previous research has begun to answer some of these and other similar questions. For example, Harrigan's (1981) research has indicated a positive association between the ratio of female to total managers and the likelihood of a woman director being elected. A recent study of women partners and associates of law firms indicated that sex roles were more stereotypical and more problematic in firms with relatively low proportions of women partners (Ely, 1995). These findings serve to empirically confirm the intuition that women directors have a positive role to play as mentors, champions and role models for other corporate women (Schwartz, 1980; Mattis, 1993).

Institutional, organizational, and individual factors affecting women directors   Given the positive patterns in women's qualifications for directorship, their relative scarcity in corporate governance calls for more impactful investigation. Questions awaiting more rigorous research include: What are the personal, institutional, and cultural factors influencing women's continued under-representation on corporate boards? What motivates boards to recruit and retain women members? What characterizes a women-friendly board of directors? What distinguishes boards that have several, as opposed to a few, women directors? What is the relationship between who controls a corporation and the representation of women on its board? How are women directors' networks different from men directors' networks? What qualifications distinguish the women who are highly sought after for corporate directorships from other women? How can CEOs and board members increase their knowledge of the available pool of women candidates for corporate directorship? What can women do to increase their visibility for corporate directorships?

Boardroom structures, processes, and operations affecting women directors More research is needed to examine boardroom dynamics affecting women corporate directors. For example, how do a board's composition, internal organization, power distribution, director information apparatus and procedures contribute to the treatment and effective usage of women members? What are the role demands (explicit and implicit) of women directors, both on the board and in the larger organization? What expectations do board members hold regarding women directors' performances and how are these expectations realized? What makes women directors satisfied with their board experiences? How valued is women's counsel to CEOs and board chairs, and on what subjects? How are the competencies of women utilized on the board in terms of their committee and task assignments? What can be done, institutionally and personally, for women directors to escape the burdens of tokenism? What organizational benefits are provided by and what dynamics are present in boards characterized by zero, one, or two or more women members?

More work is needed to document the factors influencing the effective performance of women directors in normal and crisis boardroom operations, and the productive functioning of men directors in relating with women directors. Knowledge must be gleaned on the existence of gender-specific boardroom practices and policies that influence women's performance as effective board members. Board processes and behaviours during critically important strategic decisions, such as in a takeover situation or in determining major capital investments, may shed light on the important issues of inclusion and effective usage of women directors.

Recruitment and selection of women The director recruitment and selection process to the board as a whole and the director appointment process to the various committees of the board are areas requiring more detailed investigation (cf. Dobrzynski, 1993). Research needs to be undertaken to investigate the beliefs held by board chairs, CEOs, nominating committee members, and even existing women corporate directors regarding the board's selection of women (see, for example, McGregor, 1997). Three beliefs regarding the selection of women directors, in particular, need to be singled out: (a) the belief that directors must have line business experience rather than staff experience, (b) the belief that outside directors are best drawn from the pool of active and retired CEOs of large corporations, and (c) the belief that not enough qualified women are available as candidates for directorship. While previous research, described below, has begun to question the accuracy of such beliefs, much more research needs to be undertaken before these time-honoured beliefs can be replaced.

For example, a recent study examining 164 line and staff executives suggested that significantly more women executives display leadership potential than do their male counterparts (Enslow, 1991). Additionally, this study found that men in staff positions are less likely than men in line positions to have leadership qualities (vision, charisma, innovativeness and strategic ability) and more likely to have management qualities (ability to maintain momentum, balance interests, stabilize forces and implement tactical plans) while women in staff and line positions are about equally likely to have leadership qualities. It is likely that senior management projects on to women the knowledge of men's lower leadership qualities in staff positions, and since many women hold staff positions they are most often assumed to have lower leadership qualities. As the Enslow (1991) study shows, this is an erroneous assumption.

Similarly, a Catalyst (1993) study suggests that the practice of recruiting outside directors who are active or retired CEOs should be broadened to include consideration of women who have attained senior positions in both operations and general management. The study points out two relevant facts: only three women held the title of a Fortune 500/Service 500 CEO (indicating the severe limitations of small numbers), and one-third of inside directors of corporate boards, most of whom are men, held titles below that of chief executive officer or chief operating officer. This study also recommends that the sources for recruiting women be broadened beyond the persons known to the CEO and the nominating committee. While Catalyst's recommendations are important, change is more likely to occur in corporate boards if empirical research can document the success stories of organizations effectively utilizing more innovative recruitment practices.

Affective impact of women corporate directors on powerful stakeholders Most importantly, we recommend that the content questions of research be personalized to impact individuals in positions of corporate power, thereby having the generative potential to transform organizational and boardroom systems. We suggest that research on women corporate directors is personalized when research participants and readers of research findings engage in 'learning that goes beyond understanding and explanation to producing desired changes, and therefore, learning new values and skills as well as creating new kinds of social systems' (Argyris, 1985: 104). By personalizing research on women corporate directors we specifically mean utilizing research questions that impact participants and readers not just at the cognitive levels of rationality and logic, but also at the affective levels of organizational and personal reality.

For example, we urge research on the relationship between the professional and personal lives of board members. Do the boards led by chairmen and men CEOs whose wives and daughters have professional careers differ in the number and status of women directors from the boards led by chairmen and men CEOs who do not have professional career women in their personal lives? What characteristics and patterns emerge from the personal life circumstances of women directors influencing their professional behaviours and choices? How do the boards of companies led by women CEOs differ from those led by men CEOs? Currently, the only Fortune 500 firm to achieve parity between women and men on its board has a woman CEO (Catalyst, 1997); what factors account for this composition and how effective is it? Research exploring issues such as these are likely to have a personal, gut-level impact far more potent than mere repetition of statistics and facts.

Conclusion

In this chapter we have systematically and comprehensively reviewed the extant empirical literature on women corporate directors, exploring the key thematic directions followed, and evaluating their contributions. Our overall conclusion from this analysis is that, to date, academic research has neither sufficiently nor compellingly materialized to create a cumulative body of knowledge that can substantively generate useful implications for practice, increase corporate awareness, and catalyse positive change.

We suggest that future research on the topic of women corporate directors has the potential to generate a body of insights and learnings that can spur organizational and boardroom dialogue, identify gender-biased board processes and structures, and provide personalized evidence for the construction of more progressive institutional arrangements. To engender such outcomes, however, the parameters and content of future work on corporate women directors will need to follow the general contours we have outlined in this review. By intentionally altering key dimensions such as the questions asked and the methods undertaken, academic research can achieve its transformative potential by challenging prevailing orthodoxies and spawning positive change in the representation and status of women corporate directors.

References

Argyris, C. (1985) 'Making knowledge more relevant to practice: maps for action', in E.E. Lawler III, A.M. Mohrman Jr, S.A. Mohrman, G.E. Ledford Jr, T.G. Cummings and Associates (eds), *Doing Research That is Useful for Theory and Practice*, Jossey-Bass, San Francisco.

Benson, J.K. (1977) 'Organizations: a dialectical view', *Administrative Science Quarterly*, 22: 1–21.

Benson, J.K. (1983) 'Paradigm and praxis in organizational analysis', *Research in Organizational Behaviour*, 5: 33–56.

Bilimoria, D. (1995) 'Women directors: the quiet discrimination', *Corporate Board*, July/August: 10–14.

Bilimoria, D. and Huse, M. (1997) 'A qualitative comparison of the boardroom experiences of US and Norwegian women corporate directors', *International Review of Women and Leadership*, 3 (2): 63–76.

Bilimoria, D. and Piderit, S.K. (1994) 'Board committee membership: effects of sex-based bias', *Academy of Management Journal*, 37 (6): 1453–1477.

Bilimoria, D. and Piderit, S.K. (1995) 'Sexism on high: corporate boards', *New York Times*, 5 February (section 3): 11.

Briggs, J.B. (1994) 'Cool it fellas, here comes Gretchen', *Across the Board*, 31 (6): 50–51.

Browder, D. (1995) 'Shareholders are valuing diversity', *Directors & Boards*, 19 (3): 12–15.

Burke, R.J. (1993) 'Women on corporate boards of directors', *Equal Opportunities International*, 12 (6): 5–13.

Burke, R.J. (1994a) 'Benefits of women on corporate boards of directors as reported by male CEOs', *Psychological Reports*, 75 (1): 329–330.

Burke, R.J. (1994b) 'Women on corporate boards of directors: views of Canadian chief executive officers', *Women in Management Review*, 9 (5): 3–10.

Burke, R.J. (1997a) 'Women on corporate boards of directors: a needed resource', *Journal of Business Ethics*, 16 (9): 909–915.

Burke, R.J. (1997b) 'Women directors' activism on corporate boards of directors: thriving or surviving?' *International Review of Women and Leadership*, 3 (2): 77–84.

Burson-Marsteller (1977) *Study of Women Directors*. Burson-Marsteller, New York.

Business Week (1992) 'Corporate women: how much progress?' 8 June: 74–83.

Calás, M.B. and Smircich, L. (1992) 'Using the 'f' word: feminist theories and the social consequences of organizational research', in A.J. Mills and P. Tancred (eds), *Gendering Organizational Analysis*, Sage, Newbury Park, CA, pp. 222–234.

Cassell, C. (1997) 'The business case for equal opportunities: implications for women in management', *Women in Management Review*, 12 (1): 11–16.

Catalyst (1989) *1988 Women Directors Survey Fact Sheet*, Catalyst, New York.

Catalyst (1993) *Women on Corporate Boards: The Challenge of Change*, Catalyst, New York.

Catalyst (1994) *1994 Census of Female Board Directors Fact Sheet*, Catalyst, New York.

Catalyst (1995) *CEO View: Women on Corporate Boards*, Catalyst, New York.

Catalyst (1996a) *1996 Catalyst Census of Women Board Directors of the Fortune 500*, Catalyst, New York.

Catalyst (1996b) *The 1996 Catalyst Census of Women Corporate Officers and Top Earners of the Fortune 500*, Catalyst, New York.

Catalyst (1997) *1997 Catalyst Census of Women Board Directors of the Fortune 500*, Catalyst, New York.

Collingwood, H. (1996) 'Party of one: women in the boardroom', *Working Woman*, 21 (2): 16.

Collins E.G.C. (1978) 'A woman in the boardroom: an interview with Joan Ganz Cooney', *Harvard Business Review*, 56 (January–February): 77–86.

Directors & Boards (1992) 'Spotlight on women directors', 16 (4): 66–68.

Dobrzynski, J.H. (1993) The "glass ceiling": a barrier to the boardroom, too', *Business Week*, 22 November: 50.

Dogar, R. (1997) 'Crony baloney', *Working Woman*, 22 (1): 34–37.

Dunnette, M.D. (1992) 'Blending the science and practice of industrial and organizational psychology: where are we and where are we going?' in M.D. Dunnette and L. Hough (eds), *Handbook of Industrial and Organizational Psychology*, Consulting Psychologists Press Inc., Palo Alto, CA.

Ely, R.J. (1995) 'The power in demography: women's social constructions of gender identity at work', *Academy of Management Journal*, 38 (3): 589–634.

Enslow, B. (1991) 'Why women follow', *Across the Board*, 28 (4) April: 21.

Evans, J. (1995) 'Becoming boardworthy', *Directors & Boards*, 19 (3): 26–27.

Fernandez, J.P. (1993) '*The Diversity Advantage: How American Business Can Outperform Japanese and European Companies in the Global Marketplace*, Lexington Books, New York.

Fierman, J. (1990) 'Why women still don't hit the top', *Fortune*, 30 July: 40–62.

Forbes (1995) 'Cashing in', 155 (11) 22 May: 176.

Fryxell, G.E. and Lerner, L.D. (1989) 'Contrasting corporate profiles: women and minority representation in top management positions', *Journal of Business Ethics*, 8 (5): 341–352.

Fryxell, G.E. and Lerner, L.D. 'Equity and preference: HRM programmes affecting men and women in corporate governance'. Working paper, University of Tennessee, Knoxville, TN.

Ghiloni, B.W. (1984) 'The corporate scramble for women directors', *Business and Society Review*, 51: 86–95.

Harrigan, K.R. (1981) 'Numbers and positions of women elected to corporate boards', *Academy of Management Journal*, 24 (3): 619–625.

Human Resources Magazine Update (1992) 'Women directors', 37 (January): 20–21.

Ibrahim, N.A. and Angelides, J.P. (1994) 'Effect of board members' gender on corporate social responsiveness orientation', *Journal of Applied Business Research*, 10 (1): 35–40.

Investor Responsibility Research Center (1993) 'Institutions campaign for greater board diversity', *Corporate Governance Bulletin*, 10 (6): 8–12.

Izraeli, D.N. and Talmud, I. (1997) 'Getting aboard: mode of recruitment and gender composition, the case of women directors in Israel', *International Review of Women and Leadership*, 3 (2): 26–45.

Kanter, R.M. (1977) *Men and Women of the Corporation*, Basic Books, New York.

Kesner, I.F. (1988) 'Directors' characteristics and committee membership: an investigation of type, occupation, tenure, and gender', *Academy of Management Journal*, 31 (1): 66–84.

Lawler E.E. (1985) 'Challenging traditional research assumptions', in E.E. Lawler A.M. Mohrman, S.A. Mohrman, G.E. Ledford, T.G. Cummings and Associates (eds), *Doing Research That Is Useful For Theory and Practice*, Jossey-Bass, San Francisco, pp. 1–17.

Lawler, E.E., Mohrman, A.M., Mohrman, S.A., Ledford, G.E., Cummings, T.G. and Associates (1985) *Doing Research That Is Useful For Theory and Practice*, Jossey-Bass, San Francisco.

Lear, R.W. (1994) 'Here come the women directors', *Chief Executive*, 93 (April): 10.

Mattis, M.C. (1993) 'Women directors: progress and opportunities for the future', *Business & the Contemporary World*, Summer: 140–156.

Mattis, M.C. (1997) 'Women on corporate boards: two decades of research', *International Review of Women and Leadership*, 3 (2): 11–25.

McGregor, J. (1997) 'Making the good woman visible: the issue of profile in New Zealand corporate directorship', *International Review of Women and Leadership*, 3 (2): 1–10.

Mitchell, M. (1984) 'A profile of the Canadian woman director', *Business Quarterly*, 49 (1): 121–127.

Morrison, A.M. (1992) *The New Leaders: Guidelines on Leadership Diversity in America*, Jossey-Bass, San Francisco.

National Association of Corporate Directors (1995) *The 1995 Corporate Governance Survey*, National Association of Corporate Directors, Washington, DC.

Nation's Business (1990) 'Companies court women for boards', 78 (January): 52.

Romano, C. (1993) 'All a-board! The composition of the boardroom is changing – albeit slowly', *Management Review*, 82 (10): 5.

Schwartz, F. (1980) 'Invisible resource: women for boards', *Harvard Business Review*, 58 (2): 6–18.

Schwartz, F. and Harrison, P. (1986) 'Beyond the first generation of women directors: on the other side of the roadblock', *Directors & Boards*, 11 (1): 39–41.

Sethi, S.P., Swanson, C.L. and Harrigan, K.R. (1981) *Women Directors on Corporate Boards*, working paper 81–101, Center for Research in Business and Social Policy, University of Texas at Dallas.

Stephenson, K. and Rakow, S. (1993) 'Female representation in US centralized private sector planning: the case of overlapping directorships', *Journal of Economic Issues*, 27 (2): 459–470.

Tifft, S.E. (1994) 'Board gains', *Working Woman*, 19 (2): 36–39, 70, 74–75.

von Glinow, M.A. and Mercer, A.K. (1988) 'Women in corporate America: a caste of thousands', *New Management*, 6 (1): 36–42.

11

Lessons from the Careers
of Successful Women

Barbara White

One of the greatest challenges when beginning to look at the careers of successful women is to arrive at a working definition of career success. Career success has been described as 'subjective and objective aspects of achievement and progress of an individual through an organization or an occupation (Arthur et al., 1989). Some definitions place greater emphasis on the subjective element. Derr (1986) defined career success as 'both being able to live out the subjective and personal values one really believes in and to make a contribution to the world of work'. Despite the recognition of this distinction between subjective and objective criteria for success, the subjective view is often neglected. Operational definitions generally include number of promotions, salary increases or level, current hierarchical position (e.g. Tharenou et al., 1994; Melamed, 1995). Subjective measures of success when they are employed include beliefs about success (Poole et al., 1993) and job satisfaction (e.g. Herriot et al., 1993).

In the case of women's careers the issue of definition is complicated by societal values associated with traditional notions of career success. Marshall (1995) argues that male as the norm continues to have a 'pervasive and insidious influence on thinking and valuing'. This is clearly evident in the work on career success and career development in general which often values employment primacy over other areas of life, and persists in placing hierarchic success above other forms of achievement. Marshall suggests that these are taken for granted reference points in organizations which are based on male domination. She recommends that researchers should constantly question the asssumptions which underpin the concepts and language that they use. As a contribution to this introspective process this chapter will examine some of the approaches to the study of women's career success.

The search for a universal set of determinants of career success

A number of recent studies have attempted to quantify factors which contribute to career success. Using large samples these studies apply complex regression models or structural equation modelling in an effort to discover the career paths of men and women. Predictive variables have been classified under the headings of human attributes, socio-psychological and systemic (Newman, 1993). These groups of variables are then used to predict career success (e.g. Tharenou et al., 1994; Melamed, 1995). This approach can be flawed in that it depends heavily on the appropriate selection of variables entered in the statistical equations. At the current time, much of our knowledge of careers is based on research conducted on samples of white middle-class males. This may lead to the omission of key variables which can obscure gender differences (e.g. Poole et al., 1993). Although we may have gained some useful insights into the determinants of career success, it may be premature to try to develop gender-specific models of career success using this methodology. Indeed, the pursuit of a formula for success has been labelled a somewhat futile activity, as McCall and Lombardo (1983) commented: 'There is not one best way to succeed (or even to fail). The foolproof, step-by-step formula is not just elusive; it is as Kierkgaard said of truth, like searching a pitch dark room for a black cat that isn't there.'

The comparative nature of much of the research on career success has been brought into question. Women are often studied to see how they depart from the male standard (e.g. Davidson and Cooper, 1987). Larwood and Gutek (1987) complain that, although it is likely that women's careers will be different from those of men, it does not mean that every study of women's career development should involve comparisons with men. They emphasize that there are internal dynamics of women's careers which also warrant examination. There is a need to move away from impersonal, aggregated and static data to small-scale, personal, desegregated and dynamic findings, if we are to gain any real understanding of the process by which women achieve career success.

Almost two decades ago Perun and Beilby (1981) complained that little had been done to explain changes in women's lives in developmental terms, or to incorporate them into theories of the development of occupational behaviour. The complaint continues to resound throughout the literature on women's career development. Tinsley and Heesacker (1984) commented that, although not completely bereft of theory, the topic of women at work is hardly theory driven. Fitzgerald and Betz (1987) expressed concern about the implication of the lack of theory:'there is a lack of comprehensive conceptualisations or theories which are capable of producing meaningful, testable hypotheses regarding the development of women's careers'.

Super (1990) suggested that the career patterns of men are essentially applicable to women if they are modified to take marriage and childbirth into account. He describes patterns of women's employment within which he discusses how absences, their timing and spacing affect women's career development. Super also hypothesized that there is no difference in the part self-concept plays in male and female career development. It is proposed that both make decisions on the basis of self-concept and their concept of the circumstances in which they live. This is a highly contentious issue which has been strongly criticized. Perun and Beilby (1981) state that 'we cannot assume that the process of self concept development...is identical for both sexes'. Therefore, any new model should be able to incorporate gender differences in the role self-concept plays in career development.

Career stage theory

In my own work on successful women I have attempted to conceptualize women's careers across the lifespan. This was achieved through the adoption of a career stage framework. The rationale behind the search for patterns of adjustment to life in general, and careers in particular, is to identify the issues associated with age or stages in order to help our understanding of individual behaviour in organizations, which may lead to more effective individual counselling and more effective planning. There is no claim that the stage structure is the only way or the best way to view career development, but it seems to structure or organize our knowledge in a meaningful way. This is clearly evident in the layout of many academic texts on the topic of career development theory and practice.

Age-linked stage structures

There is some controversy over whether stages should be age linked, i.e. life phases. Several stage theorists propose that developmental stages are only indirectly related to chronological age. The term 'developmental stage' refers to the frame of reference that one uses to structure the world and from within which one perceives the world (e.g. Levinson et al., 1978; Levinson, 1986; Super, 1990). Gallos (1989) has suggested that a dual focus on life stages and chronologically linked phases should be made. Both are thought to be essential parts of charting a life course perspective for women, looking at the connection between female characteristics and chronological age over the lifespan. Greenhaus (1987) strongly supports this view. He insists that age strongly shapes career aspirations, experiences and concerns and should therefore play a role in the identification of career stages. He makes the proviso that the task of the researcher in careers is not merely to classify an individual into a particular stage, but to understand how careers unfold and how people work at different stages of their lives. We should not bemoan deviations from the neat classification system; they reflect the rich diversity of careers and lives. Instead, we should try to understand the typical issues that people generally experience at each stage and consider the possible variation that can occur at each stage. Such a life course perspective may be particularly useful when studying women's development given the wide variety of patterns that women experience today.

An in-depth look at the stages in the lives of successful women

White, Cox and Cooper (1992) identified a group of 48 British women as successful. The sample was established via women's business networks in different regions of the country. The chairperson was asked to identify successful women. Due to the diversity of occupations it was not possible to outline objective

Early adult transition: 17–25 years (exploration)
Early commitment to an occupation
Testing of initial choices about preferences for living
Identity diffusion caused by role conflict

Entering the adult world: mid-20s (crystallization and implementation)
Development of sense of personal identity in relation to work and non-work
Rejection of the housewife role/separation from partner, resulting in growth of
    career sub-identity among late starters
High career centrality among early starters (go-getters)
Search for opportunities to practise chosen occupation/profession

Establishment: 25–33 years
Period of rapid learning and development
Establishing a reputation as a high achiever

Early-30s transition: 33–35 years
Raised awareness of biological clock – decision whether to have children

Settling down: 35 years (advancement)
Decision about motherhood resolved
Minimum maternity leave
Striving towards the achievement of personal goals

Late 30s transition: 38–40 years
Regret lack of children
Family–career conflict
Movement in response to glass ceiling

Achievement: 40–50 years (rebalancing)
Resolution of career–family conflict
Rationalization of decision not to have children
Realization of personal goals
Development of greater stability and consolidation of achievements to date

Maintenance: 50s onwards
Continued growth and success
Cycle of expansion and consolidation

FIGURE 11.1   *A stage model of the careers of successful women*

criteria of success such as salary, annual budget controlled, number of staff for whom the woman was responsible, or level in the occupational hierarchy, if indeed such definitions are deemed appropriate. The definition of success was deliberately left open so as not to limit the sample arbitrarily. Therefore, success was peer defined, that is, a career was seen to be successful if it was considered to be so by the organizing members of the network.

The women were asked to describe their career decision-making story (Driver, 1979). The analysis of the story was combined with issues concerning the integration of work and family to produce an age-linked stage model of women's career development. The model was based largely on the career paths of the younger women in the sample. Only five of the 48 women interviewed had taken a career break, the mean length of which was 9.4 years. These women were among the older members of the sample, their average age being 56 years. It was proposed that the sample consisted of two cohorts who were exposed to different socialization experiences. The older women in the sample were described as having an unconventional career pattern. These women had a series of challenging jobs with no logical pattern. Their employment was interspersed with periods of child rearing and voluntary work.

The results (summarized in Figure 11.1) suggested that no matter what their occupation, the successful women passed through specific life stages. The nature, duration and exact timing of the events differed, but certain life events appeared consistent. Issues did appear to emerge in chronological order, as such the mean age of the women dealing with the developmental task was given. This is compared with the portrait of women's lives presented by Bardwick in 1980. Similarly, Bardwick's work represents an attempt to describe a woman's life cycle based on observation of the issues which women in different age cohorts seem to be facing.

An age-linked stage model of women's career development

Early adult transition (17–25)

White et al. (1992) suggest that the analysis of work histories showed that over half of the successful women made a late commitment to their careers or had no coherent direction in their early working lives. This finding provides partial support for the proposal put forward by Adams (1984) that forging a vocational identity may be more complex for women, owing to the need to integrate family and career role. It would seem that for a large proportion of successful women the process of occupational identity formation is protracted, and women experience an extended period of identity diffusion.

A significant number of the successful women made an early commitment to their careers. Approximately one-third of the women interviewed decided at an early age that they would always work and entered on the bottom rung of their chosen occupation.

Entering the adult world (mid-twenties)

At this stage the late starters developed a sense of personal identity in relation to work. This was achieved through rejection of the housewife role or by separation from a partner. At this point all the women were seeking opportunities to practise their chosen occupation.

Bardwick (1980) claimed that women in the early transition years (17–28) are pushed in the direction of marriage, which she suggests is a crucial achievement for women. Almost two decades later, with the decline in marriage rates and the increased age for marriage, questions about this assertion are now raised. Gallos (1989) suggested that we replace marriage with concern for a committed relationship. In doing so, she stated that Bardwick's assertion was sound. Even with career achievements she proposed that women continue to derive a major part of their identity from traditional roles. 'Work is something important to do rather than something to be' (Gallos, 1989). During this period women are said to face a considerable challenge in balancing work and non-work issues.

Establishment (25–33)

This is a time of rapid learning and development within an occupational role. During this period the women developed a reputation for high achievement. Issues at this stage include gaining opportunities to prove oneself through challenging assignments, gaining breadth of experience and developing mentoring relationships.

Early thirties transition (33–35)

A common pattern among the successful women was to wait until their career was well established before contemplating a family. This transitional period was followed by the decision to have a child and to take minimum maternity leave, or to remain childless.

Settling down: late thirties transition

Following approximately four years of renewed commitment to their careers, the women entered another transitional phase. Some women who had decided to remain childless began to express their regrets about the decision. The women who had children began to feel the strain of career and family conflict. The conflict was often resolved by a change of organization or by becoming self-employed. It was often during this period that the women encountered the glass ceiling. These women made outspiralling moves, changing organization to gain promotion.

Bardwick also signalled this period (30–40: settling down period) as one in which the biological clock is ticking loudly for women who have not had children. She suggested that achieving professional success alone can lead to a feeling of anxiousness or wonder about what one has sacrificed. She also suggested that for those who have had children, the exhaustion of balancing multiple roles may have led to cutting back on professional work or parenting, leading to a sense of personal inadequacy.

Achievement and maintenance (forties and onwards)

The resolution of issues in the late thirties transition leads to a period of achievement and rebalancing. During this stage childless women seem to rationalize their decision not to have children, stating that they could not have achieved their current occupational success if they had children. This change of attitude may be explained in terms of Festinger's (1957) concept of cognitive dissonance. Dissonance is created in the late thirties transition because women start to feel that the sacrifices that they have made were too great. Dissonance theory suggests that people are motivated to reduce this inconsistency in cognitions; therefore women begin to place greater importance on their career achievements. These women are convinced that for them career and family are mutually exclusive.

Bardwick (1980) described middle adulthood (40–50) as a time of increased assertiveness and professional accomplishment for women. This is signalled as a time of great promise for women. She suggested that the empty nest syndrome is unlikely, given the changing expectations for women returners. Women are less confined than in previous stages and have an edge over men in terms of physical well-being. According to Bardwick, women do not seem to suffer the mid-life crisis which has been associated with male career development.

Having reached the achievement stage, women enter a maintenance stage. No evidence of further transition periods was observed. The women nearing retirement were still involved in their work, although some women mentioned that they worked fewer hours, which might be viewed as the beginning of the decline stage. Due to the small number of women in this age group it was not possible to draw any inferences about the dynamics of the decline stage.

What emerged from the study of successful women was that the age-linked stage model has a strong resemblance to the career stages described by Levinson et al. (1978), although Levinson's model was based on interviews with 40 men. This was not thought to be entirely surprising, given that these women had succeeded in a world of business which has been structured to accommodate male lives. The women in the study worked continuously and full time, fitting domestic responsibilities around work or choosing to remain childless. The fact that a large number of women are conforming to this stereotype is reflected in Osipow's (1995) comments on the vast shift in the career patterns of women, suggesting that if a modal pattern exists at all, it consists of early career entry, a brief interruption for family obligations and a return to the workforce for the rest of the lifespan.

An extension of the career stage model: exploring the dynamics of role investment

One of the key themes which emerged in the interviews with the successful women was their strength of commitment to their careers. This was clearly evident in the definitions of career given by the successful women, in which they described career as an integral part of their identity. Of the successful women in the sample, 50 per cent claimed that work took priority in their lives. As reflected in the late thirties transition, a small proportion made the reservation that although work had always taken priority in their lives, they were now beginning to have regrets. They felt that they had missed their opportunity to have children or to enjoy their children while they were young.

The process of identity investment in work or family roles is poorly understood: most research has been descriptive rather than theoretical (Kingston, 1989; Lambert, 1990). Hall's (1976) theory of sub-identities does, however, provide a useful framework for understanding the dynamics of career commitment. Hall has proposed that an individual's identity can be conceptualized as consisting of several sub-identities representing various aspects of the individual when behaving in different social roles. The career sub-identity is defined as that aspect of the person's identity which is engaged in working in a given occupation (see Figure 11.2). Hall has suggested that as the individual acquires competence relevant to the career role through the setting and achievement of challenging goals, they will experience psychological success which leads to sub-identity growth.

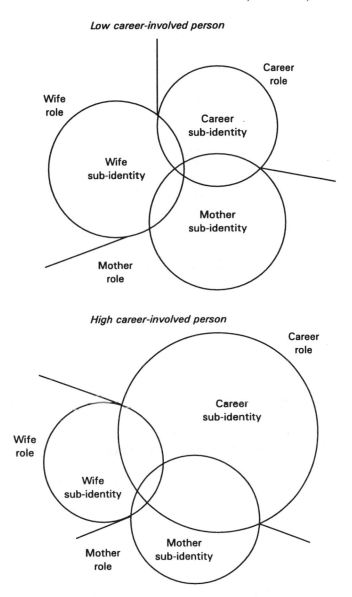

FIGURE 11.2 *Sample sub-identities of two hypothetical people: one with low career involvement and one with high career involvement (Hall, 1976)*

A segmentalist view of work and family

The observation that greater commitment to work leads to less commitment to family has been explained in terms of a utilitarian model, i.e. time is finite which means that work and family become a zero sum game. The dynamics of career sub-identity growth indicate that this explanation is incomplete. The motivations which lead to involvement in either sphere are different and individuals have different levels of need in either area. Growth needs do not stem from drive reduction but from a tendency to explore the environment and to develop mastery over it. Such motives are persistent: the mastery of a challenge requires a new one to take its place. This leads to an enhancement cycle of greater work involvement or psychological success followed by career sub-identity growth. Meeting security and nurturance needs does not seem to have the same feedback loop. Despite popular prescriptions for a balanced lifestyle, the relationship between work and family is asymmetrical (Howard, 1992). Left unchecked this process can lead to a more work, less family cycle, which may lead to diminishing life returns. Given the greater interdependence of work and family in women than men, the work enhancement cycle may be particularly problematic for women. This becomes clear when we look at an integrated model of the careers of successful women.

An integrated model of the careers of successful women

Rapoport and Rapoport (1980) have suggested that an appropriate model for thinking about career behaviour is the triple helix. Each strand in the helix has its own impetus and characteristics, and the three strands are said to interact in two distinct ways:

1   during steady states between transitions (the issue is balancing);
2   at transition points (the issue is the critical impact of events).

We may conceptualize Hall's model of sub-identities as a cross-section through the triple helix. Although there is not a direct correspondence in the diagrammatical representation, the thickness of the strands in the helix may be related to the size of the sub-identity. The timing of the growth of the career sub-identity may vary, but the majority of the successful women had resolved the conflict and crystallized their career aspirations by their mid-twenties. The points of cross-over in the helix equate to the overlap between the sub-identities. These points of cross-over correspond closely to the periods of transition in the lives of successful women.

The data derived from the current study provide information on only the career and family strands in the helical structure. These data appear to confirm Rapoport and Rapoport's description of the interaction of the two strands. The successful women experienced periods of stability during which they maintained a satisfactory balance between their work and family lives. These periods of stability are followed by periods of questioning and change, when the women have a heightened awareness of the impact of career and family upon each other. These periods of transition represent the main points of departure from the careers of men as described by Levinson et al. (1978). The schematic representation of the careers of successful women is shown in Figure 11.3.

The model of successful women's lifespan development showed that the majority of successful women displayed high career centrality. Continuous full-time employment appears to be a prerequisite for career success. These findings suggest that if we are to achieve 'genuine equality in all aspects of life' then

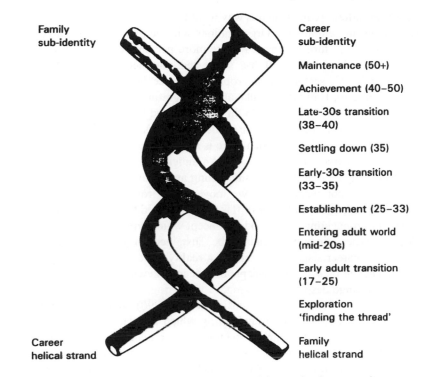

Family
sub-identity

Career
sub-identity

Maintenance (50+)

Achievement (40–50)

Late-30s transition
(38–40)

Settling down (35)

Early-30s transition
(33–35)

Establishment (25–33)

Entering adult world
(mid-20s)

Early adult transition
(17–25)

Exploration
'finding the thread'

Career
helical strand

Family
helical strand

FIGURE 11.3 *A double helix model illustrating the lifespan development of
successful women*

change is required in the prevailing stereotype of a successful career. In *Prisoners
of Men's Dreams* (1991) Gordon describes a similar pattern in the careers of successful women in the USA. She claims that women have been entrapped by male
norms and that they are accommodating to these norms rather than challenging
the rules of the game.

Conclusion

It must be acknowledged that at present it is difficult to 'get balanced' without
stepping off the fast track. There continue to be strong cultural and organizational
messages which define the requirements for a successful career as 100 per cent
commitment. Marshall (1995) suggests that although these values are now being
questioned, they continue to hold a seductive power and that many women are
committed to proving themselves in these terms.

Bailyn (1992) has suggested that we need to challenge the assumption that
100 per cent commitment in early career stages is a prerequisite for later achievement. Career may be characterized by periods of high and low commitment,
negotiated by the individual and the organization. At times when the individual
has high demands in terms of raising a family, their lower commitment should not
be interpreted as lack of motivation.

Reconceptualizing careers in this way would involve a significant shift for both organizations and employees. Organizations will have to negotiate careers with individuals who in turn will have to take more personal responsibility for their development. Marshall (1989) has suggested that people should 'creatively weave their lives', seeking an appropriate balance between work and family spheres. Similarly, Hall (1994) talks about integrating more stimuli and experience into one's sense of self. To do this women need to learn to negotiate career structures which suit their lives. The model of successful women's career stages identifies transition points at which there is a heightened awareness of the reciprocal impact of career and family roles. An understanding of important issues at these stages may be crucial in this integrating and weaving process.

Many have recommended that we move away from the linearity of career theory (Marshall, 1989; Hall, 1994). It is acknowledged that as researchers we are in danger of propagating an outmoded concept which will serve to reinforce psychological expectations that cannot be sustained in today's organizations. However, the career stage model reflects a reality, given the reluctance of many people to change their linear concepts of career. Likewise, organizations appear reluctant to change despite downsizing, restructuring, insecurity and uncertainty in job prospects. Guest and Mackensie-Davey (1996) suggest that instead of moving towards new organizational forms which are flat, flexible and project based, we are seeing a shift back to the traditional model of hierarchy, and traditional careers. If so, it seems that Arthur (1992) has legitimately questioned the urgency with which theorists need to respond to changes taking place, and as such recommends caution:

> While…career theory shows an openness to the work environment it fails to calibrate the pace of change. What appears to be a useful theoretical transformation may result in a net loss in relevance, if the environment is changing faster, or simultaneously moving in a different direction.

The career stage model does provide a framework for looking at careers that are simultaneously high on career and family commitment. The model does not assume centrality of work in women's lives; rather this depends on changing needs over the lifespan. A key point is that we should not blur the domains because different psychological meanings are attached to work and family. The implication is that a compensation model is untenable. The model continues to be useful in terms of understanding the developmental processes and age-linked issues which women face. As such, it is hoped that we may inform the development of negotiated careers which enable women to have it all.

References

Adams, J.M. (1984) 'When working women become pregnant', *New England Business*, February: 18–21.

Arthur, M.B. (1992) 'Career theory in a dynamic context', in D.M. Montross and C.J. Shinkman (eds), *Career Development: Theory and Practice,* Charles Thomas,

Arthur, M.B., Hall, D.T. and Lawrence, B.S. (1989) 'Generating new directions in career theory: the case for a transdisciplinary approach', in M.B. Arthur, D.T. Hall and

B.S. Lawrence (eds), *Handbook of Career Theory*, Cambridge University Press, New York.

Bailyn, L. (1992) 'Changing the conditions of work: implications for career development', in D.M. Montross and C.J. Shinkman (eds), *Career Development: Theory and Practice*, Charles Thomas,

Bardwick, J. (1980) 'The season's of a woman's life', in D. McGuigan (ed.), *Women's Lives: New Theory Research and Policy*, University of Michigan Center for Continuing Education of Women, Ann Arbor.

Davidson, M. and Cooper, C.L. (1987) 'Managers in Britain – a comparative perspective', *Human Resource Management*, 26: 217–242.

Derr, C.B. (1986) *Managing the New Careerist*, Jossey-Bass, San Francisco.

Driver, M.J. (1979) 'Career concepts and career management in organizations', in C.L. Cooper (ed.), *Behavioural Problems in Organizations*, Prentice Hall, Englewood Cliffs, NJ.

Festinger, L. (1957) *A Theory of Cognitive Dissonance*, Row Peterson, Evanston, IL.

Fitzgerald, L.F. and Betz, N.E. (1987) 'Issues in the vocational psychology of women', in W.B. Walsh and O.H. Osipow (eds), *Handbook of Vocational Psychology Volume One*, Lawrence Erlbaum, Hillsdale, NJ.

Gallos, J.V. (1989) 'Exploring women's development: implications for theory, practice and research', in M. Arthur, D.T. Hall and B. Lawrence (eds), *Handbook of Career Theory*, Cambridge University Press, Cambridge.

Gordon, S. (1991) *Prisoners of Men's Dreams: Striking Out for a New Feminist Future*, Little, Brown, Boston, MA.

Greenhaus, J.H. (1987) *Career Management*, Dryden Press, Fort Worth, TX.

Guest, D. and Mackensie-Davey, K. (1996) 'Don't write off traditional careers', *People Management*, 2 February.

Hall, D.T. (1976) *Careers in Organizations*, Goodyear, Santa Monica, CA.

Hansard Society (1990) *Women at the Top*, A.L. Publishing Services, London.

Howard, A. (1992) 'Work and family crossroads spanning the career', in S. Zedeck (ed.), *Work, Families and Organizations*, Jossey-Bass, San Francisco.

Kingston, P.W. (1989) 'Studying the work and family connection: a theoretical progress, ideological bias and shaky foundations for policy', in E. Goldsmith (ed.), *Work and Family*, Sage, Newbury Park, CA.

Lambert, S.J. (1990) 'Processes linking work and family: a critical review and research agenda', *Human Relations*, 43: 239–257.

Larwood, L. and Gutek, B.A. (1987) 'Working towards a theory of women's career development', in B.A. Gutek and L. Larwood, *Women's Career Development*, Sage, London.

Levinson, D.J. (1986) 'A conception of adult development', *American Psychologist*, 41: 3–13.

Levinson, D., Darrow, C.N., Klein, E.B., Levinson, M.H. and McKee, B. (1978) *The Seasons in a Man's Life*, Knopf, New York.

Marshall, J. (1989) 'Revisioning career concepts: a feminist invitation', in M. Arthur, D.T. Hall and B. Lawrence (eds), *Handbook of Career Theory*, Cambridge University Press, Cambridge.

Marshall, J. (1995a) 'Some comments on challenges and opportunities', *International Review of Women and Leadership*, 1 (1): 1–11.

Marshall, J. (1995b) *Women Managers Moving On: Exploring Career and Life Choices*, Routledge, London.

McCall, M.W. and Lombardo, M.M. (1983) *Off the Track: Why and How Successful Executives Get Derailed*, Technical Report 21, Centre for Creative Leadership, Greensboro.

Melamed, T. (1995) 'Career success: the moderating effects of gender', *Journal of Vocational Behaviour*, 47: 35–60.

Newman, M.A. (1993) 'Career advancement: does gender make a difference?' *American Review of Public Administration*, 23: 361–384.

Osipow, S.H. (1995) *Theories of Career Development*, 4th edn, Prentice Hall, Englewood Cliffs, NJ.

Perun, P.J. and Beilby, D.D.V. (1981) 'Towards a model of female occupational behaviour: a human development approach', *Psychology of Women Quarterly*, 6: 234–252.

Poole, M.E., Langan-Fox, J. and Omodei, M. (1993) 'Contrasting subjective and objective criteria as determinants of perceived success: a longitudinal study', *Journal of Occupational and Organizational Psychology*, 66: 39–54.

Rapoport, and Rapoport (1980) 'Balancing work, family and leisure: a triple helix model', in C.B. Derr (ed.), *Work, Family and the Career*, Praeger Publishing, New York.

Super, D.E. (1990) 'A life-span life-space approach to career development', in D. Brown and L. Brooks and Associates, *Career Choice and Development*, Jossey-Bass, San Francisco.

Tharenou, P., Latimer, S. and Conroy, D. (1994) 'How do you make it to the top? Examination of influences on women's and men's managerial advancement', *Academy of Management Journal*, 37: 899–931.

Tinsley, H.E.A. and Heesacker, M. (1984) 'Vocational behaviour and career development (1983): a review', *Journal of Vocational Behaviour*, 25: 139–190.

White, B., Cox, C.L. and Cooper, C.L. (1992) *Women's Career Development: A Study of High Flyers*, Blackwell Business, Oxford.

PART III

OCCUPATIONAL STRESS AND BLACK AND ETHNIC MINORITY ISSUES

12

Women, Work Stress and Health

Debra L. Nelson and Ronald J. Burke

Research interest in women and work stress has increased, and empirical evidence has been growing since the early 1980s. The burning question that has driven much of this research is 'Do men and women experience work stress differently?' Unfortunately, our review indicates that there is no clear-cut answer to this question. In this chapter, we assess the current state of the research on women and work stress by specifically focusing on three critical elements in the work stress process: stressors, coping methods, and distress symptoms. In addition, we analyse current themes and trends in the contemporary research literature on women and work stress. Finally, we propose some alternate questions to guide future research.

Why study women and work stress?

It might be argued that work life in organizations has changed. More women are in the workforce, and this has been the case now for several years. Is the study of gender and stress still relevant? Doesn't some of the evidence (e.g. Martocchio and O'Leary, 1989) indicate a striking lack of differences in males' and females' experiences of work stress? We believe that our critical review of the literature, presented next, clearly demonstrates the relevance of gender-based studies. Perhaps the most important reason to continue to study women's experience of work stress is to be able to develop specific interventions tailored to the needs of women. For instance, one distress symptom linked to work stress is smoking. In efforts to quit smoking, women encounter different problems than do men (Chesney and Nealey, 1996). It makes sense to design interventions targeted to the needs of women, bearing in mind that the goal is to increase the effectiveness of interventions for all employees.

The danger, however, is studying differences for differences' sake (Mann, 1996). Studying only women may mask the differences that exist among women, and in the hands of insensitive researchers this can lead to stereotypes and stigma. Further, when gender issues at work are focused solely on women or on men, we assume that members of each sex are more similar to each other than the opposite sex in terms of their experience of stress. We need to be sure that studies of intergroup differences are complemented by studies of intragroup differences (Matusek et al., 1995).

With this caveat, the study of women and work stress can yield important information for interventions in the workplace. We have selected three targets for interventions in this review: stressors (causes of stress), representing targets for primary interventions, coping methods, representing targets for secondary interventions, and distress symptoms, targets for tertiary interventions.

Stressors for working women

It is particularly important to understand the major sources of stress for working women. Primary preventive efforts, those that are most efficacious, focus on eliminating or changing the source of stress. The first step in prevention or intervention is to identify these sources (Burke, 1996; Langan-Fox, 1998). Common stressors for both working men and women include role conflict, role ambiguity, and responsibility for people. Studies employing measures of such stressors often fail to find significant male/female differences (Lindquist et al., 1997). Job stressors such as dull, monotonous work or having to work under time pressure and conflicting demands are associated with distress equally for men and women in dual earner couples (Barnett and Brennan, 1997). Yet some studies demonstrate overall that women report poorer psychosocial work conditions than men. One large-scale US study of professionals and non-professionals (n = 11,407) showed that women suffered particularly in terms of lack of learning opportunities and monotonous work (Matthews et al., 1998).

There are some stressors, however, that are especially salient for working women, especially those in managerial and professional careers (Burke, 1996). These include organizational politics, barriers to achievement, overload, social-sexual behaviour, and work/home conflict.

Organizational politics

At work, politics may take the form of informal behaviour, influence attempts, and struggles for control of resources and/or information. A study of 2,000 human resource managers indicated that women experienced significantly more stress from organizational politics than did men (Nelson et al., 1989). The implication of this finding is that women may be denied access to informal networks, may have trouble gaining essential information, and may lack legitimate power in organizations. When women are denied access to information and resources because of politics, they become more vulnerable to stress in the work setting.

Barriers to achievement

Part of the legitimate power deficits that women sometimes experience may be due to their lack of ability to move into the higher ranks of organizations. In the USA, few women are members of top management teams – women hold only 10 per cent of corporate officer positions in the *Fortune 500* companies (Solomon, 1998). In addition, women's salaries persist at 76 per cent of that of men in comparable positions (US Department of Labor, 1998).

The 'glass ceiling' is a transparent barrier keeping women from rising above a certain level in organizations (Morrison and von Glinow, 1990). While many explanations for this effect have been proposed, two in particular show viability (Burke, 1996). One contributing factor is discrimination, which occurs often in such subtle forms as increasing women's probability of failure, denying them access to developmental opportunities, or presenting only stereotypical challenges (Ohlott et al., 1994). Much of this discrimination is based on sex stereotypes (Heilman, 1995).

There are other obstacles to women's advancement in organizations. These include prejudices, a hostile and unsupportive environment, and the 'old boys' network' (Morrison, 1992). Other barriers identified by Auster (1993) included unwillingness by those in power to confront and eliminate sexism, biases in recruiting efforts and selection decisions, assignment of women to less influential projects and managers, and sex biases in performance appraisal criteria and processes.

Overload

There is evidence that working women experience overload as a stressor, both in the form of role overload and total workload (Hochschild, 1989, 1997). Role overload is the experience of competing or conflicting expectations from multiple roles, and women are particularly prone to this stressor. Often, working women find themselves in roles that require caring for others, and this adds to role overload. Parenting, for example, is one such role that is a major stressor for women and is consistently related to distress (Barnett and Baruch, 1985). Role overload and total workload are interrelated. Total workload includes all forms of work: paid and unpaid, vocational and domestic (Matuszek et al., 1995). Frankenhauser (1991) found that women's average total workload was 78 hours per week, whereas men's total workload was 68 hours per week. She also found that the increased workload interfered with women's ability to wind down effectively, with resultant negative effects on health. A subsequent study also showed that women had a higher total workload than men, that work stress peaked at ages 35–39, and that total workload increased with the number of children in the household (Lundberg et al., 1994).

Barnett and Shen (1997) proposed that it is not total time spent on housework tasks that is related to distress, but only the time spent on low-schedule control tasks. These include tasks that are often done under time pressure and with urgency, such as preparing meals, house cleaning, and doing dishes. These tasks must be performed regardless of other interference and cannot easily be postponed. In a study of 267 couples Barnett and Shen found that women in dual earner couples spent significantly more time on household tasks than did their husbands; however, because the husbands spent more time at work, there was no difference in total workload. They also found that the most important predictor of distress for both men and women was the time spent in low-schedule-control household tasks. Many of these tasks are typical 'female' ones, with little discretion over the nature of the task or its timing. Thus, it may be that low-schedule-control tasks, both at work and at home, are significant contributors to women's experience of overload.

Social-sexual behaviour

One form of social-sexual behaviour is sexual harassment. Other forms include flirting and making sexual jokes. Women experience more sexual harassment and non-harassing social-sexual behaviours at work (Gutek et al., 1990; Burke and McKeen, 1992). These behaviours were associated with lower levels of job satisfaction and organizational commitment and poorer well-being. In a study of police officers, women officers reported more sexual harassment from supervisors, more demeaning behaviours from peers, and more sexual joking than did men. Thirty-seven percent of the women officers reported unwanted and uninvited sexual attention from their supervisors or co-workers on the job, which is comparable to estimates in a variety of work settings (Morris, 1996).

A study of 385 office workers found that 70 per cent of the women reported exposure to gender harassment – conduct that is gender hostile and conveys insulting, hostile or degrading attitudes toward women. Frequency of gender harassment was positively related to somatic complaints, depression, and alcohol usage, and negatively associated with job satisfaction (Piotrkowski, 1998). A study of female construction workers (n = 211) demonstrated that sexual harassment and gender discrimination were positively related to headaches, nausea, and other psychological symptoms (Goldenhar et al., 1998). For some women, sexual harassment may be a chronic occupational stressor.

Work/home conflict

When work role stressors interfere with an individual's ability to fulfil home and family obligations, work/home conflict occurs. Early reports suggested that this stressor was particularly problematic for working women (cf. Nelson and Quick, 1985), and some studies provided evidence for this claim. Beatty (1996), in a study of 193 managerial and professional Canadian women, found that work/family conflict was related to anxiety, depression and irritation/hostility for the entire sample, but these relationships were stronger for women with children.

Recent work has highlighted the notion that work/home conflict is a bi-directional construct; that is work can interfere with family life, and family can interfere with work life. A study that examined both work–family and family–work conflict indicated that both forms of conflict were positively related to depression, poor physical health, and alcohol use among both sexes (Frone et al., 1996). Another study of members of dual earner families found no gender differences in work/family conflict *per se*; however, mothers in the study reported less task sharing from their partners (Schwartzberg and Dytell, 1996). A study of 501 employees in Finland demonstrated that work–family conflict was more prevalent than family–work conflict among both sexes, but no gender differences were found in either form of conflict. This result is attributed to the societal structures in Finland and the ease of combining multiple roles for both sexes (Kinnunen and Mauno, 1998).

Some studies have distinguished between the causal direction and the sign of the relationship between work involvement and family involvement. One such study included 281 dual-employed couples, and yielded different models of work/family relationships for men and women. For men, the work–family model that emerged was reciprocal in that work involvement positively affected family involvement, while family involvement negatively impacted work involvement. Males were able to trade off work for family, and vice versa. The family to work relationship was compensatory, while the work to family relationship was a positive spillover effect.

In contrast, the work–family relationship for women was unidimensional. Family involvement negatively affected work involvement, but work involvement did not impact family involvement. Females had a fixed level of family involvement that was independent of the influences of work. The results of this study indicate that there is an important and complex relationship between work involvement and family involvement, and that there are observable differences in these patterns for males and females (Tenbrunsel et al., 1995).

There has also been a body of research examining cross-over, a form of stress contagion, where a spouse's work stress creates stress for the other partner. Some of this work has also included an examination of possible effects of parents' stress on the well-being of children.

Westman and Etzion (1995) considered the crossover of psychological burnout and coping resources between male Israeli military officers and their spouses. They report that for both sexes a sense of control had the greatest relationship with their levels of self-reported psychological burnout and on their spouses' levels of psychological burnout, controlling for their own levels of job stress and resources. Spouse's sense of control served as an additional resource, which benefited the partner.

Galambos et al. (1995) noted that parent–child conflict was highest when both parents were stressed. In a similar vein, Barling, Dupre and Hepburn (1998) found that children's perceptions of their parents' job insecurity mediated the effects of parental job insecurity and layoffs on children's work beliefs and work attitudes. Other work (Barling, 1990; Stewart and Barling, 1996) provides further evidence of the effects of employment and job stress on family functioning.

In summary, some evidence suggests that women experience work/home conflict more than do men, while other evidence shows no gender difference. Still other studies point to the complex interplay of work and family, and suggest that the relationships differ for men and women (see Burke and Greenglass, 1987 and Langan-Fox, 1998 for reviews). Perhaps the gender differences in the levels of work/home conflict are not as important as recognizing that work/home conflict is an important stressor for women as well as men, and that it cannot be ignored in constructing frameworks for understanding women's stress at work. Equally important in building these guides for research is the inclusion of coping techniques that women employ in their efforts to manage these stressors.

Coping methods

One of the parts of the stress process that has received increased attention is that of coping. One model of coping suggests that methods are either problem focused, changing the source of stress, or emotion focused, managing the emotions associated with stress (Folkman et al., 1986). Some studies have shown that women tend to rely on emotion-focused methods such as venting or avoidance, whereas men rely on problem-focused methods such as taking action to change the stressor (cf. Ptacek et al., 1994). Other studies have failed to consistently support this finding (Folkman et al., 1986). A more communal view of active coping suggests that shared problem-solving, which includes turning to others for support and offering support to others, may be an effective form of coping, particularly for women (Dunahoo et al., 1996).

Exercise is a coping mechanism with positive consequences in dealing with stress, as it helps the individual recover from the experience of distress (Frankenhauser, 1991). However, women often report significantly less use of exercise and sports than men (Nelson et al., 1989). One reason for this may be that women lack the resources (time, money, childcare) to take advantage of exercise. Another may be that women simply do not see sports as a stress management technique.

Smoking is often used to cope with stress, and women smoke in order to deal with negative affect. While in the past men smoked more than women, the smoking rates of the sexes are converging, and there is a higher rate of smoking initiation among women (Chesney and Nealey, 1996).

In terms of other lifestyle factors, such as healthy eating patterns, and alcohol consumption, women may fare better. In a study of lifestyle factors, stress and blood pressure, women were more likely to use healthy coping mechanisms (e.g. positive attitude) than men. Men were more likely to use unhealthy eating, denial of stress, and alcohol consumption to cope (Lindquist et al., 1997).

Social support is a coping mechanism with demonstrated positive effects, and women are more likely to use social support than men (Matuszek et al., 1995). However, the forms and sources of social support need to be considered when examining this as a coping mechanism for women (Greenglass, 1993). Support in the workplace is particularly important. Geller and Hobfoll (1994) found that men and women received similar amounts of social support from co-workers and supervisors at work, but men benefited more from these sources. Women may have more limited access to support at work because of their exclusion from informal networks and lack of access to mentors.

Support in the home arena is also important. Family support is effective in reducing work stress for women, and employment can result in improved mental health for women if they have a supportive partner who shares in household duties (Dunahoo et al., 1996). Professional and managerial women in Beatty's (1996) study reported more depression associated with lack of spousal support.

Pretorius (1996) conducted a study in South Africa of the health-sustaining (direct effects) and stress-reducing (buffering effects) of social support among male and female undergraduate students. No gender differences were found in the receipt of social support, but differences emerged in the effects of social support. Women reported health-sustaining benefits of a number of supports and support from family and friends more than did men.

To summarize, gender differences in coping are worthy of study. Women seem to use smoking to cope, and exercise less than men. However, they eat more healthily and benefit from the use of family support. Women's access to support at work may be limited, but it is nonetheless important. Traditional notions of men's coping as problem focused and women's coping as emotion focused are coming into question.

Distress symptoms

Patterns of results are emerging from epidemiological studies and from cross-sectional studies indicating that women differ from men in their experience of distress or strain. For example, women report higher levels of distress symptoms in general, and the life expectancy for women is approximately eight years longer than that of men. The types of symptom most often reported by women tend to be non-fatal, while the symptoms reported by men tend to be the lethal illnesses such as cardiovascular disease (Quick et al., 1997). Women are more frequently ill than men, but less often with life-threatening illnesses (Jick and Mitz, 1985; Zappert and Weinstein, 1985).

The psychological distress symptoms reported most often by women include anxiety, depression and sleep disturbances, and work stress has been implicated as a primary contributor to these symptoms (Nelson et al., 1989). Women's rate of depression is approximately double that of men, and women attempt suicide at a rate 2.3 times greater than men (Philpot et al., 1997). Gender differences in physical symptoms of distress are less clear-cut; however, women do report more headaches and poorer overall physical health than men (Nelson et al., 1989; Furnham and Kirkcaldy, 1997).

There are gender differences in the behavioural consequences of distress, including smoking, alcohol and drug use, and eating disorders. Smoking may be considered a coping technique, as previously described, or as a consequence of stress. Studies demonstrate consistently that smokers smoke more when under stress. Smoking is on the rise among women, and it is the single most preventable cause of morbidity and mortality among women (Chesney and Nealey, 1996). Women's use of alcohol and drugs is rising, and problems of abuse are more likely to be undetected in women (Philpot et al., 1997). Women are more likely to drink in private, and are less likely to engage in binge drinking. Eating disorders, such as anorexia and bulimia, are more prevalent in women than in men

A number of studies have examined gender differences in psychological burnout. Psychological burnout is typically seen as a response to work stress, particularly among human service professionals. It is commonly seen as having three components: emotional exhaustion, depersonalization and lack of personal accomplishment (Maslach and Jackson, 1981). Early work (Etzion and Pines, 1986) suggested that women reported higher levels of psychological burnout than did men. Greenglass (1991) noted that gender was often confounded with occupational role and hierarchical level in these analyses. No significant gender differences are observed, except for depersonalization when confounding variables are controlled. Males consistently score higher than females on depersonalization (Ogus et al., 1990).

Researchers are focusing attention on distress symptoms unique to women. Work stress has been found to be related to reproductive outcomes such as spontaneous abortion (Schenker et al., 1997) and pre-eclampsia (Klonoff-Cohen et al., 1996). In addition, cancer incidence rates are being studied in traditionally female occupations. These include studies of 'female' cancers such as cancers of the breast, ovary and uterus (Hatch and Moline, 1997).

Gender differences in distress are difficult to detect, due in part to the fact that men use the medical system less often and are less likely than women to report symptoms (Mann, 1996). In addition, men and women are treated differently by medical professionals, who are more likely to diagnose women's conditions as psychologically related. Interestingly, some studies indicate that women are more likely to attribute their own symptoms to psychological factors (Furnham and Kirkcaldy, 1997). Women are also less likely to be diagnosed as having a stereotyped 'men's disease' such as cardiovascular problems.

Innovative studies are attempting to examine the relationships between psychosocial work factors and groups of distress symptoms, and to ascertain how these relationships differ between men and women. One such study was conducted with 13,226 employees of a French electricity company (Niedhammer et al., 1998). The major finding was that the pattern of relationships between work factors and cardiovascular disease risk factors differed between men and women. For women, low decision latitude was related to hyperlipidaemia; high psychological demands were related to being overweight; high decision latitude was associated with smoking, and low social support was related to alcohol consumption. For men, low decision latitude was associated with hypertension; high decision latitude and high social support were related to being overweight, and low decision latitude was related to alcohol consumption. These results illustrate the complexity of the stress process and show that the mechanisms through which stressors relate to distress differ between men and women.

Current themes and challenges

Because interest in women's experience of work stress has increased, the research literature has grown commensurately. In reviewing this body of work, we identified three themes that seem to characterize the contemporary literature. These include the increase in occupationally specific studies, a major paradigm shift in the study of gender differences, and innovations in the methods and measures used by researchers.

Occupationally specific studies

Within the literature on gender differences and stress, an emerging trend is the increase of occupationally specific studies. Ginn and Sandell (1997), for example, studied gender differences in the stress reported by social services workers. Their finding was that among staff, women with family responsibilities reported more stress than men in equivalent jobs. Morris (1996) examined gender differences in stress in a sample of 372 New York City police officers. Her finding was that women and minority men reported more negative social interactions on the job such as criticism and biases. In addition, women and ethnic minority men reported more positive interactions on the job than did white men, and ethnic minority women reported the greatest access to job-related guidance.

Urban bus drivers have been the subjects of study as well. No interactions between occupational stressors and gender were found (Rydstedt et al., 1998). In a study of female lawyers, Schenker et al. (1997) examined the relationship between stress and adverse reproductive outcomes. Their finding was that women working more than 45 hours per week were five times as likely to report high stress as those working 35 hours per week. In addition, women who worked more than 45 hours per week during the first trimester of pregnancy were more likely to report high work stress during pregnancy. Weekly job hours during the first trimester had a strong independent association with spontaneous abortion, after adjustment for confounding factors.

The occupationally specific studies are important in several respects. They make equivalent female/male samples easier to obtain, for one. In addition, they allow us to explore the stress experience of women in female-dominated occupations, like social services, with that of women in male-dominated occupations, like police work. Comparative studies are needed in this regard.

Paradigm shifts

In recent years, the study of gender and health has seen a change in the way researchers view gender differences. The vast majority of past studies focused on discovering differences rather than similarities in the ways men and women experience work stress. Barnett (1997) has been a vocal advocate of this paradigm shift, contending that the overlap in social role occupancy of men and women is making it possible to disaggregate gender by holding the social context of men's and women's roles constant. What is important is the study of the link between work and health, and whether it is similar for men and women. This amounts to shifting from the study of the direct effects of gender on health toward using gender as a moderator in the relationship between work and health outcomes. This allows us to isolate conditions in which gender does or does not have effects.

Barnett's (1997) work has demonstrated that after controlling for certain individual-level and couple-level variables, gender did not moderate the relationship between social roles and psychological distress. For example, she found that psychological distress was related to quality of marriage among women, but not among men. *Post hoc* analyses showed that commitment to the marriage accounted for the gender difference; that is, among individuals highly committed to marriage, changes in marriage quality were related to distress. For those with low commitment, there was no relationship, and no gender differences were found. The paradigm shift calls into question the studies that have demonstrated that women experience more distress than do men. It becomes important to identify possible covariates in these studies and to control for them.

Along these same lines, Simon (1998) proposed that gender variation in stress reactivity was contingent on individuals' marital status. Using data from the National Survey of Households and Families (n = 2,937), her analyses indicated that sex differences in parents' responses to stress depend to a large degree on the specific stressor and distress outcome studied. For example, role strain was reported by both married mothers and fathers; however, married fathers were more reactive to stressors that revolved around the breadwinner role, while mothers were more reactive to stressors revolving around the nurturant role. Additionally, role strain was manifested in depression for women, and in alcohol abuse for men. Married and unmarried mothers did not differ in their responses to work and family stress; however, parental strain was more harmful to unmarried than to married fathers.

Simon's work demonstrates that context variables that frame the meaning and psychological impact of stress, such as marital status, are important inclusions in studies of women and work stress. By focusing on marital status rather than on sex differences in distress, it is possible to isolate gender-based vulnerabilities to stressors in work and family role domains that emerge from the gendered nature of family responsibilities.

Measurement and methods innovations

Recent attention has also been directed toward improvements in measures and methods for studying women and work stress. Gross (1997) analysed studies of gender differences in physician stress and noted that those studies using inventories and closed questions were based on stressors reported only by male physicians. Consequently, stressors such as lack of role models and sexual harassment were not included. Gender differences emerged, however, when open-ended questions were used. Gross recommended that stress inventories be designed specifically to include stressors experienced by women, or studies should use open-ended questions.

The use of physiological measures of distress has increased. A recent study examined stress hormones as distress measures in 109 employed women (Luecken et al., 1997). The effects of marital and parental status on daily excretion of urinary catecholamines and cortisol were studied. Urine samples were gathered on two separate work days at three separate times (overnight, daytime and evening). Age and caffeine consumption were controlled for in a repeated measures analysis. Women with at least one child living at home excreted significantly more cortisol, independent of marital status or social support. Catecholamine levels were unrelated to marital or parental status, or social support. The use of these more objective indicators of distress in studies of women and stress is welcomed.

Researchers are increasingly using advanced analytic techniques to great advantage. Hierarchical linear modelling provides a robust way to examine change over time, and allows researchers to separate variance in distress indicators into true score and error variance (cf. Barnett and Brennan, 1997). Structural equation modelling requires more precise statements of theory and allows for refined tests of theories and for the comparison of competing theories.

Implications for interventions

The three-part preventive management framework provides a framework for integrating the preceding review into suggestions for interventions that would target the stress-related challenges of working women. Primary preventive efforts, directed at changing the source of stress, should focus on the stressors of politics, overload, barriers to achievement, sexual harassment and other social-sexual behaviours, and work/home conflict (Burke, 1996). Flexible work schedules, alternative work arrangements like telecommuting, and company assistance with childcare and eldercare can help women deal with overload and work/home issues (Mattis, 1994). Politics, barriers to achievement and sexual harassment can be effectively diminished by aggressive organizational efforts in terms of corporate policy, and a system of rewards that reinforces equitable treatment of all organizational members (Schwartz, 1992). Efforts to build in social support at work, such as in mentoring programmes, can be of special benefit to working women (Kram, 1985; Parker and Kram, 1993).

Secondary prevention efforts focus on helping women manage their own responses to stress, and usually come in the form of exercise or ways to emotionally release tension. As noted earlier, women are less likely to utilize exercise as a coping technique than are men. Interventions that educate women about the stress management benefits of exercise and encourage them to engage in exercise are warranted. Support groups to facilitate emotional release and training in relaxation methods can help women more effectively with the transition from the work to the home environment with less stress spillover.

Tertiary prevention efforts are directed at symptom management. It is essential that employee assistance programmes recognize the special needs of women in provision of services or referral to appropriate professional care. Certain behavioural distress symptoms, such as eating disorders, alcohol abuse and smoking, may be more effectively treated with gender-specific interventions.

Conclusion

Our work on this chapter has led us to view the progress in research on women and work stress with considerable optimism. The sheer volume of literature that has emerged since the late 1970s is cause for encouragement. Do men and women experience work stress differently? We believe that they do. The complication is that we, as researchers, are still not able to specify the precise differences in all aspects of the stress experience: stressors, coping methods, and distress symptoms.

The paradigm shift toward treating gender as a moderator holds promise for answering this question. The link between stressors and distress, or more broadly, between work and health, does differ between men and women. Researchers are urged to move toward considering the ways these relationships differ, and under what conditions the differences emerge. The inclusion of covariates such as marital status represents progress in this manner. We must move beyond studying differences for differences' sake, and be sure to include studies of intragroup differences. Studies on the effectiveness of interventions targeted toward women are obviously lacking and much needed.

There is substantial complexity in trying to understand the experience of work stress among women. Stressors, coping responses and distress symptoms combine in a tangled web that is still not fully comprehended. Gender can no longer be viewed solely as a predictor variable or as a classification variable. It is more appropriately viewed as a variable that interacts in complex ways with psychological, social, physiological and behavioural risk factors, as noted by Chesney and Nealey (1996). Attempting to separate out the role of gender within this complexity can be a formidable task.

References

Auster, E.R. (1993) 'Demystifying the glass ceiling: organizational and interpersonal dynamics of gender bias', *Business and the Contemporary World*, 5: 49–68.

Barling, J. (1990) *Employment, Stress and Family Functioning*, John Wiley, New York.

Barling, J., Dupre, K.E. and Hepburn, C.G. (1998) 'Effects of parents' job insecurity on children's work beliefs and attitudes', *Journal of Applied Psychology*, 83: 112–118.

Barnett, R.C. (1997) 'How paradigms shape the stories we tell: paradigm shifts in gender and health', *Journal of Social Issues*, 53: 351–365.

Barnett, R.C. and Baruch, G.K. (1985) 'Women's involvement in multiple roles and psychological distress', *Journal of Personality and Social Psychology*, 49: 135–145.

Barnett, R.C. and Brennan, R.T. (1997) 'Change in job conditions, change in psychological distress, and gender: a longitudinal study of dual-earner couples', *Journal of Organizational Behavior*, 18: 253–274.

Barnett, R.C. and Shen, Y.C. (1997) 'Gender, high- and low-schedule-control housework tasks, and psychological distress: a study of dual earner couples', *Journal of Family Issues*, 18: 403–428.

Beatty, C.A. (1996) 'The stress of managerial and professional women: is the price too high?' *Journal of Organizational Behavior*, 17: 233–252.

Burke, R.J. (1996) 'Work experiences, stress and health among managerial and professional women', in M.J. Schabracq, J.A.M. Winnubst and C.L. Cooper (eds), *Handbook of Work and Health Psychology*, John Wiley and Sons, Chichester.

Burke, R.J. and Greenglass, E.R. (1987) 'Work and family', in C.L. Cooper and I.T. Robertson (eds), *International Review of Industrial and Organizational Psychology*, John Wiley, New York, pp. 273–320.

Burke, R.J. and McKeen, C.A. (1992) 'Social-sexual behavior at work: experiences of managerial and professional women', *Women in Management Review*, 2: 22–30.

Chesney, M.A and Nealey, J.B. (1996) 'Smoking and cardiovascular disease risk in women', in P.M. Kato and T. Mann (eds), *Handbook of Diversity Issues in Health Psychology*, Plenum Press, New York, pp. 199–218.

Dunahoo, C.L., Geller, P.A. and Hobfoll, S.E. (1996) 'Women's coping: communal versus individualistic orientation', in M.J. Schabracq, J.A.M. Winnubst and

C.L. Cooper (eds), *Handbook of Work and Health Psychology*, John Wiley and Sons, Chichester, pp. 183–204.

Etzion, D. and Pines, A. (1986) 'Sex and culture in burnout and coping among human service professionals: a social psychological perspective', *Journal of Cross-Cultural Psychology*, 17: 191–209.

Folkman, S., Lazarus, R.S., Gruen, R.J. and DeLongis, A. (1986) 'Appraisal, coping and health status, and psychological symptoms', *Journal of Personality and Social Psychology*, 50: 571–579.

Frankenhauser, M. (1991) 'The psychophysiology of workload, stress, and health: comparison between the sexes', *Annals of Behavioral Medicine*, 13: 197–204.

Frone, M.R., Russell, M. and Barnes, G.M. (1996) 'Work – family conflict, gender, and health-related outcomes: a study of employed parents in two community samples', *Journal of Occupational Health Psychology*, 1: 57–69.

Furnham, A. and Kirkcaldy, B. (1997) 'Age and sex differences in health beliefs and behaviors', *Psychological Reports*, 80: 63–66.

Galambos, N.L., Sears, H.A., Almeida, D.M. and Kolaric, G.C. (1995) 'Parents' work overload and problem behavior in young adolescents', *Journal of Research on Adolescence*, 5: 201–223.

Geller, P.A. and Hobfoll, S.E. (1994) 'Gender differences in job stress, tedium and social support in the workplace', *Journal of Personal and Social Relationships*, 11: 555–572.

Ginn, J. and Sandell, J. (1997) 'Balancing home and employment: stress reported by social services staff', *Work, Employment and Society*, 11: 413–434.

Goldenhar, L.M., Swanson, N.G., Hurrell, J.J. Jr, Ruder, A. and Deddens, J. (1998) 'Stressors and adverse outcomes for female construction workers', *Journal of Occupational Health Psychology*, 3: 19–32.

Greenglass, E.R. (1991) 'Burnout and gender: theoretical and organizational implications', *Canadian Psychology*, 32: 562–572.

Greenglass, E.R. (1993) 'The contribution of social support to coping strategies', *Applied Psychology: An International Review*, 42: 323–340.

Gross, E.B. (1997) 'Gender differences in physician stress: why the discrepant findings?' *Women and Health*, 26: 1–14.

Gutek, B.A., Cohen, A.G. and Konrad, A.M. (1990) 'Predicting social-sexual behavior at work: a contact hypothesis', *Academy of Management Journal*, 33: 560–577.

Hatch, M. and Moline, J. (1997) 'Women, work and health', *American Journal of Industrial Medicine*, 32: 303–308.

Heilman, M.E. (1995) 'Sex stereotypes and their effects in the workplace: what we know and what we don't know', *Journal of Social Behavior and Personality*, 10: 3–26.

Hochschild, A.R. (1989) *The Second Shift*, Avon Books, New York.

Hochschild, A.R. (1997) *The Time Bind*, Metropolitan Books, New York.

Jick, T.D. and Mitz, L.F. (1985) 'Sex differences in work stress', *Academy of Management Review*, 10: 408–420.

Kinnunen, U. and Mauno, S. (1998) 'Antecedents and outcomes of work–family conflict among employed women and men in Finland', *Human Relations*, 51: 157–177.

Klonoff-Cohen, H.S., Cross, J.L. and Pieper, C.F. (1996) 'Job stress and preeclampsia', *Epidemiology*, 7: 245–249.

Kram, K.E. (1985) *Mentoring at Work*, Scott, Foresman, Glenview, IL.

Langan-Fox, J. (1998) 'Women's careers and occupational stress', in C.L. Cooper and I.T. Robertson (eds), *International Review of Industrial and Organizational Psychology*, John Wiley, New York, pp. 273–304.

Lindquist, T.L., Beilin, L.J. and Knuiman, M.W. (1997) 'Influence of lifestyle, coping, and job stress on blood pressure in men and women', *Hypertension*, 29: 1–7.

Luecken, L.J., Suarez, E.C., Kuhn, C.M., Barefoot, J.C., Blumenthal, J.A., Siegler, I.C. and Williams, R.B. (1997) 'Stress in employed women: impact of marital status and children at home on neurohormone output and home strain', *Psychosomatic Medicine*, 59: 352–359.

Lundberg, U., Mardberg, B. and Frankenhauser, M. (1994) 'The total workload of male and female white collar workers as related to age, occupational level, and number of children', *Scandinavian Journal of Psychology*, 35: 315–327.

Mann, T. (1996) 'Why do we need a health psychology of gender or sexual orientation in women?' in P.M. Kato and T. Mann (eds), *Handbook of Diversity Issues in Health Psychology*, Plenum Press, New York, pp.187–198.

Martocchio, J.J. and O'Leary, A. (1989) 'Sex differences in occupational stress: a meta-analytic review', *Journal of Applied Psychology*, 74: 495–501.

Maslach, C. and Jackson, S.E. (1981) 'The measurement of experienced burnout', *Journal of Occupational Behavior*, 2: 99–113.

Matthews, S., Hertzman, C., Ostry, A. and Power, C. (1998) 'Gender, work roles and psychosocial work characteristics as determinants of health', *Social Science and Medicine*, 46: 1417–1424.

Mattis, M.C. (1994) 'Organizational initiatives in the USA for advancing managerial women', in M.J. Davidson and R.J. Burke (eds), *Women in Management: Current Research Issues*, Paul Chapman, London, pp. 261–276.

Matuszek, P.A.C., Nelson, D.L. and Quick, J.C. (1995) 'Gender differences in distress: are we asking all the right questions?' *Journal of Social Behavior and Personality*, 10: 99–120.

Morris, A. (1996) 'Gender and ethnic differences in social constraints among a sample of New York City police officers', *Journal of Occupational Health Psychology*, 1: 224–235.

Morrison, A.M. (1992) *The New Leaders*, Jossey-Bass, San Francisco, CA.

Morrison, A.M. and von Glinow, M.A. (1990) 'Women and minorities in management', *American Psychologist*, 45: 200–208.

Nelson, D.L. and Quick, J.C. (1985) 'Professional women: are distress and disease inevitable?' *Academy of Management Review*, 10: 206–218.

Nelson, D.L., Hitt, M.A. and Quick, J.C. (1989) 'Men and women of the personnel profession: some similarities and differences in their stress', *Stress Medicine*, 5: 145–152.

Niedhammer, I., Goldberg, M., Leclerc, A., David, S., Bugel, I. and Landre, M. (1998) 'Psychosocial work environment and cardiovascular risk factors in an occupational cohort in France', *Journal of Epidemiology and Community Health*, 52: 93–100.

Ogus, E.D., Greenglass, E.R. and Burke, R.J. (1990) 'Gender-role differences, work stress and depersonalization', *Journal of Social Behavior and Personality*, 5: 387–398.

Ohlott, P.J., Ruderman, M.N. and McCauley, C.D. (1994) 'Gender differences in managers' developmental job experiences', *Academy of Management Journal*, 37: 46–67.

Parker, V.A. and Kram, K.E. (1993) 'Women mentoring women: creating conditions for connection', *Business Horizons*, 23: 42–51.

Philpot, C.L., Brooks, G.R., Lusterman, D. and Nutt, R.L. (1997) *Bridging Separate Gender Worlds: Why Men and Women Clash and How Therapists Can Bring Them Together*, American Psychological Association, Washington, DC.

Piotrkowski, C.S. (1998) 'Gender harassment, job satisfaction and distress among employed white and minority women', *Journal of Occupational Health Psychology*, 3: 33–42.

Pretorius, T.B. (1996) 'Gender and the health-sustaining and stress-reducing effects of social support: a South African study', *Journal of Social Behavior and Personality*, 11: 193–208.

Ptacek, J.T., Smith, R.E. and Dodge, K.L. (1994) 'Gender differences in coping with stress: when stressor and appraisals do not differ', *Personality and Social Psychology Bulletin*, 20: 421–430.

Quick, J.C., Quick, J.D., Nelson, D.L. and Hurrell, J.J. (1997) *Preventive Stress Management in Organizations*, American Psychological Association, Washington, DC.

Rydstedt, L.W., Johansson, G. and Evans, G.W. (1998) 'A longitudinal study of workload, health and well-being among male and female urban bus drivers', *Journal of Occupational and Organizational Psychology*, 71: 35–45.

Schenker, M.B., Eaton, M., Green, R. and Samuels, S. (1997) 'Self-reported stress and reproductive health of female lawyers', *Journal of Occupational and Environmental Medicine*, 39: 556–568.

Schwartz, F.N. (1992) *Breaking with Tradition*, Warner Books, New York.

Schwartzberg, N.S. and Dytell, R.S. (1996) 'Dual-earner families: the importance of work stress and family stress for psychological well being', *Journal of Occupational Health Psychology*, 1: 211–223.

Simon, R.W. (1998) 'Assessing sex differences in vulnerability among employed parents: the importance of marital status', *Journal of Health and Social Behavior*, 39: 38–54.

Solomon, C.M. (1998) 'Study confirms: women are still undervalued', *Workforce*, May: 82–83.

Stewart, W. and Barling, J. (1996) 'Fathers' work experiences affect children's behaviors via job-related affect and parenting behaviors', *Journal of Organizational Behavior*, 16: 221–232.

Tenbrunsel, A.E., Brett, J.M., Maoz, E., Stroh, L.K. and Reilly, A.H. (1995) 'Dynamic and static work–family relationships', *Organizational Behavior and Human Decision Processes*, 63: 233–246.

US Department of Labor (1998) 'Usual weekly earnings summary', *Labor Force Statistics from the Current Population Survey*, US Government, Washington, DC.

Westman, M. and Etzion, D. (1995) 'Crossover of stress, strain and resources from one spouse to another', *Journal of Organizational Behavior*, 16: 169–181.

Zappert, L.T. and Weinstein, H.M. (1985) 'Sex differences in the impact of work on physical and psychological health', *American Journal of Psychiatry*, 142: 1174–1178.

13

Stress and the Unemployed Woman Manager – A Comparative Approach

Sandra L. Fielden and Marilyn J. Davidson

The greatest social change over the last two decades has been the increase of women in paid employment. In 1997 women accounted for just over half of the UK workforce (*Labour Force Survey*, 1997) and this figure will continue to rise until the year 2006, according to recent government projections (Employment Service, 1995). This increase has not been across all occupations or occupational levels; occupational segregation by sex persists as a primary characteristic of the UK labour market. Women are concentrated in service industries, especially retail, educational and medical services. They tend to work in smaller workplaces than men, i.e. with fewer than 50 employees, and 'get paid less for working with other women' whereas men 'get paid more for working with other men' (Equal Opportunities Commission, 1998). Women are still seriously under-represented at all senior management levels (Rigg and Sparrow, 1994). Although a third of all UK managers and administrators are now women (Equal Opportunities Commission, 1998) the majority are employed at the lowest levels of the managerial hierarchy.

Employment is important to women both as a source of income and as a defining factor in self-conceptions. Attitudes and social patterns which deny the legitimacy of women's employment persist and ignore the importance that work has come to occupy in the lives of many women (Ratcliff and Brogden, 1988). It has often been proposed that women will actually experience less stress than men during unemployment because the work/family interface, which is a major source of stress for working women, is removed (Newell, 1993). This approach has been used to further devalue the worth of women's employment but research does not support this view. Studies that have included unemployed women show no significant difference between unemployed men and women in terms of self-esteem, hostility and personal distress. However, they have found that unemployment is experienced differently by each sex (Stokes and Cochrane, 1984; Leana and Feldman, 1991). Further research has shown that women are faced with additional sources of stress, and the denial of the importance of work in women's lives often results in non-supportive social 'support' and an undermining of self-worth (Ratcliff and Brogden, 1988). Employment, and specifically managerial employment, still appears to be intrinsically linked with masculinity, resulting in few studies of women's unemployment and only one previous study relating to unemployed female managers, conducted by the authors (Fielden and Davidson, 1996).

Managerial unemployment has traditionally been viewed as a male bastion that was limited to a few unfortunate individuals. Until the late 1980s the number of unemployed managers was relatively low but job loss through economic pressures and structural changes is increasingly affecting this occupational group, especially middle managers. The 1990s have seen record levels of organizational downsizing, and this has had a major impact on managers, who have borne the brunt of these cutbacks (Capell, 1992). Much of the work performed by middle management has been eroded by information technology and the drive for efficiency, which has placed many managers under the enormous pressure of ever increasing workloads (Malo, 1993). Growing numbers of managers are being discarded as surplus to requirement because they are unable to perform at the required levels; those who have few or no formal qualifications are particularly susceptible to redundancy (White, 1991).

Restructuring has not only led to a significant increase in managerial unemployment, but has also resulted in the decline of the generous employment conditions previously enjoyed by middle and senior managers. Although managers have historically enjoyed better employment conditions than clerical or blue-collar workers, recent developments have diminished or eroded many of those benefits. In a recent survey by the Institute of Management over 80 per cent of managers expressed anxiety about their future financial security (*Women in Management Review*, 1996a). Long notice periods and access to pensions had offered some degree of financial security for managers but as their positions change, they are becoming more disposable and hence more vulnerable to job loss (White, 1994). More and more managers are having to face career direction changes, with fewer career opportunities available, and less and less job security (*Women in Management Review*, 1996b). Recent and foreseeable developments may further weaken managers' positions (White, 1991). This affects not only those in work but those seeking work.

The increases in managerial unemployment affects both female and male managers, yet to date only one major study has been conducted which explores the comparative experiences of female and male managers (Fielden, 1997). The findings of that study indicate that the impact of unemployment on the psychological well-being of male managers is significant but the impact on the psychological and physical well-being of unemployed female managers is substantially greater. This chapter presents the findings of the authors' study and considers the overall effect of unemployment on male and female managers, and what can be learned from their comparative experiences, based on research conducted in UK-government-funded agencies (Executive Job Clubs) designed to assist unemployed managers back into work.

Methodology

An extensive review of the literature by the authors has identified many potential sources of stress that male and female managers may face during unemployment.

TABLE 13.1   *Participants' demographic details*

Personal details	Females (n = 115)	Males (n = 169)
Age range (mean)	22–58 (39.47)	24–62 (45.9)
Previous position –		
senior management	23%	40%
middle management	31%	41%
junior management	25%	12%
Supervisory	21%	7%
Length of		
unemployment (mean)	1–56 months (11 months)	1–36 months (14 months)
Time at Executive Job		
Club (mean)	0.25–12 months (2.3 months)	0.25–18 months (2.9 months)

Although the relationship between stressors, mediators and stress outcomes is a complex one, the comparative effects of unemployment upon male and female managers could only be summarized from the literature. This study sought to identify both gender differences and similarities, in its investigation of the comparative experiences of unemployed male and female managers. A questionnaire was developed based upon the content analysis of semi-structured interviews (two hours in duration) with unemployed female (n = 20) and male (n = 20) managers, in conjunction with an extensive literature review.

Questionnaires were distributed to all the Executive Job Clubs (EJCs) throughout England, i.e. government-funded agencies specifically operated to assist unemployed managers in their search for work and the only formal register of unemployed managers in England. A random, matched sample of 115 female and 169 male managers (see Table 13.1) were recruited from 47 of the 80 EJCs that were operating throughout England. The overall return rate was estimated at 47 per cent for the main questionnaires, based on the availability of female managers registered at EJCs. Quantitative data were on a number of independent variables: personal and job demographics, sources of unemployment stress (including job loss, finance, relationships, and job search), Type A coronary prone behaviour patterns, locus of control, and behavioural and cognitive coping strategies; and two dependent measures: well-being (mental and physical health) and negative emotions.

Stressors experienced during managerial unemployment

The main source of stress reported by unemployed female managers resulted from the stigma associated with unemployment. Although this was a significant source of stress for both unemployed female and male managers, unemployed female managers perceived substantially greater levels of stigma than their male counterparts. This difference in perception was frequently linked to the occupational stereotypes encountered by female managers in all aspects of their unemployment experiences. These stereotypes, especially those they had to contend with at government agencies, for example the Employment Service, were a major source of stress. This stress was exacerbated by the loss of occupational identity which, along with their male counterparts, they experienced as a direct result of job loss. In contrast, the main sources of stress reported by unemployed male managers arose from the financial impact of unemployment and the extensive ageism that they faced during job search. In general, the stressors encountered by unemployed male managers were similar to those found by previous research (e.g. Swinburne, 1981) studying the effects of unemployment on non-managerial males, with the only marked differences being the loss of the creativity outlet suffered by unemployed male managers as a result of job loss, a managerial characteristic traditionally viewed as a female attribute (Schein and Mueller, 1992).

The financial impact of unemployment on female and male managers was equally devastating but frequently in qualitatively different ways. Lack of adequate food was a deprivation of primary lifestyle experienced by both female and male managers as a direct result of the financial effects of unemployment. Unemployed female managers also experienced further primary lifestyle deprivation, reporting lack of adequate heating as a significant effect of their financial situation. The main and most striking financial effect reported by unemployed male managers, surpassing any primary lifestyle deprivation they had experienced, was the loss of their company car. The removal of this status symbol had a significant impact on the physical well-being of unemployed managers, producing high levels of stress in unemployed male managers, a loss for which no substitute was available. This finding clearly illustrates the degree of status placed by male managers on their cars and, because it is such a public display of their employment status, the effect of this loss is devastating for unemployed male managers. No such effect was found for unemployed female managers but this may result from the fact that very few female managers are afforded such status symbols or from a lack of value placed on such outward displays of status.

The reactions of others encountered by unemployed female and male managers differed significantly. Unemployed male managers reported substantial support from both friends and family members, with many unemployed female managers feeling that they would have received more support had they been male. This may arise because of the greater acceptance of men as managers (Schein and Mueller, 1992), combined with a lack of recognition of the importance of work in the lives of female managers. It may also be compounded by scarcity of unemployed female managers who could increase understanding and acceptance of their situation. Conversely, it may lead to the appearance that few unemployed managers are female because of the persistence of the stereotypical perception that 'male = managers' (Sheridan, 1994), with their existence being denied rather than ignored. Thus, if unemployed female managers are only offered the support afforded other unemployed women, they are likely to perceive it as unsupportive and possibly even destructive. This was clearly illustrated by one unemployed female senior manager who commented,

> 'They [friends and family] were great at first because I was less stressed, now they can't understand why I haven't got a job. The other day one of my friends told me to get off my backside and get a job.'

This situation is compounded by the impact of the stigma experienced by female managers during unemployment, with the degree of stigma perceived having a direct influence on their ability to access social support networks. As one unemployed junior manager in her twenties said, 'They [friends] ask why I haven't got a job yet. I lie and say I'm not looking, I avoid these conversations at any cost.'

Unemployed male managers reported that they had no one to talk to significantly more often than their female counterparts. Yet it was unemployed female managers who expressed a desire for increased social contact. Overall, unemployed male managers desired to keep their situation private, a fact underlined by their reluctance to discuss their situation with anyone outside of their family circle, with partners being the main source of emotional support. The expression of feelings was not seen as a priority by unemployed male managers, many of whom preferred to keep their thoughts to themselves. It is not possible to say whether or not these men would have benefited from increased social support, but it is likely that those who found it easier to disclose their feelings experienced less negative emotions and better mental well-being as a result. This again points to the differences in the desire of unemployed female and male managers for the emotional support provided by social contact. In light of this finding it may seem surprising that both female and male managers experienced high levels of isolation during unemployment, although unemployed female managers consistently reported more loneliness than their male counterparts.

As anticipated, the job search experiences of unemployed female and male managers differed substantially. The main barrier faced by unemployed male managers during job search was ageism and this was believed to be a significant factor in explaining their lack of success in securing employment. Unemployed female managers encountered numerous barriers in their search for work. Discrimination on the grounds of gender was the primary form encountered, although discrimination on the grounds of race and sexuality were also reported. These types of discrimination were found in all facets of recruitment and unemployed female managers even reported significant levels of patronization by their fellow male Executive Job Club members.

Previous research may suggest that unemployed female managers would have greater difficulty finding suitable positions to apply for than their male counterparts (Cooper and Davidson, 1984; Ray, 1990). However, the level of perceived difficulty may have been influenced by prior expectations rather than the actual number of suitable positions available (Davies and Esseveld, 1989). This may be indicated by the finding that unemployed female managers reported a lack of suitable jobs as a reason for unsuccessful job search significantly more often than their male counterparts. In addition, unemployed female managers applied for significantly fewer jobs than their male counterparts, again suggesting the existence of fewer suitable vacancies. The high ambition reported by unemployed female managers interacted with their lack of relevant male-based experience and their lack of access to effective networks. This resulted in decreased confidence and a tendency for unemployed female managers to apply for positions they were overqualified for; unemployed female managers strongly believed that they would have access to more vacancies if they were male. Thus, it would appear that recruitment literature is still being targeted at male rather than female candidates.

It may have been anticipated from these findings that unemployed male managers would secure more interviews than their female counterparts, yet there were no significant differences in the number of interviews attended by unemployed female and male managers. In addition, there were no differences in the interview experiences of unemployed female and male managers. However, one similarity was likely to have different repercussions for male and female unemployed managers, which was the significant predominance of male interviewers. According to Stuart (1992), interviewers frequently choose the candidate who most closely resembles themselves. This means that male interviewers are more likely to recruit male candidates, as they provide greater congruence with their 'ideal candidate' in terms of occupational and personal characteristics. This may result in unemployed female managers being excluded from the selection process or being evaluated less favourably.

Previous research into discrimination and recruitment has concentrated on employers, excluding other participants such as employment agencies. These agencies are often used in managerial recruitment as a method of short-listing potential candidates and, whilst the employer is still ultimately responsible for final selection, employment agencies can successfully block any application. Although employment agencies have to conform to the Sex Discrimination Act (1975), over a third of those unemployed female managers who used employment agencies reported that they had experienced discrimination on the grounds of gender. In contrast, over a third of the unemployed male managers who had used employment agencies reported experiencing discrimination on the grounds of age. As one unemployed male middle manager in his fifties stated, 'Employment agencies are useless if you're over 40, they "pigeonhole" people simply because of their age.' This indicates that employment agencies may be a substantial barrier during job search and is an area which needs further research, to establish the extent and impact of this form of discrimination on unemployed female and male managers.

These findings clearly show that the prevalence of sex discrimination in the recruitment process persists, with almost a third of unemployed female managers reporting discrimination on the grounds of gender. Further support for this position comes from the comments of Executive Job Club leaders, two-thirds of whom believed that unemployed female managers were constantly faced with prejudice and discrimination in their search for managerial work. As one female leader wrote,

> Genderism is still the main barrier faced by women because of outmoded perceptions of female abilities and the place females are perceived to hold in society.

Because unemployed female managers face extensive discrimination on the grounds of both gender and age, they are likely to suffer greater negative affect as a result of unsuccessful job search than their male counterparts.

Moderators of the stress process

Unemployed female managers were significantly more likely to be single than their male counterparts. As partners were a key source of social support, this meant that unemployed female managers were frequently deprived of this effective moderating factor. However, unemployed male managers were also more likely to have dependants to support. This increased many of the financial pressures experienced during unemployment, both directly through its impact on the availability of economic resources and indirectly through the psychological impact resulting from the loss of the breadwinner role. Nevertheless, this role also provided unemployed male managers with more supportive social support, because of the increased understanding of their situation promoted by stereotyped societal attitudes.

Age was perceived by unemployed male managers as a significant factor in their experience of unemployment but it also strongly influenced the experiences of unemployed female managers. The high levels of gender discrimination reported by female managers tended to mask the degree of ageism they also encountered during unemployment. In some cases this was felt to be even more of an issue for unemployed female managers because of the lower retirement age. In addition, they had significantly higher educational qualifications than their male counterparts. This provided drawbacks for both unemployed female and male managers during job search. The availability of suitable positions was restricted to some degree by the lack of educational qualifications held by unemployed male managers, although it did not appear to go against them after the initial application stage. In contrast, unemployed female managers were often overqualified for the positions for which they applied, a situation compounded by the predominance of male interviewers with comparatively lower educational status.

A lack of personal control, reported by both unemployed female and male managers, was also a significant moderator of their experience during unemployment. However, unlike their male counterparts, unemployed female managers were also affected by decreasing self-confidence and self-efficacy. These were exacerbated by high employment commitment and low levels of Type A coronary prone behaviour, i.e. the overall style of behaviour observed in those who are hard-driving, competitive, aggressive, time-conscious and ambitious (Greenglass, 1993). In contrast, unemployed male managers experienced high levels of self-esteem and self-concept, which appeared to be aided by high levels of Type A coronary prone behaviour rather than hindered, as suggested by previous research (Edwards et al., 1990). These personal factors were strongly influenced by the availability of social support: as unemployed female managers reported significantly poorer levels of social support than their male counterparts, the detrimental effects of this interaction on the mental well-being of unemployed female managers were severe.

In addition, negative emotions were a very important predictor of mental and physical well-being for both unemployed female and male managers. This is of particular significance when considering the comparative effects of unemployment on female and male managers, with unemployed female managers experiencing significantly more negative emotions during unemployment than their male counterparts. Unemployed female managers experienced significantly greater anxiety, upset, fear and degradation, and lower personal confidence. This would suggest that these aspects are continually reinforced throughout unemployment, being affected both independently and interactively. For example, the gender discrimination experienced by unemployed female managers may result in reduced personal confidence, which in turn increases anxiety levels and fear of future prospects. Alternatively, a lack of confidence can inhibit interview performance, again leading to greater anxiety and an increased fear of future interviews.

The negative emotions experienced by the unemployed managers may result from the impact of job loss on their self-concept. Unemployment deprives an individual of the part of their *perceived self* which is derived from their occupational status, increasing the disparity between the *real self* and the *ideal self* (Bala and Lakshmi, 1992). The impact of this type of deprivation is greater where work is central to an individual's self-image (Fineman, 1983). Yet previous research has shown that unemployed male managers frequently maintain their self-image and self-esteem by retaining their perceived self (Hartley, 1980), i.e. by continuing to see themselves as managers rather than as people who are unemployed. This may provide an explanation as to why loss of car is significantly related to the physical well-being of unemployed male managers, as it deprives unemployed male managers of an important aspect of their self-image, for which there is no alternative. In contrast, previous work by the authors has suggested that unemployed female managers do not retain their perceived self (Fielden and Davidson, 1996). This theory is supported by the comments of one unemployed female middle manager in her forties who wrote, 'I have no idea anymore how to manage, or even who I am or where I am going.'

The impact of unemployment on the self-concept of female managers appears to be linked to the degree of stigma that they perceive as connected with their situation. Unemployed female managers perceived significantly more stigma than their male counterparts, which in turn was significantly related to their ability to cope with unemployment. Previous research has also found that, compared to men, unemployed women hold more negative reflected appraisals, i.e. the perceived opinions of others (Sheeran and Abraham, 1994). These have a substantial impact, as working women tend to hold more positive reflected appraisals than working men (Bala and Lakshmi, 1992). Thus, the disparity between how they feel and how others view them during unemployment, compared to when they are working, is likely to be significantly greater than that experienced by their male counterparts. Although the effect of negative emotion is a major factor in determining both mental and physical well-being, the findings suggest that the disparity in reflected appraisals experienced by unemployed female managers has a greater impact on their self-concept and consequently a greater impact on their mental and physical well-being.

The sources of stress experienced during unemployment by female and male managers were also moderated by the coping strategies they employed. In comparison to their female counterparts, unemployed male managers were significantly more affirmative in their approach to unemployment when they had accepted their situation. In general, unemployed male managers maintained high levels of self-esteem and self-confidence through their positive approach to their situation. Although both unemployed female and male managers actively sought to maintain a positive attitude, unemployed male managers were substantially more successful in maintaining their self-belief by seeing unemployment as a challenge. The self-belief of many male managers appears to arise from their ability to retain their self-image and self-concept throughout unemployment. This is likely to result from a strong sense of occupational identity: when they become unemployed they may lose their job but not their occupational identity. Unemployed male managers continue to be managers even when they are not officially employed in that position, although this does not necessarily increase their chances of job search success; unemployed female managers achieved this by taking a more flexible approach to their job search activities.

Stress outcomes of managerial unemployment

In comparison with the general adult population, results from the authors' study revealed that unemployed male managers did suffer poorer mental well-being, as would be expected from previous unemployment research (Warr et al., 1988), but they experienced little decrease in their physical health. Overall, the mental and physical outcomes, in conjunction with the sources of stress and stress moderators experienced by unemployed male managers, are compatible with previous research (Hartley, 1980; Swinburne, 1981) and even indicate that male managers may be less affected by unemployment than their non-managerial counterparts. However, in comparison with their male counterparts unemployed female managers suffered significantly poorer mental and physical well-being. The main reason for this difference appears to be accounted for by the significantly high levels of negative emotions reported by unemployed managers. Negative emotion was a highly significant predictor of the mental and physical well-being experienced by both unemployed female and male managers. This factor, in conjunction with the loss of self-concept and self-confidence plus decreased levels of self-efficacy experienced by female managers as a result of the stressors encountered during unemployment, was not only responsible for reduced mental and physical well-being during unemployment but resulted in an increased probability of long-term health problems compared to their male counterparts.

These findings are not surprising, considering that female managers reported substantial stress arising from all aspects of their experiences during unemployment. The basis of the majority of these stressors lies in the 'male = manager' stereotype still so prevalent throughout society. Gender discrimination was encountered everywhere by unemployed female managers: in their search for work, in their contact with government agencies, and in their family and social circles. This, combined with the general lack of recognition given to the importance of work in the lives of unemployed female managers, means that unemployed female managers feel increasingly isolated and undervalued. The enormity of the stressors faced by unemployed female managers not only impacts on their overall well-being, but affects their ability to cope with their situation. Their coping abilities become less effective, leading to a sense of learned helplessness. This position is frequently exacerbated by the lack of access to or availability of social support experienced by many unemployed female managers. As social support is the main coping strategy they use, the search for effective support can become a further source of stress, especially when its unavailability results from the same stereotypical assumptions as the majority of other stressors.

Overall, the impact of unemployment on the psychological and physical well-being of female managers was substantial and, the long-term effects of this may be devastating. In addition, unemployed female managers suffered a number of behavioural effects, the most damaging of which was their inability to relax; this placed a further strain on their mental and physical well-being. Lack of relaxation, combined with negatively altered sleeping patterns, adversely affected not only the health of unemployed female managers but also their ability to cope effectively. Moreover, unemployed female managers suffered from a loss of self-confidence, self-efficacy and self-esteem which is likely to perpetuate their lack of job search success, trapping them in a situation which progressively erodes their self-concept and self-image.

The results of this study clearly indicate that unemployed female managers experience significantly greater sources of stress than their male counterparts, have less access to effective moderators of the stress process, and suffer significantly poorer mental and physical well-being as a result of their experiences during unemployment. This conflicts with the majority of previous work on the effects of unemployment on non-managerial women, which has suggested that non-managerial women encounter less stress than their male counterparts, are better able to cope and subsequently enjoy better mental and physical well-being during unemployment.

Previous research has ignored the experiences of unemployed female managers, and a number of studies (e.g. Warr and Parry, 1982; Dilnot and Kell, 1988) have theorized that the impact of unemployment on female managers would be less than that experienced by male managers. They have proposed that women are affected less by unemployment than men because of the assumption that the removal of the home/work interface will decrease the stress they experience (Stokes and Cochrane, 1984; Leana and Feldman, 1991). This stereotypical view was also held by unemployed male managers, who felt that unemployment was easier for female managers because they were more home oriented. The view of unemployed female managers differed dramatically from that of unemployed male managers; as one unemployed female middle manager interviewed in the pilot study explained, 'I hate being at home, I feel so trapped. I hate housework...I'd much rather be at work, it's where I belong.'

In addition, many unemployed female managers experienced greater stress from the home/work interface, rather than less, because of the lack of support they receive from their families. This illustrates the dangers of making assumptions about female managers based on traditional stereotypes and demonstrates that the reactions of female managers cannot be based on findings relating to unemployed male managers and non-managerial women.

The way forward

Unemployed managers have to deal with additional sources of stress to their non-managerial counterparts. These include:

1 isolation, often resulting from a lack of access to managers in a similar position;
2 a reduced availability of suitable positions, decreasing as managerial level is increased;
3 the fact that time periods in the recruitment process tend to be extended; and
4 the fact that many employers appear to be ill-equipped to recruit managers, often being less qualified than those applying for the available position.

These stressors mean that, for unemployed managers, finding work can take much longer than for their non-managerial counterparts. Many of the stereotypes relating to female managers are perpetuated by such assumptions, which have a dual effect: they inhibit the understanding of the true impact of unemployment on female managers and maintain the stereotypes which are the main source of stress for female managers during unemployment. This results in a lack of adequate services for unemployed female managers, which in turn becomes a self-fulfilling prophecy, i.e. few unemployed female managers use Executive Job Clubs therefore they must have substantially lower employment commitment than their male counterparts. This belief is wholly unsupported by the views of unemployed female managers and is contrary to the extensive knowledge of managerial unemployment held by Executive Job Clubs' leaders.

The Employment Service must address its own approach to unemployed managers. Staff were frequently reported as unhelpful and rude, with many unemployed managers feeling degraded and demoralized by the treatment they received. There was an overwhelming belief that Employment Service staff had minimal or no understanding of what the term 'manager' means, or how the needs of unemployed managers differ from those of the general unemployed population. This was especially distressing for unemployed female managers and the level of gender discrimination encountered at the Employment Service came as a shock to the majority of them. This discrimination was fuelled by the 'male = manager' stereotype, which negatively affected the approach taken by Employment Service staff towards female clients who had previously held managerial positions. These attitudes can be addressed only by breaking down gender stereotypes and by an increased awareness of the effect the stereotypes held by an individual have on their behaviour.

Overall, the Employment Service could be instrumental in reducing many of the stressors faced by unemployed female and male managers. Earlier access to Executive Job Clubs would provide unemployed managers with an effective means of job search, before they experienced the full impact of unemployment on their psychological and physical well-being. It would also provide some protection against discrimination on the grounds of being unemployed, a barrier which inevitably increases with the length of unemployment. Staff training and attitudinal change would result in a service to unemployed managers that demonstrates understanding and a recognition of the differences between managerial and non-managerial job search. This would not only minimize the sources of stress originating from unemployed managers' contact with the Employment Service, but it would help to maintain the self-concept and self-image of managers during unemployment.

Conclusion

Special provision for unemployed female managers, if marketed correctly, could not only reduce the stressors they encounter but could also help to maintain their self-confidence and self-esteem. This in turn would provide unemployed female managers with a more effective means of coping with their situation, especially through the increased access to social support that these provisions would open up. A higher profile and greater recognition of the impact of unemployment on female managers may also provide a basis for a change in wider social attitudes towards unemployed female managers.

The 1990s have seen a growing body of literature concerned with the comparative experiences of employed female and male managers. The findings of this study indicate that the barriers faced by female managers and many of the sources of stress they encounter in their working-lives are mirrored in their experiences of unemployment. However, those reflections are not equal: they are amplified by the lack of occupational identity afforded to unemployed female managers. Unlike their male counterparts, female managers have yet to experience a strong sense of being 'a manager' regardless of their employment status, a situation which will not change while female managers' experiences are so undermined by academia, the government and society as a whole.

References

Bala, M. and Lakshmi (1992) 'Perceived self in educated employed and educated unemployed women', *International Journal of Social Psychiatry*, 38 (4): 257–261.

Capell, P. (1992) 'Endangered middle managers', *American Demographics*, January, 44–47.

Cooper, C.L. and Davidson, M.J. (1984) *Women in Management*, Heinemann, London.

Davies, K. and Esseveld, J. (1989) 'Factory women: redundancy and the search for work: toward a reconceptualization of employment and unemployment', *Sociological Review*, 37: 219–252.

Dilnot, A. and Kell, M. (1988) 'Male unemployment and women's work', *Fiscal Studies*, 8 (3): 1–16.

Edwards, J.R., Baglioni, A.J. and Cooper, C.L. (1990) 'Stress, type-a, coping, and psychological and physical symptoms: a multi-sample test of alternative models', *Human Relations*, 43 (10): 919–956.

Employment Service (1995) 'The JUVOS Cohort: a longitudinal database of the claimant unemployed', *Employment Gazette*, September: 345–350.

Equal Opportunities Commission (1998) *Facts about Women and Men in Great Britain 1998*, EOC, Manchester.

Fielden, S.L. and Davidson, M.J. (1996) 'Sources of stress in unemployed female managers – a pilot study', *International Review of Women and Leadership*, 2 (2): 73–97.

Fielden, S.L. (1997) 'Sources of stress experienced by unemployed female and male managers: a comparative study'. Unpublished, UMIST PhD.

Fineman, S. (1983) *White Collar Unemployment*, John Wiley, Chichester.

Greenglass, E.R. (1993) 'Structural and social-psychological factors associated with job functioning by women managers', *Psychological Reports*, 73 (3): 979–986.

Hartley, J.F. (1980) 'The impact of unemployment upon the self-esteem of managers', *Journal of Occupational Psychology*, 53: 147–155.

Labour Force Survey (1997) Spring, Office for National Statistics, London.

Leana, C.R. and Feldman, D.C. (1991) 'Gender differences in response to unemployment', *Journal of Vocational Behaviour*, 38: 65–77.

Malo, S. (1993) 'Game, set and match to the human jungle', *New Scientist*, July: 45.

Newell, S. (1993) 'The superwoman syndrome: gender differences in attitudes toward equal opportunities at work and towards domestic responsibilities at home', *Work, Employment & Society*, 7 (2): 275–289.

Ratcliff, K.S. and Brogden, J. (1988) 'Unemployed women: when "social support" is not supportive', *Social Problems*, 35 (1): 54–63.

Ray, M. (1990) *Recruitment Advertising*, McCorquodale (Newton) Ltd, Newton-le-Willows, Lancs.

Rigg, C. and Sparrow, J. (1994) 'Gender, diversity and working styles', *Women in Management Review*, 9 (1): 9–16.

Schein, V.E. and Mueller, R. (1992) 'Sex role stereotyping and requisite management characteristics: a cross cultural look', *Journal of Social Behaviour*, Vol. 13, 439–447.

Sheeran, P. and Abraham, C. (1994) 'Unemployment and self-conception: a symbolic interactionist analysis', *Journal of Community & Applied Social Psychology*, 4: 115–129.

Sheridan, A. (1994) 'Managers in cartoons – they are still men in the *Harvard Business Review*', *Women in Management Review*, 9 (4): 20–24.

Stokes, G. and Cochrane, R. (1984) 'A study of the psychological effects of redundancy and unemployment', *Journal of Occupational Psychology*, 57: 309–322.

Stuart, P. (1992) 'What does the glass ceiling cost you?' *Personnel Journal*, 71 (11): 70–73.

Swinburne, P. (1981) 'The psychological impact of unemployment on managers and professional staff', *Journal of Occupational Psychology*, 54: 47–64.

Warr, P.B. and Parry, G. (1982) 'Paid employment and women's psychological well-being', *Psychological Bulletin*, 91: 498–516.

Warr, P.B., Jackson, P.R. and Banks, M. (1988) 'Unemployment and mental health: some British studies', *Journal of Social Issues*, 44 (4): 47–68.

White, M. (1991) *Against Unemployment*, Policy Studies Institute, London.

Women in Management Review (1996a) 'News & views: is marriage an advantage for men but an obstacle for women job seekers?' 11 (3): 37–38.

Women in Management Review (1996b) 'News & views: management anxiety exposed despite economic recovery', 11 (3): 35–36.

14

Refracted Lives: Sources of Disconnection between Black and White Women

Ella L.J. Edmondson Bell and Stella M. Nkomo

For over a decade we have studied the dynamics of race, gender and class, and the ways in which these constructs interconnect in women's lives. In 1992, we advocated a new way to 'revision' managerial women's lives (Bell and Nkomo, 1992). We argued for a feminist analysis, one taking into consideration the following factors: (1) group identity variables, (2) a biographical approach, and (3) an incorporation of the historical forces that help to determine women's lives. Our implicit assumption was to employ a holistic approach to explore the everyday realities working women experienced – regardless of their race and position – not just in their professional worlds, but in their professional lives throughout their life course (Bell et al., 1992).

Being 'woman-centred' was a core epistemological value for us. At the heart of woman-centred scholarship are the experiences of women, their relationships with other women, and issues of power ensuing between them. Kamala Visweswaran thinks of 'woman-centred' approaches as those that 'can consider how identities are multiple, contradictory, partial, and strategic' (1996: 50–51). She believes the 'underlying assumption' of this method is to recognize how a woman 'represents a constellation of conflicting social, linguistic, and political forces' (Visweswaran, 1996: 50).

Still in the early stages in our work, our woman-centred concepts were merely propositions. We had yet to test out how these concepts were related to or manifested in a woman's life. This all changed when we were funded by both the Ford and Rockefeller foundations to conduct a study on the career and life experiences of black and white professional women. We hoped our study would enable us to understand how race, gender and class impacted all dimensions of a woman's life. More than understanding the obstacles that discriminatory barriers created in women's lives, our goal was broader. We sought to discover how a woman's identity informed her life course, especially her relationship to the world of work, and her ability to pursue an alternative career path. Building upon adult development theories, research on women managers, and the legacy of scholarly work on race and gender relations, we wanted to learn how their backgrounds, families and educational levels influenced managerial women. How did a woman make sense of her life, the opportunities, the incongruencies and the regrets?

In this chapter we share what we learned from our study. At the end of our journey, we come away not with hard facts, but with striking images of what the women's narratives reveal. Race and class certainly impact and differentiate women's lives, but these are not the only factors. Their stories reveal much about what separates black and white women, in both their professional and personal lives.

Methodological approach

The method we employed in our research was life history. The life history approach provided a framework in which the meaning of experience is revealed from narratives told by a woman. We selected this approach for two reasons. First, it allowed us to capture a systematic, holistic portrait of women's lives. Second, it provided a way to understand the interwoven components of a woman's life, as well as the complexities. Life history is more than a woman's personal story. Her story reveals the differing and changing dimensions of her identity: changing in that identity, as Stuart Hall reminds us, 'is a matter of "becoming" as well as "being"' (Hall, 1989: 68). A woman's identity is located within a particular historical time, geographic place and multiple cultural contexts. Hall suggests that 'identities are the names we give to the different ways we are positioned by, and position ourselves within, the narratives of the past' (1989: 68). Thus, their self-representations tells us much about women's continuing role in history, ways they have influenced the communities they live and work in, and both the choices they made and the opportunities they had in navigating their lives.

Life history interviews were conducted with 120 executives and managers: 80 African-American and 40 European-American. We intentionally over-sampled African-American women since this professional group was underinvestigated. A cross-race interview team was employed in order for black women to be interviewed by a black female researcher and white women to be interviewed by a white female interviewer. Research studies indicate significant race-of-interviewer effects in cross-race interview situations (Schafer, 1986; Bailey, 1987). Just as the gender barrier was eliminated by the fact that women were interviewing women, we also wanted to eliminate potential racial barriers that might hinder the quality of the interaction during the interview. Put simply, we wanted our participants to feel comfortable and unjudged when sharing their stories. Interviews were conducted over two to three sessions, with each session lasting three to four hours. Women were interviewed in their homes and at their offices, early in the morning or late in the night, depending on the women's hectic schedules.

The stories you will read in this chapter come from managerial and executive women. They are employed in a wide variety of executive, administrative and managerial positions in private sector companies. These women were recruited through different professional women's networks, by referral from participants and alumnae from educational institutions. Selected participants demonstrated a positive motivation for self-exploration, a willingness to share their life stories and a commitment to the research project by giving their time. Participants lived in the northeast and southeast regions of the country. A majority were part of what Gail Sheehy identifies as the 'Vietnam generation', born between 1945 and 1955 (Sheehy, 1995). However, a small number of the women were from the 'Me Generation', being born in the late 1950s. For purposes of this chapter, all the women's names and other pertinent facts that could reveal their identities were changed.

Metaphors of disconnection

> *Your train is traveling*
> *South at 73 miles per hour.*
> *Mine is headed North doing 68.*
> *How long will it take us to arrive at*
> *our separate definitions?*
> *What time shall we begin, for real?*
> *What time can we call it home?*
>
> *Kate Rushin (1993)*

Metaphors enable us to move beyond our normal image of a situation by creating alternate images that both enhance and expand our present understanding. As John van Maanen adds, metaphors 'provide the constructive force for representing experience and thus help shape what we know and how we think' (Van Maanen, 1994: 2). When reading Kate Rushin's poem, the image of the trains struck us as a powerful metaphor for illuminating what we had learned about the separate life realities of black and white women. History, culture and social location all contribute to us often finding ourselves riding on two separate trains, heading in opposite directions, travelling at different speeds. These forces have certainly led to black and white women arriving at separate definitions of themselves. Or, as Louise Bernikow poignantly relates, 'Let everyone speak of racism but never tell what they have known as a dark woman and as a light woman, Black and Caucasian, Jew and Christian, eye each other, in a book or an office building' (Bernikow, 1980: 239).

Another way we tend to think of the disconnection between women is the image one has when looking into a mirror. Imagine a black woman and a white woman standing face to face, each as if peering into a mirror. But, instead of seeing a mirror likeness, what they see is a distortion. This distortion is caused by the refraction that occurs as their images travel through a filter of collective history combined with a cultural milieu of social relationships attributed to gender, race and class. The filter constantly distorts each woman's perception of the other. At certain angles, these distortions become so magnified as to block out any form of similarity. We refer to this filtering process as the disconnection between black and white women. Ironically, it is this disconnection that intricately binds their lives together. By unravelling an enmeshed web of disconnection, we can begin to more fully comprehend the nature and degree of their separateness. But, we also discover how their collective stories are needed in order to understand their life experiences in totality. We move on from here to discuss what we discovered to be the key sources of their disconnection: the historical forces shaping their lives, the cultural context where they live their lives out, and the social location in which their lives are embedded.

Sources of disconnection

History

Women's lives are bounded by a specific time and space. Erik H. Erikson, one of our most prominent thinkers on adult development, referred to time as the 'historical moment'. As he puts it, human life is 'inextricably interwoven with history' (Erikson, 1975: 5). The eminent sociologist, C. Wright Mills coined the term 'sociological imagination' to capture the same sentiment: 'Neither the life of an individual or the history of a society can be understood without understanding both' (Mills, 1959: 3–4). According to Mills' line of thinking, 'the success and failure of men and women' were mitigated by history (Mills, 1959: 6).

When reading the women's stories, we quickly discovered the difficulty of interpreting their lives without taking into consideration the historical context in which they lived (Iroquoian, 1975). Other researchers of gender, race and class have reached similar conclusions. Amott and Matthaei suggest that the socially constructed categories of gender, race-ethnicity and class 'arise and are transformed in history, and themselves transform history' (Amott and Matthaei, 1996: 12). They continue by stating that 'central to the historical transformation of gender, race-ethnicity, and class processes have been struggles of subordinate groups to redefine or transcend them'.

Consider, for example, the women's club movement during the late nineteenth and early twentieth centuries. Both educated, middle-class black and white women responded to the negative, male-dominated exclusive and volatile conditions in which they lived by forming women's clubs. Of course, these clubs were racially segregated. For white women the club movement was a response to exclusion from male occupational and professional groups. For black women, it was more a question of doing race work to improve the often volatile social conditions for both black women and men. Historian Paula Giddings has referred to this as the period of 'the cult of true womanhood' (Giddings, 1984: 47–48). Bridges between the women were not built because their social and economic interests were different, complicated by the white women's emphasis on gender issues only. Their aim was to join side by side with White men in enjoying the power, privileges and status customarily accorded to White men to the exclusion of all blacks. Black women, on the other hand, were seeking liberation from the racist policies, the inhuman lynching of black men and women, and economic equity for their community.

The historical moment in which the women who participated in our study live was just as complex, striking and rich. What was most striking about their life stories, however, was their dichotomous experience of history. For the black women, especially, coming to age during the civil rights movement era left an indelible imprint on their lives. Theirs was the experience of living the historical moments of black nationalism and the black arts movement. They lived the drama of history, making them more aware of the conditions, intricacies, paradoxes and forces that ultimately changed the state of race relations in this country. For the black women these were periods of drama which gave them stronger voices to articulate their stories, while also giving them a different story to tell.

A story told to us by Karen Brown, an African-American woman, underscores this point. Karen is a senior-level human resource executive for a Fortune 100 company, where she is responsible for the company's overall recruitment and administering compensation benefits. She currently resides in New York City, but she is originally from Los Angeles. Her old neighbourhood was Watts. Karen was 16 years old when the 1965 race riots broke out only four blocks away from her house. She remembers this day and the chain of events that followed as vividly as if it all took place yesterday.

The street where Karen lived was sealed off by the LAPD. On the days when the rioting was at its height, Mrs Brown remained home with her children. Karen remembers her mother keeping the blinds and curtains closed tight. She and her sisters were kept away from the windows. Mrs Brown feared that straying bullets from a sniper's or policeman's gun would come tearing through the window. On television the family watched in horror news reports on the looting, shootings, killings and the burning of their community. Nights were filled with nerve-racking sounds of screaming police sirens that endlessly went on until dawn.

The stories of the other black women we interviewed were equally illuminating. Martin Luther King was revered as their modern-day Moses, leading black people to the mountain top of racial equality. As young girls Julia Smith, Patricia Triggs, Karen Brown and Whitney Hamilton were taught by their parents, extended kin folks and members of their communities to believe they were special, gifted and talented because of their race. Because the historical moment of the 1960s empowered black people to declare themselves black and beautiful, Dawn Briggs and Brenda Boyd wore their hair in soft, curly Afros to symbolize their racial pride and solidarity.

The voices of the white women we interviewed, who grew up in the same period as the black women, were suppressed in contrast. What can be gathered from their narratives, at this particular historical moment, is that they experienced the turbulence of the 1960s at a distance. They certainly did not experience this moment on their doorsteps where they lived or even in their everyday realities. Race riots were something they sometimes watched on television in the safety and comfort of their living rooms – far, far away from burning inner cities. Consider the story of Joyce Canton. She has done well in the dynamic and volatile consumer products industry as a marketing director for a Fortune 100 company. Joyce grew up in a small town in the western panhandle of Maryland near the old Mason-Dixon line separating North from South, freedom from slavery. She remembers, 'My neighbourhood, my entire town was White, very White.' During the summers, her father would send Joyce and her sister off to visit her grandmother who lived in Mississippi.

Joyce recalls her experience of the civil rights movement: 'There were civil rights riots in Mississippi where my grandmother lived. We went down there,

I guess around 1964 or 1965. The National Guard was posted all over town. My sister and I thought this was lots of fun, because we would see the big machine guns and tanks. We would sort of race around the tanks and jump up and down. I think actually as a kid it was exciting. I don't think I had any notion that there had been violence in the town, or windows had been smashed. I don't even remember if anyone was killed.'

Karen Brown and Joyce Canton are referring to the same cultural and historical moments. Yet, these examples starkly show contrasting experiences: one of a teenage girl witnessing her community's struggle for racial equality; and the other a young girl's sheltered innocence, playfulness and sense of adventure of seeing soldiers in her grandmother's town. Black and white women have always had divergent historical experiences, dating back to the legacy of slavery. However, the historical moment of the civil rights movement did not shape the white women's self-perception, strengthen their sense of group identity or heighten their consciousness. There was another interesting discovery in the white women's stories. They were equally silent about the events and foremothers surrounding the women's movement. While we believe this is understandable in the accounts of the black women, since they never fully participated in the women's movement, we were quite puzzled to find this for the white women. Perhaps it underscores the fact that not all white women were touched by the women's movement, and helps to explain why some disclaim being feminists.

Cultural context: Black women's perceptions

We have described how black and white women's experiences of history differ, but the women also gave contrasting accounts of the cultural contexts that shaped their lives from childhood through adulthood. Culture is not detached from history, however. The two are closely interlocked. Historian Gerda Lerner views history as a critical component of our 'cultural tradition'. For Lerner history is embedded within multiple 'national, ethnic, religious and racial' contexts, and is manifest in the 'body of ideas, values and experiences' of the cultural traditions (Lerner, 1997: 116). These women's life stories are a retelling of their past, encompassing not only their personal history but also a collective history. Yet, their personal and collective histories are richly coloured and loosely bounded by the culture contexts of the women.

Culture is one of those complex, shifting social constructs where true agreement on what it means still befuddles social scientists. 'Like most powerful ideas in the human sciences,' writes anthropologist Clifford Geertz, '[culture] came under attack virtually as soon as it was articulated; the clearer the articulation, the more intense the attack' (Geertz, 1995: 42). Given the slippery slope of the terrain, Stuart Hall has been tremendously helpful in shaping our understanding of culture, especially in our interpretation of our participants' life stories. Hall conceptualizes culture this way: 'to say that two people belong to the same culture is to say that they interpret the world in roughly the same ways and can express themselves, their thoughts and feelings about the world, in ways which will be understood by each other' (Hall, 1997: 2). Hall's thinking on culture embraces three key concerns: shared meanings between individuals within groups, the cultural practices emerging between them, and the everyday effects of such practices in terms of power and social regulation. How did culture contribute to a woman's identity, her sense of group identity and affiliation, her sense of society and her place in it?

For black women, their self-identity was fortified by their sense of racial identity. There was a need for these women to embellish their racial self, particularly in the corporate setting where they felt invisible, unappreciated, unsupported, along with their sense of self-worth being constantly undermined. We were struck, when reading the responses of the black women together, by a powerful like-mindedness among them. Most, if not all, described an internal strength of mind and spirit. They believed their inner strength came from maternal ancestors, both those who were blood-kin or those who were legendary. These women conjured up women such as Sojourner Truth, Harriet Tubman, Lena Horne, Lorriane Hansberry, Ella Baker and Madame T.J. Walker. Their comments suggest that African-American women's strength is partly derived from their knowledge of past generations of black women who stood up to, endured and changed a society that oppressed their race, gender and class. The words of Brenda Boyd truly underscore this point.

Brenda Boyd is Director of Human Resources for a Fortune 100 consumer products company. She is a confident woman, very comfortable with herself. Her external demeanour is matched by the words she uses to describe herself. 'I experience myself as being exotic and mysterious to most white people. I think it is both the thing that I enjoy the most and it is the most difficult part of me...Being a black woman enables me, in spite of not having the right degrees, not being the right colour or the right gender, to be what I am today. On the other hand, being a black woman is the thing that probably keeps me from moving ahead, because in a white world black women are simply unfathomable.'

She continues: 'I think that part of the majesty about being a black woman is that we have a great strength to draw from our grandmothers and great-grandmothers throughout our history. Our strength runs in our veins. We always know our way home on some fundamental level. Home is our anchor, our centre. As long as we keep dusting off, or do not let the dust stay on us too long, then we realize that there is something quite extraordinary about being a black woman.'

Black women are raised in a culture of resistance by their families and the African-American community. Hagestad reminds us that 'families not only transmit, reinforce, and interpret standards of the wider society, they also generate expectations and create their own set of meanings – their own construction of reality' (Hagestad, 1986: 688). The culture of resistance has its genesis in the subordinate status of the African-American community due to racism, classism and sexism. Subordinate groups have consistently struggled to find ways to resist and to fight systems of oppression in order to overcome dominance. Black women, according to historian Stephanie Shaw, in particular 'were encouraged and prepared to resist, wherever possible the constraints the larger society sought to impose on them' (Shaw, 1996: 38). The culture of resistance left an indelible mark on the black women's life stories.

All of the black women who shared their life stories were taught by their parents, extended kin and other significant adults to give something back to their communities. The value of self-help was not unusual in the black community. Shaw points out, 'At a time when relatively few African-Americans achieved much formal education, those few who did were looked to, encouraged to, and expected to take up the crosses of those who were less able than they. Community and educational mentors joined with the families to imbue such women with a determination to use their education in a socially responsible way' (Shaw, 1996: 2). Our black women participants were no exception to this tradition.

Julia Smith's story is a good case in point. She is a mover and shaker in the financial industry, where she became the first Black woman to be brought into the company's executive ranks. It would be hard to guess that this sophisticated, intellectually strong woman's family origins can be traced to the deep South. Her parents, grandparents and great-grandparents were all born and raised in Mississippi. Julia has fond recollections of her maternal grandparents. Her grandfather owned the only black grocery store in town. Black people travelled for miles to buy their supplies from him. Grandfather Butler not only was a shopkeeper, but he was also a stonemason: he learned this craft as a small boy. Over the years, he had developed a fine reputation for his workmanship in both the white and black communities. A compassionate man, he trained young Black men in stonemasonry. They worked with him on various projects. On holidays, he provided small bonuses for his workers and he made sure that each of their families received a ham. His generosity and assistance made him one of the most respected black men in the county.

Julia's grandfather modelled the importance of giving back to the community. Her grandparents and parents reinforced the idea of 'lifting as you climb'. That is, helping other black people with fewer resources. Thus, an image of 'practices of commitment' was instilled in her at an early age (Bellah et al., 1985: 154). And she has found ways to carry out this value as an adult. Julia serves on the board of the Studio Museum, a premier showcase for African-American art. She believes serving on the board fits into what she likes to do. She said, 'I've always enjoyed art, and I've never been particularly talented enough to do anything on the creative side. But certainly bringing a business sense to a museum that is situated in our community is important today. Our kids in New York don't have a whole lot else.'

Julia is quick to point out that her mother and dad also demonstrated daily practices of commitment in their lives. Together they stressed, 'you've got to give something back. You cannot be content just to rest on your laurels.' She continued with this interpretation: 'my grandparents, as a matter of survival, support and a sort of deep religious conviction, always gave something back to the community. Their need to contribute was motivated very much by an understanding of racial dynamics in the United States, the fact that Black folks are only as strong as their weakest link.'

Service on the boards of cultural institutions is the traditional conservative means for such institutions to gain access to the elite (Ostrower, 1995). However, this service takes on a different character for black women. Black women have different motivations and make very different choices about where and how they serve. Many of the black women we interviewed leveraged their resources, expertise and company stature to bolster the limited staff resources and technical know-how of black community organizations. Indeed Julia's board service to the Studio Museum became a regular part of her 80-hour work week. Somehow, too, she also gave considerable leisure time to other community work.

Another cultural dimension unique to black women was their biculturality. According to Bell, 'a bicultural life experience requires a black woman to create a dynamic, fluid life structure that shapes the patterns of her social interactions, relationships, and roles both within and between two cultural contexts': one black, the other white (Bell, 1990: 462). Structuring one's life biculturally is often a conscious choice, permitting a woman to hold on to her African-American rootedness without being totally assimilated into the dominant culture. Just how far do black professional women go to organize their lives biculturally? The woman who told us the next story gave us a wonderful illustration. She is director of a Southern regional branch of a Fortune 100 financial services corporation.

To celebrate the holiday season, she plans and hosts two separate Christmas parties at her home. The first is a small gathering organized for her white colleagues. It is scheduled early Friday evening. For this event she hires a professional caterer. Together they plan an array of hot and cold hors-d'oeuvres and order a case of vintage California wine. On the night of the affair, elegantly dressed guests arrive promptly at five o'clock. Hired waiters serve the guests. In the living room an elaborate decorated table sits by the Christmas tree blanketed with sumptuous desserts. Classical music plays softly in the background. Guests mingle and talk throughout the evening, chatting about work, their families and social events. By eight o'clock the last of the guests have left, and the caterer is busy cleaning up.

The second Christmas party she organizes for friends, Delta sorority sisters, brothers of Omega Psi Phi, extended family members and professional associates – all of whom are black. It takes place the following Saturday, after the Christmas gathering for her white colleagues. The same caterer is hired. However, this time a bountiful ethnic feast is planned: honey-baked ham, turkey, chitterlings, potato salad, marinated blackeye peas and collard greens. There is a huge bread basket filled with corn bread and yeast rolls. This soulfully abundant banquet is presented on a magnificent oak table in the kitchen. Guests help themselves, over and over again. The dessert table, again set up by the Christmas tree, is now laden with pound cake and coconut cake, sweet potato pie, peach cobbler, banana pudding and a huge crystal punch bowl filled to its brim with egg nog spiked with rum, brandy and bourbon. Guests do not start arriving until nine o'clock. The pulsating sounds of the Temptations, Aretha Franklin, Marvin Gaye, the Whispers and Luther Vandross emanate from the stereo. Some people talk, but most of them dance. This Christmas party does not wind down until 3.30 in the morning.

The holding of two very different Christmas parties represents the way this particular African-American woman chooses to manage her sense of membership in two different cultures. We found the African-American women did not wish to abandon their cultural identity. Nevertheless, they also felt it was important to participate in the culture that dominated their professional lives. The women did not appear to want to integrate the two cultures in their social lives.

White women's perceptions

The white women were raised in a culture of individualism. American individualism is at the core of this culture. The idea of American individualism first appeared in the writings of Alexis Tocqueville, the French sociologist, whose observations of US culture appear in his book, *Democracy in America*. He used the concept of individualism to label a social relationship distinctive to US society:

> Individualism is...the feeling, which
> disposes each member of the community
> to sever himself from the mass of his
> fellows and to draw apart with his family
> and his friends, so that, after he has thus
> formed a little circle of his own, he
> willingly leaves society at large to itself. (Tocqueville, 1945: 104–106)

Clearly, early notions of individualism were rooted in patriarchy, being male formulations based on men's experiences. Linda Kerber, a historian, rightfully points out that individualism was the ultimate experience of educated, middle-class, white men, who had the luxury to discover themselves and the world around them (Kerber, 1997: 598). Women were left to play support roles. Throughout Western history women have been forced to be dependent on men, with less opportunity for free choice. Ironically, historians point out that early white feminists embraced individualism as an important value and used it as an argument for their right to the vote and to self-actualization. In what is referred to as her greatest speech, Elizabeth Cady Stanton proclaims the significance of the individual self:

> The point I wish plainly to bring before you on this occasion
> is the individuality of each human soul – our Protestant idea,
> the right of individual conscience and judgment – our republican
> idea, individual citizenship. In discussing the rights of woman,
> we are to consider, first, what belongs to her as an individual,
> in a world of her own, the arbiter of her own destiny, an
> imaginary Robinson Crusoe with her woman Friday on a
> solitary island....The strongest reason for giving woman all
> the opportunities...for the full development of her faculties,
> her forces of mind and body...is the solitude and personal
> responsibility of her own individual life...as an individual
> she must rely on her self. (Stanton, 1902: 189–90)

Individualism has remained a constant feature of US culture although its relative intensity has varied during particular periods. The white women in our study came of age during one of the periods in which individualism enjoyed a resurgence. The postwar period of the 1950s and 1960s saw a heightened emphasis on individualism or what was commonly referred to as the 'me generation'. The words of Stanton echo in the narratives of the white women in our study. As educated white women they were no longer simply defined by the domestic sphere. Particularly due to the influence of the women's movement, these women were able to choose the professional, public sphere even though the road was not fully paved and was extraordinarily uneven compared to the men's road.

Contemporary sociologists like Robert Bellah and his colleagues describe the culture of individuality as one that 'encourages us to cut free from the past, to define our own selves, to choose the groups with which we wish to identify' (Bellah et al., 1985: 154). Self-reliance, a strong sense of individuality, a belief in meritocracy and a high achievement orientation were central components of the white women's identity.

Both the explicit and implicit messages the women were given had to do with being a person, not with being a girl or a woman. Jean Hofbrau is a senior vice-president in the cosmetics industry who grew up in an upper middle-class family. She is an energetic, assertive and highly animated woman. Jean remembers: 'My mother never gave me advice about being a woman. She gave me advice about being a person. I knew I would become something, not just somebody's wife.' Anne Gilbert tells a story that echoes Jean's comments. 'I was madly in love in my first year of high school. One day I was with my grandmother and mother. My grandmother asked what were my plans for college, and I said jokingly, Well, I didn't intend to go to college, that I was going to marry Jim and have six kids. My mother was aghast! I can remember her taking me aside and saying, "Ann, I don't ever want to hear you say that to your grandmother again. It's very important that you be able to support yourself – that you go college – that you have the ability to earn a living. That's very important."'

Those kinds of message made them feel they were not constrained by gender. The women did not remember being made aware they might face discrimination and sexism because of their gender. Instead what they seem to have taken away from their families was a gender-neutral message – they could be anything they desired. Achievement was assured if they simply did their individual best. At an early age, they were imbued with the notion of meritocracy – that is, individuals who work hard will succeed. According to Maureen Scully, meritocracy is a 'taken-for-granted idea. . . . A social system in which merit or talent is the basis for sorting people into positions and distributing rewards, such that the positions of highest authority are occupied by those of the greatest merit' (Scully, 1997: 452).

The communities where the women grew up were not strong socializing forces. In fact, these women grew up in what appear to be lifestyle enclaves, a term first coined by Bellah and his associates. They define a lifestyle enclave as a group 'of people who express their identity through shared patterns of appearance, consumption, and leisure activities... they are not interdependent, do not act together politically, and do not share a history' (Bellah et al., 1985: 335).

An artefact of the culture of individualism is a strong sense of the nuclear family and the insularity of family life. When asked who were the significant adults in the women's lives as young girls, their responses were consistently the same. Every woman talked of her mother and father. When probed about other adults who were influential in their lives, the women would refer once again to their parents. Occasionally a woman would mention her grandparents, aunts or uncles. Brothers and sisters were also spoken of as central people in their lives. For these women it was their parents who were primarily responsible for preparing their daughters to go out into the world. The nuclear family provided these women with the support, encouragement and nurturance needed for them to become self-actualizing adults. The family also insulated the women from any negative influences from the broader society.

The families they described also had a limited number of friendships. Jean Hofbrau says, 'I didn't get the habit as a child of really reaching out. I was friendly and had plenty of friends. My family never worked at being friends with a lot of people. We were really self-contained.' For Gina Davidson, too, her sisters and her parents were the most significant people in her life. She describes a very close-knit family with activities centred around six family members. 'My folks had lots of energy. They were in their twenties. We travelled a lot. They would bundle us up in the car and go places. They still liked to go to drive-in movies. They'd put me in my pajamas and I'd go with them. We played a lot together and worked a lot together.'

In part the economic status of the women's families allowed them to be largely insular. These families had the resources to be self-sufficient and to offer their daughters a secure, comfortable childhood. Additionally, many of their mothers stayed home and there was less need to rely upon relatives for childcare support. This resulted in the relatives playing a less vital role in the women's early upbringing.

As black women drew strength from their collective past and racial identity, White women's identity seems to be strengthened by their sense of individuality. Because of their membership in the advantaged social group and blindness to race, they did not have to deal with racism or struggles to overcome racial oppression. It was easier for them to understand sexism because they encountered gender discrimination. White women did not understand their role and participation as members of a privileged racial group. What they did see were the negatives and disadvantages associated with being black.

Social location

While history and culture explain a great deal about the disconnection between black and white women, we also found that the social location of the women contributed to understanding their disconnection. The experience of gender and race for women depends on how they intersect with other sources of oppression and inequality. A powerful source of difference in the life experiences of women is class. Generically, class refers to the degree of access to resources and to power. The resources that distinguish economic privilege from economic deprivation are tangible. Resources can also be elaborated culturally and defined in various ways but they remain real and quantifiable (Lerner, 1997). According to Lerner, 'location in the ranking order of hierarchical societies consists of various sets of relations whereby people gain access to a variety of resources and privileges' (Lerner, 1997: 181). These include economic resources, land, political power, education, technology and access to the formal and informal networks through which societies organize power. 'Power in patriarchal societies has always been maintained through gender and/or racial dominance' (1997: 181). Class creates multilayered locations, relations and experiences that differ according to gender, race, ethnicity and stage in the life cycle (Sacks, 1989). As Stuart Hall has noted, race and gender are the modalities through which class is lived; disentangling them is impossible (Hall, 1992).

Scholars use the term 'social location' to capture the differential placement of various groups in the nexus created by the intersection of class with race, gender, and other sources of inequality. In our analysis the term refers to a woman's social location not in a strictly spatial sense, but within a social structure where gender, race and class are linked to positions that in turn shape experience. Consequently, it is important to recognize that class positions women in different social locations. Another way to think about a woman's social location is in terms of the economic resources, experiences, relationships, status and wealth available to her. As Zinn and Thornton argue, 'social location is a complex (and often contradictory) determinant of women's distinctive experiences' (1994: 9). The differential social locations of Black and White women generate significant cleavages in their life experiences (Drugger, 1991: 38–59). Although we use the concept of social location, we do not intend to imply that women occupy static positions. To the extent that race and gender are socially constructed and class positions can change, social location can be dynamic. In our study, we were most interested in the women's social locations during their early lives. Social location meshed with race and culture tended to lock black and white women into positions of no contact, or relationships that were superficial and distant, or superior–subordinate relationships.

Because of social location and racial segregation, black and white women from middle-class families had little meaningful interaction with each other as girls. The disconnection created by differential social locations can be illustrated by the experiences of Maxine German and Karen Brown. While Maxine is white and Karen is black, both women were raised in middle-class families.

Maxine, a director of corporate affairs for a Fortune 500 communications company, grew up in a middle-class family in a suburb of Chicago. She attended a parochial school in her neighbourhood of comfortable single family homes. Her father was a successful entrepreneur who provided a good lifestyle for his family. Maxine recalls a district that was '100 per cent white'. For Maxine, it was idyllic: 'When you sold Girl Scout cookies, you just knocked on your neighbours' doors and they were supportive. On Hallowe'en you ran from house to house. It was just the perfect growing up.' During her childhood, Maxine's contact with blacks occurred when the family ventured outside of their suburban home. Her only interaction with blacks was at a distance. On family excursions to downtown Chicago, Maxine's parents had to drive through the South side. Driving through this inner city neighbourhood, her mother cautioned Maxine to check that car doors were locked and not to stare at black people on the street so as not to attract their attention.

Karen Brown grew up in the middle-class section of Watts, the portion of Los Angeles reserved for blacks during the 1960s. She lived with her parents in a single family house with a large porch complete with a swing on a tree-lined street. The block was filled with homes occupied by businessmen, doctors, lawyers and teachers. Karen remembers white folks passing through Watts, never stopping. In

Karen's mind, their passing made them remote and her neighbourhood was a place where they did not belong. White people passed through but they lived in a separate world.

Even though some middle-class black families had the resources to live in newly integrated suburbs, they were socially isolated from their white neighbours. Their social activities were with clubs and organizations in the black community. White families socialized in racially segregated country clubs. As a result, the black and white women in our study like Karen and Maxine had few stories to tell about having playmates of another race. Formal education was usually the first place black and white girls in our study had contact. Even this contact was minimal. It is difficult for black and white women to connect meaningfully when they have been isolated from each other through the course of their lives. When the boundaries separating them are encrusted by racism their social location became a vast gulf for them to cross.

For the white women raised in upper middle-class families, their social location gave them a different experience as young girls than that of women like Maxine German. Their interactions were with black women and girls who worked for their families taking in laundry and doing other domestic services. Our interviewees' stories illuminate both sides of the superior–subordinate relations engendered by these different social locations. In her 25-year corporate career, Colleen Powell has risen from her initial position as a financial analyst to corporate treasurer for a Fortune 50 consumer products company. Her success today belies the difficult challenges of her early years. The oldest of five children and the only girl, Colleen grew up poor in rural Arkansas. Colleen started working at age 12 after her mother left home to escape an abusive husband. When her father remarried and started a new family, Colleen and her brothers were taken in by her grandmother. Colleen cleaned White people's houses and took in their laundry to supplement her grandmother's meagre wages. Her earnings were essential not only to her survival but to that of her younger brothers.

In North Carolina, Gina Davidson's mother carried the family laundry to a Black woman who lived across town. Gina grew up in one of the wealthiest families in her rural town. Her father owned just about every revenue-generating business, including the only cotton gin. In his later years, her father became a state legislator. She grew up well cared for and in a very comfortable home. Gina, who is today a plant manager for a large industrial company, remembers always having black women or black girls working for her family. She even had her own handmaid who was hired to play with her and attend to her personal needs. The stories of Colleen and Gina underscore the subordinate and superior relationships created by the differential social location of poor black women and upper middle-class white women. When black and white women's experience with one another is unequal and tainted by hierarchical oppression, how can a genuine conversation start between them?

A compelling example of the complex weave of social location, race and culture and the divergent effects that result, occurs when we examine the lives of a black woman and white woman both raised in dire poverty. Even though both women grew up in very poor families the differences in culture resulted in very different early life experiences. Take the story of Ruthie Mae Washington, a poor

Black girl whose childhood was 'snuffed out'. Ruthie Mae grew up in one of the poorest counties in the Carolinas during the 1950s. The oldest of eight children born to Johnnie Mae and Jonathan White, Ruthie Mae was raised by her mother, who tried to provide for the family by sharecropping and cleaning and cooking for white folks. Scraping by and getting enough to eat was an everyday reality for Ruthie and her family. She does not remember her father being around much or giving any financial help after he divorced her mother. Other family members could not help because they were busy trying to feed themselves. Ruthie Mae and her sisters and brothers were working in the tobacco fields, cleaning white folks' houses, and picking watermelons by their eighth birthday. When she wasn't in the field, Ruthie Mae was 'mother' to the younger children. She loved school but often she couldn't go because she had to stay home with her youngest brother.

Finally, one of her teachers visited her home to find out why Ruthie Mae had stopped coming to school. When she learned the reason, she gave Ruthie Mae permission to bring her younger brother to school. What saved Ruthie Mae from a cycle of poverty that could have enveloped her young life was a culture of resistance in the larger black community in which she grew up. When Ruthie went to her segregated school, her teachers made sure she had food to eat. They gave her hand-me-down clothes, cleaned and pressed. The principal encouraged her to continue her education. He took the college application forms to her house and told her mother of the importance of education for Ruthie Mae. He even showed Ruthie Mae's mother how to fill out the college application. Others in the community provided encouragement, support and guidance. They became her guardian angels. Ruthie Mae Washington, who today is a senior vice-president in the financial industry, has never forgotten the people in her community who made sure she got the resources she needed to get an education.

Linda Butler's social location during her early years had a very different effect. Linda never knew her father because he divorced her mother before she was born. Her time with her mother was very short. After the death of her mother when she was seven, Linda was taken from town to town by her stepfather, an itinerant worker who got work wherever he could. They always lived in the poorest part of town, sometimes in a trailer or worse. Despair won out one day and Linda was abandoned by her stepfather. Linda had to grow up fast. For the next few years, she was passed from one relative to another where she was tolerated. In exchange for her keep, she was responsible for all the domestic work in the house. She went to school hungry but told no one, choosing instead to go the school library at lunchtime and read a book. Linda was an intellectually gifted child and graduated valedictorian – the student with the highest academic standing – in her class. But the school principal told her that because she was poor she must go to work. No one encouraged her to go to college or gave her information about college. Linda remembers: 'There were no counselors to tell me there were actually scholarships that one could get.' Her only choice was to get a job after high school and forgo college. Linda's social class combined with a culture of individualism led to a situation where she had to fend for herself. There are no guardian angels.

A poor black girl is encircled with support and encouragement. She is not taught shame. Instead the community affirms her self-worth. She makes it because of the collective support she receives. And she recognizes that once she succeeds, it is her chance to help someone else who may be struggling. A poor white girl is isolated and must fend for herself. Her poverty is secretive and shameful. She learns she is responsible for herself and must pull herself up literally by her own initiative and hard work.

Conclusion

When we called for a 're-visioning' of managerial women's lives, we were challenging the traditional image of the universal professional female, and the methods used for enquiring into their lives. What we have learned from our scholarship is that race, gender and class are inseparable forces in these managers' lives. By using these lenses to understand women's lives, we gleaned new insights into the deep fractures operating to separate their realities. The division is more complex and multilayered than the combined effects of racism and sexism; however, it is directly related to both of these systems of oppression. The divisions existing between them are embedded in culture, history, their sense of identity and their implicit designated place in society. In addition to the women's life histories, applying cultural and historical analyses to their narratives enabled us to capture the dynamic and fluid distinctions between these two groups of women. One thing is for certain, however: we can no longer afford to talk about the shared experiences of women, not even within the same racial group. As Gerda Lerner points out, 'gender is constructed racially and through class and ethnicity', causing differences among individuals and groups (Lerner, 1997). While we do not discuss within-group differences in this chapter, they certainly did exist, particularly along the lines of class.

In a period when black and white women are entering the managerial and executive ranks in numbers greater than ever before, are there a few cautionary notes we can strike? We believe there are. First of all, it should not be assumed that alliances will naturally develop between black and white women. Nor should it be assumed they will be allies when it comes to career support and developing networks. Based on the evidence from our study, quite the contrary will be true. A combination of personal, intergroup and organizational measures is needed to correct the distortion existing in their relationships.

Socio-psychological bridges are necessary for these two groups to come together in order to develop authentic, trusting relationships. That is, to repair the refractured distortion. Based on their history and culture, these two groups of women enter into a relationship from vastly different spaces. Their connections to the powers that be – white men and privilege – have traditionally been, and continued to be, polar opposites. White women because of their race are attached economically and socially to the privileges available to members of the dominant culture. But the price of success in the male-dominated work world often requires them to suppress their voices by relinquishing their femininity and diminishing their power. Black women are in a different position. They start on the margins. Working from the edges, they experience the full force of racialized sexism. What they soon discover is that the agenda they bring into the company is not the agenda the company has envisioned.[1] Still, they are not easily blind-sided by the corporate game. Instead, they find ways to challenge the system.

On the personal level, a deep transformative dialogue might make a good first step, so women can tell and listen to the stories of the 'other'. Deep transformative dialogue means emotionally opening to the one who is different, so healing and supportive ways for dealing with each other are discovered. On the organizational level, until companies fully recognize and legitimize the power and authority of both black and white, they will continue to jostle for influence in ways that can undermine all women, while white males remain in dominance.

Notes

Portions of this chapter are based on the unpublished manuscript, 'Our separate ways: black and white women's paths in corporate America'.

1 We are indebted to Michelle Fine for her helpful framing and wonderful language in describing the situation of professional minority women.

References

Amott, T. and Matthaei, J. (1996) *Race, Gender and Work*, South End Press, Boston, MA.

Bailey, K.D. (1987) *Methods of Social Research*, The Free Press, New York.

Bell, E. (1990) 'The bicultural life experience of career-oriented black women', *Journal of Organizational Behavior*, 11 (6): 462.

Bell, E. and Nkomo, S. (1992) 'Revisioning women managers' lives', in A.J. Mills and P. Tancred (eds), *Gendering Organizational Analysis*, Sage, Newbury Park, CA.

Bell, E., Denton, T. and Nkomo, S. (1992) 'Women of color in management: towards an inclusive analysis', in L. Larwood and B. Gutek (eds), *Women in Management: Trends, Issues and Challenges in Managerial Diversity*, Sage, Newbury Park, CA.

Bellah, R., Madsen, R., Sullivan, W., Swindler, A. and Tipton, S. (1985) *Habits of the Heart: Individualism and Commitment in American Life*, University of California Press, Berkeley.

Bernikow, L. (1980) *Among Women*, Harmony Books, New York.

Drugger, K. (1991) 'Social location and gender-role attitudes: a comparison of black and white women', in J. Lorber and S. Farrell (eds), *The Social Construction of Gender*, Sage, Newbury Park, CA.

Erikson, E. (1975) *Life History and the Historical Moment*, W.W. Norton, New York.

Geertz, C. (1995) *After the Fact: Two Countries, Four Decades & One Anthropologist*, Harvard University Press, Cambridge, MA.

Giddings, P. (1984) *When and Where I Enter: The Impact of Black Women on Race and Sex in America*, William Morrow, New York.

Hagestad, G. (1986) 'Dimensions of time and the family', *American Behavioral Scientist*, 29 (6): 688.

Hall, S. (1989) 'Cultural identity and cinematic representation', *Framework*, 36: 68.

Hall, S. (1992) 'The questions of cultural identity', in S. Hall, D. Held and T. McGraw (eds), *Modernity and Its Futures*, Polity Press, Cambridge.

Hall, S. (1997) *Representation: Cultural Representation and Signifying Practices*, Sage, London.

Iroquoian, E. (1975) *Life History and the Historical Moment: Diverse Presentation*, W.W. Norton, New York.

Kerber, L. (1997) 'Women and individualism in America', *Massachusetts Review*, 1 (1): 598.

Lerner, G. (1997) *Why History Matters: Life and Thought*, Oxford University Press, New York.

Mills, C. (1959) *The Sociological Imagination*, Oxford University Press, New York.

Ostrower, F. (1995) *Why the Wealthy Give: The Culture of Elite Philanthropy*, Princeton University Press, Princeton, NJ.

Rushin, K. (1993) *Opposite Directions*, Unpublished essay.

Sacks, E. (1989) 'Toward a unified theory of class, race, and gender', *American Ethnologist*, 16: 534–550.

Schafer, N.C. (1986) 'Evaluating race-of-interviewer effects in national survey', *Sociological Methods and Research*, 8: 400–419.

Scully, M. (1997) 'Meritocracy', in R. Freeman and P. Werhane (eds), *Dictionary of Business Ethics*, Blackwell, Oxford.

Shaw, S. (1996) *What a Woman Ought to Be and to Do*, University of Chicago Press, Chicago.

Sheehy, G. (1995) *New Passages: Mapping Your Life across Time*, Random House, New York.

Stanton, E. (1902) 'The solitude of self', in S. Anthony and I. Harper (eds), *The History of Woman Suffrage IV*, Rochester, New York.

Tocqueville, A. (1945) *Democracy in America*, A.A. Knopf, New York.

Van Maanen, J. (1994) 'Metaphor', Unpublished essay.

Visweswaran, K. (1996) *Fictions of Feminist Ethnography*, University of Minnesota Press, Minneapolis.

Zinn, M. and Thornton, B. (1994) *Women of Color in US Society*, Temple University Press, Philadelphia.

15

Black and Ethnic Minority Women Managers in the UK – Continuity or Change?

Reena Bhavnani and Angela Coyle

Over the last decade or more, there has been significant labour market restructuring in the UK and other industrialized economies as they have sought to adapt to major global economic change processes. This has given rise to transformations in labour markets, work organizations and the economic activity of women. Indeed the feminization of work is a key feature of this new 'global' economy. Whether this represents progressive change is another matter. Public and private sector employers have engaged in reducing wage costs, deskilling labour and promoting greater 'flexibility' with the increasing use of part-time, fixed contract and casual employment (Acker, 1992; Hutton, 1995). Although there has been some analysis of the impact of these changes on women in the UK (for example Lindley, 1994; Coyle, 1995; Dex and McCulloch, 1995), the impact on black and ethnic minority women has just begun (Jones, 1993; Modood et al., 1997).

In the UK the growth of a services-based economy has led to an increase in jobs for women, mostly in part-time and low-status work but also in managerial and professional occupations. Women are expected to share in this growth of management jobs (Rubery and Fagan, 1994), as are black and ethnic minority groups, amongst whom there has been a strong growth of employment as managers, administrators and professionals (Owen and Green, 1992). This chapter raises questions about the impact of these changes on black and ethnic minority women managers. In addition, the authors draw on evidence from their own study in the National Health Service (NHS) which aimed to evaluate a series of training and development initiatives designed for black and ethnic minority women managers.

Social mobility and progressive change

These labour market changes may not represent opportunities for progress and real change in the relative status of black and ethnic minority women and men compared to white women or men or for white women, compared to white men. Several questions arise. Does this apparent growth in black and ethnic minority women managers indicate social mobility? To what extent are these changes a reflection of the changes in the occupational structures of the professions and managerial jobs into which black men, black women and white women are entering? To what extent are these occupational areas declining in status and pay as black men and women enter them? Further, as some 'new' sectors become gender segmented (Coyle, 1995) are we also witnessing the racialization of some feminized work?

Research about women and organizational change suggests that the nature of management itself is being redefined. Women make up 33 per cent of those in managerial and administrative posts and 40 per cent of those in professional occupations (EOC, 1998) and the long-term trends suggest women are entering management-graded jobs in increasing numbers. *However, the types of new management jobs being created through restructuring are different from those previously taken by men.* They are mostly in public and private service sectors and new forms of gendered labour market segmentation seem to be occurring, with the trend for women to increase their predomination in the low-paid service sector (Wilson, 1994). So, for example, there is evidence to suggest that women make up 50 per cent of all hotel managers currently, but that women in this area earn below the average of all women's earnings (Rubery and Fagan, 1994).

Research analysing black and ethnic minority women managers' and professionals' position is as yet just beginning. According to recent British Labour Force Survey data, 9 per cent of ethnic minority females in the UK are found in the category 'Professional, Manager, Employer, Employees, and Managers – large establishments', compared to 11 per cent of white females (Davidson, 1997). It is also argued that relative to white women, black and ethnic minority women continue to be under-represented in higher-grade employment (Bhavnani, 1994, 1996). For example:

> of the general managerial and administrators jobs held by women in 'national/local government, large companies and organizations' in the UK in 1991, 1.4 per cent were filled by Afro Caribbean women. Moreover, only 1.3 per cent of women in the 'other managers and administrators' category were Afro Caribbean, 0.7 per cent of women who are 'specialist managers' and 'managers in transport and storing' and 0.6 per cent of women who were 'financial institutions and office managers, and civil service executive officers'. (Davidson, 1997: 14)

Although a recent report of the Employment Policy Institute (Employment Policy Institute, 1998) indicates that black women's pay is outstripping that of white women, Bruegel (1994) suggests that the position of black and ethnic minority women may actually have worsened in recent years. Her analysis shows there has been a small overall rise in the proportion of black and ethnic minority women in managerial and skilled manual jobs. However, they account for a smaller proportion of women in professional jobs, and a higher proportion of women in manual work than in the late 1970s, suggesting they have actually experienced a *deterioration* of their position relative to white women.

In fact, there is not enough information to make clear statements about the pay differences between women and men from the different ethnic groups. It *appears* as if a pay difference, to the advantage of black Afro-Caribbean women, exists relative to white women, but once qualification levels, different ethnic groups, age, region, full-time and part-time work, work in the informal economy and self-employment are considered, as well as how information about earnings is actually obtained, we may see a more fragmented picture (Bhavnani, 1998), suggesting a pay difference to the advantage of white women.

What we do know is that black women on the whole are disadvantaged compared to white women in the labour market. They are less likely to become managers, are on lower grades within the same occupations, are more likely to do shift work, are more likely to be unemployed. This information has been borne out by studies for the Equal Opportunities Commission (Bhavnani, 1994) as well as studies carried out in the public sector (Beishon et al., 1995; Andrew, 1996).

It is also clear that many of the managerial jobs taken by black and ethnic minority women relate to the increase in self-employment amongst black people, and to the tendency for black women and men to work in small firms, where the label 'manager' may connote different status and responsibilities, relative to being a manager in a large private or public sector organization (Bruegel, 1994). As managers, they are more likely to be self-employed owner-managers of very small units, where employment is badly remunerated (1994). Secondly, they are more likely to be managers in the severely cash-strapped public sector. Table 15.1 taken from the British Labour Force Survey confirms the view that Afro-Caribbean/ African and black-other women are more likely to work in the public sector than other groups.

Although white people are more likely than ethnic minority employees to be in the private sector (62 per cent compared to 57 per cent), the difference is most marked between women. Sixty per cent of white women work in the private sector compared to 54 per cent from ethnic minorities. This difference is primarily accounted for by the fact that Afro-Caribbean, African and black-other women are much more likely to work in the public sector – 51 per cent compared to 31 per cent for all women – as well as the fact that South Asian women are more likely to be self-employed – 19 per cent compared with an average of 7 per cent for all women (DOE *Employment Gazette*, 1995). Thirdly, black and ethnic minority women are more likely to be employed in segregated positions, in services directed at black and ethnic minority service users (Bhavnani, 1994; Bruegel, 1994).

These trends look set to continue and may also be happening in the professions. Studies of doctors and teachers contain some evidence of the fact that black and ethnic minority teachers are more likely to be employed in areas where there was a shortage of teachers as well as being on the lower end of the salary scale (Ranger, 1988). The household sample of anonymised records (SARs) represents a 1 per cent sample of households enumerated in the 1991 Census and identifies 10 ethnic groups. Recent work has analysed occupational distribution by race and gender using categories from the Women and Employment Survey (Martin and Roberts, 1984).

Holdsworth and Dale (1996) found certain key differences to be apparent; 24 per cent of black-Caribbean women in employment work in the nursing sector compared to 9 per cent of white women. Those of South Asian origin represent 6–7 per cent, with Chinese and other at 14 and 19 per cent respectively. Those

TABLE 15.1 *People in employment by sex, ethnic origin and employment status: Great Britain, spring 1994 (not seasonally adjusted)*

Per cent

Employment status	All origins	White	Ethnic minority groups			Pakistani Bangladeshi	Mixed/other origins
			All	Black	Indian		
All							
All in employment							
(thousands =							
100 per cent	*24,942*	*23,909*	*1,025*	*294*	*343*	*156*	*233*
All employees	85	85	82	90	79	73	82
Private sector	61	62	57	49	60	61	60
Public sector	24	24	25	41	19	12	23
Self-employed	13	13	15	7	18	22	14
Male							
All in employment							
(thousands =							
100 per cent	*13,716*	*13,139*	*574*	*146*	*190*	*110*	*128*
All employees	81	81	77	87	74	71	77
Private sector	63	63	59	55	58	65	60
Public sector	18	18	18	32	16	*	17
Self-employed	17	17	20	10	23	26	19
Female							
All in employment							
(thousands =							
100 per cent	*11,226*	*10,770*	*451*	*148*	*153*	*46*	*105*
All employees	91	91	88	94	84	79	89
Private sector	59	60	54	43	62	53	59
Public sector	31	31	34	51	22	26	30
Self-employed	7	7	8	*	11	*	*

Source: Labour Force Survey *Employment Gazette*, June 1995: 257

from the South Asian groups are more likely to be in the skilled or semi-skilled categories, which include factory work. Black African, Chinese and Indian women are more likely to be in the professional category. There is also some evidence from the public sector that segregated patterns of black and ethnic minority women's professional areas actually block access to senior management positions. For those women in education who were appointed for their background experience into Section 11 posts (posts originally created for servicing Commonwealth immigrants) this work experience itself became 'a barrier to parity of status with most senior posts in schools and inhibited access to these posts' (Taylor, 1991).

This may have parallels with research in the USA. The increasing mobility of the black middle class has been explained by the fact that it now services the poor and minority populations that had previously been underserved or unserved by white professionals (Sokoloff, 1992).

It could be argued that it is extremely difficult to judge real mobility because of changes in occupational structure and because of the occupational levels of black and ethnic minority women prior to migration:

the apparent progress made by Britain's blacks needs to be qualified in two ways. Over the same period, the white population has also experienced a shift to non manual work and Britain's blacks therefore had to gain social mobility in order to prevent their status being eroded. Secondly we need to remind ourselves of the loss of status that many blacks experienced on arrival in Britain. Upward social mobility is therefore only returning many blacks to positions they enjoyed prior to migration. (Robinson, 1990: 277)

Thus far then, labour market changes may give the illusion of mobility for black and ethnic minority women but in reality could be largely explained by changing occupational structures and definitions of management. When we take into account the relative status of black compared to white women, we may see a picture of no real change, but more in-depth research is clearly needed.

The impact of equal opportunities policies

Global and economic change and the growing numbers of highly qualified women entering the labour market have forced organizations to consider their responses to the presence of women in managerial jobs and to introduce equal opportunities policies to counter disadvantage in employment based on 'race' and gender. In some instances employers have also responded to the presence and career aspirations of black and ethnic minority women staff by providing positive action training and development. As black and ethnic minority women are frequently to be found employed in a level and type of work far below their actual level of qualifications and abilities, such employer initiatives have the potential to effectively support such women's career development. But do they? To what extent do such training and development initiatives have a positive impact on the status and promotion prospects of black and ethnic minority women?

The last 10 years has seen a growing interest in the position and experience of women in management, with a rapid rise in the provision of positive action courses for women run by a range of organizations in the UK (see Glucklich, 1985; Clarke, 1991; Knight and Pritchard, 1994; Tanton, 1994). There have also been recent initiatives on black people and management (LGMB, 1992; Andrew, 1996), but many initiatives go unrecorded and are not evaluated (Clarke, 1991).

Organizational responses to black and ethnic minority women managers

Black and ethnic minority women fall into the gap between 'race' and gender. They are invisible in texts on 'race' and employment and on gender and employment. They have not often been considered *separately* in positive action initiatives or by employers generally in their equal opportunity policies. Recent work has, however, brought their particular position to light, pointing out the complex interaction of 'race', gender and class and establishing that black and ethnic minority women are at a disadvantage in the labour market relative to white women, white men and black and ethnic minority men on the whole (e.g. Brah,

1993; Bhavnani, 1994; Bruegel, 1994), although there are some differences between the sexes in some of the ethnic minority groups (see Jones, 1993; Modood et al., 1997).

Growing interest and awareness in black and ethnic minority women as managers has led some employers to take positive action aimed specifically at them. But what are the effects of positive action training courses on women themselves and the organization? Are these change strategies part of the process of entrenching labour market segmentation or do they represent a real change for black and ethnic minority women managers?

The authors undertook an evaluation of a series training and development initiatives that were specifically designed to meet the needs of black and ethnic minority women managers working in the National Health Service. We wanted to address some of these questions; whether such 'positive action' training has been able to further black and ethnic minority women's skills development and career progression; and the extent to which their participation in such training has been supported by their managers and organizations as part of a concerted effort to overcome the many barriers that black and ethnic minority women face in the labour market (Bhavnani, 1994).

We found that black and ethnic minority women managers who have participated in training programmes such as these were unequivocal about the value of these programmes for their own personal development. Three related points are made by them in relation to this area. Firstly the sharing of experience, which was commonly understood, provided a context for discussing their experiences of racism:

> These training programmes are important because they provide a safe environment to discuss sensitive issues among people who can appreciate the problem we face – people who are not faced with racism have great difficulty understanding the problem and sometimes are unaware of it.

Secondly, they also recognized that targeted programmes were important in securing black and ethnic minority women's access to training and development opportunities, as they are frequently overlooked or not considered suitable for 'mainstream' programmes. Thirdly, they rated very highly the ways in which the programmes had contributed to the development of their skills and knowledge and overall considered that they had become markedly more effective in their management roles, as well as in various aspects of their personal lives.

> I use it [the programme] every day both at work and at home. Planning before tackling any task, negotiation, settling conflicts or issues of contention, I am more conscious of my personality. It has equipped me in special ways in dealing with my children. I have learned to talk through things that I used to internalize.

So far, so good. These programmes have clearly been influential in black and ethnic minority women managers' personal development. However, the rest of the story is more illustrative of the ways that the organization itself did not change; barriers continued to exist, such that a large proportion of black and ethnic minority women managers felt their long-term aspirations to become part of senior management would remain a dream. The achievement of such long-term career goals was not just up to them:

I think the racism in the NHS is too strong. Development programmes for ethnic minorities will not be enough to change this.

I wish myself happiness in life. Promotion seems an unachievable dream.

Thus there is an intrinsic, inbuilt danger with targeted training interventions in that they can raise hopes and expectations which may subsequently be dashed when career ambitions are not recognized or supported.

Instead of increased motivation, black and ethnic minority women managers are more likely to feel that there is no real commitment to bringing about change and that the informal methods of career succession which advantage white managers still flourish:

In reality there has not been much impact as equality of opportunity and career development is not an issue or a concern for them. Many white managers still progress with minimum qualifications. Many use the informal networks to good effect to gain advantage in the job market. Some white managers are 'groomed' for succession, others are protégés or have an influential mentor.

Consequently positive action in these and other ways can actually make things worse. Sometimes there is hostility from others:

White colleagues: threatened, bemused, attempts to undermine the professionalism of the course i.e. it must be of dubious value if targeted at black and ethnic minorities. Black colleagues: either 'how can I access something like this?'; or 'why do you have to attend a programme that highlights our difference?'

Furthermore, we found that the status of training and development that is informed by 'positive action' is frequently constructed as being inferior:

The course was valuable for developing individuals. It raises morale, provides learning experience in different settings and assists in career planning. But for getting promotion I don't think it is of value. The course has a stigma attached to it. It is seen as an 'ethnic course'. It does not carry the necessary weight in an organizational setting.

Organizational barriers

Organizational obstacles remain the paramount problem for black and ethnic minority women managers. There are fewer management job opportunities within the occupational areas in which they tend to work, and they are clustered in the more marginal areas of their health care organizations:

Middle managers' jobs are graded at a much lower level so black and ethnic minority professionals (such as nurses and health visitors) have no financial incentive to move into middle management jobs. Within the professional structures, heads of services are few and black and ethnic minority women are not always supported to develop their skills at middle management level. Rather they are encouraged to take up jobs that address race and health issues, thus marginalizing them from mainstream services.

Racism operates in many and diverse ways but the most often cited aspect we found was the failure of white managers to recognize or acknowledge the capabilities of black and ethnic minority women managers. Sometimes this occurs because notions of managerial competence are based on white and male models.

Sometimes it is a more active resistance either due to fear, to white people's resistance to being managed by black or ethnic minority managers, or to an opposition to relinquishing a position of relative privilege:

> As a 'young' black woman, I feel that (and I have been told this by senior management) some of my colleagues are very threatened by me.

> White managers are still of the opinion that we cannot manage and do not recognize our potential. A number of white people resent being managed by black and ethnic minority women. There is a lack of respect for black women as managers. Either we are not taken seriously or our 'power' presence and effectiveness is seen as a threat. Our faces will never 'fit in' to the corporate whole or the images of those in positions of power. Being 'different' is viewed negatively instead of viewed positively.

Black and ethnic minority women as the problem

For us this study is illustrative of the failure of organizational responses to the presence of black and ethnic minority women in management. It is clear that the segregation of management is both structural and cultural. There are occupational barriers in career paths which prevent black and ethnic minority women getting on. Processes of exclusion are organizationally determined rather than self-imposed and these need to be addressed through other forms of intervention.

The culture of the organization which constructs women as 'different' or 'other' makes us perceive them as inferior. Although based on the sincerest of motives to tackle under-representation, these programmes and the research have also constructed these women as 'deficient' in skills, knowledge and experience, which should be tackled by these programmes. Our study itself continues this process, and was set up to assess how far the women *themselves* had been successful in overcoming organizational barriers, to become successful managers. The women demonstrate that they take on the barriers and change their behaviour in order to be promoted, but the organization is entrenching the processes of gender and 'race' segmentation.

Positive action programmes put the responsibility for change on to black and ethnic minority women: it is up to them to tackle racism, whereas, they are the recipients of its impact, not its creators! Thus only black and ethnic minority staff bear the label 'race', whilst the white staff are not at all racialized (see Ware, 1992, for a fuller discussion on problematizing the label 'white', in considering 'race' and gender). Whiteness is not seen as a racial identity and questions of 'race' usually mean focusing on black people who are constructed as problems (Maynard, 1994). This separation of 'race', class, gender and age places people firmly in only one category: black or white, women or men, young or old, with little possibility of the construction of all staff as having multiple identities which are constantly shifting, according to context and situation.

Lessons from positive action and the implementation of equal opportunity policies suggest that positive action may be an inappropriate change strategy to challenge what are essentially unequal power relations. Perhaps we need to rethink concepts of equality in organizations to encompass a view which argues that difference based on power can add value to the organization itself. It is not enough to increase numbers and expect women to blend in. It is also not enough to recruit black and ethnic minority women based on an assumption that their main virtue lies in what they can offer as knowledge of their 'own people'. Black and ethnic minority women, like other diverse groups,

> bring different, important, and competitively relevant knowledge and perspectives about how to actually do work – how to design processes, reach goals, frame tasks, create effective teams, communicate ideas, and lead. When allowed to, members of these groups can help companies grow and improve by challenging basic assumptions about an organization's practices, and procedures. And in doing so, they are able to bring more of their whole selves to the workplace and identify more fully with the work they do, setting in motion a virtuous circle. (Thomas and Ely, 1996: 80)

Who are the change agents?

Our research suggests to us that unless positive action training for black and ethnic minority women is part of a wider strategy of organizational development and change, it can actually entrench racialized notions of difference. For the time being at least there is little evidence that equal opportunities policies in the UK have made any significant impact on minority women's social mobility. There is evidence however that black and ethnic minority women themselves are taking matters into their own hands. Their responses suggest that they are and will continue to be the change agents.

Women themselves are pursuing managerial and professional jobs by undertaking higher education and are at least as well trained and educated as their male counterparts (Davidson and Burke, 1994).

Table 15.2 shows recent census evidence in this area for black and ethnic minority women. It suggests that they are enrolling into further and higher

TABLE 15.2   *Great Britain: possession of higher-level qualifications and unemployment by ethnic group*

Ethnic group	% of all aged 18 and over with A levels and above	% aged 18–29 with A levels and above	Overall unemployment rate	Unemployment rate for highly qualified persons
White	13.4	12.3	8.8	3.6
Minority ethnic groups	15.4	12.7	18.3	8.2
Black groups	13.7	9.8	21.1	10.4
Black-Caribbean	9.2	7.0	18.9	5.8
Black-African	26.5	16.7	27	16.1
Black-other	12.7	8.2	22.2	8.0
South Asian	11.9	11.3	18.2	6.9
Indian	15.0	15.0	13.1	5.7
Pakistani	7.0	7.1	28.8	12.0
Bangladeshi	5.2	3.3	31.7	9.8
Chinese and others	25.4	20.1	14.1	8.0
Chinese	25.8	27.5	9.5	5.7
Other-Asian	24.4	15.9	13.4	6.2
Other-Other	26.0	18.1	17.7	11.1
Entire population	13.4	12.3	9.3	3.8

Source: Owen (1994: 117)

education at rates of 40 per cent to 77 per cent , compared to 25 per cent for white women. African-origin women experience a high unemployment rate despite the fact they are twice as likely as white women to possess qualifications above A levels (Owen, 1994). Barriers in the labour market and responsibility for family and domestic tasks may encourage women to become self-employed.

How do black and ethnic minority women who are committed to raising their qualification levels in response to labour market changes view their prospects? Certainly careers officers may be entrenching racialized segmentation at work: research shows that their attitudes are described as ethnocentric and stereotypical (Cross et al., 1988).

However, Afro-Caribbean women students, for example, clearly recognized restrictions in the labour market, as has been ably demonstrated in recent research by Safia Mirza (1992). Her interviews with white and Afro-Caribbean women and men show that young Afro-Caribbean women indicated they both expected and aspired to take jobs in the highest social groupings, social classes 1 and 2, particularly in the social and welfare fields. Young Afro-Caribbean men expected to find employment as skilled manual workers, and young white women expected to achieve employment in social class 3 as non-manual and skilled manual workers. The author argues that Afro-Caribbean women opted for jobs in traditionally female sectors because of their recognition of the constraints of a sexually and racially segregated labour market, that is, they recognized the limited occupational opportunities open to black women (Safia Mirza, 1992). Asian women students are also expressing growing ambition, but not 'ridiculously so given their achievements and commitment to education' (Cross et al., 1988).

The expansion of self-employment since 1979 in the UK has also had a major impact on black and ethnic minority women. Whilst men's self-employment increased by two-thirds nationally, women's rates doubled (Owen and Green, 1992). In 1993, women accounted for a total of 24 per cent of the self-employed (Meager and Court, 1993) and in 1990 black groups comprised 10 per cent of the 3.4 million self-employed.

Self-employment rates for black and white women are similar (Owen, 1994), but in any case the figures are not a true reflection of black women and self-employment. Firstly, they disguise the role of black women within business. These may include those women who are engaged in running a family business and mediating on a family's behalf. Secondly, they may include women who are home workers who may designate themselves as self-employed even though they are in a genuinely subordinate relationship with their employer. Thirdly, self-employment is not always synonymous with entrepreneurship; entrepreneurs are defined as those who employ at least one other person (Phizacklea, 1988). Analysis of the 1991 census shows higher rates of entrepreneurship for black and ethnic minority women as a whole, relative to white women. Bangladeshi women have the highest rates, followed by Pakistani, Indian and Chinese women (Owen, 1994).

Self-employment amongst black and ethnic minority women, therefore, shows a complex picture. For example, their family businesses may be successful and there is evidence that women are using this experience to set up on their own (Bhavnani, 1996). Their businesses operate in a local competitive economy and are not necessarily racially segregated. A recent survey found that the East African Asian community had a high degree of self-employment and that 70 per cent of London newsagents are Asian owned (Lyon and West, 1995). Furthermore, the businesses run by the East African Asians were not marketing 'ethnic' products; they were highly competitive and in the market for general food and provisions. On the other hand, another small-scale study on London black businesses found that Afro-Caribbean origin women worked in the food products distribution and hair care services (Kangula, 1988).

Conclusion

Recent economic and political changes have had contradictory effects on black and ethnic minority women. On the one hand, there is evidence that they have not experienced social mobility, even though they have entered management positions. What we may be seeing therefore, is a re-segregation of the labour market in terms of both 'race' and gender. Furthermore, organizational change initiatives to promote them appear, in the limited research available, to be reinforcing these trends. On the other hand black and ethnic minority women have growing aspirations and qualifications to enter skilled jobs.

Research in the future may need to examine in depth how far we are witnessing the re-racializing and re-gendering of labour markets. The role of organizations in promoting equality needs to be re-examined as equal opportunities policies increasingly look ineffective and out of date.

Women in growing numbers are recognizing the operation of these barriers and aiming to challenge organizations and increase their opportunities through qualifications and self-employment. The presence of qualified articulate women working independently or within organizations, who will no longer be silent, may offer a hope of real change for the future.

References

Acker, J. (1992) 'The future of women and work: ending the twentieth century', *Sociological Perspectives*, 35 (1): 53–68.

Andrew, F. (1996) *An Exploration of Opportunities and Barriers to the Development of Black Managers in Public Services*, Office for Public Management, London, July.

Beishon, S., Virdee, S. and Hagel, A. (1995) *Nursing in a Multi-Ethnic NHS*, Policy studies Institute, London.

Bhavnani, R. (1994) *Black Women in the Labour Market: a Research Review*, Manchester, Equal Opportunities Commission.

Bhavnani, R. (1996) *Black and Ethnic Minority Women in the Labour Market in London*, Fair Play, London.

Bhavnani, R. (1998) 'The real story on black women's pay', in *Visible Women*, Commission for Racial Equality, London, November.

Brah, A. (1993) '"Race" and "culture" in the gendering of labour markets: South Asian young Muslim women and the labour market', in *New Community: Race, Ethnicity and Gender Relations*, 19 (3), April pp. 441–458.

Bruegel, I. (1994) 'Labour market prospects for women from ethnic minorities', in Institute for Employment Research (ed.), *Labour Market Structures and Prospects for Women*, Institute for Employment Research/Equal Opportunities Commission, Warwick University.

Clarke, K. (1991) *Women and Training*, EOC research discussion series 2, EOC, Manchester.

Coyle, A. (1995) *Women and Organizational Change*, EOC, Manchester.

Cross, M., Wrench, J. and Barnett, S. (1988) *Ethnic Minorities and the Careers Service: an Investigation into the Processes of Assessment and Placement*, Department of Employment Research Paper 73, Department of Employment, London.

Davidson, M. (1997) *The Black and Ethnic Minority Woman Manager: Cracking the Concrete Ceiling*, Paul Chapman, London.

Davidson, M. and Burke, R. (1994) *Women in Management: Current Research Issues Vol. 1*, Paul Chapman, London.

Department of Employment *Employment Gazette* (1995) 'Ethnic origins and the labour market: analyses from the spring 1994 *Labour Force Survey Employment Gazette*', Department of Employment, London.

Dex, S. and McCulloch, A. (1995) *Flexible Employment in Britain: a Statistical Analysis*, EOC research discussion series, EOC, Manchester.

Equal Opportunities Commission (1998) *Facts about Women and Men in Great Britain*, EOC, Manchester.

Glucklich, P. (1985) 'Women's management training in a ghetto?' *Personnel Management*, September 1983 pp. 40.

Holdsworth, C. and Dale, A. (1996) 'Modelling ethnic group differences in women's employment'. Paper presented at conference on 'The Research Value of the SARs', Manchester Business School, 13–14 March.

Hutton, W. (1995) *The State We're In*, Jonathan Cape, London.

Jones, T. (1993) *Britain's Ethnic Minorities*, Policy Studies Institute, London.

Kangula, W. (1988) 'Black business among Ugandan Asians and Caribbeans in London', unpublished thesis, MA in Public Policy Studies, University of Bristol.

Knight, J. and Pritchard, S. (1994) 'Women's development programmes: "No we're not colour consultants!"' in M. Tanton (ed.), *Women in Management: a Developing Presence*, Routledge, London.

Lindley, R. (ed.) (1994) *Labour Market Structures and Prospects for Women*, Institute for Employment Research, University of Warwick/Equal Opportunities Commission, Manchester.

Local Government Management Board (LGMB) (1992) *Management Development and Black Managers*, LGMB, Luton.

Lyon, M. and West, J. (1995) 'London Patels: caste and commerce', *New Community*, 21 (3): 399–419.

Martin, M. and Roberts, C. (1984) *Women and Employment: a Lifetime Perspective*, HMSO, London.

Maynard, M. (1994) 'Race gender and the concept of difference in feminist thought', in H. Afshar and M. Maynard, *The Dynamics of Race and Gender: Some Feminist Interventions*, Taylor & Francis, London and Pennsylvania.

Meager, N. and Court, G. (1993) *TECS and Equal Opportunities: a Review Paper*, Institute of Manpower Studies, London.

Modood, T., Berthaud, R., Lakey, J., Nazroo, J., Smith, P., Virdee, S. and Beishon, S. (1997) *Ethnic Minorities in Britain: Diversity and Disadvantage. The Fourth National Survey of Ethnic Minorities*, Policy Studies Institute, London.

Owen, D. (1994) *Black and Ethnic Minority Women in the Labour Market: 1991 Census Analysis*, EOC, Manchester.

Owen, D. and Green, A. (1992) 'Labour market experience and change among ethnic groups in Great Britain', *New Community*, 19 (1): 7–29.

Phizacklea, A. (1988) 'Entrepreneurship, ethnicity and gender', in S. Westwood and P. Bhachu (eds), *Enterprising Women: Ethnicity, Economy and Gender Relations*, Routledge, London.

Ranger, C. (1988) *Ethnic Minority School Teachers: a Survey of Eight Local Education Authorities*, CRE, London.

Robinson, V. (1990) 'Roosts to mobility: the social mobility of Britain's black population 1971–1987', *Ethnic and Racial Studies*, 13 (2): 274–286.

Rubery, J. and Fagan, C. (1994) 'Occupational segregation: *Plus ça change...*' in R. Lindley (ed.), *Labour Market Structures and Prospects for Women*, Institute for Employment Research, University of Warwick/Equal Opportunities Commission, Manchester.

Safia Mirza, H. (1992) *Young, Female and Black*, Routledge, London and New York.

Sokoloff, N. (1992) *Black Women and White Women in the Professions*, Routledge, London and New York.

Tanton, M. (1994) 'Developing women's presence', in M. Tanton (ed.), *Women in Management: a Developing Presence*, Routledge, London.

Taylor, H. (1991) 'Management development for black women teachers', *Women in Management Review and Abstracts*, 6 (2).

Thomas, D.A. and Ely, R.J. (1996) 'Making differences matter: a new paradigm for managing diversity', *Harvard Business Review*, September–October.

Ware, V. (1992) *Beyond the Pale: White Women, Racism and History'*, Verso, London.

Wilson, R. (1994) 'Sectoral and occupational change: prospects for women's employment', in R. Lindley (ed.), *Labour Market Structures and Prospects for Women*, Institute for Employment Research, University of Warwick/Equal Opportunities Commission, Manchester.

PART IV

THE FUTURE – ORGANIZATIONAL AND GOVERNMENT INITIATIVES

16

The Glass Ceiling: Explaining the Good and Bad News

Gary N. Powell

The glass ceiling has been defined as 'a barrier so subtle that it is transparent, yet so strong that it prevents women and minorities from moving up in the management hierarchy' (Morrison and von Glinow, 1990: 200). Calás and Smircich (1996: 226) stated that 'we can conceive almost all of women-in-management research as *glass ceiling* research, since assuring women fair access to managerial positions has been its overriding objective'. Reviewing women-in-management research as a whole is a task suitable for this entire book. The scope of this chapter is more limited. It begins by reviewing prior reviews and related statistics about the status of women in the managerial ranks. Based on this review, the chapter poses questions about trends in such statistics and addresses each question in turn.

Reviewing prior reviews and statistics

Numerous review articles, books and book chapters have considered the status of women in the workplace in general and the glass ceiling in particular since women-in-management research was first published in the 1970s. Dipboye's (1987) review listed nine prior reviews that had appeared since 1974 (e.g. O'Leary, 1974; Kanter, 1977). In turn, at least 10 reviews have appeared since Dipboye's (1987) review (e.g. Morrison and von Glinow, 1990; Davidson and Cooper, 1992; Powell, 1993). Since there have been so many reviews of research in this field, this review of reviews is necessarily selective and focuses on trends. It also presents statistics about the status of women in the workplace that provide insight into the change in emphasis of reviews over time. Statistics on the American workplace are presented initially and are supplemented with statistics from other countries.

In 1970, the proportion of women in the American labour force was 38 per cent (US Department of Labor, 1998a). However, the proportion of women in management positions in 1970 was only 16 per cent, a proportion that had held constant for over a decade (US Department of Labor, 1983). There were no systematic surveys of the proportion of women in top management positions at this time. However, there were so few female executives in the late 1960s that a study attempted by the Harvard Business School was abandoned due to lack of sufficient subjects (Epstein, 1975).

In response to such statistics, the first generation of reviews of women in management research primarily addressed the question, 'Why are there so few women in management?' For example, Riger and Galligan (1980) categorized causal explanations for the scarcity of women in management as focusing on either the person or the situation. *Person-centred explanations* suggested that socialization practices directed toward females encouraged the development of personality traits, skills and behaviours that were contrary to the demands of the managerial role. These explanations, which had received greater attention in prior research, were depicted as inadequate in accounting for women's low status in management. In contrast, *situation-centred explanations* suggested that the nature of the work environment faced by women who aspired to management positions determined their fate more than their own traits, skills and behaviours. The work environment for women included factors such as group dynamics directed towards 'token' female members (Kanter, 1977) and attitudes of workers towards female managers (O'Leary, 1974). Riger and Galligan (1980) called for greater research attention directed towards the influence of situation-centred variables, as well as the interaction of person-centred and situation-centred variables, on the status of women in management.

Bartol (1978) also attempted to account for the relatively small number of women in managerial positions. She first considered the person-centred explanation that women in leadership positions behave differently and generate different outcomes than men in such positions. However, upon reviewing research on sex differences in three leadership-related areas, Bartol rejected this explanation. She then offered a situation-centred explanation based on the existence of filtering points for women at different career stages that keep them from progressing up organizational hierarchies. Like Riger and Galligan (1980), Bartol (1978) stressed the utility of situation-centred explanations over person-centred explanations in explaining why so few women were in management positions.

Moving forward in time, the proportion of women in management positions in the United States dramatically increased during the 1970s and 1980s. This proportion grew from 16 per cent in 1970 to 26 per cent in 1980 and 39 per cent in 1990 (US Department of Labor, 1983, 1990). The proportion of women in the American labour force also grew during this period, from 38 per cent in 1970 to

43 per cent in 1980 and 45 per cent in 1990, but at a slower rate (US Department of Labor, 1998a). By the end of the 1980s, the gap between the proportions of women in the labour force and in management had narrowed.

However, the proportion of women in top management positions was much smaller. Government statistics are not kept regarding the proportion of women at various management levels, and various surveys have differed in how 'top management' has been defined. However, whatever definition was used, the proportion of women in top management positions was never reported as higher than 5 per cent during the 1970s or 1980s. For example, the proportion of female executives in large American corporations was reported as 0.5 per cent in 1979 and 2.9 per cent in 1989 (Korn/Ferry International, 1990). Also, the proportion of female corporate officers in Fortune 500 corporations was reported as 1.7 per cent in 1986 (Morrison et al., 1987) and 2.6 per cent in 1990 (Morrison et al., 1992).

In response to such statistics, the second generation of reviews of women in management research primarily addressed the question, 'Why are there so few women in top management?' For example, Dipboye (1987: 118 and 119) found both good news ('there are clearly more women in management today than there were 10 or 20 years ago') and bad news ('women are still a distinct minority in management, particularly at the higher levels, and there are signs that this situation will continue for some time to come'). The balance of the chapter was devoted to possible person-centred and situation-centred explanations for the bad news.

Similarly, Morrison and von Glinow (1990) presented good news and bad news about the status of women in management. The good news, contained in one sentence and not discussed thereafter, was that 'the number of women, Blacks, and Hispanics in management has quadrupled since 1970, and the number of Asians has increased eightfold' (1990: 200). The remainder of the review reported and offered possible person-centred and situation-centred explanations for the bad news regarding the low rate of upward movement of women and minority managers. Morrison and von Glinow suggested that white women and people of colour encounter a glass ceiling within the managerial ranks. However, little attempt was made in either Dipboye's or Morrison and von Glinow's review to explain the recent increase in the proportion of women in management positions. Instead, the focus of both reviews was on explaining the pervasive problems that women face in attaining positions at higher levels within the managerial ranks.

Turning to the most recent statistics available, the proportion of women in the American labour force was 46 per cent in 1998, representing a 1 per cent increase since 1990 (US Department of Labor, 1998b). The proportion of women in management positions was 44 per cent in 1998, representing a 5 per cent increase since 1990. The proportion of female corporate officers in Fortune 500 corporations was 8.7 per cent in 1994, 10.0 per cent in 1995, and 10.6 per cent in 1996 (Catalyst, 1997); these statistics compare favourably with earlier statistics regarding the same proportion in 1986 (1.7 per cent: Morrison et al., 1987) and 1990 (2.6 per cent: Morrison et al., 1992). However, it should be noted that definitions of what constitutes a 'corporate officer' vary from company to company and may have expanded over time to include positions at lower levels where there tend to be more women. Also, the statistics reported in Morrison et al. (1987, 1992) and Catalyst (1997) were compiled by somewhat different methods.

We can see that the proportions of women in the American labour force, in management overall, and in top management have increased in recent years. Also, the gap between the proportions of women in the labour force and in management overall has virtually disappeared. However, the gap between the proportions of women in management overall and in top management remains large. In fact, the proportion of women in management overall in 1970 (16 per cent; US Department of Labor, 1983) was larger than the most recent estimate of the proportion of women in top management (10.6 per cent in 1996; Catalyst, 1997).

Similar trends have been exhibited in other countries that report labour statistics to the International Labour Office (ILO). For example, between 1985 and 1995, the proportion of women in the labour force increased by 2–9 per cent in countries as diverse as Australia, Brazil, Egypt, Israel, Italy and Swaziland. Between 1985 and 1991, the proportion of women in management positions increased in 39 of 41 countries for which figures were available (ILO, 1993). The proportion of women in management varies widely between countries; for example in 1991 this proportion was about 40 per cent in Australia and Canada, about 25 per cent in Peru and Norway, and about 5 per cent in Turkey and Korea (ILO, 1993). Since the definition of 'manager' used in ILO statistics also varies between countries, precise comparisons are not appropriate. Nonetheless, the proportion of women in top management, although increasing slightly over time in some countries, has typically been reported as less than 5 per cent (e.g. Davidson and Cooper, 1992, 1993). Within all countries, the proportion of women decreases at progressively higher levels in organizational hierarchies (Parker and Fagenson, 1994).

Thus, the challenge for the next generation of reviews of women in management research is to explain both the good news and the bad news in recent trends regarding the status of women in management. The present chapter represents an attempt to respond to this challenge. It addresses the following questions: (1) Why has the proportion of women in management overall increased in recent years? (2) Why has the proportion of women in top management remained relatively small?

Explaining the good news

Why has the proportion of women in management overall increased in recent years? Human capital theory suggests that the quality of the labour supply is influenced by investments in human capital; resources that are invested in individuals today are likely to enhance their future productivity and career prospects. In particular, higher education enhances individuals' credentials by increasing their skills and knowledge, ranging from specific skills applicable only to certain jobs (e.g. computer programming) to general skills applicable to a wide variety of jobs (e.g. writing skills, reasoning ability, maths proficiency). In addition, educational institutions teach behaviours that are valued in the workplace, such as punctuality, dependability, and the ability to follow instructions (Blau et al.,

1998). Women have taken significant steps to increase their human capital through higher education in recent years. Between 1970 and 1995, the proportion of women earning college degrees in all disciplines in the United States increased from 43 per cent to 55 per cent at bachelor's level and from 40 per cent to 55 per cent at Master's level. Moreover, during the same 25-year period, the proportion of women earning college degrees in business administration increased from 9 per cent to 48 per cent at bachelor's level and from 4 per cent to 37 per cent at Master's level (US Department of Education, 1997). Increases in the proportion of women receiving college degrees at all levels in all disciplines and in business have also been exhibited in many other countries (UNESCO, 1997). These trends in statistics depict a major societal shift toward the enhancement of women's academic credentials, as well as an increased commitment of women to managerial and professional careers.

The quantity of the supply of available labour also influences women's employment in management. For example, the fertility rate of American women decreased by about half from 1957 to 1975 and remained at about the same level through 1990 (Schwartz, 1992). Let's assume that the average entry-level manager is about age 30. In 1987, 30-year-old managers were born in 1957, when the fertility rate was at its postwar peak. In 1997, managers of the same age were born in 1967, when the fertility rate was declining. Looking ahead to 2005, 30-year-old managers will have been born in 1975, when the fertility rate reached its low point. A reduced fertility rate contributes to a shortage of new entrants to the workforce, including candidates for entry-level managerial positions. When there are fewer candidates for such positions, there are more opportunities for women (Schwartz, 1992).

Simultaneously, the demand for labour has affected the status of women in management. When an economy is expanding, the increased demand for labour tends to result in a larger proportion of women in the labour force (Adler and Izraeli, 1988). In a growing economy, the rising demand for managers leads to a shortage of equally qualified men and thereby boosts the proportion of women in lower-level managerial jobs. In such cases, the women hired do not replace male managers, as much as they fill newly created jobs.

Other economic developments, such as the global shift from a manufacturing-based to an information- and service-based economy, benefit women's employment in management positions. In an economy that increasingly values 'brain power' over 'muscle power', highly educated workers are in greater demand, (Schwartz, 1992). This advantage dovetails with women's enhanced levels of educational attainment.

Social policies as exhibited in laws promoting equal employment opportunity (EEO) and executive orders requiring affirmative action (AA) programmes have contributed to substantial gains by women and people of colour in the workplace in many countries (Hodges-Aeberhard and Raskin, 1997). Konrad and Linnehan (1999) documented improvements attributable to AA in women's access to education and employment in both the public and private sectors of the American economy. AA has also led to the development of formalized human resource management (HRM) structures that in turn have enhanced the status of women and people of colour in management. Overall, EEO laws, AA programmes, and resulting HRM practices have contributed to the enhancement of opportunities for women to enter the managerial ranks (Konrad and Linnehan, 1999).

Characteristics of organizations other than their commitment to EEO, AA programmes and HRM practices affect the proportion of women in management positions. Blum et al. (1994) found that an organization's proportion of women in management positions at all levels was positively related to the proportion of women in non-management positions, proportion of non-whites in management positions, number of annual management vacancies, proportion of employees in professional and skilled positions, industry type (non-manufacturing rather than manufacturing), and emphasis on training, development and promotion from within the organization; this proportion was negatively related to the average management salary. Blum et al. (1994) concluded that the organizational context may facilitate as well as restrict women's access to management positions.

Finally, the presence of women at higher managerial levels may influence the entry and retention of women at lower managerial levels. Cohen et al. (1998) found that women are more likely to be hired and promoted into a given managerial level when there is a substantial minority of women above that level, but not when women constitute the majority of managers in higher-level positions. Using an organizational-level analysis, Goodman, Fields and Blum (1995) found that an organization's proportion of women in top management was positively related to its proportion of women in managerial jobs at all levels.

The proportion of women in top management may influence the proportion of women at lower managerial levels indirectly as well as directly. Folcy (1998) found that female associates in law firms with a smaller proportion of women and minority partners were more likely to perceive the existence of a glass ceiling that would prevent them from attaining partner status themselves, which in turn led to greater intentions to quit the firm. Other studies have found that a smaller proportion of women at upper levels results in greater intentions to quit (Burke and McKeen, 1996) and actual turnover (Cohen and Elvira, 1997) for women at lower levels. These results suggest that a smaller proportion of women in top management may indirectly lead to a smaller proportion of women in lower-level managerial positions through its effect on women's voluntary departures from organizations.

In summary, both situation-centred and person-centred explanations account for the increased proportion of women in management in recent years. Situation-centred explanations include a decrease in the supply of candidates for entry-level managerial jobs, an increased demand for managers due to a growing global economy, a global shift to an economy that is based less on manufacturing and more on information and services, social policies promoting equal employment opportunity and affirmative action within organizations, and other organizational characteristics and practices. Person-centred explanations include women's increased educational attainment in all disciplines in general and in business in particular, which has accompanied as well as contributed to women's increased commitment to managerial and professional careers. In addition, within individual organizations, the presence of women in higher managerial levels may have both direct and indirect effects on the proportion of women in lower managerial levels.

Explaining the bad news

Why has the proportion of women in top management remained relatively small? The forces that have driven the increase in the proportion of women in management overall have had less effect on the proportion of women in top management. The higher the position within the managerial ranks, the less the importance attached to 'objective' credentials such as education that women may acquire (Antal and Krebsbach-Gnath, 1988). As a result, women's increased educational attainment, which represents a change in the quality of the labour supply, has had a greater effect on hiring and promotion into entry-level management positions than into top management positions. Also, increases in the demand for labour due to a growing economy have relatively little effect on the proportion of women in top management because the number of executive positions in any organization is limited and there is seldom a scarcity of interested and qualified male candidates (Adler and Izraeli, 1994). Further, discriminatory selection practices are more easily prevented or addressed when there is a greater reliance on objective credentials in making the selection decision. Thus, the effects of social policies such as equal employment opportunity laws and affirmative action programmes are seen more in women's access to entry-level management positions than top management positions. To answer this question, we need to consider other forces.

The most basic force to be considered is the societal context. Throughout recorded history, a patriarchal social system in which the male has power and authority over the female has almost always prevailed (Marshall, 1984; Powell, 1993). Women's presence in top management positions violates the norm of men's higher status and superiority to a greater extent than women's presence in lower-level management positions. One way to enforce this norm would be simply to ban women from occupying higher-level positions, but such a ban would not be especially subtle and would be resisted by women, as well as by men with any sense of justice. Instead, the norm is reinforced in more subtle ways, such as in stereotypes of what constitutes an effective leader and in the cognitive processes of decision-makers.

In most societies, leadership in general, and management in particular, tends to be regarded as a masculine domain, i.e. one associated with men (Marshall, 1984; Hearn and Parkin, 1988). Schein (1973, 1975) compared middle managers' beliefs about the characteristics associated with women in general, men in general, and successful middle managers. She found that both female and male managers believed that successful middle managers possessed an abundance of characteristics that were more associated with men in general than with women in general. Similarly, Powell and Butterfield (1979) found that female and male business students at both the MBA and undergraduate levels described a good manager in predominantly masculine terms. Replications of both studies with different types of samples and in different countries have yielded essentially the same results: women and men continue to describe good managers as higher in stereotypically masculine traits than stereotypically feminine traits (Powell, 1993). These stereotypes work to women's disadvantage at all levels of management. However, they are most often invoked when women are being considered for top-level management positions, because women's presence at such levels most violates the norm of male superiority.

The cognitive processes of decision-makers about top management positions also reinforce the norm of male superiority. Perry et al. (1994) noted that individual decision-makers develop schemata or mental models about the attributes of job holders that influence their hiring and promotion decisions. Schemata may be either gender based, incorporating the gender of job holders in some way, or gender neutral, ignoring the gender of job holders. According to Perry et al. (1994), gender is most likely to be incorporated into decision-makers' job holder schemas when primarily persons of one gender occupy the job under consideration and/or the applicant pool. Gender-based schemata favouring men are more likely to arise in large firms than in small firms, because large firms (1) have more formal job ladders from which women may have been systematically excluded in the past, thus providing greater stimuli for the triggering of gender-based schemata; (2) have more job titles, thus providing greater opportunity for the formation of gender-based schemata; and (3) fill more jobs and evaluate more candidates for jobs, thus providing greater opportunity for the use of gender-based schemata.

People make the most positive evaluations of and decisions about people whom they see as similar to themselves (Byrne and Neuman, 1992). Kanter (1977) characterized the results of such a preference in management ranks as homosocial reproduction. She argued that the primary motivation in bureaucracies in all decisions is to minimize uncertainty. Uncertainty is always present when individuals are relied upon, and the effects of such uncertainty are greatest when the individual holds significant responsibility for the direction of the organization. One way to minimize uncertainty in the executive suite is to close top management positions to people who are regarded as 'different'. Thus, women have a difficult time in entering the male-dominated ranks of top management (Kanter, 1977).

Gender-based schemata and preferences for similar job holders as a way to minimize uncertainty are cognitive processes that decision-makers may use when filling any type of job. However, these processes are especially likely to be used when top management jobs are filled because the gender composition of the executive ranks most determines whether a societal norm of male superiority is upheld in the workplace. Cohen et al. (1998) found that women are more likely to be hired and promoted into a particular management level when more women are already there. In turn, when women already hold some of the top management jobs in an organization, gender-based schemata favouring men are less likely to be used when top management jobs are filled (Perry et al., 1994) and the prospect of adding women to top management is less fraught with uncertainty (Kanter, 1977). As Cohen et al. (1998) noted, the challenge then becomes getting women into top management jobs in the first place.

The entry of women into top management is also influenced by how the decision-making process is structured and whether decision-makers are held accountable for their decisions. Most organizations do not have a systematic procedure for making promotions to top management positions, handling each case on an *ad hoc* basis instead, and records are seldom kept of the promotion process. As a result, decisions about top management positions are relatively unstructured and subjected to little scrutiny, providing the opportunity for decision-makers' biases to influence the outcome of decisions. In contrast, decisions for lower-level management positions that are more based on objective credentials may be scrutinized more readily, rendering decision-makers more accountable for their decisions.

Powell and Butterfield (1994) found that women's access to top management positions may be influenced by such practices. In their study of a cabinet-level department of the US federal government, the sex of applicants for open top management positions that were not political appointments influenced promotion decisions to the advantage of women. Powell and Butterfield (1994) suggested that women's advantage in such decisions may have been due to the federal government's special promotion procedures in addition to its strong commitment to EEO. First, all open positions are made known through a public announcement. Second, all promotion decisions are made using the same procedure. Third, records must be kept of the entire decision-making process for at least two years. These practices provide structure to the decision-making process and enable identification of decisions not properly made, thereby making decision-makers accountable for how promotion decisions are made. However, such practices are rare, especially in the private sector.

The proportion of women in top management is further influenced by the developmental experiences of lower-level managers. If lower-level female managers are not groomed for top management positions as much or as well as lower-level male managers, they will be at a disadvantage when competing for scarce top management positions. Ohlott et al. (1994) found that male managers experienced greater task-related developmental challenges in their jobs, whereas female managers with equivalent backgrounds and jobs experienced greater developmental challenges stemming from obstacles faced in their jobs. In particular, men's jobs were higher in the need to handle high stakes, manage business diversity, and handle external pressure. In contrast, women's jobs were lower in personal support due to their being excluded from key networks and receiving little encouragement from others. According to female executives, the developmental challenges faced more by male managers in Ohlott et al.'s (1994) study contribute to women's career advancement (Mainiero, 1994; Ragins et al., 1998), and the challenges faced more by female managers hinder women's career advancement (Morrison et al., 1987).

Another key developmental experience is having a mentor. Mentors significantly contribute to their protégés' career success and satisfaction. In addition, mentors buffer women from both overt and covert discrimination and help them to overcome obstacles to their attaining top management positions (Ragins, 1999). However, potential male mentors, who are in greater abundance than potential female mentors, may be reluctant to select female protégés because of concerns about possible sexual innuendoes and rumours or simply because they prefer to mentor people like themselves (Byrne and Neuman, 1992), i.e. male protégés. If lower-level female managers have more difficulty in obtaining a mentor or have mentoring relationships that are more problematic, they will experience the career-enhancing benefits of being mentored less than lower-level male managers (Ragins, 1999).

Thus far, this section has offered situation-centred explanations for why the proportion of women in top management is relatively small. Situation-centred explanations support the existence of a glass ceiling that acts as a barrier to women moving up management hierarchies (Morrison and von Glinow, 1990). However, moving up management hierarchies is not necessarily good in itself, and not everyone wants to make such moves. We also need to consider person-centred explanations for why some women do not move up management hierarchies, at least in large organizations.

Consider the nature of the typical executive job. It is one that has enormous responsibilities, time demands and pressures, and it calls for considerable sacrifices in personal life. Who wants to hold such a job? According to theoretical models of what people are looking for in their lives, men do more than women. Powell and Mainiero (1992), upon comparing theories of women's and men's career development, differentiated between the traditional 'male model' of career success and what may be called a 'female model' of career success in two ways. First, the traditional male model emphasizes objective measures of career success such as salary, title and number of levels from the top of the management hierarchy, whereas the female model places greater emphasis on subjective measures of career success such as satisfaction with the current job and prospects for future satisfaction at work. Second, the traditional male model focuses primarily on work life, whereas the female model includes greater consideration of non-work as well as work life. Thus, according to the female model of career success, women attempt to strike a balance between their relationships with others and their personal achievements at work and seek some level of personal or subjective satisfaction in both realms (Powell and Mainiero, 1992). Top management jobs do not encourage this kind of balancing act and so tend to attract individuals who adhere to the traditional male model of career success.

Of course, not all women adhere to the female model of career success, nor do all men adhere to the traditional male model. Indeed, many women would like to attain top management jobs. However, given the same level of perceived career opportunities, female managers are more likely to quit their organizations than male managers (Stroh et al., 1996). Thus, women managers have a lower tolerance for lack of career opportunities. Perry et al. (1994) suggested that female managers have fewer career opportunities in larger organizations due to decision-makers' greater use of gender-based schemata.

Where do these women go when they quit their organizations? Increasingly into business for themselves. Moore and Buttner (1997) reported that women have been starting businesses at more than twice the rate of men in recent years. Female entrepreneurs tend to give five reasons for why they left their prior organizations to go into business for themselves: challenge, self-determination, family concerns, blocks to advancement, and organizational dynamics. Women who leave the corporate world to run their own businesses do not show up in published statistics about the proportion of women in top management, because such statistics typically focus on large publicly held firms such as Fortune 500 corporations (e.g. Morrison et al., 1987, 1992; Catalyst, 1997). However, such women in effect have become the top management of their own firms.

In summary, both situation-centred and person-centred explanations account for the relatively small proportion of women in top management, at least in the large firms for which such statistics have been compiled. Situation-centred explanations include a patriarchal social system, stereotypes of effective leaders, decision-makers' tendencies to use gender-based schemata when making hiring and promotion decisions for top management positions and their preferences to work with people like themselves, organizational practices in making such decisions that are unstructured and hidden from scrutiny, and sex differences favouring men in developmental experiences at lower managerial levels such as challenging assignments, personal support, and access to mentoring. Person-centred explanations include sex differences in the desire to hold the kinds of jobs that exist at top management levels and in the inclination to quit organizations and the corporate world altogether when faced with a lack of career opportunities in the current organization.

Conclusion

According to this review, an intricate web of interrelated forces that differ according to managerial level and are common to many countries has influenced the status of women in management in recent years. These same forces seem likely to influence the future status of women in management as well. However, we must be cautious in our predictions. After all, the forces that will shape the future cannot be predicted with certainty. Also, individual women and men managers must decide how important moving up the management hierarchies of large organizations is in their own lives.

We have reason to be concerned whenever women who attempt to move up management hierarchies are unsuccessful because of external barriers that are encountered only by people like themselves. Such barriers serve to create and maintain a glass ceiling that restricts women's career advancement and satisfaction, especially in large organizations. Thus, the objective that Calás and Smircich (1996) describe as underlying 'glass ceiling' research is sound: women deserve fair access to managerial positions at all levels.

Note

The author extends grateful appreciation to Laura Graves, Marcia Kropf, Mary Mattis, Patricia Ohlott, Marian Ruderman and Mary Ann von Glinow for their reactions to the ideas presented in this chapter.

References

Adler, N.J. and Izraeli, D.N. (eds) (1988) *Women in Management Worldwide*, Sharpe, Armonk, NY.

Adler, N.J. and Izraeli, D.N. (eds) (1994) *Competitive Frontiers: Women Managers in a Global Economy*, Blackwell, Cambridge, MA.

Antal, A.B. and Krebsbach-Gnath, C. (1988) 'Women in management: unused resources in the Federal Republic of Germany', in N.J. Adler and D.N. Izraeli (eds), *Women in Management Worldwide*, Sharpe, Armonk, NY.

Bartol, K.M. (1978) 'The sex structuring of organizations: a search for possible causes', *Academy of Management Review*, 3: 805–815.

Blau, F.D., Ferber, M.A. and Winkler, A.E. (1998) *The Economics of Women, Men, and Work*, 3rd edn, Prentice Hall, Upper Saddle River, NJ.

Blum, T.C., Fields, D.L. and Goodman, J.S. (1994) 'Organization-level determinants of women in management', *Academy of Management Journal*, 37: 241–268.

Burke, R.J. and McKeen, C.A. (1996) 'Do women at the top make a difference? Gender proportions and the experiences of managerial and professional women', *Human Relations*, 49: 1093–1104.

Byrne, D. and Neuman, J.H. (1992) 'The implications of attraction research for organizational issues', in K. Kelley (ed.), *Issues, Theory, and Research in Industrial/ Organizational Psychology*, Elsevier Science, Amsterdam.

Calás, M.B. and Smircich, L. (1996) 'From "the woman's" point of view: feminist approaches to organization studies', in S.R. Clegg, C. Hardy and W.R. Nord (eds), *Handbook of Organization Studies*, Sage, London.

Catalyst (1997) *Census of Women Corporate Officers and Top Earners*, Catalyst, New York.

Cohen, L.E. and Elvira, M.M. (1997) 'The effects of organizational sex composition on the turnover of men and women: is leaving just the same?' Paper presented at the Meeting of the Academy of Management, Boston.

Cohen, L.E., Broschak, J.P. and Haveman, H.A. (1998) 'And then there were more? The effect of organizational sex composition on the hiring and promotion of managers', *American Sociological Review*, 63: 711–727.

Davidson, M.J. and Cooper, C.L. (1992) *Shattering the Glass Ceiling: The Woman Manager*, Chapman, London.

Davidson, M.J. and Cooper, C.L. (eds) (1993) *European Women in Business and Management*, Chapman, London.

Dipboye, R.L. (1987) 'Problems and progress of women in management', in K.S. Koziara, M.H. Moskow and L.D. Tanner (eds), *Working Women: Past, Present, Future*, Bureau of National Affairs, Washington, DC.

Epstein, C.F. (1975) 'Institutional barriers: what keeps women out of the executive suite?' in F.E. Gordon and M.H. Strober (eds), *Bringing Women into Management*, McGraw-Hill, New York.

Foley, S. (1998) 'The effects of the actual and perceived glass ceiling on perceptions of promotion fairness', Doctoral dissertation, University of Connecticut, Storrs, CT.

Goodman, J.S., Fields, D.L. and Blum, T.C. (1995) 'An organizational level study of the glass ceiling'. Paper presented at the Meeting of the Academy of Management, Vancouver.

Hearn, J. and Parkin, P.W. (1988) 'Women, men, and leadership: a critical review of assumptions, practices, and change in the industrialized nations', in N.J. Adler and D.N. Izraeli (eds), *Women in Management Worldwide*, Sharpe, Armonk, NY.

Hodges-Aeberhard, J. and Raskin, C. (eds) (1997) *Affirmative Action in the Employment of Ethnic Minorities and Persons with Disabilities*, International Labour Office, Geneva.

International Labour Office (1993) 'Unequal race to the top', *World of Work: The Magazine of the International Labour Office* (US edn), 2: 6–7.

Kanter, R.M. (1977) *Men and Women of the Corporation*, Basic Books, New York.

Konrad, A.M. and Linnehan, F. (1999) 'Affirmative action: history, effects, and attitudes', in G.N. Powell (ed.), *Handbook of Gender and Work*, Sage, Thousand Oaks, CA.

Korn/Ferry International (1990) *A Decade of Change in Corporate Leadership*, Korn/Ferry International, New York.

Mainiero, L.A. (1994) 'Getting anointed for advancement: the case of executive women', *Academy of Management Executive*, 8 (2): 53–67.

Marshall, J. (1984) *Women Managers: Travellers in a Male World*, Wiley, Chichester.

Moore, D.P. and Buttner, E.H. (1997) *Women Entrepreneurs: Moving beyond the Glass Ceiling*, Sage, Thousand Oaks, CA.

Morrison, A.M. and von Glinow, M.A. (1990) 'Women and minorities in management', *American Psychologist*, 45: 200–208.

Morrison, A.M., White, R.P., Van Velsor, E. and the Center for Creative Leadership (1987) *Breaking the Glass Ceiling: Can Women Reach the Top of America's Largest Corporations?* Addison-Wesley, Reading, MA.

Morrison, A.M., White, R.P., Van Velsor, E. and the Center for Creative Leadership (1992) *Breaking the Glass Ceiling: Can Women Reach the Top of America's Largest Corporations?* updated edn, Addison-Wesley, Reading, MA.

Ohlott, P.J., Ruderman, M.N. and McCauley, C.D. (1994) 'Gender differences in managers' developmental job experiences', *Academy of Management Journal*, 37: 46–67.

O'Leary, V.E. (1974) 'Some attitudinal barriers to occupational aspirations in women', *Psychological Bulletin*, 81: 809–826.

Parker, B. and Fagenson, E.A. (1994) 'An introductory overview of women in corporate management', in M.J. Davidson and R.J. Burke (eds), *Women in Management: Current Research Issues*, Chapman, London.

Perry, E.L., Davis-Blake, A. and Kulik, C.T. (1994) 'Explaining gender-based selection decisions: a synthesis of contextual and cognitive approaches', *Academy of Management Review*, 19: 786–820.

Powell, G.N. (1993) *Women and Men in Management*, 2nd edn, Sage, Newbury Park, CA.

Powell, G.N. and Butterfield, D. A. (1979) 'The "good manager": masculine or androgynous?' *Academy of Management Journal*, 22: 395–403.

Powell, G.N. and Butterfield, D.A. (1994) 'Investigating the "glass ceiling" phenomenon: an empirical study of actual promotions to top management', *Academy of Management Journal*, 37: 68–86.

Powell, G.N. and Mainiero, L.A. (1992) 'Cross-currents in the river of time: conceptualizing the complexities of women's careers', *Journal of Management*, 18: 215–237.

Ragins, B.R. (1999) 'Gender and mentoring relationships: a review and research agenda for the next decade', in G.N. Powell (ed.), *Handbook of Gender and Work*, Sage, Thousand Oaks, CA.

Ragins, B.R., Townsend, B. and Mattis, M. (1998) 'Gender gap in the executive suite: CEOs and female executives report on breaking the glass ceiling', *Academy of Management Executive*, 12 (1): 28–42.

Riger, S. and Galligan, P. (1980) 'Women in management: an exploration of competing paradigms', *American Psychologist*, 35: 902–910.

Schein, V.E. (1973) 'The relationship between sex role stereotypes and requisite management characteristics', *Journal of Applied Psychology*, 57: 95–100.

Schein, V.E. (1975) 'Relationships between sex role stereotypes and requisite management characteristics among female managers', *Journal of Applied Psychology*, 60: 340–344.

Schwartz, F.N. (1992) *Breaking with Tradition: Women and Work, the New Facts of Life*, Times Warner, New York.

Stroh, L.K., Brett, J.M. and Reilly, A.H. (1996) 'Family structure, glass ceiling, and traditional explanations for the differential rate of turnover of female and male managers', *Journal of Vocational Behavior*, 49: 99–118.

United Nations Educational, Scientific and Cultural Organization (UNESCO) (1997) *Statistical Yearbook 1997*, UNESCO, Paris, table 3.12, pp. 3-332–3-378.

US Department of Education, National Center for Education Statistics (1997) *Digest of Education Statistics 1997*, Government Printing Office, Washington, DC, tables 244 and 281, pp. 261 and 308.

US Department of Labor, Bureau of Labor Statistics (1983) *Handbook of Labor Statistics*, Government Printing Office, Washington, DC, table 16, pp. 44–48.

US Department of Labor, Bureau of Labor Statistics (1990) *Employment and Earnings*, 37 (2): table A-22, p. 29.

US Department of Labor, Bureau of Labor Statistics (1998a) *Employment and Earnings*, 45 (1): table 2, p. 163.

US Department of Labor, Bureau of Labor Statistics (1998b) *Employment and Earnings*, 45 (9): tables A-2 and A-19, pp. 7 and 27.

17

The Business Case and the Management of Diversity

Catherine Cassell

As the chapters within this book highlight, the last 30 years have seen an increase in the number of women entering management, yet the statistics show that the number of women in senior positions is still not as high as would be expected, given shifting demographic trends (Davidson and Cooper, 1993; Tanton, 1994). This chapter focuses on one particular set of arguments that have recently been used to support the entry and progression of women into management. These arguments are based upon a business case. The business case is not a unitary approach, nor a specific set of interventions; rather the label has been used to describe any approach to equal opportunities which focuses upon the business benefits that employers can accrue through making the most of the skills and potential of all their employees. The argument is that the loss or lack of recognition of these skills, as a result of everyday discriminatory practices, can be very costly to companies. A key development within the realm of business cases for equal opportunities is that of managing diversity (e.g. Thomas, 1990; Cox, 1992; Jackson et al., 1992; Kandola and Fullerton, 1994). Managing Diversity initiatives, which originated in the United States, are beginning to emerge in UK organizations.

The aim of this chapter is to critically assess the underpinnings and implications of the business case for the progression of women managers. The chapter begins by outlining some of the problems with the conventional approaches to the furtherance of equal opportunities in order to set the context within which the business case has arisen. The key principles and characteristics underlying the business case and management of diversity initiatives are then outlined. Evidence for the success of these initiatives in relation to both the experiences and progression of women in management is then considered. The chapter concludes by detailing a research agenda that stems from an assessment of current evidence.

Equal opportunities (EO) and the progression of women in management

In Britain a lot of research has focused on the experiences of discrimination faced by women managers (e.g. Davidson and Cooper, 1992, 1993; Green and Cassell,

1996). The context for examining discriminatory practices has long been associated with the philosophy of equal opportunities. The basic premise of equal opportunities is that talent and ability are equally spread throughout all groups, including between men and women, able-bodied and people with disabilities, and all ethnic groups (Wilson, 1995). Therefore equal opportunities policies and codes of practice (in theory) are aimed at ensuring that organizations make the most of a diverse workforce rather than losing those talents through discriminatory processes. Today many employers in Britain refer to themselves as 'Equal Opportunity Employers', implying that they are keen to dissociate themselves from discriminatory practices based on gender, race, disability, etc. In practice groups of employees within those organizations can still experience considerable discrimination, as many studies show (Cockburn, 1991; Wilson, 1995; Cassell, 1996). At the root of equal opportunities initiatives are assumptions about social justice, equality and fairness. Organizations have approached the institutionalization of these values in different ways. However, despite the existence of equal opportunities legislation, Wilson (1995) suggests that the notion that equal opportunity exists now for women is a myth. Indeed there seems to be considerable disappointment and disillusionment about the current state of women's position at work, given 20 years of EO legislation. A number of reasons have been given for the lack of success of equal opportunity initiatives, such as disappointing legislation for example. Cassell (1996) suggests that equal opportunities policies and practices have been attracting a bad press, linking in with the 'backlash' that has occurred against women's progression in the 1980s and 1990s (Faludi, 1992).

Aside from the problems associated with gaining a bad press, Kandola and Fullerton (1994) suggest that the body of ideas seen to represent conventional wisdom in equal opportunities has changed very little during the last 15 years. Despite this, they argue that the face of equal opportunities is changing as a result of a number of factors. These include a more overt emphasis on the business case; an increased amount of research and recognition that a wide range of groups within the workplace face discrimination and harassment (for example on the basis of age, sexuality or disability); and an increasing concern about ethics and ethical behaviour in the workplace, a key element of which is equal opportunities (Kandola and Fullerton, 1994: 13). They suggest that the implication of this changing face is a recognition that the time is right for a reconsideration of conventional approaches to EO. They propose a focus on managing diversity as an alternative approach which is more appropriate to the challenges facing organizations in the 1990s.

The business case

Given the problems outlined with the equal opportunities approach, it is not surprising that an alternative approach has emerged. The business case focuses on the business benefits that employers accrue through making the most of the skills and potential of women employees. The argument is that the loss or lack of recognition of these skills and potential is very costly. Consequently the business case is fundamentally linked to the principles of strategic HRM where the human resource and its full utilization is seen to give a company the competitive edge

(Biswas and Cassell, 1996). Additionally, it is crucial that equal opportunities initiatives are seen to tie in with the overall strategic direction of a company. A business case sees achieving equality as essential to achieving organizational goals. Again in the same way that strategic HRM is linked into the general strategy of a firm, so equal opportunities pervades every aspect of business policy, rather than being merely an add-on.

In 1995 the Equal Opportunities Commission launched a campaign to highlight the business case for equal opportunities. The aim was to demonstrate that in economic terms, equality made good business sense. A leaflet produced at the time outlines the 'Benefits of Equality' and 'Costs of Inequality'. The benefits of equality include:

- best use of human resources (reduced staff turnover; motivated workforce and better recruitment);
- flexible workforce to aid restructuring;
- workforce representative of the local community;
- improved corporate image with potential employees and customers;
- attracting ethical investors;
- managers can integrate equality into corporate objectives;
- new business ideas from a diverse workforce.

The costs of inequality include:

- inefficiency in use of human resources (high staff turnover; low productivity; and restricted pool of talent);
- inflexible workforce limiting organizational change;
- poor corporate image with prospective employees and customers;
- management time spent on grievances;
- losing an industrial tribunal case (no ceiling on awards; management/staff time; legal fees; bad publicity).

Underlying these costs and benefits are a series of demographic trends that were seen to be placing pressure on businesses. The UK labour force has experienced considerable change over the last 30 years with women entering the labour market in large numbers. As Ross and Schneider (1992: 50) suggest, as a result of such demographic trends, a shift in thinking was required:

> The shift that was necessary was one away from external drives, towards internal economic and business ones. There is an ethical argument for EO. It is these principles which led to the legislation being enacted in the first place. There is also, however an unquestionable economic and business case for change. The projected need for skills and the sheer number of women and ethnic minorities who will be qualifying over the next few years and entering the work force, will mean that the labour market will dictate the need to review recruitment methods. Practical business sense will mean that organizations will need to widen the recruitment pool to include non-traditional recruits.

They continue by warning that 'it will no longer be about being a "good employer" and will instead have everything to do with long-term survival' (1992: 51).

Through becoming associated with a business case, it is assumed that equal opportunities is now back on the map. The business case is seen to be more attractive to employers precisely because it talks of issues such as 'business benefits' and 'competitive advantage'. This in itself is perceived to have advantages in terms of who 'owns' the EO issues. Maddock (1995) suggested that because equality measures in the past were typically focused on the disadvantaged groups, rather than on those who managed them, it was assumed that equality was solely concerned with special cases. Ross and Schneider (1992) point out that within a business case the wider ownership of equal opportunities becomes possible. They argue that once the issue is seen as a business issue and becomes an integral part of the organization's culture and widely owned it will be understood in a different way:

> In time, equal opportunities will therefore not be a topic of controversy and debate. It will not be viewed as something in favour of minorities and against whites. It will, however, be normal to be different and equal opportunities principles will be integrated into the values of an organization. (1992: 55)

But the key development that has arisen from the business case and changing demographic trends is that of managing diversity. This approach, whilst claiming to be distinctive from conventional approaches to EO, offers to enhance the working lives and opportunities of women managers.

Managing diversity

One example of a clearly defined approach using a business case is a set of interventions based upon the effective management of diversity in organizations. The management of diversity presents a business case for moving towards a diverse workforce where the skills of all groups are recognized. The argument is that given the current shortage of skilled labour (particularly in the United States) the effective use of diverse skills within an organization makes good business sense. Diversity management is particularly popular in the United States where the skill shortages are more pronounced than in Britain. Management of diversity is based on the notion of difference and the effective management of difference. Valuing difference is seen as an important concept because it is specifically linked to an organization's culture and values. A key element is to move towards 'cultures of inclusion' (Thornberg, 1994) recognizing that various organizational practices often lead to certain groups feeling left out or unwelcome. Exponents of the management of diversity perspective (Thomas, 1990; Cox, 1992; Jackson et al., 1992; Kandola and Fullerton, 1994) argue that all differences must be valued including those of white males.

To take an example, Walker and Hanson (1992) describe some of the components of the 'Valuing Differences' philosophy that has been introduced and implemented at DEC (Digital Equipment Corporation), a company with 120,000 employees in 64 countries throughout the world. The philosophy

> focuses employees on their differences. Employees are encouraged to pay attention to their differences as unique individuals and as members of groups, to raise their level of

comfort with differences, and to capitalize on differences as a major asset to the company's productivity. (1992: 120)

The 'Valuing Differences' work is done in a variety of ways including awareness and skills training; celebrating differences events (e.g. Gay and Lesbian Pride week, Hispanic Heritage month); and leadership groups and support groups. A particularly radical intervention is that of the establishment of an informal network of small ongoing discussion groups, known as core groups described as 'groups of 7–9 employees who commit to coming together on a monthly basis to examine their stereotypes, test the differences in their assumptions, and build significant relationships with people they regard as different' (1992: 121). The authors conclude that 'capitalizing on diversity means helping employees become their very best by learning to accept, trust and invest in others' (1992: 136).

The benefits of the successful management of diversity are seen to be very rich. Cox (1992: 34) for example describes them as 'better decision-making, greater creativity and innovation, and more successful marketing to different types of customers'. Thornberg (1994) outlines three phases which represent a company's evolution towards a more diverse heterogeneous culture. The first is to bring in more women and minorities; the second to emphasize working on problems of individual and group behaviour associated with race and gender, that is to begin to understand how people are different and why; and the third a focus on company culture which involves evaluating all of the organization's policies and procedures. Diversity interventions are characterized as comprehensive and inclusive.

Robinson and Dechant suggest that developing a business case for diversity is more difficult than for other business issues, mainly because 'evidence of diversity's impact on the bottom line has not been systematically measured and documented for easy retrieval and use' (1997: 21). They suggest that in putting the case, a number of business reasons can be suggested. These include cost savings such as decreased turnover and absenteeism and the avoidance of lawsuits. More positively they outline a range of ways in which diversity can drive business growth. These include improving marketplace understanding; increasing creativity and innovation; producing higher-quality problem-solving; enhancing leadership effectiveness; and building effective global relationships. The authors report a survey where human resource executives from 15 Fortune 100 companies were asked to identify the main business reasons for engaging in diversity management. The top reasons given were better utilization of talent (93 per cent); increased marketplace understanding (80 per cent); enhanced breadth of understanding in leadership positions (60 per cent); enhanced creativity (53 per cent); and increased quality of team problem-solving (40 per cent). As Robinson and Dechant suggest, the executives focus more on the added value that emerges from diversity initiatives rather than the more negative penalties of mismanagement, such as the avoidance of lawsuits.

Kandola and Fullerton (1994) suggest that managing diversity must pervade the entire organization, if it is to be successful. They propose a MOSAIC vision, which summarizes the key characteristics of the diversity-oriented organization. MOSAIC is an acronym for **M**ission and values, **O**bjective and fair processes,

Skilled workforce: aware and fair, Active flexibility, Individual focus, and Culture that empowers. In highlighting these key characteristics it is clear that the managing diversity approach is considerably different from previous conventional approaches to equal opportunities. The focus becomes that of ensuring that all individuals within an organization can maximize their potential, regardless of any groups they may belong to. It is an all-embracing concept where the focus is cultural change and learning, rather than promoting fairness and avoiding discrimination. Crucially, managing diversity is seen as a key element of overall business policy, linked into an organization's strategy, rather than a personnel or HR policy. Given that, the emphasis is clearly on the business benefits that the successful management of diversity can accrue for a company. From a cursory overview it would appear that the management of diversity approach has much to offer the woman manager struggling to enhance her position in the workplace. However, it is important to examine the extent to which the claims made about the potential of diversity initiatives match with empirical evidence as to their relative success or failure.

Assessing the impact of managing diversity programmes: the evidence

The search for empirical evidence to validate the success of managing diversity programmes can be a fairly frustrating exercise. One of the problems is that many of the case studies of diversity programmes that are reported in the literature do not contain any evaluative element. Indeed sometimes these case study reports focus more on promoting a particular company approach with evangelical zeal, rather than assessing and evaluating the success of a given programme. An additional source of concern is that most of the studies that do look at diversity interventions are American based. This in itself is not a problem, but there is the issue of how transferable the context is, given that the demographic trends experienced in the USA are a considerably exaggerated version of what is currently happening in the UK labour market. Finally, in assessing the evidence it is worth noting that management of diversity initiatives are unlikely to focus specifically on women managers. Given the underlying philosophy of valuing all differences, women managers are just a group of individual employees, like any other.

As was suggested earlier, the impact of diversity on the business bottom line is difficult to assess. Studies are starting to emerge however that consider the financial benefits of diversity programmes. One such analysis is provided by Wright et al. (1995). Using data from 1986 to 1992, they examined the impact that announcements of US Department of Labor awards for exemplary affirmative action had upon the stock returns of winning corporations, together with the effects that announcements of damage awards from the settlement of discrimination lawsuits had on the stock returns of guilty corporations. Their results indicated that announcements of quality affirmative action programmes were associated with an increase in stock prices, and conversely, announcements of discrimination settlements were associated with significant negative stock price changes. The authors conclude from this study that:

the prevalent organizational ethnic and gender bias (Hitt and Barr, 1989) should be eradicated not only because such bias is not ethical or moral, but also because it does not make economic sense. As the climate of competition becomes more intense, no enterprise can afford the senseless practice of discrimination. In fact, America's cultural diversity may provide a competitive advantage for unbiased US corporations over both domestic rivals that discriminate and European and Japanese companies in the world marketplace. (1995: 284)

Other discussions of diversity programmes focus on particular companies. Totta and Burke (1995) outline the processes by which the Bank of Montreal became committed to workforce diversity. The aim was to integrate issues of diversity and equality into the day to day life of the bank, so that each and every business decision was influenced by diversity issues. The leaders of the organization recognized that this would require a cultural transformation, at the centre of which would be climate of workplace equality where individuals felt welcomed. A series of interventions were created to further these aims, including changes in a wide range of procedures and practices, and 26 action plans: 'initiatives that would dramatically transform every aspect of the way business was conducted at the bank, from hiring practices to performance review criteria, from approaches to learning to the definition of corporate values' (1995: 35). Totta and Burke's account is that of work in progress, rather than a systematic evaluation of the programme, but it provides an example of many of the cases that are published about the introduction of diversity programmes. Other examples include: American Express (Wolfe Morrison and Mardenfeld Herlihy, 1992); Pepsi-Cola (Fulkerson and Schuler, 1992); DEC (Walker and Hanson, 1992); and International Distillers and Vintners (Kandola and Fullerton, 1994).

A different approach is taken by Kandola and Fullerton (1994). After reviewing a range of managing diversity models from the literature they produced their own strategic implementation model that focuses on eight processes (the clarity of the organization vision; the extent of top management commitment; the auditing and assessing of needs; the setting of clear objectives; the degree of accountability; the degree of communication within the organization; the extent of co-ordination; the degree to which the strategy and actions are evaluated). The authors then conducted two surveys. The first was a study of 285 organizations examining the initiatives that each had put in place to manage diversity, and how successful they were perceived to be. The second survey was conducted with 49 organizations to test out the model proposed. The results from the surveys validated the model proposed, which, as the authors suggest, makes it the 'first ever to have been empirically tested and validated' (1994: 97).

Results from their survey demonstrate that the initiatives perceived to be the most successful by HR managers were those that were related to equalizing treatment between staff, or actions for universal benefit, as Kandola and Fullerton describe them. This is important given the focus of managing diversity philosophy on all individuals rather than specific groups. Such initiatives include eliminating age criteria from selection procedures and introducing the same benefits for part-time workers as full-time workers. The initiatives perceived to be the least successful were those focused on specific groups in the workforce.

Such measures included setting targets for the composition of the workforce and using positive action in recruitment training. Additionally, 'Including equal opportunities as part of business plans' was also seen as unsuccessful by 53 per cent of the organizations who had sought to implement it. The authors point out that this result could be an indication that the importance of diversity as a central business issue has not yet been recognized by many organizations.

The Kandola and Fullerton work is an asset to the literature in that it does have an empirical base. The limitations of the study are that its focus is the views of one senior manager within each of the companies studied, rather than the impact of diversity initiatives on the ground. It is however a useful starting point for those keen to evaluate the success or otherwise of diversity initiatives.

A number of authors have pointed to some of the problems that emerge when trying to implement diversity initiatives in organizations. Ellis and Sonnenfeld (1994) review three pioneering diversity programmes currently operating in US companies. They conclude that although it makes sense that the benefits of such programmes may translate into higher productivity and lower turnover, few organizations actually measure the transfer of the educational interventions into actual changes in human resource practices such as recruiting, management development and promotion. Their article highlights some of the emerging pitfalls with new corporate diversity programmes. They suggest that the programmes:

> are positive in tone, yet often lack systematic firm-wide integration into other human resource policies and do not tap the passionate disagreement that often rages beneath a platitudinous facade. (1994: 80)

One of the problems they highlight is the lack of time actually spent on training in some diversity initiatives:

> These programmes seem to be based on the premise that contact with members of different ethnic groups – if only for a few hours – or propaganda announcing the benefits of diversity, will clear up any misperceptions or ill will that some employees feel towards certain ethnic groups. Evidence often shows the contrary: simply pointing out differences among various groups, if not handled sensitively, can increase hostility and misunderstanding. (1994: 83)

Of significance here is the danger that diversity training may actually reinforce old stereotypes, or create new tensions. Ellis and Sonnenfeld point out that when evaluating a 'Valuing Diversity' seminar they found that a minority of respondents disliked it. In particular white males complained that they were 'vilified' in the training materials which depicted bias and miscommunication in their interactions with women and minorities. The authors suggest that leaders need to continuously monitor the messages that are being put across through diversity initiatives. They also conclude that studies of the effects of managing diversity programmes are rarely conducted. So although an individual may be asked to evaluate the training they've received through an evaluation questionnaire, the impact is rarely measured at the level of the firm, for example through the business benefits accrued.

Kossek and Zonia (1992) describe the importance of the diversity climate in an organization, suggesting that climate and context, not numbers, are the real issues pertaining to the implementation of diversity policies. They conducted a study based on intergroup theory to examine relationships between perceptions of diversity climate and group and organizational characteristics. Their results suggest that diversity initiatives were embraced more by white women and ethnic minorities, most of whom were not high up enough in the company hierarchy to effect any change. Their results also point to:

> the need to better understand issues of backlash and perceptions of equity regarding employer activities to promote a diverse workforce. In an era of shrinking resources and downsizing, the competition between groups for scarce organizational resources will intensify.... Our results suggest that conducting cosmetic diversity activities in an organization that is still overwhelmingly dominated by white males may, in fact, exacerbate negative intergroup processes such as hostility and splitting. (1992: 77)

In conclusion it would seem that the jury is still out on whether or not diversity initiatives meet their long-term goals. This is understandable given that compared to other forms of organizational interventions, diversity initiatives are relatively new. At this stage however, we can speculate on some of the implications of business case approaches for the work experience and progression of women managers.

Implications of the business case for the progression of women managers

In outlining the business case for the progression of women managers, it is evident that it is considerably different from the ways in which advocates have traditionally argued for equal opportunities. At the root of the business case are the goals of business success and competitive advantage. Equal opportunities policies are seen as one of the many means to achieve that end. At the root of traditional approaches to equal opportunities, however, are the goals of justice and fairness. The implications of the change in goals is a debate in itself. Indeed there is no reason why these goals should be mutually exclusive. An organization can strive to be both competitively successful and an equal opportunities employer. What is interesting is the relative attractiveness of these goals. It seems likely that a focus on business goals may be more attractive to employers.

The context within which the business case has emerged is of key significance. As suggested earlier, some authors have argued that we have recently seen a backlash against equal opportunities at work (Faludi, 1992). The existence of such a backlash has implications for the work experience of women. It creates a context where it is difficult for women to challenge discrimination at work. Indeed those who try may be marginalized or punished as a result (Cockburn, 1991; Cassell and Walsh, 1993). One way of dealing with a backlash and the effective silencing of discussions around inequality is to reframe them in a more socially acceptable language. When discussing the business case for equality, women managers and equal opportunities activists can invoke concepts such as 'added value', 'competitive advantage' and 'business benefits'. These concepts, couched in business language, appear to be neutral, and consequently more rational, than the language traditionally associated with equal opportunities, where concepts such as fairness and equality can be perceived as having a more emotional (and therefore irrational) appeal. Recently the author and a colleague (Susan Walsh) conducted a piece of research about the barriers to the progression of women into senior management positions within the publishing industry (Walsh and Cassell, 1995). The client group who commissioned the research were very senior women managers, some at director level. In presenting our findings and recommendations to the group we talked about notions of diversity management and the business benefits of making the most of women's skills and experience at senior levels. The group were particularly enthused about our recommendations because it gave them an apparently neutral language with which they could talk about equal opportunities at board level. Rather than focusing on what were considered to be emotive terms such as 'discrimination' the group took on 'Managing diversity for competitive advantage' as its theme.

In a backlash situation, the business case provides us with a way of talking about issues such as equality and fairness in what is perceived as a businesslike framework, in an organizationally acceptable manner. Legitimacy is provided for discussions about inequality because they are framed in terms of business advantage. Women managers in the position of defending equal opportunities can use the new language without the risk of being marginalized.

Part of the business case is to recognize that different groups of people have different types of skills which they can usefully bring to their work. Traditionally the skills of women have been undervalued at the workplace yet as suggested earlier there is now a move to argue that it is precisely women's distinctive skills that make them well suited for positions in senior management. In essence this approach is attractive to women managers. For a long time women have wrestled with how to manage their 'difference' in organizations and have struggled to 'fit in' (Sheppard, 1989). The paradox of managing difference whilst trying to appear the same is at the heart of many of the accounts of women who have made it into the more senior management positions in organizations (Kanter, 1977; Marshall, 1984; Davidson and Cooper, 1992; Walsh and Cassell, 1995). An approach based on not just a recognition of, but a celebration of, difference is potentially extremely appealing to such women managers. It is perhaps a liberation to be free to argue that women are different and therefore better at some aspects of managerial work than men. Of equal appeal is the notion that there are individual differences within groups of women. One of the frustrations so often faced by token senior women is that they are perceived as the epitome of women generally (Kanter, 1977). A focus on individuals is significant given that the discrimination women face at work is often based on stereotypes, which by definition expect all women to be the same.

However, there is a danger lurking in the seductive attraction of the language of difference. Within the context of managing diversity all differences that are psychologically meaningful to individuals are apparently recognized. Yet our knowledge of organizational life reminds us that some differences have a higher value attached to them than others (Liff, 1993). Given this concern it is important to question the extent to which a focus on women's 'distinctive' skills is useful for encouraging their progression at work. There is an argument that women are better at doing some managerial tasks, and those tend to be associated with more participative and transformational management styles. Although research demonstrates that women favour these kinds of management styles (Rosener, 1990; Martin, 1993), we must question the benefit to women of such perspectives. To what extent are these perspectives really a challenge to traditional organizational thinking that is associated with the gendered division of labour? As Antal and Izraeli (1993) suggest, although it may be intended to be 'women-friendly', this analysis carries the risk of a new form of stereotyping and ghettoization of women into areas perceived as 'women's work'. For women managers to reclaim the notion of difference as a positive force is appealing, but caution needs to be exercised about the potential of such an approach to inform radical change.

Conclusion

From the account provided above it would seem that this area is ripe for investigation. Clearly a considerable amount of literature is now devoted to the subject, particularly in relation to managing diversity. As Hall and Parker (1993) suggest, the last few years have generated a vast amount of descriptive research and prescriptive directives for intervention based on the management of diversity. There is also a large amount of advice now available to the senior manager who wishes to progress diversity management in their own workplace (e.g. Joplin and Daus, 1997). Some of this advice is based on the learning that has already occurred as a result of the experiences of those practitioners and consultants who have taken part in the implementation of diversity initiatives. Additionally, research from an economic tradition is starting to emerge that provides evidence for the economic case for equal opportunity initiatives (e.g. Equal Opportunities Commission, 1995).

What is missing is the systematic evaluation of diversity programmes. In particular the views of those on the receiving end, members of diverse groups, need to be investigated more fully. In the long-term we need to know the impact that a company's commitment to diversity has on the position and status of various groups within the workplace. Included in that pool are women managers who in theory have much to gain from diversity approaches. Additional to this is the need for further theoretical development. Hall and Parker (1993) suggest that what is needed within the diversity literature is a conceptual framework that is capable of integrating both theory and practice. Though the Kandola and Fullerton model is a start in this direction, further development would provide a structure from which key research questions can be defined.

Inevitably what underlies all approaches to equal opportunities based on a business case is the notion that the policies with regard to women are in an organization's commercial interests. The business case and management of diversity are a product of the economic climate in which we currently find ourselves. Any change to this climate may alter the pervasiveness of the arguments. So, as to the long-term prospects of this approach for improving women's current position in the management arena, only time will tell.

Note

This chapter is a development of an article previously published by the author: C.M. Cassell (1997) 'The business case for equal opportunities: implications for women in management', *Women in Management Review*, 12 (1): 11–16. Reproduced with permission.

References

Antal, A.B. and Izraeli, D.N. (1993) 'A global comparison of women in management: women managers in their homelands as expatriates', in E.A. Fagenson (ed.), *Women in Management, Trends, Issues and Challenges in Managerial Diversity*, Sage, Newbury Park, CA.
Biswas, R. and Cassell, C.M. (1996) 'The sexual division of labour in the hotel industry: implications for strategic HRM', *Personnel Review*, 25 (5): 51–66.
Cassell, C.M. (1996), 'Business ethics and discriminatory behaviour in organisations', in K. Smith and P. Johnson (eds), *Business Ethics and Business Behaviour*, International Thomson Business Press, London.
Cassell, C.M. and Walsh, S. (1993) 'Being seen but not heard: barriers to women's progression in the workplace', *The Psychologist*, 61 (6): 110–114.
Cockburn, C. (1991) *In the Way of Women: Men's Resistance to Sex Equality in Organisations*, Macmillan Education, Basingstoke.
Cox, T. Jr (1992) 'The multi-cultural organization', *Academy of Management Executive*, 5 (2): 34–47.
Davidson, M.J. and Cooper, C.L. (1992) *Shattering the Glass Ceiling*, Paul Chapman, London.
Davidson, M.J. and Cooper, C.L. (1993) *European Women in Business and Management*, Paul Chapman, London.
Ellis, C. and Sonnenfeld, J.A. (1994) 'Diverse approaches to managing diversity', *Human Resource Management*, 33 (1): 79–109.
Equal Opportunities Commission (1995) *The Economics of Equal Opportunities*, EOC, Manchester.
Faludi, S. (1992) *Backlash: the Undeclared War against Women*, Chatto & Windus, London.
Fulkerson, J.R. and Schuler, R.S. (1992) 'Managing worldwide diversity at Pepsi-Cola International', in S.E. Jackson and Associates (eds), *Diversity in the Workplace: Human Resource Initiatives*, Guilford Press, New York.
Green, E. and Cassell, C.M. (1996) 'Women managers, gendered cultural processes and organisational change', *Gender, Work and Organization*, 3 (3): 168–178.
Hall, D.T. and Parker, V.A. (1993) 'The role of workplace flexibility in managing diversity', *Organizational Dynamics*, 5–18.
Hitt, M.A. and Barr, S.H. (1989) 'Managerial selection decision models: examination of configural cue processing', *Journal of Applied Psychology*, 59: 705–711.
Jackson, S.E. and Associates (1992) *Diversity in the Workplace: Human Resource Initiatives*, Guilford Press, New York.
Joplin, J.R.W. and Daus, C.S. (1997) 'Challenges of leading a diverse workforce', *Academy of Management Executive*, 11 (3): 32–47.
Kandola, R. and Fullerton, J. (1994) *Managing the Mosaic: Diversity in Action*, Institute of Personnel and Development, London.
Kanter, R.M. (1977) *Men and Women of the Corporation*, Basic Books, New York.
Kossek, E.E. and Zonia, S.C. (1992) 'A field study of reactions to employer efforts to promote diversity', *Journal of Organisational Behaviour*, 14: 61–81.
Liff, S. (1993) *From Equality to Diversity, Organisations, Gender and Power*, Warwick Papers in Industrial Relations 48, University of Warwick.

Maddock, S. (1995) 'Rhetoric and reality: the business case for equality and why it continues to be resisted', *Women in Management Review*, 10 (1): 14–20.

Marshall, J. (1984) *Women Managers: Travellers in a Male World*, John Wiley & Sons, Chichester.

Martin, P.Y. (1993) 'Feminist practices in organizations: implications for management', in E.A. Fagenson (ed.), *Women in Management: Trends, Issues and Challenges in Managerial Diversity*, Sage, Newbury Park, CA.

Robinson, G. and Dechant, K. (1997) 'Building a business case for diversity', *Academy of Management Executive*, 11 (3): 21–31.

Rosener, J. (1990) 'Ways women lead', *Harvard Business Review*, November–December: 119–125.

Ross, R. and Schneider, R. (1992) *From Equality to Diversity: a Business Case for Equal Opportunities*, Pitman, London.

Sheppard, D.L. (1989) 'Organizations, power and sexuality: the image and self-image of women managers', in J. Hearn, D.L. Sheppard, P. Tancred-Sherrif and G. Burrell (eds), *The sexuality of Organizations*, Sage, London.

Tanton, M. (1994) *Women in Management: Developing a Presence*, London: Routledge.

Thomas, R.R. Jr (1990) 'From affirmative action to affirming diversity', *Harvard Business Review*, 68 (2): 107–117.

Thornberg, L. (1994) 'Journey towards a more inclusive culture', *HRMagazine*, February: 79–96.

Totta, J.M. and Burke, R.J. (1995) 'Integrating diversity and equality into the fabric of the organization', *Women in Management Review*, 10 (7): 32–39.

Walker, B.A. and Hanson, W.C. (1992) 'Valuing differences at Digital Equipment Corporation', in S.E. Jackson and Associates (eds), *Diversity in the Workplace: Human Resource Initiatives*, Guilford Press, New York.

Walsh, S. and Cassell, C.M. (1995) *A Case of Covert Discrimination: Report on the Women in Management Study*, Book House Training Centre, London.

Wilson, F.M. (1995) *Organizational Behaviour and Gender*, McGraw-Hill, London.

Wolfe Morrison, E. and Mardenfeld Herlihy, J. (1992) 'Becoming the best place to work: managing diversity at American Express Travel related services', in S.E. Jackson and Associates (eds), *Diversity in the Workplace: Human Resource Initiatives*, Guilford Press, New York.

Wright, P., Ferris, S.P., Hiller, J.S. and Kroll, M. (1995) 'Competitiveness through management of diversity: effects on stock price valuation', *Academy of Management Journal*, 38 (1): 272–287.

18

Critical Studies on Men, Masculinities and Managements

David L. Collinson and Jeff Hearn

In the study of work, organizations and management the critical analysis of men and masculinities is fundamentally important. Yet an examination of the available literature reveals the recurring paradox that men are often an 'absent-presence' in organizational studies. The categories of men and masculinity are frequently central to analyses, yet they remain taken for granted, hidden and unexamined. Men are talked about but rarely the focus of interrogation rendered simultaneously explicit and implicit. Many scholars have seemed extraordinarily unaware of the men in organizations about whom they write. The study of management is a case in point. Most managers in most organizations in most countries are men (Collinson and Hearn, 1996). Yet the conditions, processes and consequences of men's historical and contemporary domination of management have received little scrutiny. There has been a strange silence, reflecting a taken for granted association, even conflation, of men with organizational power, authority and prestige. This association persists in both 'theory' and 'practice', with consequences for organizations, employees and managers. Although not all managers are men, the male domination, particularly of senior levels within management, tends to persist across different societies. The development of transnational organizations, international trade, communication and world financial systems could well reinforce the globalized nature of these male-dominated networks and processes.

The association of men and managements can be seen in the biographies and autobiographies of famous twentieth-century entrepreneurial male managers/owners, such as Ford (Ford, 1923; Sward, 1948), Iacocca (Iacocca, 1984), Geneen (Geneen, 1985) Hughes (Drosnin, 1987) and Maxwell (Davies, 1992). These accounts reveal evangelical, personal and lifelong preoccupations with military-like efficiency, ruthless business practices based on bullying and coercion and autocratic control based on the humiliation of subordinates. Equally, they implicitly disclose the masculine assumptions and practices that frequently predominate in management. In the 1980s particularly aggressive forms of masculinity increasingly seemed to characterize managerial discursive practices.

Highly autocratic managerial styles were widely celebrated as the primary means of generating corporate success. Journalistic profiles of male executives consistently emphasized their 'heroic' qualities of struggle and battle, a willingness to be ruthless and brutal, a rebellious nature and an aggressive, rugged individualism (Neale, 1995). Managers and senior executives were often depicted and portrayed themselves as 'hard men', virile, swashbuckling and flamboyant entrepreneurs who had reasserted their managerial prerogative (Denham, 1991). Management came to be defined in terms of the ability to control people, events, companies, environments, trade unions and new technology.

In the 1990s gendered assumptions can still be discerned in managerial initiatives such as total quality management and business process re-engineering. The language of management also frequently remains gendered, for example, both in terms of its highly (hetero)sexualized talk about 'penetrating markets' and 'getting into bed with suppliers/customers/competitors', and in the extensive use of sporting metaphors and sexual joking in rationalizing managerial decisions and practices (Cockburn, 1991). Equally, managerial presentational styles which emphasize 'professional', 'competent' and 'rational' self-images infused with an air of total confidence, detachment and control frequently reveal masculine assumptions, particularly when presenters use sexist and racist jokes as 'ice-breakers' (Cockburn, 1991). Participation in male-dominated sports can still significantly shape managerial interactions and indeed career progress within and between organizations, networks, labour markets and professional alliances (Collinson et al., 1990; Kanter, 1997/1993). Increasingly, a considerable amount of business is also conducted through the 'corporate entertainment' of client 'guests' in male-dominated sporting spheres such as tennis and golf clubs, in 'executive boxes' at football grounds and in the men-only business clubs of which many managers are members. Japanese 'hostess clubs' are a very clear example of the way that corporate-funded entertainment for managers can reflect and reinforce dominant masculinities (Allison, 1994).

Feminist writers have demonstrated how management often excludes women, especially those who are black and/or from ethnic minorities (Bell and Nkomo, 1992; Ibarra, 1995). This chapter attends to the Other side, that is taken for granted in malestream discourses and is theorized implicitly and sometimes explicitly in feminist discourses: the problem of men, masculinities and managements. Its purpose is to examine critically the conditions, processes and consequences of men's persistent dominance of management. Why, when we 'think manager' do we still tend to 'think male'? (Schein, 1976). The first section below briefly illustrates how much of the literature on management has neglected issues of gender, men and masculinity. The main argument of the chapter is then developed through a review of recent studies that have begun to explore and analyse the complex gendered processes of power that characterize contemporary management. This review demonstrates how a more integrated analysis of gender, men and managements can facilitate a rereading of traditional issues in management. It suggests that a re-examination of themes such as power, structure and decision-making can produce challenging new insights, understandings and perspectives.

Agendered management

The emergence of management as the central organizational activity of twentieth-century corporations is reflected in the burgeoning literature that explores the function's assumptions, responsibilities and practices (for example Drucker, 1979; Stewart, 1986; Reed, 1989, Grint, 1995). Despite – possibly even because of – the frequently pervasive association between men, power and authority in organizations, the literature on management has consistently failed to question its gendered nature. Whether adopting prescriptive, descriptive or critical perspectives, studies typically subscribe to images of middle and senior management that are imbued with particular notions of masculinity. This tendency can be seen in the development of management theory, from scientific management to human relations, systems and contingency theories, and more recently population ecology and institutional perspectives. In conventional organizational psychology, where the major contribution to the prescriptive study of leadership has emerged, leadership is frequently assumed to be synonymous with men (Hearn and Parkin, 1988). For example, Bennis' (1989) prescriptions on how to 'become a leader' exclude women and fail to problematize men and masculinity in relation to leadership.

The influential work of Mintzberg (1973, 1975, 1983, 1989) challenges the prevailing highly rational and 'scientific' view of management. Mintzberg examines the political alliances and strategies played out by managers in their search for power, influence and organizational security. In many ways, such descriptions of managerial work are similar to those of Dalton's (1959) classic study that graphically examined the hidden agendas of intra-managerial collusion and conflict. While both authors may be writing primarily (or even exclusively) about men, they fail to analyse men and masculinities as socially produced, reproduced and indeed changeable. Mintzberg uses 'manager' and 'he' interchangeably and even when he critiques the 'Great Man' theory for revealing 'almost nothing about managerial work' (1973: 12), he remains silent about its inherently gendered imagery and assumptions. He does not seem to recognize that within, between and across managerial and organizational hierarchies, masculine discourses and practices are often a crucial basis for alliances, divisions and conflicts between men in senior positions.

More critical studies of management examine the function's overriding concern with the control of labour and the extraction of production and profit (Braverman, 1974; Edwards, 1979). They seek to make explicit and then to question management's extensive power and control (Alvesson and Willmott, 1996). Increasingly, critical writers have also contextualized managerial power and discretion within broader social, economic and political conditions (Willmott, 1987; Linstead et al., 1996) and have examined the diversity, differences and contradictions that can characterize managerial hierarchies (Hyman, 1987; Jermier et al., 1994). They show how managers may also be highly sensitized to career advancement in ways that can produce tension and conflict as managers seek to differentiate and elevate themselves and their departments (Watson, 1994). Outlining the patronage, intrigues and conspiracies characterizing relations within management, Jackall (1988) describes how managers seek to survive by 'currying favour' with senior managers and 'managing reputation' with colleagues. Yet even these more critical analyses of management rarely attend to the continued predominance of men in managerial positions, the relatively limited presence of women and the processes, networks and assumptions through which the latter are intentionally and unintentionally excluded and/or subordinated.

To summarize, whether we refer to the 'ideal' prescriptive models of management of early academic writers, descriptive accounts of managerial work or even more critical analyses, the masculine imagery of management and managers seems to be taken for granted, neglected, and thereby reproduced and reinforced. Having highlighted this tendency to ignore gender completely in the literature on management, we wish to emphasize that our approach is not intended to be an extension of the 'women in management' literature (for example Helgesen, 1990; Rosener, 1990; Fagenson, 1993). Such analyses have also tended to neglect a critical examination of the hierarchical and gendered power of either men as managers or managers as men. Their recurrent emphasis upon women's different ways of managing and leading and the need to develop women's skills to fit into contemporary managerial hierarchies reflects a focus primarily upon women that is in danger of blaming the victim and/or essentialism. Research has found few consistent differences between female and male managers in terms of managerial behaviours, commitment, decision style, stress or subordinates' responses (Donnell and Hall, 1980; Boulgarides, 1984). We subscribe to a much more critical approach to gender relations, as the following section outlines.

Gender, feminism and critical studies on men

Feminist studies constitute the major influence in developing the explicit analysis of gender in organizations. Some feminist writers (Cockburn, 1983; Walby, 1986) focus upon patriarchy as a separate system of men's control over women. They reveal how organized groups of male workers have historically opposed the entry of cheaper female labour by demanding the 'breadwinner wage' and by controlling both the provision of training and gendered definitions of skill (Phillips and Taylor, 1980). Other feminist analyses combine a focus on structure with that of agency, contradiction and difference (for example Hollway, 1984; Ferguson, 1984; Pringle, 1989). Examining the contradictions of male power and control, as well as highlighting female agency and resistance, such studies criticize theories of patriarchy for treating 'men' and 'women' as unified groups and undifferentiated categories. For Connell (1987), such 'categorical' theories about patriarchy neglect differences and relations that can shift over time and place. Post-structuralist feminism has increasingly recognized men's and women's diverse, fragmented and contradictory lives in and around organizations. Attention has focused on gendered subjectivities and their ambiguous, fragmented, discontinuous and multiple character within asymmetrical relations (Henriques et al., 1984; Kondo, 1990).

Informed by the growing interest in gendered power, subjectivity and agency, critical studies on men highlight not only male power, but also the material and symbolic differences through which that power is reproduced (Brittan, 1989). While both men and masculinities are dominantly categories of power and social value, they are by no means homogeneous, unified or fixed categories but diverse, differentiated and shifting (Hearn, 1987, 1992b; Hearn and Morgan, 1990; Connell, 1995). Hence the use of the term 'masculinities', rather than just 'masculinity' (Carrigan et al., 1985). Such studies also examine relations between men themselves as well as between women and men (Collinson, 1992; Morgan, 1992). Likely to vary in specific situations, in different historical times, particular masculinities may also be internally contradictory, in tension and differentiated by, for example, age; class; ethnicity; religion; sexuality; nationality; paternal/marital kinship status; occupation and size (Hearn and Collinson, 1994). Such debates have in turn led to critiques concerning the increasing diversity of what is meant by 'masculinity', the imprecise nature of some usages, and the need to focus on 'men's practices', material and discursive (McMahon, 1993; Hearn, 1996).

While many of the foregoing gender analyses have explored women's and indeed men's experience of subordination, and of being managed, comparatively less attention has been paid to the gendered conditions, processes and consequences of those who exercise considerable hierarchical power in organizations. Some feminist writers have examined the gendered character of the managerial function from the perspective and experience of women managers (e.g. Davidson and Cooper, 1983; Sheppard, 1989; Martin, 1990; Calás and Smircich, 1993; Marshall, 1995; Sinclair, 1995; Wajcman, 1998). Yet little attention has been paid to men in management. This is particularly surprising in the case of critical studies on men given the central focus in these studies on the way that 'hegemonic masculinities' (for example white, heterosexual, middle class) may dominate other masculinities (for example black, gay, working class).[1] From the perspective of gender, hierarchy and class, men in management, especially those in accounting, engineering and strategic functions, often most closely represent 'hegemonic masculinity/ies' in the workplace. Accordingly, men's organizational dominance both 'as managers' and 'as men' requires further analysis.

Men, masculinities and managements

Most of the work examined in the two previous sections has not explicitly considered the interrelations of gender, men and managements. This section discusses a growing number of studies attempting to 'break the silence' on men and management. It recognizes the seminal importance of Kanter's (1977/1993) groundbreaking work – one of the first studies explicitly to focus on the interconnections between men as managers and managers as men. The following discussion considers how recent accounts of the connections between management, men and masculinities can shed new light on traditional themes in management writing and managerial practice. In what follows, we consider three 'classic' and closely interrelated issues in management: power, structure and decision-making.

Power

In examining how the gendered nature of management is reproduced, Kanter refers to 'homosexual reproduction' (1977: 48) to describe the way that men managers can appoint in their own image and thereby exclude women. She then uses the term 'homosocial reproduction' (1977: 48) to characterize the processes by which certain men managers are selected according to their ability to display appropriate social credentials. In the former case, Kanter suggests that men are selected for managerial positions because they are perceived to be more reliable, committed and predictable, free from conflicting loyalties between home and work. In the latter case, she argues that the extensive pressures on managers to conform to corporate expectations and demands can exclude not only women, but also many men. The typical profile of managers, she argues, is 'invariably white and male, with a certain shiny, clean-cut look' (1977: 42). While Kanter's study usefully describes how elitist practices can characterize management, it is less valuable in analysing the gendered nature of these persistent interrelations and networks (see also Pringle, 1989; Witz and Savage, 1992). Kanter contends that what appear to be differences between men and women in organizations are related not to gender, but to work position and the structure of opportunity. In seeking to deny difference, she fails to recognize how organizational power relations are frequently heavily gendered. Her concern to separate 'sex' from 'power' (1977: 202), inevitably neglects the way that particular masculinities may help to reproduce and legitimize managerial power and authority (see also Collinson and Hearn, 1995).

Managerial power is both hierarchical and gendered. Typically, it is in the managerial function that organizational power formally (and often informally) resides. In most contemporary organizations, managerial prerogative over key decisions remains the taken-for-granted norm. Managerial prerogative can be seen as part of a highly masculine discourse. Indeed managerial masculinities are also hegemonic within organizations in the sense that those in senior positions enjoy comparatively high salaries and ancillary remuneration packages in the form of secretarial support, share options, company cars, pensions, extensive holiday entitlements and other material and symbolic benefits. Even when they are dismissed, managers may receive substantial 'golden handshakes', and poor performance does not seem to prevent re-employment in other lucrative, senior positions (Pahl, 1995).

There are also innumerable ways in which the authority and status of managers can signify 'men' and indeed vice versa, just as there are many signs that can simultaneously signify the power of both 'manager' and 'men'. These cultural processes of signification include the company car, the size and position of personal offices; the office furniture and the display of pictures, paintings and plants; the use or control of computers and other technological equipment; and of course the choice of clothing. While business suits appear to have a transnational significance, their particular style, cut and cost are also important, not least as a means of managing impressions through 'power dressing' (Feldman and Klich, 1991). The colour and style of shirts, braces, shoes and socks as well as the size and pattern of ties (see Gibbings, 1990) can all carry context-specific meanings for both managers and men that may reflect and reinforce their organizational hegemony. Men's continued domination of senior positions results in many interconnections between particular masculinities and managerial practices. Specific managerial masculinities, such as paternalism or autocratic control methods, may not only reinforce the power of those men concerned, but also confirm the 'rights' of management and men to manage (Collinson and Hearn, 1994, 1996b; Hearn and Collinson, 1998).

In organizations where the manager is also the owner, power relations can be especially asymmetrical and gendered. Reed (1996) examines changes in Australian management over the last century. Highlighting the gendered nature of the so-called 'self-made man', she contrasts the lives of David Syme (1827–1908), the nineteenth-century, Scottish-born Australian publisher of *The Age* newspaper with Rupert Murdoch, the contemporary Australian-born international media entrepreneur. While Syme conformed to the Weberian image of the sober, self-made modern capitalist who adopted a paternalistic and dutiful approach to management, Murdoch's style is adventurist and more akin to pre-modern forms of capitalism and management. Studies of entrepreneurialism also reveal the interdependence of organizational power, gender and the family. Mulholland (1996) conducted research on 70 of the richest entrepreneurial families in a Midlands county of England. She found that, while men consistently claimed all of the credit for their business success, in practice their capital accumulation was highly dependent on the hidden household (and workplace) services provided by wives/women. Other studies report similar dynamics where men's managerial careers and identities are constructed through the invisible support of women as secretaries and wives (e.g. Finch, 1983; Grey, 1994).

In elaborating the connection between gendered power and subjectivity in management, Roper (1991, 1994) describes how British men managers in the postwar era frequently identified strongly with machinery and products. Undervaluing the role of labour in the manufacture of products, male managers engaged in a kind of fetishizing of the masculine self through the idolization of products. These managers were persistently concerned to display a masculine air of confidence and control that concealed anxiety and self-doubt. Kerfoot and Knights (1993) develop similar themes. They contend that paternalism and strategic management are concrete manifestations of historically shifting forms of masculinity. Arguing that these managerial approaches both reflect and reinforce 'discourses of masculinism', they suggest that 'paternalistic masculinity' and 'competitive masculinity' have the effect of privileging men *vis-à-vis* women, ranking some men above others, and maintaining as dominant certain forms and practices of masculinity. Kerfoot and Knights (1996) have also examined the contemporary and privileged form of masculine identity associated with dominant management practice – abstract, rational, highly instrumental, controlling of its object, future-orientated, strategic and, above all, masculine and wholly disembodied. These masculine managerial subjectivities are typically expressed in aggressive and competitive practices concerned to master and dominate. Highlighting the self-defeating nature of the search for masculine and managerial identity in these discourses of control, Kerfoot and Knights also show how the desire for a secure and stable sense of self tends to reproduce rather than eliminate anxiety and insecurity.

Indeed men's asymmetrical control and authority as managers is more contradictory, precarious and heterogeneous than often it at first appears. For example, in the 1990s the security of gendered power relations and masculine identities has been threatened by considerable social change. Equal opportunity initiatives, the need to compete with women for particular jobs, career bottlenecks and redundancies may all constitute significant challenges to men managers' conventional gender identities. Widespread organizational downsizing, short-term contracts and work intensification seem to be reinforcing the anxiety and insecurity of middle-range men managers in particular, who are increasingly having to recognize that their working lives are constantly being evaluated and assessed. One central criterion of these evaluation practices is the masculinist concern with personal power and the ability to control others and self. Managers are increasingly assessed according to their ability to control their lives. Consequently men managers have frequently 'distanced' themselves from children and family responsibilities. Within organizations, such 'distancing' strategies are often interpreted in a positive light as evidence both of commitment to the company and of individual ability to control 'private life' (Collinson and Hearn, 1994). Accordingly, it is important to recognize that in the changing organizations of the 1990s, managers are self-evidently objects as well as subjects of the organization. These patterns that are restructuring gendered power relations require sophisticated analyses that incorporate the contradictory and ambiguous practices through which are reproduced the authority and status of men managers.

Organizational structure

Throughout the twentieth century organizational structures and managerial practices have been heavily influenced by the principles of scientific management and bureaucracy. Kanter (1977) argued that the emphasis in scientific management on rationality and efficiency is infused with an irreducible 'masculine ethic'. This assumes that only men hold the requisite qualities of the 'new rational manager': a tough-minded approach to problems, analytical abilities to abstract and plan, a capacity to subordinate personal concerns in order to accomplish the task and a cognitive superiority in problem-solving. Recent contributions have developed Kanter's interest in organizational structure by adding an analysis that is more sensitive to the connections between men, masculinities and managements. Rereading her own earlier work (Hollway, 1991) through the lens of competing masculinities, Hollway (1996) analyses the transition from the disciplining of bodies (scientific management) to self-regulation (human relations) in terms of diverse masculinities. Hollway pursues her approach through the application of psychoanalytic theory located within a social analysis of gendered power relations, both between women and men, and between men. Highlighting the reproduction of 'defensive masculinities', Hollway (1996: 40) outlines a variety of forms of splitting, desire for control and mastery over the other. Hearn (1992b) has also addressed the gendered conditions and consequences of management's establishment in the late nineteenth and early twentieth centuries.

Morgan (1996) critically reflects on the modern history of bureaucracy. Rereading classic sociological contributions, he identifies some of the concealed themes around gender that lie within these apparently genderless texts that subsequently influenced management theory and practice. Morgan shows how men have been and are more likely to carry out managerial functions within bureaucracies, while bureaucracies were, and are, major sites for the development and elaboration of modern masculinities. In marked contrast with Weberian bureaucratic models of impersonal relations, Roper (1996) suggests that organizations and managements are locales of emotion managed by men. He explores relations between men, not simply in terms of power, authority or competition, but specifically in terms of homosocial desire. Examining management as a complex series of processes that involve and invoke seduction and succession between men, his analysis suggests that these power relations may entail flows of power from the less formally powerful to the more formal, as well as vice versa. Using detailed case study material from a management college, Roper argues that the relations between men in management can consist of circuits of desire.

The gendered nature of control and scientific management, and rationality and bureaucracy has also been examined by Burris (1996). Concentrating on the interrelation of technocracy, patriarchy and management and its specific implications for men and masculinities, she reviews the specific types of and shifts in patriarchy and their association with different forms of organizational control. In particular, she examines technocratic patriarchy – a new type of managerial practice that is highly gendered. Its key features include polarization of both occupational status and gender segregation; valuing of expertise as authority; 'adhocracy', informality and, indeed, sexuality, among the expert sector; and technocratic patriarchal ideology. These developments, she contends, shape the gender identity of managers and the gendering of others. Increasingly, organizational structures have to be understood as part of global economic processes (Lehman, 1996). Connell (1998) has spelt out the form of transnational business masculinity. Woodward (1996) has examined 'rationality', in the context of the European Union administration, designed on the 'rational' principles of bureaucratic practice in order to be above national and party loyalties. Using a framework which emphasizes the interconnections of gender, organization, systems, culture and power, Woodward has examined international organizations as gendered bureaucracies in which the 'male' norm is dominant and masculine practices of resistance to female leadership persist. Demonstrating how specific masculinities can shape bureaucratic management, she pays special attention to selection of Eurocrats within the European Commission, and how these structure masculinities and femininities.

In the light of changing forms and practices of management worldwide, interrelations of men, masculinities and management in contemporary organizations are likely to be all the more important. As the previous section outlined, these changes include the introduction of more tightly controlled performance targets and work schedules for managers themselves, their increasing employment on fixed-term, insecure contracts and the possible proletarianization of some, perhaps many, managers (Smith, 1990; LaNuez and Jermier, 1994). On the one hand, these tendencies across private and public sectors for managerial work to be intensified, measured, evaluated and even delayered problematizes the view that management constitutes the most clear-cut form of hegemonic masculinity. On the other hand, working long hours in post-delayering cultures can become a test of manhood, with some men managers enjoying 'the buzz' of staying late at the office. Consequently management may be re-colonized as an inherently masculine function (Collinson and Collinson, 1997). Relatedly, it is possible that junior-level managerial positions, confined to national-level concerns, will continue to be feminized, downgraded and deskilled, while men appropriate the more powerful, prestigious and strategic globalized functions of transnational corporations (Calás and Smircich, 1993). The result will be the reinforcement of men's managerial hegemony at senior levels.

Decision-making

In recent years Kanter's work on the way that homosocial/sexual reproduction can shape managerial decision-making has been updated with a particular focus on men and masculinity. Yancey-Martin (1996) has demonstrated how managers' evaluations of employees can be shaped by particular masculinities. She identifies three evaluational frames which link masculinism and patriarchal masculinities: 'differing potential' (of men and women); 'normative legitimacy' (in rights to hierarchical power); and 'performance' (valuing men's and women's contributions and failures). She describes typical styles of gendered interactions: 'promotion of men', 'requests for paternalistic aid', 'open criticism of women, not men', and 'ganging up on a woman'. By studying managerial decision-making, she reveals the cultural and structural embeddedness of gender in organizations, the importance of power as a constitutive aspect of gender relations in organizations, and the proactive gendering of individuals through the discursive, relational and material dynamics and arrangements of organizations. Similarly, in our own work we have explored the ways that (men) managers can routinely discriminate against women in recruitment and promotion practices whilst privileging male candidates (Collinson et al., 1990; Hearn and Collinson, 1998). We have also examined how men managers can mismanage cases of sexuality and sexual harassment as a result of flawed decision-making shaped by deep-seated misconceptions about gender (Collinson and Collinson, 1989, 1992, 1996).

Pierce (1996) has highlighted the extent to which legal decision-making is based on explicitly masculine managerial practices. She describes how men lawyers use emotion to perform 'Rambo-like' courtroom presentations to win litigation contests. Arguing that 'Rambo litigators' are actually required and reinforced by the legal profession itself with its adversarial model of dispute resolution, she shows how men lawyers seek to secure their domination through intimidation and 'strategic friendliness'. Pierce found that women litigators who adopted similar strategies (thereby contravening traditional notions of femininity) were denigrated while women who were more supportive were seen as 'too soft' and too compliant.

The potentially negative and indeed disastrous impact of hegemonic masculinities on key managerial decisions has been graphically documented in relation to the *Challenger* space shuttle explosion (Messerschmidt, 1996; Maier and Messerschmidt, 1998). This research reveals that the flawed decision-making leading up to the disaster took a specifically gendered form. Messerschmidt (1996) shows how the all-male management team overruled engineering advice about the threat to safety in launching the shuttle in very cold conditions, labelling this as 'an acceptable risk'. According to Messerschmidt, the managers were willing to make such a high-risk decision precisely because risk-taking was embedded in their managerial masculinity. Managers used previously successful launches to rationalize risk-taking while also confirming that managers were in control through the suppression of doubt, fear and uncertainty. In addition they suppressed any acknowledgement that human beings were on the shuttle. As they stated: 'the task was to get Challenger up' (Messerschmidt, 1996: 43). Concerned to maintain their lucrative but fixed-term production contracts, managers were indifferent to the human consequences of their decision making. Messerschmidt argues that this high-risk decision-making process was a resource for accomplishing not only profit, but also masculinity.

The foregoing studies demonstrate how conventional managerial decision-making can be shaped by multiple masculine subjectivities that, in turn, can result in intensified competition, hostility between employees, increased anxiety and, fundamentally, flawed decision-making. The tragedy of the *Challenger* space shuttle is merely one example of the disastrous organizational consequences that can result from the continued male hegemony of senior managerial positions. Conversely, these perspectives on the socially constructed and gendered nature of men managers and men's management raise the possibility of anti-oppressive and even pro-feminist management by men (Hearn, 1989, 1992a, 1994).

Conclusion

This chapter has attempted to demonstrate the growing importance to organizational analysis of critical perspectives on men, masculinities and managements. It has shown how the emergent literature in this area enables us to re-examine traditional issues relevant to the study of management, such as power, structure and decision-making. In turn, these detailed historical, theoretical and empirical studies raise many general questions for management. For example, could the continued dominance of management by men and masculinities and the exclusion of alternative views actually constitute crucial barriers to 'effective', 'efficient' and 'rational' decision making and organizational practices? Will women managers challenge or reproduce the masculine hegemony of management? Conversely, how is men's power in management maintained by the gendered structuring of largely unpaid domestic work and childcare? Less obviously, what are the implications for both women and men of the tendency for increasing organizational power in management to be associated with growing encroachments of business into personal and domestic time? These studies also raise important issues about the impact of gender on the historical emergence of particular managerial functions (marketing, production, sales, etc.) and in relation to the different (gendered) meanings and values associated with managements in and across cultures and societies. There is also a need to explore the possible connections between workplace bullying, sexual harassment and violence and managerial masculinities. In sum, studies of men, masculinities and managements have the potential to develop new forms of analysis of power in management and organizations.

All of these issues suggest major changes in the theorizing of management. Management theory itself until recently has remained very much a domain of men. These arguments raise important questions: what perceptions and priorities are emphasized and neglected by men management educators? Why do men as management and organization theorists find so many 'good reasons' for avoiding these issues? Self-reflexive questions such as these speak to the very heart of management theory and practice as it has been constructed historically. Not least, they critically examine what counts as 'theory', and how 'theory' is developed, defined, written, refereed, rejected or acclaimed, published and circulated. The practice of critical self-reflexivity is an important precondition for the development of management theorizing. There is a pressing need for explicit, critical, feminist/pro-feminist and self-reflexive studies on the enduring dominance and interrelations of men, masculinities and managements. How is it that the 'great' and 'classic' theories of management consistently managed to avoid these obvious questions?

Note

1 When we try to apply the notion of 'hegemonic masculinities' specifically to organizational analysis, its meaning is not always obvious. For example, white, male-dominated shopfloor masculinities may be simultaneously hegemonic in terms of gender or ethnicity but subordinated with regard to class and hierarchy. This also highlights the difficulties of specifying what exactly is hegemonic, in the Gramscian sense of determining without necessary coercion the dominant definitions and realities of others, about particular masculinities, and how this in turn differs from more overt dominance, whether in organizational or other social contexts.

References

Allison, A. (1994) *Nightwork: Sexuality, Pleasure and Corporate Masculinity in a Tokyo Hostess Club*, University of Chicago Press, Chicago.

Alvesson, M. and Willmott, H. (1996) *Making Sense of Management*, Sage, London.

Bell, E.L. and Nkomo, S.M. (1992) 'Re-visioning women managers' lives', in A. Mills and P. Tancred-Sheriff (eds), *Gendering Organizational Theory*, Sage, Newbury Park, CA, pp. 235–247.

Bennis, W. (1989) *On Becoming a Leader*, Warren Bennis, Wilmington, MA.

Boulgarides J.D. (1984) 'A comparison of male and female business managers', *Leadership and Organisation Development Journal*, 5 (5): 27–31.

Braverman, H. (1974) *Labour and Monopoly Capital*, Monthly Review Press, New York.

Brittan, A. (1989) *Masculinity and Power*, Basil Blackwell, Oxford.

Burris, B. (1996) 'Technocracy, patriarchy and management', in D.L. Collinson and J. Hearn (eds), *Men as Managers, Managers as Men*, Sage, London, pp. 61–77.

Calás, M. and Smircich, L. (1993) 'Dangerous liaisons: the "feminine-in-management" meets "globalization"', *Business Horizons*, March–April: 73–83.

Carrigan, T., Connell, R.W. and Lee, J. (1985) 'Toward a new sociology of masculinity', *Theory and Society*, 14 (5): 551–604.

Cockburn, C. (1983) *Brothers*, Pluto Press, London.

Cockburn, C. (1991) *In the Way of Women. Men's Resistance to Sex Equality in Organizations*, Macmillan, London.

Collinson, D.L. (1992) *Managing the Shopfloor: Subjectivity, Masculinity and Workplace Culture*, Walter de Gruyter, Berlin.

Collinson, D.L. and Collinson, M. (1989) 'Sexuality in the workplace: the domination of men's sexuality', in J. Hearn, D. Sheppard, P. Tancred-Sheriff and G. Burrell (eds), *The Sexuality of Organization*, Sage, London and Newbury Park, CA, pp. 91–109.

Collinson, D.L. and Collinson, M. (1992) 'Mismanaging sexual harassment: blaming the victim and protecting the perpetrator', *Women in Management Review*, 7 (7): 11–17.

Collinson, M. and Collinson, D.L. (1996) 'It's only Dick: the sexual harassment of women managers in insurance', *Work, Employment and Society*, 10 (1): 29–56.

Collinson, D.L. and Collinson, M. (1997) 'Delayering managers: time-space surveillance and its gendered effects', *Organization*, 4 (3): 375–408.

Collinson, D.L. and Hearn, J. (1994) 'Naming men as men: implications for work, organization and management', *Gender, Work and Organization*, 1 (1): 2–22.

Collinson, D.L. and Hearn, J. (1995) 'Men managing leadership? *Men and Women of the Corporation* revisited', *International Review of Women and Leadership*, 1 (2): 1–24.

Collinson, D.L. and Hearn, J. (eds) (1996a) *Men as Managers, Managers as Men*, Sage, London.

Collinson, D.L. and Hearn, J. (1996b) '"Men" at "Work": multiple masculinities in multiple workplaces', in M. Mac an Ghaill (ed.), *Understanding Masculinities: Social Relations and Cultural Areas*, Open University Press, London.

Collinson, D.L., Knights, D. and Collinson, M. (1990) *Managing to Discriminate*, Routledge, London.

Connell, R.W. (1987) *Gender and Power*, Polity Press, Cambridge.

Connell, R.W. (1995) *Masculinities*, Polity Press, Cambridge.

Connell, R.W. (1998) 'Globalization and masculinities', *Men and Masculinities*, 1 (1): 3–23.

Dalton, M. (1959) *Men Who Manage*, John Wiley & Sons, New York.

Davidson, M. and Cooper, C. (1983) *Stress and the Woman Manager*, Martin Robertson, Oxford.

Davies, N. (1992) *The Unknown Maxwell*, Pan Macmillan, London.

Denham, D. (1991) 'The "Macho" management debate and the dismissal of employees during industrial disputes', *Sociological Review*, 39 (2): 349–364.

Donnell, S.M. and Hall, J. (1980) 'Men and women as managers: a significant case of no significant difference', *Organizational Dynamics*, 8: 60–77.

Drosnin, M. (1987) *Citizen Hughes*, Henry Holt, New York.

Drucker, P. (1979) *The Practice of Management*, Heinemann, London.

Edwards, R. (1979) *Contested Terrain: The Transformation of the Workplace in the Twentieth Century*, Heinemann, London.

Fagenson, E. (1993) 'Diversity in management: introduction and the importance of women in management', in E.A. Fagenson (ed.), *Women in Management: Trends, Issues and Challenges in Managerial Diversity*, Sage, Newbury Park, CA, pp. 3–19.

Feldman, D. and Klich, N. (1991) 'Impression management and career strategies', in R. Giacalone and P. Rosenfeld (eds), *Applied Impression Management*, Sage, Newbury Park, CA, pp. 67–80.

Ferguson, K.E. (1984) *The Feminist Case against Bureaucracy*, Temple University Press, Philadelphia, PA.

Finch, J. (1983) *Married to the Job: Wives' Incorporation in Men's Work*, Allen & Unwin, London.

Ford, H. (1923) *My Life and Work*, Heinemann, London.

Geneen, H.S. (1985) *Managing*, Collins, London.

Gibbings, S. (1990) *The Tie: Trends and Traditions*, Studio Editions, London.

Grey, C. (1994) 'Career as a project of the self and labour process discipline', *Sociology*, 28 (2): 479–498.

Grint, K. (1995) *Management: A Sociological Introduction*, Polity Press, Cambridge.

Hearn, J. (1987) *The Gender of Oppression: Men, Masculinity and the Critique of Marxism*, Wheatsheaf, Brighton. St Martin's, New York.

Hearn, J. (ed.) (1989) 'Men, masculinities and leadership: changing patterns and new initiatives', special issue, *Equal Opportunities International*, 8 (1).

Hearn, J. (1992a) 'Changing men and changing managements: a review of issues and actions', *Women in Management Review and Abstracts*, 7 (1): 3–8.

Hearn, J. (1992b) *Men in the Public Eye. The Construction and Deconstruction of Public Men and Public Patriarchies*, Routledge, London and New York.

Hearn, J. (1994) 'Changing men and changing managements: social change, social research and social action', in M.J. Davidson and R. Burke (eds), *Women in Management – Current Research Issues*, Paul Chapman, London, pp. 192–209.

Hearn, J. (1996) 'Is masculinity dead? A critique of the concept of masculinity/masculinities', in M. Mac an Ghaill (ed.), *Understanding Masculinities. Social Relations and Cultural Arenas*, Open University Press, London.

Hearn, J. and Collinson, D.L. (1994) 'Theorizing unities and differences between men and between masculinities', in H. Brod and M. Kaufman (eds), *Theorizing Masculinities*, Sage, Newbury Park, CA and London, pp. 148–162.

Hearn, J. and Collinson, D. L. (1998) 'Men, masculinities, managements and organisational culture', *Zeitschrift für Personalforschung*, 12 (2): 210–222.

Hearn, J. and Morgan, D.H.J. (eds) (1990) *Men, Masculinities and Social Theory*, Unwin Hyman, London and Boston.

Hearn, J. and Parkin, W. (1988) 'Women, men and leadership: a critical review of assumptions, practices and change in the industrialized nations', in N.J. Adler and D. Izraeli (eds), *Women in Management Worldwide*, M.E. Sharpe, New York, pp. 17–40.

Hearn, J. and Parkin, W. (1995) *'Sex' at 'Work': The Power and Paradox of Organisation Sexuality*, Prentice Hall/Harvester Wheatsheaf, London. St Martin's, New York.

Helgesen, S. (1990) *The Female Advantage: Women's Ways of Leadership*, Doubleday, New York.

Henriques, J., Hollway, W., Urwin, C., Venn, C. and Walkerdine, V. (1984) *Changing the Subject*, Methuen, London.

Hollway, W. (1984) 'Gender difference and the production of subjectivity', in J. Henriques, W. Hollway, C. Urwin, C. Venn and V. Walkerdine (1984) *Changing the Subject*, Methuen, London, pp. 227–263.

Hollway, W. (1991) *Work Psychology and Organizational Behaviour*, Sage, London.

Hollway, W. (1996) 'Masters and men', in D.L. Collinson and J. Hearn (eds), *Men as Managers, Managers as Men*, London, Sage, pp. 25–42.

Hyman, R. (1987) 'Strategy or structure? Capital, labour and control', *Work, Employment and Society*, 1 (1): 25–55.

Iacocca, L. (1984) *Iacocca: An Autobiography*, Bantam, New York.

Ibarra, H. (1995) 'Race, opportunity, and diversity of social circles in managerial networks', *Academy of Management Journal*, 38 (3): 673–703.

Jackall, R. (1988) *Moral Mazes: The World of Corporate Managers*, Oxford University Press, New York.

Jermier, J., Knights, D. and Nord, W. (eds) (1994) *Resistance and Power in Organizations*, Routledge, London.

Kanter, R.M. (1977) *Men and Women of the Corporation*, Basic Books, New York. (republished in 1993).

Kerfoot, D. and Knights, D. (1993) 'Management masculinity and manipulation: from paternalism to corporate strategy in financial services in Britain', *Journal of Management Studies*, 30 (4): 659–679.

Kerfoot, D. and Knights, D. (1996) 'The best is yet to come? The quest for embodiment in managerial work', in D.L. Collinson and J. Hearn (eds), *Men as Managers, Managers as Men*, Sage, London, pp. 78–98.

Kondo, D. (1990) *Crafting Selves: Power, Gender and Discourses of Identity in a Japanese Workplace*, Chicago University Press, Chicago.

LaNuez, D. and Jermier, J. (1994) 'Sabotage by managers and technocrats: neglected patterns of resistance at work', in J. Jermier, D. Knights and W.R. Nord (eds), *Resistance and Power in Organizations*, Routledge, London, pp. 219–251.

Lehman, C. (1996) 'Quiet whispers: men accounting for women, west to east', in D.L. Collinson and J. Hearn (eds), *Men as Managers, Managers as Men*, Sage, London, pp. 150–166.

Linstead, S., Grafton Small, R. and Jeffcutt, P. (eds) (1996) *Understanding Management*, Sage, London.

Maier, M. and Messerschmidt, J. (1998) 'Commonalities, conflicts and contradictions in organizational masculinities: exploring the gendered genesis of the *Challenger* disaster', *Canadian Review of Sociology and Anthropology*, 35 (3): 325–344.

Marshall, J. (1995) *Women Managers Moving On*, Routledge, London.

Martin, J. (1990) 'Deconstructing organizational taboos: the suppression of gender conflict in organizations', *Organizational Science*, 1 (4): 339–359.

McMahon, A. (1993) 'Male readings of feminist theory: the psychologization of sexual politics in the masculinity literature', *Theory and Society*, 22: 675–695.

Messerschmidt, J. (1996) 'Managing to kill: masculinities and the space shuttle *Challenger* explosion', in C. Cheng (ed.), *Masculinities in Organizations*, Sage, London, pp. 29–53.

Mintzberg, H. (1973) *The Nature of Managerial Work*, Prentice Hall, Englewood Cliffs, NJ.

Mintzberg, H. (1975) 'The manager's job: folklore and fact', *Harvard Business Review*, July/August: 49–61.

Mintzberg, H. (1983) *Power in and around Organizations*, Prentice Hall, Englewood Cliffs, NJ.

Mintzberg, H. (1989) *Mintzberg on Management*, Macmillan, New York.

Morgan, D.H.J. (1992) *Discovering Men*, Unwin Hyman/Routledge, London and New York.

Morgan, D.H.J. (1996) 'The gender of bureaucracy', in D.L. Collinson and J. Hearn (eds), *Men as Managers, Managers as Men*, Sage, London, pp. 29–53.

Mulholland, K. (1996) 'Entrepreneurialism, masculinities and the self-made man', in D.L. Collinson and J. Hearn (eds), *Men as Managers, Managers as Men*, Sage, London, pp. 123–149.

Neale, A. (1995) 'The manager as hero'. Paper presented at Labour Process Conference, Blackpool, April.

Pahl, R. (1995) *After Success: Fin-de-Siècle Anxiety and Identity*, Polity Press, Cambridge.

Phillips, A. and Taylor, B. (1980) 'Sex and skill: notes towards a feminist economics', *Feminist Review*, 6 (7): 79–83.

Pierce, J. (1996) 'Rambo litigators: emotional labour in a male dominated organization', in C. Cheng (ed.), *Masculinities in Organizations*, Sage, London, pp. 1–28.

Pringle, R. (1989) *Secretaries Talk*, Verso, London.

Reed, M. (1989) *The Sociology of Management*, Harvester Wheatsheaf, London.

Reed, R. (1996) 'Entrepreneurialism and paternalism in Australian management: a gender critique of the self-made man', in D.L. Collinson and J. Hearn (eds), *Men as Managers, Managers as Men*, Sage, London, pp. 99–122.

Roper, M.R. (1991) 'Yesterday's model: product fetishism and the British company men 1945–85', in M.R. Roper and J. Tosh (eds), *Manful Assertions, Masculinities in Britain since 1800*, Routledge, London and New York, pp. 190–211.

Roper, M.R. (1994) *Masculinity and the British Organization Man since 1945*, Oxford University Press, Oxford.

Roper, M.R. (1996) 'Seduction and succession; circuits of homosocial desire in management', in D.L. Collinson and J. Hearn (eds), *Men as Managers, Managers as Men*, Sage, London, pp. 210–226.

Rosener, J. (1990) 'Ways women lead', *Harvard Business Review*, 68 (6): 119–125.

Schein, V.E. (1976) 'Think manager – think male', *Atlanta Economic Review*, March–April: 21–24.

Sheppard, D. (1989) 'Organizations, power and sexuality: the image and self-image of women managers', in J. Hearn et al., *The Sexuality of Organization*, Sage, London, pp. 139–158.

Sinclair, A. (1995) 'Sex and the MBA', *Organization*, 2 (2): 295–319.

Smith, V. (1990) *Managing in the Corporate Interest: Control and Resistance in an American Bank*, California Press, Oxford.

Stewart, R. (1986) *The Reality of Management*, Heinemann, London.

Sward, K. (1948) *The Legend of Henry Ford*, Russell & Russell, New York.

Wajcman, J. (1998) *Managing Like a Man*, Polity Press, Cambridge.

Walby, S. (1986) *Patriarchy at Work*, Polity Press, Cambridge.

Watson, T. (1994) *In Search of Management*, Routledge, London.

Willmott, H. (1987) 'Studying managerial work: a critique and a proposal', *Journal of Management Studies*, 24 (3): 249–270.

Witz, A. and Savage, M. (1992) 'The gender of organizations', in M. Savage and A. Witz (eds), *Gender and Bureaucracy*, Blackwell, Oxford, pp. 3–62.

Woodward, A.E. (1996) 'Multinational masculinites and European bureaucracies', in D.L. Collinson and J. Hearn (eds), *Men as Managers, Managers as Men*, Sage, London, pp. 167–185.

Yancey-Martin, P. (1996) 'Gendering and evaluating dynamics: men, masculinities and managements', in D.L. Collinson and J. Hearn (eds), *Men as Managers, Managers as Men*, Sage, London, pp. 186–209.

19

Affirmative Action in Australia: Employment Equity at the Crossroads

Andrew Hede

Like most other Western countries, Australia's workforce has developed along markedly sex-segregated lines based on prolonged discrimination against women in employment. Although this threefold sex segregation (in terms of industry, occupation, and managerial representation) has eased over the past two decades as a result of employment equity reforms, it is still quite pronounced today (Hede and O'Brien, 1996). There are a number of indications that Australia is losing the political will to maintain efforts to redress sex discrimination in employment (Norris, 1997). The most proactive programme, affirmative action, is currently undergoing a major regulatory review that some see as threatening a watering down of its present provisions (Bagwell, 1998a). This chapter explores the issues being addressed in Australia in relation to affirmative action, issues which are common to many other countries. In keeping with the theme of this book the focus will be on affirmative action as it affects women in management.

Affirmative action framework

Although Australian feminists, like those in the US and UK, pressed for equality for women throughout most of this century (Bomford, 1993), it was not until the 1970s that significant progress was made towards equality of opportunity and elimination of discrimination (Ronalds, 1987; Sawer, 1989; Poiner and Wills, 1991). Several Australian states introduced anti-discrimination legislation in the late 1970s, but federal legislation was not introduced until the 1980s. The two key pieces of federal legislation are the Sex Discrimination Act 1984 (SD Act) and the Affirmative Action (Equal Employment Opportunity for Women) Act 1986 (AA Act). The SD Act is based on a reactive approach to redressing specific instances of direct or indirect discrimination via conciliation in response to complaints (Ronalds, 1987; Thornton, 1990). The AA Act, on the other hand, embodies a proactive approach to eliminating all forms of discrimination including systemic discrimination and to promoting the principles of equal employment opportunity (EEO) (Ronalds, 1987; Kramar, 1994).

Current affirmative action provisions and practice

Affirmative action legislation in Australia originally covered all organizations with more than 100 employees in the private and higher education sectors. Following an effectiveness review in 1992 the coverage was extended to community organizations, unions, non-government schools and group training organizations still with a threshold of 100 employees (see AA Agency, 1992). The two key requirements under the AA Act are that organizations implement an eight-step affirmative action programme and that they submit an annual report to the AA Agency on progress with their programme (see Kramar, 1994). The debate about affirmative action in the 1980s centred on the issue of hard quotas (e.g. Moens, 1985). Although the AA Act opted for 'forward estimates' in order to provide soft targets which preserve merit and avoid positive discrimination, this term is still widely seen as a 'dirty word' (Poiner and Wills, 1991: 15).

The AA Agency introduced a rating system with five-level performance standards in 1994 as a basis for assessing affirmative action programmes and encouraging best practice rather than simple compliance. Those organizations that achieve best practice standards as evidenced in their reports over three consecutive years are eligible to have their reporting requirements waived. In 1996–97, a total of 311 organizations (11 per cent of those covered) had their programmes assessed as best practice (AA Agency, 1997). Those organizations that either fail to report or fail to meet the minimum standard in their programmes are deemed to be in breach of the AA Act. As a penalty such organizations may be named in Parliament and become ineligible to win government contracts (note that the former provision is specified in the AA Act whereas the latter is a government policy introduced in 1993 without legislative basis). A total of 63 organizations were named in 1997 (i.e. 2.2 per cent of those covered) though a further 44 organizations failed to meet legislative requirements but were not named at the director's discretion (AA Agency, 1997). Finally, the AA Agency has introduced national awards for 'Best Employers in Affirmative Action' (AA Agency, 1996).

Status of women in management

The current status of women in management in Australia was reviewed by leading employment equity consultant, the late Dr Clare Burton, for public and private sector executives (Burton, 1997a) and also for public and private sector boards (Burton, 1997b). In the case of boards, women held only 7.3 per cent of private sector board positions in 1996 (up from 4 per cent in 1994) as compared with 29.3 per cent for public sector boards (22.7 per cent in 1994) (Burton, 1997b). Australia lags well behind the US in women's board representation in the private sector. In the US, 95 per cent of Fortune 100 companies and 81 per cent of Fortune 500 companies have at least one woman board member, whereas in Australia the figure is only 28 per cent for the 200 large companies surveyed annually by Korn/Ferry (Burton, 1997b).

Women's managerial representation in the Australian public sector ranks well against other comparable countries. A comparative analysis across several senior public services shows that if future trends continue at the rate for the past 10 years, women should achieve 50 per cent of executive positions in both Australia and Canada by the year 2021 as compared with 2034 for the US and 2036 for the UK (Hede, 1995b). A recent audit of 61 agencies comprising the Australian Public Service found that 28 of them had already reached the year 2000 target of 20 per cent women in the Senior Executive Service (SES) but that 27 agencies had not achieved the 1995 target of 15 per cent women (Australian National Audit Office, 1997). Currently, the Australian SES comprises 19.7 per cent women (Burton, 1997a).

Of particular interest in the present context is the status of women in the private sector which is covered by the AA Act. Still and associates conducted surveys of 239 companies in 1984 and 140 companies in 1992 and found that women's managerial representation increased only marginally from 10.9 per cent to 11.8 per cent between the two surveys (Still, 1985; Still et al., 1994). These researchers also found that women managers were less represented at higher levels with the proportions in top management actually decreasing from 2.5 per cent to 1.3 per cent between 1984 and 1992.

Related evidence comes from a longitudinal study which tracked women's managerial representation in the overall Australian workforce using official statistics compiled over almost 30 years (Hede, 1995a). This study examined trends in three periods: 1966–74, 1975–84, 1986–94, the periods defined by International Women's Year in 1975 and the introduction of the AA Act in 1986. The study introduced a performance indicator for EEO effectiveness, namely, the 'Managerial Inequity Index' (MI Index) which is designed to control for variations in workforce participation of different demographic groups. It specifies the representation of a demographic group in managerial positions relative to that group's representation in the workforce using the formula:

$$\text{MI Index} = (\%\ \text{Managers}/\%\ \text{Workforce}) \times 100$$

Where managerial representation equals workforce representation that group has managerial equity and the MI Index takes a value of 100. Index values greater than 100 indicate over-representation and values less than 100 indicate under-representation. The MI Index for women in Australia is currently 54, indicating that women's managerial representation is only 54 per cent of what it would be if there were employment equity. It is worth noting that the MI Index can precisely specify the extra discrimination effects suffered by indigenous women (viz. MI Index value of 23).

The results of the study indicated that the MI Index for women decreased significantly during the first period up to 1974 (at an annual rate of – 1.61), then increased significantly for the second period up to 1984 (at + 0.95 per year). However, for the third period after the introduction of the AA Act, the trend line was found to be flat with no significant increase (+ 0.22 per year). Although the percentage of women in management did increase significantly during the third period (from 22.5 per cent in 1986 to 25.3 per cent in 1994), the fact that the MI Index was flat shows that this increase was an artefact of women's increased representation in the workforce (from 39.3 per cent to 42.5 per cent) (Hede, 1995a). For the Australian workforce women's representation in the managerial occupational category has remained essentially static for the past four years:24.1 per cent in 1995, 23.4 per cent in 1996, 24.3 per cent in 1997, and 23.0 per cent in 1998 (ABS, 1995–97; ABS, 1998).

Current debate on affirmative action

Debate about affirmative action in Australia has been crystallized by a regulatory review initiated in late 1997 as part of a broad programme to ensure that all legislation does not restrict competition or impose excessive burdens on business. The government appointed a five-person independent committee which implemented a review process involving a national call for submissions, release of an issues paper, roundtable discussions in all capital cities, and public release of the review report in mid-1998. The government undertook to announce its response within six months of the report.

The regulatory review issues paper identifies as the central issues to be addressed by the affirmative action review committee: (1) the costs and benefits to business of the AA Act; (2) the costs and benefits to the community; and (3) the efficiency and effectiveness of the AA Act, including possible amendments or non-legislative alternatives. The issues paper also poses 73 specific questions and sub-questions under these broad central issues (Review Committee, 1998a). Rather than attempting to duplicate the regulatory review by assessing the submissions in terms of the review's stated issues and questions, the present chapter will analyse a number of points which encapsulate the current debate about affirmative action in Australia and which may have lessons for other countries.

Point 1: Appropriateness of the term 'affirmative action'

There is a growing consensus in Australia that the term 'affirmative action' is inappropriate. The term connotes preferential treatment and positive discrimination largely because of its association with US legislation which is perceived (some would argue misperceived) to encourage such practices (Thornton, 1997; Walpole, 1997). The press in Australia uses the term for both the programme under the AA Act and for proposals to use hard quotas for women (e.g. in political party preselection – see Kingston, 1994). The term has always been controversial in Australia. Whereas Canada opted for the politically safer term 'employment equity' for its 1986 Act, Australia chose 'affirmative action' but tried to placate the critics by adding the title reference to 'EEO for women' (Thornton, 1989). When the legislation was debated in the early 1980s, according to Susan Ryan who championed the AA Act as the then Minister Assisting the Prime Minister on the Status of Women:

> Affirmative action…was seen by many nervous employer organizations as being a Stalinist plot to force otherwise profitable companies to sack their male employees and replace them with incompetent women. (Ryan, 1997: 47)

Although the AA Act clearly specifies that affirmative action in Australia is to be based strictly on merit without quotas or preferential treatment, this has not been sufficient to prevent widespread misinterpretation of positive discrimination, a fact the inaugural director of the AA Agency recalls as a major frustration in implementation (Pratt, 1997). Evidence of misinterpretation is given in two surveys of managerial attitudes, the first of 1,492 senior executives in the public sector (Hede and Renfrow, 1990) and the second of 486 managers mainly in the private sector (Hede and Dingsdag, 1994). The results indicated that more than a third of managers agreed with the statement that 'Affirmative action legislation in Australia encourages positive discrimination in favour of women' (38 per cent in the public sector and 44 per cent in the private sector). Although women were less likely than men to agree with the statement, it is notable that as many as one in five women in both surveys felt that affirmative action encourages positive discrimination in their favour. Further evidence comes from a study of employee attitudes which found that more than 40 per cent of employees were unsure whether affirmative action involved quotas (Sheridan, 1995).

Three of the key stakeholders, namely, the main feminist body (Women's Electoral Lobby – WEL), the peak business body (Australian Chamber of Commerce and Industry – ACCI), and the AA Agency all agree on the need to change the name of both the legislation and the programme (WEL, 1998; ACCI, 1998; AA Agency, 1998). The AA Agency has not stated a preference. However, WEL favours the term 'employment equity' while the ACCI suggests 'equal opportunity'. But neither of these terms connotes the proactive approach which characterizes affirmative action as it is currently practised in Australia and which distinguishes it from both the reactive approach of sex discrimination legislation and the relatively neutral approach of EEO. It is to be hoped that appropriate market research will be conducted before any new term is adopted. The peak trade union organization (Australian Council of Trade Unions – ACTU) warns, however, that a name change could send unintended messages to the community about a change in focus of affirmative action policy (ACTU, 1998).

Point 2: Effectiveness of current legislation

Perhaps the single most important question regarding affirmative action is whether it is effective, whether after more than a decade in operation in Australia it has improved the equity of women in employment generally and of women in management specifically. As we saw above, the longitudinal studies by Still et al. (1994) and Hede (1995a) seem to show no significant improvement. However, the former study suffered from methodological problems (low response rate and unmatched samples for the two surveys) which led the researchers to warn that 'few generalizations can be made from the data regarding the status of women managers in *all* Australian commercial organisations' (Still et al., 1994: 9). The latter study, on the other hand, was based on data for the whole Australian workforce not just organizations covered by the AA Act (Hede, 1995a).

A study by Hede and O'Brien (1996) was designed to test the effectiveness of affirmative action by tracking women's managerial representation in private sector organizations covered by the legislation. The methodology involved a census comprising every firm that had submitted a report to the AA Agency each year over the period 1990–95, a total of 1,228 firms with more than a million employees and 90,000 managers overall. Using the employment profiles included in the annual reports, data were obtained on women in the managerial occupational category and on the industry category of the firm in terms of the ASCO and ANZSIC classification systems, respectively (see Hede and O'Brien, 1996).

The major finding was that the percentage of women in management in the 1,228 firms increased significantly over the six years, from 17.2 per cent in 1990 to 21.7 per cent in 1995. This was confirmed using the Managerial Inequity Index to control for women's increasing workforce representation, the MI Index values moving from 46.2 in 1990 to 51.9 in 1995, again a significant increase. In terms of industry, the Health/Education/Services sector has the highest representation, with women close to managerial equity (48.1 per cent), followed by Entertainment/ Recreation (38.1 per cent) and Wholesale/Retail Trade (35.0 per cent). By contrast, women have very low managerial representation in Mining (5.4 per cent), Construction (6.7 per cent) and Agriculture (8.5 per cent). Over the six years, five industries showed significant improvement in women's managerial representation, namely, Entertainment/Recreation, Wholesale/Retail Trade, Finance, Property/ Insurance, and Manufacturing. The MI Index confirmed this increase for the first three of these industries and indicated that the percentage increase in the last two was due to women's increased representation in employment in these industries (Hede and O'Brien, 1996). The conclusion is that affirmative action is effective insofar as it is producing small but significant improvements for women in management, though this improvement is confined to three industries. What about other indicators of effectiveness?

There is some evidence that affirmative action is having an effect on the quality of policies and practices within companies that comply with the legislation. Over the period 1994 to 1996, the AA Agency reports an improvement in the quality of affirmative action programmes, with 5.4 per cent of organizations moving from Level 2 (minimum standard) to Level 3 (medium standard) (AA Agency, 1997). Also, there has been an increase in the proportion of organizations assessed as achieving 'best practice' (Level 4 or 5 standard), namely, 11 per cent in 1997 as compared with 7.8 per cent in 1995 (AA Agency, 1998). But the AA Agency assessments are based on documentary evidence only. Stronger tests of effectiveness require an examination of what is happening at the workplace in terms of both employee attitudes and actual practice.

Sheridan (1995, 1996) surveyed employees in three best practice affirmative action companies one of which had won an award for affirmative action. The results indicated that large proportions of women believed that they did not have equal opportunity in their company, that senior management was not committed to EEO, and that recruitment and promotion practices were not fair for both women and men. Because this study did not assess changes over time it is not possible to determine whether affirmative action is proving effective – it could be that these companies started from a low base and are making steady progress towards EEO by means of their affirmative action programmes. Ideally, effectiveness of affirmative action in Australia would be monitored via annual surveys of a fixed sample of companies across all industry groups measuring employee attitudes and obtaining first-hand reports of their experiences in key equity practice areas such as recruitment, promotion, training and development.

From companies themselves there is mixed evidence on the cost-effectiveness of affirmative action, the difference largely dependent on top-level commitment with those who support the programme seeing the benefits as worth the costs and those who oppose it seeing only the costs. Those companies that have embraced affirmative action as a means of achieving employment equity for both ethical and economic reasons seem to have no doubts about its effectiveness. The review submission from the AA Agency includes supportive 'testimonials' from 10 organizations across a diverse range of industries (AA Agency, 1998).

There is a minority view in Australia that affirmative action is not effective because it is having unintended consequences. The 'blokes backlash' from men's groups, for example, is fuelled by vigorous though questionable arguments about the alleged social and economic consequences of affirmative action, namely, that women's increasing participation in the workforce is destroying the family, that the increase in the proportion of high-income women is distorting the 'economic balance' of society, that affirmative action discriminates against men, that women workers impose extra costs on employers, etc. (see Institute of Men's Studies, 1998; Men's Confraternity Inc., 1998).

Point 3: *Coverage of affirmative action*
At present, less than a third of the Australian workforce is covered by the AA Act (non-government organizations with more than 100 employees). The AA Agency estimates that the current legislation covers about 2,700 organizations which employ about 2 million workers out of about 7 million in the total workforce (AA Agency, 1998). There is evidence that no significant progress is being made towards employment equity in organizations not presently covered by the AA Act (excluding the Commonwealth and state public sectors where equivalent systems are generally operating under separate legislation).

As mentioned above, the longitudinal study by Hede and O'Brien (1996) found that in private sector firms covered by the AA Act, the MI Index for women improved significantly from 46 to 52 over the six years to 1995. But over the same period women's managerial representation in the overall workforce, as evidenced in Australian Bureau of Statistics data, did not increase at all (MI Index values of 57 in 1990 as compared with 56 in 1995). The only possible reason for this difference in results is that in non-government organizations not covered by the AA Act, women's managerial representation actually got worse. This study strongly suggests that affirmative action legislation is working where it has coverage but that the Australian workforce is not moving towards managerial equity because medium and small-sized firms (< 100 employees) are slipping backwards. If women are not getting into management in firms not covered by the AA Act then they are sure to be suffering from other effects of discrimination as well. The clear policy implication is that unless firms with fewer than 100 employees start proactive EEO programmes the goal of an equitable Australian workforce will never be achieved.

The above evidence provides a strong case for lowering the threshold for coverage of the AA Act. Both the feminist main body and the AA Agency advocate a lower threshold of 50 (WEL, 1998; AA Agency, 1998). However, it is clear that Australian business will fight any attempt to lower the threshold. One of the catch-cries of business in Australia, as in many countries, is that there is too much 'government red tape'. The main business submission to the regulatory review argues for more exemptions from the AA Act and for retention of the current threshold, warning that 'any attempt to amend it would be extremely controversial' (ACCI, 1998: 6).

Most Australian governments are very responsive to the red-tape argument from business and several of them have created taskforces specifically to reduce the paperwork burden on small business. So strong is this government commitment to reducing paperwork for business in the State of Queensland that the review submissions from the central employment agency for the public service and the agency responsible for women's affairs both argue ironically against lowering the threshold on these grounds (Office of the Public Service, 1998; Office of Women's Affairs, 1998). In any case, the terms of reference for the regulatory review give a clear hint that lowering the threshold is simply not an option – the review objectives emphasize minimizing compliance costs, particularly for small business (Review Committee, 1998a). It is most unlikely, therefore, that the review committee would recommend that the compliance threshold be lowered and even less likely that the current government would accept any such recommendation.

Point 4: Compliance requirements

The only requirement under the AA Act besides implementing an eight-step affirmative action programme is that organizations report annually on their programme. Reporting is generally quite unpopular though only one in 50 organizations refuse to report at all (AA Agency, 1997). One company's review submission expresses a common claim that reporting is 'an enormous waste of scarce resources' but concedes that the reported statistics are 'useful to our organisation' (Anonymous, 1998).[1] Some claims about the costs of reporting (e.g., 20 + person-days) appear either exaggerated or reflective of inefficiencies. As one commentator puts it, organizations 'could avoid much grief by simply paying a consultant $500 to fill in an AAA report' (Bagwell, 1998a: 17).

According to one authority on affirmative action law, 'the legislative mandate is concerned with procedure' (Thornton, 1997: 300). Thus, the current AA Act simply ensures that organizations report without requiring them actually to achieve any equity outcomes by implementing effective programmes. It is possible for organizations to produce impressive paperwork while allowing systemic discrimination to continue unabated. Many of the review submissions recommend legislative amendments to ensure an outcome focus rather than the current focus on process. Where opinion differs, however, is on how this is to be achieved. Some seem to harbour the notion that equity outcomes can somehow be achieved without any processes which proactively eradicate systemic barriers to women and ensure the ongoing adherence to EEO principles in day-to-day practice. Although the legislation should have more emphasis on outcomes, the education function of the AA Agency and the programmes in organizations themselves must still focus on the processes which comprise best practice in employment equity. Nevertheless, in line with an outcome focus, the reporting form could be greatly simplified (from the current 20 pages) and still serve its primary purpose.

If there was a shift to a focus on outcomes, then the annual report could become a simple two-page statement of the basic statistics including the employment profile of the organization specifying the proportion of women and men across occupational categories and at the various managerial levels. Instead of an emphasis on reporting, the legislation could provide for a system of audits to monitor reported outcomes and identify causes of systemic discrimination. Auditing could involve a range of measures from a postal 'please explain' to a full workplace investigation. A number of key submissions to the regulatory review support the introduction of auditing (AA Agency, 1998; AMP, 1998; IEU, 1998; WEL, 1998). Most see it as a possible function for the AA Agency but at least one submission suggests that organizations should pay for an independent equity audit as they would a financial audit (Osborne Associates, 1998). The main business lobby, however, 'strongly opposes any auditing function' again warning that this 'would be extremely controversial' (ACCI, 1998: 14–15).

Although there is a demonstrable need to bring more organizations under the AA Act (see Point 3 above), there is little chance of any lowering of the current threshold of 100 employees. One alternative would be to require that all organizations with 20–99 employees implement a proactive employment equity programme but to totally exempt them from any reporting requirements. The rationale would be that employment equity is good for both business competitiveness and business ethics: 'It's good for business, so just do it without any paperwork burden!' Of course, there would have to be some mechanism for ensuring compliance. Here a system of random audits could be effective without being excessively burdensome ('If you're doing it then demonstrate it!').

A highly contentious aspect of compliance is that of sanctions. At present, the only offence under the AA Act is failure to report satisfactorily, and the only sanctions are naming in Parliament and ineligibility for government contracts. Mild though these sanctions are (some would say ineffectually so – e.g. WEL, 1998), business is keen to see them reduced (ACCI, 1998). The contract provision is resented even though no company has yet been denied a contract because of it (AA Agency, 1998). The fact that this provision gets a specific mention in the review's terms of reference may signal a government intention to remove it if possible. There is, however, considerable non-business support for increasing sanctions and also changing their rationale (AA Agency, 1998; IEU, 1998; WEL, 1998). Were an auditing system to be introduced it would seem appropriate to impose tough financial penalties on organizations which are identified as refusing to take action to eradicate discriminatory practices and foster employment equity.

Future directions

The future directions for affirmative action in Australia depend primarily on which political party wins the next election due by early 1999 but likely in late

1998. The AA Act was introduced by the Hawke Labor government and is still strongly supported by Labor now in opposition. The Liberal/National Coalition in 1993 had a policy to repeal the legislation and some see the current review as 'a back-door way for the Coalition to rid it of troublesome affirmative action regulations' (Bagwell, 1998a: 17). If the Coalition is returned to government, the review report may well give them an excuse to make major concessions to business. Whether or not the Labor Party wins government they have indicated that 'Labor will oppose any measures which weaken the current act and the incentives for companies to comply' (Macklin, 1998). Either way any changes are unlikely to be radical.

Australian governments are not known for their revolutionary approach to public policy reform, generally preferring to use incremental means to modify policy by systematic adjustment without upsetting stakeholders and risking political backlash. The original affirmative action legislation resulted from a policy compromise between the interests of women versus employers. According to Thornton (1997: 301) 'the AA Act is a prime example of the mediation of dichotomous interests by the government of the day'. Today, as Australia debates the future of affirmative action, the same compromise between women and business is a political certainty. There will be change, but only incremental change, the direction being dictated more by the results of the next federal election than by the report of the regulatory review.

In an ideal world employers would see that employment equity is both ethically and economically an imperative. They would view employment equity as contributing positively to their bottom-line performance and would want to achieve it regardless of any regulatory requirements. In a perfect market in the long-term, firms with employment equity will win out over those who allow discriminatory practices to continue. This message is proclaimed loudly in the financial sector of Australian business by a company which specializes in strategic advice on diversity management (Osborne Associates, 1998). This company gives CEOs of the top financial firms an annual rating of their commitment to gender equality based on a survey of women executives across the sector (Bagwell, 1998b).

Even though many firms are pursuing employment equity for their own strategic reasons, we are still a long way from having the majority of firms in such a position. We have seen that small-to-medium firms (20–100 employees) are generally making no progress towards employment equity. Unless something proactive is done to bring employment equity into such organizations which collectively employ more than a third of the Australian workforce, equity for women will still be a distant dream into the twenty-second century – on current trends women will not reach managerial equity until the year 2170 (Hede and O'Brien, 1996). It is far too early to consider relying solely on the reactive systems of sex discrimination regulation and the maintenance systems of EEO. As for suggestions about self-regulation or integration of employment equity into managerial practice, they are ideals which are currently met by a very small proportion of organizations. A proactive system such as that provided by affirmative action legislation is still essential if any real progress is to be made towards employment equity.

Australia is at the crossroads on employment equity. The choice is between a direct route involving constructing an 'equity highway' which requires considerable effort and challenges established vested interests versus the least-resistance route involving the construction of an 'equity country road' at low cost with no controversy. The trouble is that any country opting for the equity country road will take more than a hundred years to reach the destination of employment equity for women.

Conclusion[2]

The report of the regulatory review on affirmative action was presented to the relevant minister in June 1998 (Review Committee, 1998b), but was not released until December 1998 when the newly re-elected Howard government issued its response to the report's 19 recommendations (Coalition Government, 1998). Perhaps the most significant outcome will be a change in the name of the Act and the Agency from 'affirmative action' to 'equal opportunity for women in the workplace'. While a name change is essential to overcome confusion, it is significant that the government has accepted the name recommended by business (ACCI, 1998) rather than 'employment equity' recommended by the women's lobby (WEL, 1998), or 'equity for women in the workplace' (and 'workplace equity agency') proposed by the review committee or best of all, a market-researched term signifying proactive equity. The term 'equal opportunity' has been around in Australia for a long time – it is now rather stale and denotes a neutral rather than a proactive approach to employment equity. Despite government claims to being 'firmly committed' (Coalition Government, 1998: 1), the new name subtly symbolizes a predictable softening of government support for women's employment equity.

In fact, the broad thrust of the changes announced by the government is to make it easier for business to comply. Reporting is to be simplified and will be required biennially rather than annually (to save business a paperwork burden of $3.5 million per year – Review Committee, 1998b: 30). Reports will no longer be assessed by the Agency using a rating system to encourage best practice, but only in terms of compliance versus non-compliance. The current eight-step programme will be replaced with a more flexible one. Also, it will be easier in future for organizations to have their reporting requirements completely waived. In addition, there will be no increase in the current mild sanctions of naming and contract compliance (see Point 4 above).

Further, although the review committee recommended that all relevant employers be required to self-identify and register with the Agency, the government rejected this recommendation. The government also rejected, without explanation, a recommendation that the Agency or 'alternative bodies' conduct audits via workplace visits to confirm 'waived status' and to supplement reporting (Review Committee, 1998b: 34). Finally, the review committee recommended that the Act be extended to require *all* employers to provide EEO for women but suggested, questionably, that those with fewer than 100 employees 'not [be] required...to take any specific actions' (Review Committee, 1998b: 21). As any equity practitioner can testify, employment equity cannot be achieved without specific actions. In any case, the government response specifically rejects any extension in the coverage of the Act, thereby ensuring that small-to-medium businesses can continue to discriminate against women in management (as argued in Point 3 above). Overall, it is clear that Australian business has had a major win over women in the regulatory review changes to affirmative action.

On the positive side, the government has accepted a review committee recommendation that a ministerial advisory board be established comprising representatives of the key stakeholders to oversee administration of the new Act, to advise on equity policy and to foster communication. The government has also supported the review committee's call for an enhancement of the Agency's facilitative and educative functions including the provision of implementation guidelines. Notably, however, such guidelines will be 'wholly voluntary' (Coalition Government, 1998: 5) and, therefore, will be less than fully effective.

The Affirmative Action Agency 'welcomed' the review outcomes (AA Agency, 1999: 1). This surprising reaction may indicate relief that the Agency is to survive under a new name and a new act. But the Agency will have reduced powers and a lower national profile. It will be monitored by the proposed advisory board and will have to seek board approval for decisions on report-waiving, naming and contract compliance. The Agency will have a reduced load in relation to reporting but will not have its requested auditing function involving site visits. Most significantly, the government response failed to endorse the review committee's recommendation that 'the Agency and its Director retain their current statutory basis and remain based in Sydney' (Review Committee, 1998b: 40). Instead, the government response to this recommendation states: 'Over the longer term, we will consider whether co-locating Agency staff in the States and Territories or contracting out advisory and support functions to the jurisdictions would improve service delivery to women and the businesses covered by the Act' (Coalition Government, 1998: 7). This is surely an ominous warning about the future of the Agency.

By withholding the report for six months and then releasing it together with its own response, the government seems to have succeeded in quelling opposition to what is effectively a scaling back of affirmative action (and employment equity) in Australia. There has been no outcry, though the federal opposition did criticize the government's response and a few prominent commentators have questioned some of the proposed changes (Sawer, 1998). Affirmative action has achieved results during its 12 years of operation in Australia. The new changes indicate that Australia is not going to take the 'equity highway'. Whether it opts for an 'equity country road' or something in between, will become clear when the new legislation is implemented.

Notes

1 Some companies provided a copy of their submission on condition of confidentiality.

2 This chapter was written in mid-1998 during the regulatory review. This section provides an update as of mid-1999.

References

AA Agency (Affirmative Action Agency) (1992) *Quality and Commitment: The Next Steps*, Australian Government Publishing Service, Canberra.
AA Agency (1996) *Best Employers in Affirmative Action: Case Studies*, Affirmative Action Agency, Sydney.
AA Agency (1997) *Annual Report 1996–97*, Affirmative Action Agency, Sydney.
AA Agency (1998) Submission, *Regulatory Review of the Affirmative Action (EEO for Women) Act*, April.
AA Agency (1999) *Action News*, 37 (January), Affirmative Action Agency, Sydney.
ABS (Australian Bureau of Statistics) (1995–97) *The Labour Force Australia*, Australian Bureau of Statistics, Monthly Reports for August each year, cat.no.6203.0, Canberra.
ABS (1998) *The Labour Force Australia*, Australian Bureau of Statistics, Monthly Report – May, cat.no.6203.0, Canberra.
ACCI (Australian Council of Commerce and Industry) (1998) Submission, *Regulatory Review of the Affirmative Action (EEO for Women) Act*, April.
ACTU (Australian Council of Trade Unions) (1998) Submission, *Regulatory Review of the Affirmative Action (EEO for Women) Act*, April.
AMP (1998) Submission, *Regulatory Review of the Affirmative Action (EEO for Women) Act*, April.
Australian National Audit Office (1997) *Equity in Employment in the Australian Public Service*, Australian National Audit Office, Canberra.
Bagwell, S. (1998a) 'New opportunity with equal opportunity', *Australian Financial Review*, 20 May: 17.
Bagwell, S. (1998b) 'CEOs rate badly on sex equality', *Australian Financial Review*, 6 February: 53.
Bomford, J.M. (1993) *That Dangerous Persuasive Woman: Vida Goldstein*, Melbourne University Press, Melbourne.
Burton, C. (1997a) *Women in Public and Private Sector Senior Management*, Research report, Office of the Status of Women, Canberra.
Burton, C. (1997b) *Women's Representation on Commonwealth and Private Sector Boards*, Research report, Office of the Status of Women, Canberra.
Coalition Government (1998) *Promoting Equal Opportunity for Women – Coalition Government Response to the Report of the Regulatory Review of the Affirmative Action (Equal Employment Opportunity for Women) Act 1986*, Parliament House, Canberra, 16 December.
Hede, A.J. (1995a) 'Managerial inequity in the Australian workforce: a longitudinal analysis', *International Review of Women and Leadership*, 1 (1): 11–21.
Hede, A.J. (1995b) 'Women managers in the Civil Service: the long road towards equity in Britain', *International Review of Administrative Sciences*, 61: 587–600.
Hede, A.J. and Dingsdag, D. (1994) 'Equity in selection: managerial attitudes and practices', *International Journal of Selection and Assessment*, 2 (1): 37–44.
Hede, A.J. and O'Brien, E. (1996) 'Affirmative action in the Australian private sector: a longitudinal analysis', *International Review of Women and Leadership*, 2 (2): 15–29.
Hede, A.J. and Renfrow, P. (1990) *Survey of Executives in Queensland Public Service Departments and Statutory Authorities*, Public Sector Management Commission, Brisbane.
Independent Education Union of Australia (IEU) (1998) Submission, *Regulatory Review of the Affirmative Action (EEO for Women) Act*, April.
Institute of Men's Studies (1998) Submission, *Regulatory Review of the Affirmative Action (EEO for Women) Act*, April.
Kingston, M. (1994) 'Conference vote for 35% quota a "defining moment", Keating hails victory for women', *Sydney Morning Herald*, 28 September: 1.

Kramar, R. (1994) 'Affirmative action in Australian organizations', in M.J. Davidson and R.J. Burke (eds), *Women in Management: Current Research Issues*, Paul Chapman, London.

Macklin, J. (1998) 'Affirmative action', email communication from the Assistant to the Leader of the Opposition for the Status of Women, 22 May.

Men's Confraternity Inc. (1998) Submission, *Regulatory Review of the Affirmative Action (EEO for Women) Act*, April.

Moens, G. (1985) *Affirmative Action: The New Discrimination*, The Centre for Independent Studies, St Leonards, NSW.

Norris, R. (1997) 'The will and the way: Australia's legislative response to international agreements on human rights and its effect on equal employment opportunity and human resource practice', Conference of the Association of Industrial Relations Academics of Australia and New Zealand, Brisbane, February.

Office of the Public Service (Qld) (1998) Submission, *Regulatory Review of the Affirmative Action (EEO for Women) Act*, April.

Office of Women's Affairs (Qld) (1998) Submission, *Regulatory Review of the Affirmative Action (EEO for Women) Act*, April.

Osborne Associates (1998) Submission, *Regulatory Review of the Affirmative Action (EEO for Women) Act*, April.

Poiner, G. and Wills, S. (1991) *The Gifthorse: A Critical Look at Equal Employment Opportunity in Australia*, Allen & Unwin, Sydney.

Pratt, V. (1997) 'Hindsight is easier than foresight', in E. Davis and V. Pratt (eds), *Making the Link 8: Affirmative Action and Industrial Relations*, Affirmative Action Agency and Macquarie University, Sydney.

Review Committee (1998a) *Issues Paper: Regulatory Review of the Affirmative Action (Equal Employment Opportunity for Women) Act 1986*, Affirmative Action Review Secretariat, Canberra, March.

Review Committee (1998b) *Unfinished Business – Equity for Women in the Australian Workplace: Final Report of the Regulatory Review of the Affirmative Action (Equal Employment Opportunity for Women) Act 1986*, Affirmative Action Review Secretariat, Canberra, June.

Ronalds, C. (1987) *Affirmative Action and Sex Discrimination*, Pluto Press, Sydney.

Ryan, S. (1997) 'In the beginning was a bill to tackle discrimination', in E. Davis and V. Pratt (eds), *Making the Link 8: Affirmative Action and Industrial Relations*, Affirmative Action Agency and Macquarie University, Sydney.

Sawer, M. (1989) 'Women: the long march through the institutions', in B. Head and A. Patience (eds), *From Fraser to Hawke*, Longman Cheshire, Sydney.

Sawer, M. (1998) 'The future of affirmative action', email communication on ausfempol-net, 18 December.

Sheridan, A. (1995) 'Beyond the rhetoric: the practice of affirmative action in Australia', doctoral thesis, University of New England, Armidale, NSW.

Sheridan, A. (1996) 'Affirmative action for women: learning from experience', in M. Browne (ed.), *ANZAM '96 Conference Refereed Papers*, University of Wollongong, Wollongong, NSW.

Still, L.V. (1985) 'Women in management: the case of Australian business', *Human Resource Management Australia*, 24 (1): 32–37.

Still, L.V., Guerin, C.D. and Chia, W. (1994) 'Women in management revisited: progress, regression or status quo?' in A. Kouzmin, L.V. Still and P. Clarke (eds), *New Directions in Management*, McGraw-Hill, Sydney.

Thornton, M. (1989) 'Hegemonic masculinity and the academy', *International Journal of the Sociology of Law*, 17: 115–130.

Thornton, M. (1990) *The Liberal Promise: Anti-Discrimination Law in Australia*, Oxford University Press, Melbourne.

Thornton, M. (1997) 'Deconstructing affirmative action', *International Journal of Discrimination and the Law*, 2: 299–315.

20

Towards Short-term Contract Cultures: The Future Impact on Women in Management

Cary L. Cooper

Our failure to adjust to change is one of the greatest causes of stress in our lives. The stationmaster's cry 'All change, please' means getting off the train at the end of the line and getting on to another that is going somewhere. But we don't find it easy to do that. Sometimes we sit on the old empty train of our lives and pretend that it's moving. We don't like change. When we don't understand what's going on, we feel trapped. When change is rapid and overwhelming, as it has been throughout this century, we feel confused and powerless. The last half of this century in particular has seen enormous change in the workplace, and it is understanding where we have come from and where we are likely to be going, that will help us explore the future impact of these trends on women in management in the new organizational environments of the future. This chapter will start with a brief history of work over the last 40 years, then explore where we are likely to be going and what the implications of this are for men and women in management (Cooper, 1998b).

A brief history of work

The 1960s epitomized the limitless possibilities of change, as society confronted the horrors of the Vietnam War and the traditional and established lifestyles of the postwar period. It was an era that embraced new technology, with Harold Wilson, the British Prime Minister, proclaiming that the 'white heat of technology' was about to transform our lives, producing a leisure age of 20-hour weeks. This was followed by the 1970s, a period of industrial strife, conflict and retrenchment. The workplace became the battleground for employers and workers, the middle classes and the working classes, liberal and conservative thinkers. This industrial confrontation was highlighted by Studs Terkel (1972: xiii) in his acclaimed book of the period *Working*: 'Work is by its very nature about violence – to the spirit as well as to the body. It is about ulcers as well as

Walpole, S. (1997) 'On the right track, but don't lose momentum', in E. Davis and V. Pratt (eds), *Making the Link 8: Affirmative Action and Industrial Relations*, Affirmative Action Agency and Macquarie University, Sydney.

WEL (Women's Electoral Lobby) (1998) Submission, *Regulatory Review of the Affirmative Action (EEO for Women) Act*, April.

accidents, about shouting matches as well as fistfights, about nervous breakdowns as well as kicking the dog around. It is, above all, about daily humiliations. To survive the day is triumph enough for the walking wounded among the great many of us.'

Out of the turmoil of the 1970s came the 'enterprise culture' of the 1980s, a decade of privatizations, statutory constraints on industrial relations, mergers and acquisitions, strategic alliances, joint ventures, process re-engineering and the like, transforming workplaces into free market, hothouse cultures. Although this entre-preneurial period improved economic competitiveness in home and in international markets, there were also the first signs of strain, as 'stress' and 'burnout' became concepts in the everyday vocabulary of many working people (Cartwright and Cooper, 1997).

By the end of the 1980s and in the early 1990s, the sustained recession, together with the privatizing mentality regarding the public sector during the decade, laid the groundwork for potentially the most profound changes in the workplace since the industrial revolution. The early years of the 1990s were dominated by the effects of recession and efforts to get out of it, as organizations 'downsized', 'delayered', 'flattened' or 'right-sized'. Whatever euphemism you care to use, the hard reality experienced by many was job loss and constant change in the developed world. There were fewer people, doing more work and feeling more job insecure. The rapid expansion of information technology also meant the added burden of information overload and the accelerating pace of work, with people demanding more and more information, and quicker and quicker (Cooper, 1998a). From the middle 1980s throughout the 1990s, we also saw the massive expansion of women in the workplace, with a noticeable pushing (not shattering) of the glass ceiling further upwards (White et al., 1992). The changing role of men and women at work and at home added another dimension to the enormity of change taking place in the offices, factory floors and techno-cultures of many developed countries (Cooper and Lewis, 1998).

The downsizing and the rapidity of change has certainly taken its toll in the 1990s, particularly in the UK, where the restructuring of industry in terms of short-term contracts and a more flexible workforce has outpaced all other European countries and has led to what is being referred to as the Americanizing of UK industry. An Institute of Survey Research of 400 companies in 17 countries employing over 8 million workers throughout Europe, found that in 10 years the UK's employee satisfaction level dropped from 64 per cent in 1985 to 53 per cent by 1995, the biggest drop of any European country (ISR, 1995).

In addition, the sickness absence rates rose during much of this period, recently hitting an all-time high of £12 billion cost to UK industry in one year (CBI, 1998). This had effects on the family, as more and more two-earner families/couples emerged in a climate which was anything but 'family friendly'. The British Telecom Forum's report, *The Cost of Communication Breakdown* (Walker, 1995) found that in 1991 the UK had the highest divorce rate in Europe, with over 171,000 divorces, while the proportion of people living in one-parent families increased fourfold between 1961 and 1991; they predicted that over 3 million children and young people will grow up in stepfamilies by the year 2000. This is in no small measure partly a result of a 'long working hours' culture in most public and private sector organizations in the UK. DEMOS' (1996) report *Time Squeeze* in 1995 found that 25 per cent of British male employees worked more than 48 hours a week; a fifth of all manual workers worked more than 50 hours; one in eight managers worked more than a 60-hour week and seven out of 10 British workers want to work a 40-hour week, but only three out of 10 do.

The short-term contract culture

While this scenario is cause enough for concern, the underlying trend toward out-sourcing and market testing is leading inexorably toward a more insidious work environment, the short-term contract or freelance culture (Makin et al., 1996). This 'privatizing of the private sector' no doubt stems from our insatiable appetite to mas-sively privatize the public sector in the 1980s in many developed countries, particu-larly in the UK. This has led to what employers refer to euphemistically as 'the flexible workforce', although in family friendly terms it is anything but flexible. The psychological contract between employer and employee – 'reasonably permanent employment for work well done' – is truly being undermined, as more and more employees no longer regard their employment as secure and many more are engaged in part-time working. From 1984 to 1994 in the UK, for example, the number of men working part time doubled, with the number of people employed by firms of more than 500 employees having slumped to just over a third of the employed population and with over one in eight British workers now self-employed (Cooper, 1998a).

There may be nothing inherently wrong with this trend, but a recent 'Quality of Working Life' survey by the Institute of Management and UMIST (Worrall and Cooper, 1998), which has surveyed and will continue to survey 5,000 man-agers each year over the next five years, found some disturbing results among Britain's managers. First, organizations at the end of the 1990s were found to be in a state of constant change, with nearly two-thirds of this national UK sample of managers having undergone a major restructuring over the last 12 months. The consequences of this change, even among a group supposedly in control of events, were substantially increased job insecurity, lowered morale, and the ero-sion of motivation and loyalty (Worrall and Cooper, 1998).

Most of these changes involved downsizing, cost reduction, delayering and outsourcing. Yet, the perception was that although inevitably these changes led to an increase in profitability and productivity, decision-making was slower and, more importantly, the organization was deemed to have lost the right mix of human resource skills and experience in the process. In addition, the impact on working patterns, contract hours and evening and weekend working was penal. It was found that 79 per cent of managers in the UK regularly work more than 40 hours a week, just under 40 per cent report working over 50-hour weeks and 41 per cent 'always or often' work at weekends (see Figure 20.1). What was even more disturbing was that although, as one might expect, 59 per cent of them said these long hours damaged their health, 56 per cent their morale and 55 per cent their productivity, an overwhelming 73 per cent acknowledged that it severely damaged their relationship with their children and 72 per cent their relationship with spouse/partner.

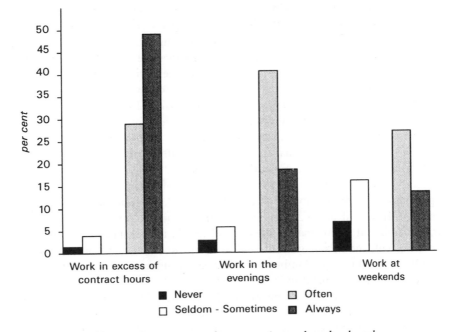

FIGURE 20.1 *Working patterns, contract hours, evening and weekend work (Worrall and Cooper, 1998)*

This snapshot of corporate life from Britain's organizations, which is at the forefront of the short-term contract culture, highlights the likely destination of the workplace of the future. As Cooper and Jackson (1997) predict in *Creating Tomorrow's Organizations*, most organizations will have only a small core of full-time, permanent employees, working from a conventional office. They will buy most of the skills they need on a contract basis, either from individuals working at home and linked to the company by computers and modems (teleworking), or by hiring people on short-term contracts to do specific jobs or carry out specific projects. In this way companies will be able to maintain the flexibility they need to cope with a rapidly changing world. Much of this change is already happening, with BT claiming that more than 3 million people are already working wholly or partly from home and predicting that this will rise to 4 million by the millennium. There is also a significant rise in the provision of 'interim management' agencies to supply senior management on a project management basis to industry. All the trends are in the direction of what is being referred to as the 'contingent workforce', an army of blue-collar, white-collar and managerial temps.

The future impact on women in management

So what are the consequences of this change? First, since more and more women have experienced short-term contracts, part-time working and intrinsic job insecurity, will women end up as the main breadwinners of the future? With employers increasingly looking for and recruiting 'flexible workers', won't women be preferred to men for managerial jobs, given their history of flexibility? For example, there are currently, in the UK, five times as many women working part time than men, and although twice as many men are now working part time than a decade ago, women are historically more experienced at discontinuous career patterns, flowing in and out of the labour market, working part time and on short-term contracts (Equal Opportunities Commission, 1998). What will this all mean for organizations, for their management style and for the future of male and female employees? The questions and possible scenarios are legion. If women begin to take significant managerial roles, how will the culture of organizations change and how will men cope with these changes? What might a female senior executive culture mean for the management style of organizations, for the management of change, and for the future of family friendly policies within organizations? How will organizations develop their male employees in accepting a more feminized senior management? Will men's role change in the domestic environment, and how might this spill over into work organizations, or will the conflicts caused by a predominance of female executives encourage a mass exodus of women, a downshifting revolution?

Second, as more and more people are likely in the future to work from their homes, whether in portfolio careers, part-time working or on short-term contracts, we will be increasingly creating 'virtual organizations'. With two out of three families/couples, two-earner or dual career, how will working from home affect the delicate balance between home and work, affect the roles of men and women both at home and work, and how will this impact their children? Will women executives be at the forefront of flexible working arrangements or will they want to separate work from home?

Third, since the industrial revolution many white-collar, managerial and professional workers have not experienced high levels of job insecurity. Even many blue-collar workers who were laid off in heavy manufacturing industries of the past were frequently re-employed when times got better. The question that society has to ask itself is, 'Can human beings cope with permanent job insecurity, without the safety and security of organizational structures, which in the past provided training, development and careers?' The European survey by ISR on employment security provides some cause for concern in this regard, showing the UK with the worst decline in employee satisfaction in terms of employment security of any of its competitors, from 70 per cent satisfaction levels in 1985 to 48 per cent by 1995; at a time when UK Plc has been moving faster toward a contingent workforce than all of its European counterparts. The ISR survey (Figure 20.2) also shows other European countries experiencing greater job insecurity as they begin to dismantle their permanent, long-term contract cultures.

Will this trend toward job insecurity, freelance working and virtual organizations be embraced by women executives when they get into positions of power, since they have experienced these in the past, or will a predisposition toward a more nurturing management style encourage women to engage in more reward-orientated, more secure family cultures in the workplace? And, more importantly, can organizations, virtual or otherwise, continue to demand commitment from

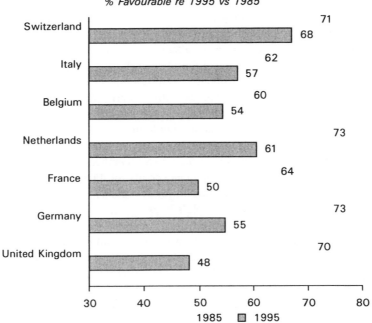

Employment Security: 1995 vs 1985
% *Favourable re 1995 vs 1985*

FIGURE 20.2 *Employee satisfaction (ISR, 1995)*

employees they don't commit to? Although short-term contract cultures like the UK are doing remarkably well, their levels of job insecurity and dissatisfaction are fairly high. Developing and maintaining a 'feel good' factor at work and an ever-changing economy generally is not just about bottom-line factors, such as higher salaries, a lower income tax or increased profitability. It is, or should be, in a civilized society, about quality of life issues as well, like hours of work, family time, manageable workloads, control over one's career and some sense of job security. As the social anthropologist Studs Terkel suggested, work 'is about a search for daily meaning as well as daily bread, for recognition as well as cash, for astonishment rather than torpor, in short, for a sort of life rather than a Monday through Friday sort of dying' (1972: xiii).

Developing an agenda for change

Cooper and Lewis (1998) have suggested that all stakeholders have to develop a 'shared vision' of the sort of organizations, families and society we want for the future, particularly in light of the changing nature of work. They outline a number of steps for their 'agenda for change'.
Integrating work–family issues into core thinking
and strategic planning in organizations
Organizations need to be proactive. They need to anticipate the changing needs of the workforce in strategic planning; that is, they must recognize that the ways

in which organizations have operated in the past are not necessarily appropriate to today's workplace.

More diversity in decision-making

It is not necessarily the most rational decision outcomes which are acted upon in organizations, but often the decision outcome favoured by the most powerful individual or groups of individuals (Pettigrew, 1993). Often these are men with non-career wives or women without family commitments. For example, in a recent study of over 1,300 US male executives over 50 per cent of those who were married had non-working wives. Although these men reported some interference of work with family, they reported little interference by family with work (Judge et al., 1994). It is unlikely that this group will have an understanding of the work–family issues confronting more typical members of the workforce, nor the stress that standard ways of working can create for dual earner couples. More diversity in decision-making may help to focus organizations on issues relating to the achievement of balance in people's lives.

A rethinking of notions of time

Currently, men's time is valued more than women's, and time in the marketplace more than time with family. A critical evaluation of the ways in which values are assigned to time will be a necessary precursor to changes to benefit all stakeholders. Within the workplace the definition of time as symbolic of productivity, commitment and value belittles the contribution of those who work shorter or more flexible hours and disguises the fact that long hours at the workplace reflect inefficiency (Schor, 1991). Different ways of thinking about time in the workplace might include a focus on quality of outcome rather than quantity of time spent on activities.

Developing flexibility and autonomy

There needs to be openness about the expectations of particular jobs and the demands they make on incumbents' personal lives as a means of clarifying boundaries, and an acknowledgement that people can be highly committed contributors to both work and family life.

Redefining careers

Organizations need people who can do different types of work at different times and be flexible in a way which is currently not encouraged by the traditional career ladder. If careers, as well as time and commitment, can be redefined, this will have important effects. For example, a temporary lower time investment at work, to enable individuals to meet family needs, would reduce only the tasks which people are allocated at a particular stage and not undermine what they can achieve in the future. This will be easier to achieve in flatter, less hierarchical organizations (Lewis and Taylor, 1996).

New approaches to management

Traditional management theory and supervisor behaviour presume a work–family split and assume that a concern for family will interfere with organizational needs. Traditionally supervisors have tended to think in terms of forcing workers to prioritize career or family rather than considering ways of helping them to integrate and manage both. Managing a flexible workforce requires trust, support rather than control, and collaboration rather than confrontation, in finding mutually acceptable ways of achieving goals.

Redefining success

Success is another dynamic and changing concept and it is useful to reflect on its meaning in the context of current changes and tensions. As Handy (1994) points out, successes such as the invention of the motor car or of new manufacturing technology were made without thought to the long-term consequences such as pollution or a redundant workforce. It is important to consider the possible long-term impact of the ways in which we currently define success. Current emphasis tends to be on profits and responsibilities to shareholders, and these are assumed to be independent of other needs.

A report on ways of achieving sustainable business growth in the face of substantial global competition argues that tomorrow's company will have to adopt an inclusive approach to the definition of success, considering all stakeholders (Royal Society of Arts, 1994).

Public policy support and partnership with industry

Public policy-makers also need to recognize the changes in family structures and to adapt to meet the needs of these families, recognizing that the single-breadwinner family is no longer the norm.

An infrastructure of quality childcare, eldercare and other care is a basic need of all working families. Government has an important role to play here, in partnership with local government and employers if appropriate, to ensure that local needs are met. Social policy-makers also need to consider the value of statutory entitlement to appropriate paid leave for family care. Lack of provision for family leave is based on the assumption that one family member (usually the woman) is either not employed or that their income is not necessary for family upkeep. There is evidence (Holterman, 1995), that the costs of providing leave can be balanced by benefits for employers and for the economy as a whole. Apart from the more obvious advantages of greater sex equality, reduced stress and absenteeism, there is some evidence that parental leave encourages androgynous behaviour (Haas and Hwang, 1995), and this blurring of traditional male/female roles is increasingly recognized as a characteristic of good.

Conclusion

As we approach the millennium, I hope employers will reflect on where they are going and what that might mean for employees and society in the future, and try to action their often espoused but rarely implemented view that 'our most valuable resource is our human resource'. Will the increasing army of women executives make a difference and support the words of John Ruskin in 1871: 'in order that people may be happy in their work, these things are needed: they must be fit for it; they must not do too much of it; and they must have a sense of success in it'. The future is female in the workplace, but where it goes will depend on the answers to some of the questions presented above.

References

Cartwright, S. and Cooper, C.L. (1997) *Managing Workplace Stress*, Sage Publications, Newbury Park, CA.

Confederation of British Industry (CBI) (1998) Sickness Absence Survey. CBI, London.

Cooper, C.L. (1998a) *Theories of Organizational Stress*, Oxford University Press, Oxford.

Cooper, C.L. (1998b) 'The psychological implications of the changing nature of work', *RSA Journal*, 1 (4): 74–78.

Cooper, C.L. and Jackson, S. (1997) *Creating Tomorrow's Organizations: A Handbook for Future Research in Organizational Behavior*, John Wiley & Sons, Chichester and New York.

Cooper, C.L. and Lewis, S. (1998) *Balancing your Career, Family and Life*, Kogan Page, London.

DEMOS (1996) *Time Squeeze*, DEMOS, London.

Equal Opportunities Commission (1998) *The Fact About Women Is*, EOC, Manchester.

Haas, L. and Hwang, P. (1995) 'Company culture and men's usage of family leaves in Sweden', *Family Relations*, 44: 28–36.

Handy, C. (1994) *The Empty Raincoat*, Hutchinson, London.

Holterman, S. (1995) 'The costs and benefits to British employers of measures to promote equality of opportunity', *Gender, Work and Organization*, 2: 102–112.

Institute of Survey Research (ISR) (1995) *Employee Satisfaction: Tracking European Trends*, ISR, London.

Judge, T.A., Boudreau, J.W. and Bretz, R.D. (1994) 'Job and life attitudes of male executives', *Journal of Applied Psychology*, 79: 767–782.

Lewis, S. and Taylor, K. (1996) 'Evaluating the impact of family friendly employment policies: a case study', in *The Work – Family Challenge*, Sage, London.

Makin, P., Cox, C. and Cooper, C.L. (1996) *Organisations and the Psychological Contract*, British Psychological Society Books, Leicester.

Pettigrew, A. (1993) *The Politics of Organizational Decision Making*, Tavistock, London.

Royal Society of Arts (1994) *Tomorrow's Company: The Case for an Inclusive Approach*, Royal Society of Arts, London.

Schor, J. (1991) *The Overworked American*, Basic Books, New York.

Terkel, S. (1972) *Working*, Avon Books, New York.

Walker, J. (1995) *The Cost of Communication Breakdown*, BT Forum, London.

White, B., Cox, C. and Cooper, C.L. (1992) *Women's Career Development*, Blackwell, Oxford.

Worrall, L. and Cooper, C.L. (1998) *IM-UMIST Quality of Working Life Survey*, Institute of Management, London.

Index